when nature turns nasty

PUBLISHED BY THE READER'S DIGEST ASSOCIATION LTD
LONDON · NEW YORK · SYDNEY · MONTREAL

Contents

Defying the Elements   10

Earth   12

Air   74

Fire   134

Water   192

Life   254

Index   310

Acknowledgements   318

when nature turns nasty

Earth

14 **The Day the Earth Shook**
A devastating earthquake wrecks Turkish cities

28 **East African Drought**
Widespread starvation as rains fail

36 **Nature's Icy Grip**
An ice storm paralyses eastern Canada

40 **Black Blizzard**
Swirling dust clouds smother the Midwest

44 **The Great Blizzard**
Snowstorms rage from Florida to Maine

46 **Buried Alive**
A mudslide engulfs a Philippine village

52 **White Death**
A freak avalanche strikes an Alpine ski resort

58 **Heatwave over Europe**
Europe swelters during the 2003 heatwave

64 **Taken by the Tide**
Cocklers die in the sands of Morecambe Bay

68 **Russia's Big Freeze**
Bitter Siberian cold grips western Russia

Air

76 **Tornado Super Outbreak**
148 tornadoes swirl through 13 US states

88 **Clouds of Sand**
The desert descends on Beijing

94 **Destroyed by Wind and Wave**
Hurricane Katrina devastates New Orleans

108 **England's Great Storm**
Hurricane-force winds across southern England

114 **Typhoon Havoc**
A typhoon tears into the coast of South Korea

118 **A Deadly Storm Surge**
A cyclone floods Bangladesh's delta region

124 **A Noxious Cloud of Gas**
Carbon dioxide erupts from a West African lake

128 **London's Great Smog**
A five-day smog smothers the British capital

Fire

136 Keeper of the Fire
Mount St Helens erupts in the USA's north-west

146 Rivers of Lava
A volcano in central Africa spews out deadly lava

150 A 20th-century Pompeii
Mont Pelée in the Caribbean wipes out an entire city

152 Deadly Mudflows
Thousands die in volcanic mudflows in Colombia

158 Angry Mountain
Mount Pinatubo explodes in the Philippines

166 A Bolt from the Blue
Spectacular and deadly lightning strikes

172 Yellowstone Ablaze
Wildfires rage out of control

182 Smog over South-east Asia
Forest fires in Indonesia cause hazardous pollution

184 Fire from the Sky
Meteorites crash to Earth in north-west India

188 Impact from Outer Space
A fireball explodes above Tunguska in Russia

Water

194 Boxing Day Tsunami
Thousands of people are swept to their deaths

206 The Black Dragon Roars
The largest tidal bore ever recorded

210 Hard Rain in Mumbai
A freak storm floods India's most populous city

216 Hailstorm over Sydney
Cricket ball-sized hailstones bombard Sydney

218 The Restless Sea
Monstrous 'freak' waves batter ocean shipping

222 Into the Whirlwind
Yachts off Australia sail into a waterspout

224 El Niño 1997-8
A year of weather chaos around the world

232 Drowned in Sight of Shore
Rip currents drown eight off the Florida coast

234 Central Europe Under Water
Floods in Europe after record-breaking rainfalls

242 Over the Edge
A Norfolk village disappears into the North Sea

250 Denmark's *Titanic*
An iceberg sinks the Danish ship *Hans Hedtoft*

Life

256 Shark Attack
The ocean's top predator strikes close to shore

264 Something in the Water
A major cholera epidemic takes hold in Angola

268 Lethal Injection
A snake's defence is a deadly weapon

272 Trouble Breathing
SARS, a deadly respiratory disease, spreads in Asia

274 Beautiful but Deadly
Plants and fungi that can injure or kill

278 In the Blood
Malaria kills and traps millions in poverty

284 The Eighth Plague
A plague of locusts sweeps across north-west Africa

290 The Swarm
Hybrid 'killer' bees make savage attacks in the USA

292 The Next Pandemic?
The H5N1 strain of avian flu spreads west from Asia

296 Superbug
The spread of antibiotic-resistant MRSA

298 Cold-blooded Killers
Terrifying crocodile and alligator attacks around the world

304 Africa's Darkest Secret
Hundreds die a gruesome death from the Ebola virus

308 A Grizzly End
A bear kills and eats two eco-campaigners in Alaska

Defying the Elements

New Orleans was awash. It was Tuesday, August 30, 2005, the day after Hurricane Katrina had smashed into the Louisiana and Mississippi coasts, unleashing terrifying storm surges. These huge walls of water reared up over the low-lying shore and swept far inland.

Driving up the Mississippi river and shipping canals, the surges of water thrust right into the heart of New Orleans, breaching the levees, or embankments, designed to protect the city. With the floodwaters pouring in, thousands of people trapped there were in danger of drowning. 'The devastation is worse than our worst fears,' Louisiana Governor Kathleen Blanco told news reporters that day. 'Pray for patience, pray for courage.'

Energy unleashed

When Nature turns nasty, no one is safe, for the forces involved are colossal. An earthquake that shook north-western Turkey in August 1999 released, in just 37 seconds, energy equivalent to the simultaneous explosion of 20 million tonnes of TNT. When a huge pulse of warmer-than-average water started washing the coasts of Peru and Ecuador in July 1997 – part of a periodic phenomenon in the Pacific called an El Niño event – it contained more energy within it than a million Hiroshima bombs.

Sophisticated modern technology may protect some of us from these events for some of the time. But, in the face of violent winds and waves, raging fires, or the tectonic forces in the ground beneath us, there is nothing we can do that will

guarantee our safety. Hurricane Katrina struck a major city in the USA, the world's richest country, yet all that nation's economic and technological might could not forestall the catastrophe, which left more than 1,800 people known to be dead and about the same number missing.

When such disasters strike less developed nations, they can kill not just hundreds, but tens or hundreds of thousands, injure thousands more and make millions homeless. The Boxing Day tsunami of 2004 left more than 250,000 dead around the Indian Ocean. Less than a year later, in October 2005, after a devastating earthquake shook Kashmir on the edge of the Himalayas, the official death toll was put at some 75,000 people, but the true count was almost certainly far higher.

This book tells the stories of these and many other natural catastrophes of recent times. They are stories of nightmare mingled with astonishing instances of human resilience and courage, of human error and even incompetence mixed with inspiring examples of compassion and solidarity. They tell of people such as Australian fireman Ranald Webster, who suffered horrific burns when fighting a bushfire near Melbourne in 1983, made a near-miraculous recovery and now helps other burns victims ... or Felix

> ❛ **The devastation is worse than our worst fears. Pray for patience, pray for courage.** ❜
>
> *Kathleen Blanco*

Rojas from the Colombian town of Armero, which was devastated when a nearby volcano erupted, sending deadly mudflows pouring down its slopes and into the town. Felix lost his father and seven sisters and brothers, yet worked on tirelessly to rescue others.

The quest for solutions

Each event is examined and analysed. Experts present the latest theories on cause and effect – outlining, for instance, how quantum physics can explain monstrous 'freak' waves, which rear terrifyingly and unexpectedly from an ocean swell, rising as high as a ten-storey building and capable of snapping in two even the largest and apparently safest ships.

Artworks illustrate the explanations, while 'Top 10' boxes create perspective – listing the deadliest tornadoes in US history, for example, or the deadliest volcanic eruptions since 1900. Photographs provide visual drama, such as an astonishing sequence by German tourist Georg Mader, who captured the progress of an avalanche as it thundered down an Alpine valley in February 1999.

'Future profile' features offer expert predictions, such as the probable effects of global warming and climate change. Are these processes likely to trigger more extreme weather events, from heatwaves to hurricanes to torrential rainstorms, bringing severe flooding? How will rising sea levels affect communities living on eroding coastlines?

'Silver lining' features, meanwhile, focus on positive, sometimes unexpected outcomes – such as the exceptional blossoming of wildflowers in devastated woodland after southern England's Great Storm of October 1987 and after the Yellowstone fires of 1988; or the building of a power plant in the African country, Rwanda, that will turn deadly methane gas trapped in the waters of Lake Kivu into a much-needed source of energy for the nation; or the high hopes for an effective vaccine against the malaria parasite, which blights the lives of millions across Asia, Africa and South America.

Our place in the world

In 1985, Australian academic Val Plumwood had a terrifying encounter with a saltwater crocodile while on a canoeing trip in Kakadu National Park. Three times, it pitched her into a death roll; she escaped

❝ In the West, there is a strong effort to deny that we humans are also animals positioned in the food chain. ❞

Val Plumwood

its jaws, only to fall back into them once more; finally, she struggled to freedom, horribly wounded. It was an experience that has, not surprisingly, shaped the rest of her life – but without bitterness. 'In the West,' she says, 'there is a strong effort to deny that we humans are also animals positioned in the food chain.'

That vision of our inextricable interdependence with the rest of Nature is also the vision of this book. Nature's often fearsome power makes no distinction between humans and other victims and, even today, our ability to control it is far from assured.

The Editors

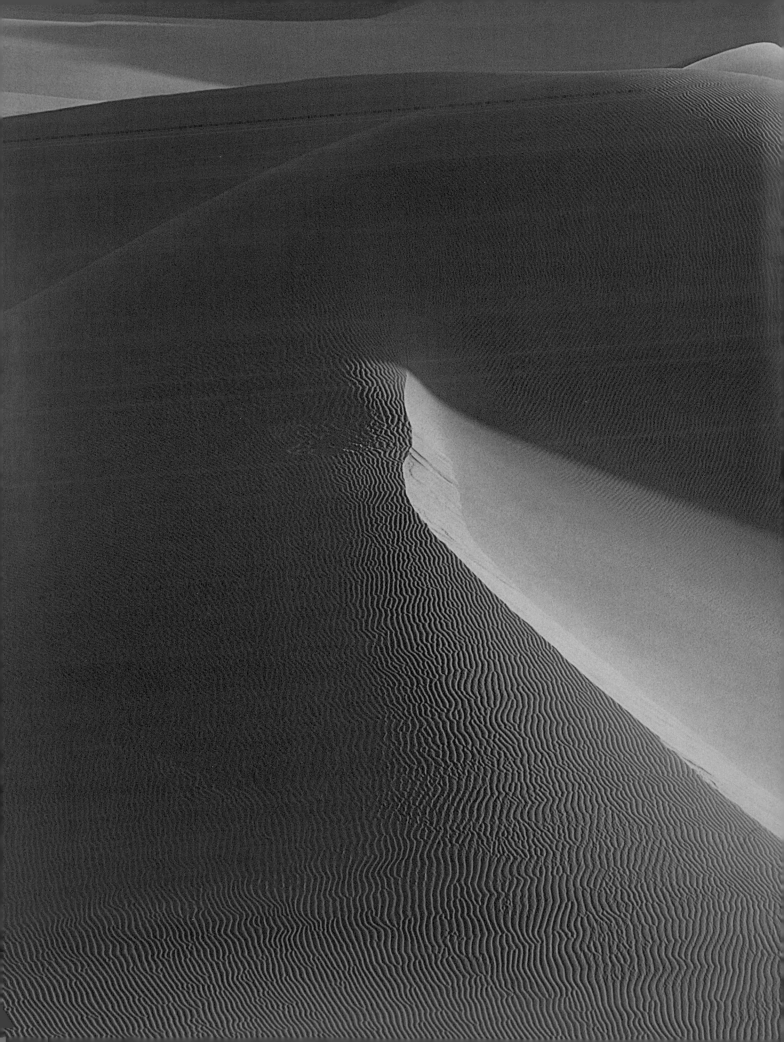

Earth

The Day the Earth Shook

T he Turkish city of Izmit was unusually busy in the small hours of August 17, 1999. It had been a hot and airless evening, and even at 2 am, people were still strolling along the city's sea front or fishing from its harbour walls.

An hour later, at 3.01 am, a colossal booming sound reverberated across the water, accompanied by the first in a series of massive jolts. By then, most people had turned in for the night, but a few stunned eyewitnesses who were still up reported seeing a red light in the sky, before cracks opened up in the ground. The waterfront collapsed, and in this city built of concrete, thousands of buildings tipped over or slumped where they stood. An earthquake measuring 7.4 on the Richter scale (see box, page 25) had struck, releasing energy equivalent to the simultaneous explosion of 20 million tonnes of TNT.

An immense shaking

About 100 km (60 miles) west of Izmit, Turkey's biggest city, Istanbul, also felt the quake, as it set tower blocks vibrating and woke millions of people from their sleep. Among them was Zeynep Uygun, whose immediate fear was for her son: 'I jumped out of my bed and stood up for a split second before running into the next room where my ten-month-old baby boy was sleeping,' she recalls. 'Our flat on the seventh floor of an apartment building was shaking wildly but I could not exactly see or hear what the quake was doing from the throbbing in my head

PULLED TO SAFETY *In Istanbul, rescue workers tug 30-year-old survivor, Umran Savus, from the rubble of a collapsed building.*

HOMES IN RUINS *In the city of Adapazari, 50 km (30 miles) east of Izmit, buildings were tossed like dice on a board and 3,891 people died.*

At least 17,000 people died in August 1999 when an earthquake measuring 7.4 on the Richter scale hit north-western Turkey.

and chest … I could never think I could be scared so much.' To add to the terror, the city's power supply had shut down, leaving people in blackness. 'It was as if a beast was chasing us in the darkness,' says Zeynep, 'and we were trying to find a place to hide from it but knew that we could not.'

English lecturer Nihat Ozen remembers the 'immense shaking' that jolted him awake. 'The bed I was on went up and down like a piece of paper for a couple of seconds. At first, I thought this was another dream – this time a bad one … I looked out of the window, electricity was cut and ambulance sirens got stronger and people started shouting "Get out of your houses!".' He could not decide what to do. 'First, I thought, "I will go under a table", then I felt maybe underneath the door was safer. Finally, I picked up a T-shirt and started running out of the apartment.'

Kadir Bahcecik, another Istanbul resident, had no hesitation in getting out – fast. 'I ran down eight floors of stairs and got in the open,' he says. 'I saw a starry Istanbul sky for the first time in more than a decade as

AGAINST THE CLOCK
Izmit residents look on in horror as rescuers hunt for survivors in the remains of their shattered homes.

> **❝ Our flat … was shaking wildly but I could not exactly see or hear what the quake was doing from the throbbing in my head and chest. ❞**
>
> *Zeynep Uygun, Istanbul resident*

the city was in total darkness, bar the headlights of the cars driving around aimlessly …' The behaviour he witnessed was mirrored throughout the earthquake zone. Once people were in the open, many of them felt that a car was the safest place to be, heading out of town. Around Istanbul, the exodus of panicking motorists was so great that some exit roads were blocked with traffic. The city escaped with relatively minor damage, largely because it is built on rock and lies 90 km (56 miles) from the quake's epicentre.

A divided landmass

For people who live above the Earth's tectonic fault lines, earthquakes are a constant and deadly threat. That hot August night, the threat had turned to terrifying reality in north-western Turkey, when part of the North Anatolian Fault – one of the world's most

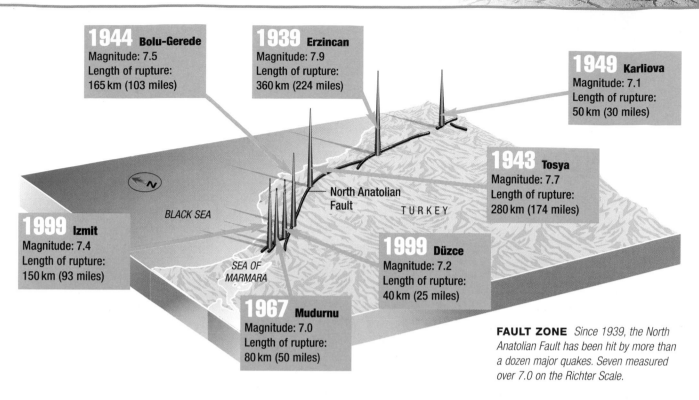

1944 Bolu-Gerede
Magnitude: 7.5
Length of rupture:
165 km (103 miles)

1939 Erzincan
Magnitude: 7.9
Length of rupture:
360 km (224 miles)

1949 Karliova
Magnitude: 7.1
Length of rupture:
50 km (30 miles)

1943 Tosya
Magnitude: 7.7
Length of rupture:
280 km (174 miles)

North Anatolian
Fault

BLACK SEA

T U R K E Y

1999 Izmit
Magnitude: 7.4
Length of rupture:
150 km (93 miles)

SEA OF
MARMARA

1999 Düzce
Magnitude: 7.2
Length of rupture:
40 km (25 miles)

1967 Mudurnu
Magnitude: 7.0
Length of rupture:
80 km (50 miles)

FAULT ZONE *Since 1939, the North Anatolian Fault has been hit by more than a dozen major quakes. Seven measured over 7.0 on the Richter Scale.*

active fracture zones – ruptured about 17 km (10.6 miles) below ground level.

Although Turkey looks like a single landmass, deep down it is split into two, by the North Anatolian Fault. This tear in the Earth's crust stretches more than 900 km (560 miles) from east to west, running roughly parallel with the country's northern, Black Sea coast. It passes close to several major cities, including Izmit, before reaching the Sea of Marmara – the inland sea that separates Europe from Asia, linked to the Black Sea to the north and the Aegean to the south – and then disappears under the seabed.

The two parts of the country sit on different tectonic plates – the plates composing the Earth's crust. The narrower section, lying north of the fault line, is part of the giant Eurasian plate, which extends

from western Europe as far as China and Japan. The rest of the country forms the much smaller Anatolian plate, which continues south underneath the Mediterranean. Relative to Eurasia, the Anatolian plate is moving westwards at an average rate of about 3 cm a year. Instead of sliding smoothly, however, it moves in a series of jerks. Each jerk is marked by tremors and earthquakes, generated by the sudden release of energy as the plates slip past each other and then lock together again.

The earthquake of August 1999 lasted just 37 seconds, but in that time, the two plates jolted past each other along a 150 km (93 mile) stretch of the fault line, from the city of Düzce, 100 km (60 miles) east of Izmit, as far as the Sea of Marmara. Twenty minutes later, the first

continued on page 20 »

THE SEA INVADES *There was severe flooding where parts of the Gulf of Izmit coast subsided and when tsunamis, triggered by the earthquake, smashed onto the shoreline.*

COLLAPSED *Gölcük, on the south side of the Gulf of Izmit, also suffered badly. In its shattered town centre (overleaf), broken apartment blocks seem slumped together for support.*

August 17 The initial rupture occurs in the western section of the North Anatolian Fault. Tsunamis wash across the Sea of Marmara, flooding Gölcük and other coastal towns.

August 18 The death toll stands at 4,000. Turkey's bestselling daily paper, *Hurriyet*, blames building contractors, denouncing them as murderers.

August 19 Hundreds of thousands of people are now camping outside. Turkey's prime minister, Bülent Ecevit, announces plans to build tent cities to house the homeless.

August 24 The official death toll stands at 14,000, and a further 200,000 people are without homes. The Turkish government appeals for bulldozers and body bags.

August 31 Panic breaks out when a tremor, measuring 5.2 on the Richter scale, hits Izmit. One person is killed, and nearly 200 injured in the rush for safety out of doors.

September 13 The most powerful aftershock, a quake of magnitude 5.8, hits the Izmit region. Six people die, and several hundred are injured as damaged buildings collapse.

October 17 According to official figures, issued two months after the quake, 17,000 died. But with so many missing, the true figure is thought to be much higher.

November 12 The year 1999 comes to a catastrophic close as a quake of magnitude 7.2 devastates the city of Düzce, leaving more than 600 people dead.

in a series of aftershocks hit the region, measuring 4.6 on the Richter scale – strong enough to be a significant earthquake in its own right, and as powerful as a small atomic bomb. Its psychological effect was huge, making already terrified people more frightened still.

Scenes of devastation

Izmit was worst hit. Home to more than 200,000 people, it lies on the narrow Gulf of Izmit, which forms the eastern tip of the Sea of Marmara. During the day, factories and apartment blocks dominate its skyline, while at night, the lights of tankers and ferries glimmer in the dark as they sail past.

On August 17, that peaceful scene was shattered. Along the city's sea front, some apartment blocks lay on their sides in pieces, while other buildings had collapsed completely, their floors sandwiched together,

HOPE IN THE DARK *Working through the night, Japanese rescue workers in Düzce dig down towards a crying baby.*

crushing everything – and everybody – in between. In the streets, terrified survivors stumbled about in the darkness, desperately trying to discover what had become of their relatives.

As dawn broke that day, and the rest of the world listened to the morning news, the extent of the disaster started to become clear. Calls saturated Turkey's telephone system, as millions of Turks living and working abroad tried to get information about family members and friends. The earliest reports spoke of several hundred casualties, but given the strength of the quake, the true toll was sure to be higher. How much higher, no one could yet guess.

In Izmit, the city centre and suburbs were the scene of frantic activity. Survivors pulled at the rubble with their bare hands as they tried to locate people trapped beneath shattered concrete and broken glass. Even at this early stage, it was painfully evident that poor workmanship had cost many lives. For, amid the ruins throughout the city, stood other, better-constructed buildings which had survived almost unscathed. Developers who had skimped on materials or ignored safety regulations were quickly blamed for adding to the death toll.

The city's industrial zones had also taken a massive hit. In the oil refinery, several storage tanks were on fire, pouring out black smoke into the morning air. One of the chimneys, originally 115 m high, had been reduced to a 40 m stump. Oil was spilling out into the Gulf of Izmit, and the smell of hydrocarbons hung heavily in the air. In the city's electrical substations, transformers weighing several tonnes had slid about during the quake as if they were on skates. Much of the city was now without electricity.

As the morning progressed, more news of the night's horrors emerged. At Gölcük, opposite Izmit on the southern side of the Gulf of Izmit, the sea had receded from the shoreline before smashing its way through the town and its naval base in a succession of tsunamis. The fault where the earthquake occurred cut right through the town and, to make matters worse, the sediment on which it is built is soft there – it rippled like liquid as each shock wave passed. The land then slumped and subsided, allowing the sea to flood in. Buildings near the shore were inundated, killing several thousand people.

Wave power

At the nearby holiday resort of Degirmendere, the entire shoreline subsided by around 2 m, and tsunamis also struck, smashing wooden fishing boats and sea-front cafés to pieces. They swept a passenger ferry inland, where it became marooned in the remains of an amusement park. The size of the waves could be seen by what they left behind. An industrial refrigerator, for instance, used by ice-cream sellers, was swept onto on a second-floor balcony where it stuck fast.

Supermarket manager Cengic Tayfur saw the tsunamis roar in. 'It was like watching a whirlpool,'

An echo from the past

The earthquake of August 1999 bore an uncanny resemblance to one that shook exactly the same region 16 centuries earlier, on August 24, AD 358. Roman historian Ammianus Marcellinus described the destruction and suffering it inflicted in the city of Nicomedia, built on the same site as modern Izmit.

'Since most of the buildings were built along the slope of the hill, they collapsed onto each other, while everything reverberated with the almighty clamour of their ruin. Meanwhile, the highest places were echoing with the mingled cries of those seeking their loved ones and children and whatever relatives were nearby.

'Eventually, after two hours … the air, now fine and clear, revealed the deadly wreckage lying below. For some had been buried under the great mass of rubble and crushed to death by its weight. Others, indeed, buried in mounds up to their necks, could have survived, if someone had come to rescue them – they died only for lack of assistance. Others again hung fixed to the points of protruding wooden beams.

'Most had been killed at once, and where shortly before men could be seen, now there was a chaotic mass of dead bodies. Some were saved, unharmed, by falling pediments inside their houses, but were later consumed by suffocation or starvation. Among these was Aristaenetus, governor of the recently created diocese [administrative district] … of Pietas …, who choked out his life for a long time in this torturous fate.

'Others, crushed by the sudden, great ruin, are hidden to this day under the same rubble. Yet more, indeed, with fractured skulls or broken arms or legs, were poised between life and death, begging for help from others in similar suffering. But they were abandoned, despite their loud entreaties.

'And the majority of the buildings – sacred, private and those of the citizens – could yet have survived, had not a sudden sweep of flames, burning for five days and nights, destroyed whatever was left to be consumed.

Ammianus Marcellinus

SAVED! *Triumphant Turkish soldiers free a man who has been trapped in the rubble for 52 hours.*

he says. 'It looked as if someone had pulled the plug out from the seabed. The sea was gurgling and then a wind came rushing at us, like a typhoon. The sea level dropped, but moments later a wave came rolling at us, getting bigger and faster all the time. After the two tidal waves, there must have been over 200 big waves that kept crashing onto the road.' He was lucky. He was able to run upstairs in a building that stayed in one piece. Even so, the sea flooded the corridors behind him, and the second wave lapped at his feet as he ran.

Huge waves continued to ebb and flow across the Gulf of Izmit, swamping the shoreline. By the time they subsided, most of the resort's sea-front buildings were flooded. At least 300 people were killed as apartments and hotels collapsed or were shattered by the power of the waves. In the eerie calm of the days that followed, fish killed on impact rotted in ground-floor rooms.

Two days passed before an international rescue programme finally got under way. At Gölcük, many survivors felt that the authorities had forgotten them. 'They are more

interested in looking after the armed forces,' said Bulent Ertekin, who had lost his mother. The town's naval headquarters had collapsed, and the initial rescue efforts seemed to be concentrated there.

Odds against

Despite the two-day delay, rescuers succeeded in pulling many out alive – people such as Sema and Ahmed Bulte. The couple had spent four days lying side by side in bed, surviving the overpowering heat by placing cool bricks on their stomachs. The following day, a Russian team found a six-year-old girl in the remains of her parents' home. Her mother and father had died, but she had survived thanks to an air pocket.

But the real story of the Turkish earthquake was one of overwhelming tragedy, as people bled to death under the rubble or died slowly from suffocation, and the delay had undoubtedly cost many lives. 'If somebody has plenty of room, and lots of water and they are not injured in any way, then it's possible they can survive in those situations for up to five days,' said Dr Beat Kunzi, a member of a Swiss medical team. 'If any of those factors are against them, then their chances are drastically reduced.' Altogether, nearly a quarter of a million survivors were made homeless and at least 17,000 people lost their lives, although many estimates put the figure much higher – more than 35,000.

TENTED CITY *Outside Gölcük, a survivor sets up one of thousands of emergency tents flown in by the Turkish Red Crescent.*

Shaken but not stirred

San Francisco's 48-storey Transamerica Pyramid stands just a few miles north of the San Andreas Fault, one of the world's most dangerous fault lines. Completed in 1972, it is the city's tallest building, yet also, in this earthquake-prone region, one of its safest. When the Loma Prieta quake struck in October 1989, causing widespread damage, the Pyramid's top floor shook by about 30 cm, but there was no structural damage, and no one suffered a serious injury. It was said, jokingly, that not even a paper clip moved.

For the Pyramid's architect, William Pereira, earthquake resistance was a top priority. The skyscraper stands on an open plinth of diagonal trusses, to protect it from sideways and up-and-down movements, while its flaring shape, converging in a spire 280 m above ground level, gives it great structural stability. It has become a symbol of pioneering earthquake-proof design.

HARSH LESSON *In 1995, the collapse of the Kobe Expressway showed the importance of earthquake-proofing.*

Architects have learned much about earthquake resistance in the past few decades. On the far side of the Pacific from San Francisco, the world's tallest inhabited building is also in an active earthquake zone. Finished in 2004, the Taipei 101 Tower rises 509 m high. Most of its 101 floors contain offices, restaurants and shops, but the 88th houses something very different: a massive 660-tonne metal ball, called a 'tuned mass damper', suspended from 16 cables. If a quake or typhoon hits, the weight starts to swing in the opposite direction to the movement of the skyscraper, damping down the oscillations.

Engineers can also add protection to existing structures. During the 1995 earthquake at Kobe in Japan, parts of the city's raised expressway system toppled over. Replacing the entire system would have been prohibitively expensive, so the authorities used 'seismic retrofitting' instead – a way of updating structures to make them earthquake-proof. They replaced collapsed sections, but gave intact piers protective jackets, to stop them cracking in future. They also replaced steel supports with rubber ones, which are better at damping down an earthquake's vibrations.

SILVER LINING

Regions at risk

Several of the world's most densely populated places lie in earthquake-prone regions. While many developed countries have constructed carefully to withstand powerful tremors, other less developed nations have not – and the potential loss of life from a major quake could be considerable.

Earthquakes are most likely to occur with significant force on fault lines – the cracks in the Earth's crust, where the slabs, or tectonic plates, that make up the crust rub alongside each other. Worldwide, there are seven major plates – the African, Antarctic, Australian, Eurasian, North American, South American and Pacific plates – and many more minor ones. Meshed together like gigantic shards of pottery, they are continually on the move, driven by the intense heat at the Earth's core.

One of the most famous fault lines is the San Andreas Fault, which slices through California, along the boundary between the Pacific and North American plates. Destructive earthquakes along this restless gash in the Earth's surface have included the San Francisco quake of 1906, which left at least 3,000 people dead, and the Loma Prieta quake in 1989, which caused damage estimated at $6 billion.

The San Andreas Fault is dangerous, and Californians live in dread of what they call the 'big one', a massive earthquake which is bound to happen one day and could strike with a thousand times the strength of the 1999 Izmit quake. But the San Andreas Fault is just one portion of a far greater danger zone – the Pacific Ring of Fire, a horseshoe-shaped arc around the Pacific Ocean, where the Pacific and other plates meet. Ninety per cent of all the world's earthquakes occur on the Ring of Fire, including the largest earthquake ever recorded, the so-called Great Chilean Earthquake of 1960, which hit 9.5 on the Richter scale, and the Kobe quake in Japan in 1995, which left 6,433 people dead.

The second most earthquake-prone zone lies along the southern edge of the Eurasian plate, where the African, Arabian and Indian plates push northwards against it. Some of the

QUAKE PRONE *Most of the world's earthquakes occur in two zones – the Pacific Ring of Fire and the so-called Alpide belt along the southern margin of the Eurasian plate.*

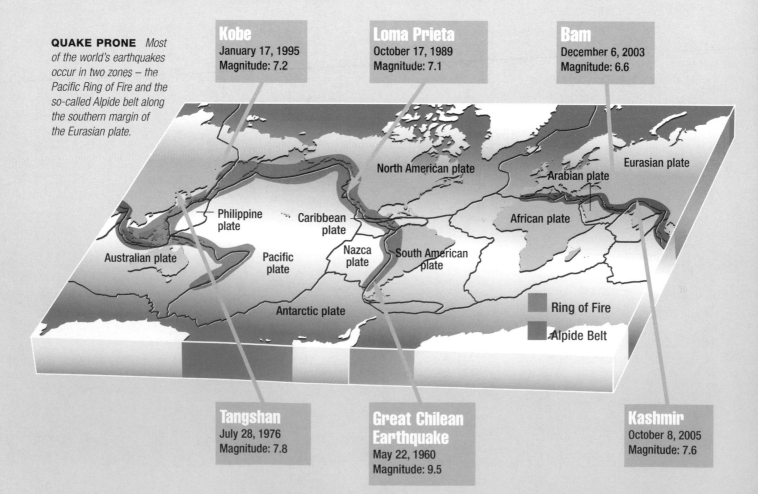

Kobe
January 17, 1995
Magnitude: 7.2

Loma Prieta
October 17, 1989
Magnitude: 7.1

Bam
December 6, 2003
Magnitude: 6.6

North American plate

Eurasian plate

Arabian plate

Philippine plate

Caribbean plate

African plate

Australian plate

Pacific plate

Nazca plate

South American plate

Antarctic plate

Ring of Fire

Alpide Belt

Tangshan
July 28, 1976
Magnitude: 7.8

Great Chilean Earthquake
May 22, 1960
Magnitude: 9.5

Kashmir
October 8, 2005
Magnitude: 7.6

most devastating quakes of recent times have occurred in this belt, which extends from the Atlantic, across the Mediterranean, through west Asia to the Himalayas and as far as Indonesia. They included the quakes at Bam in Iran and in Kashmir (see pages 26 and 27) and the undersea quake that triggered the 2004 Boxing Day tsunami.

What worries experts is that these zones include some of the most heavily populated places on Earth. For example, half of the world's ever-growing megacities (cities with a population of 10 million or more) lie in earthquake-prone regions – huge urban agglomerations including Tokyo and its metropolitan area, Manila in the Philippines, Tehran, Istanbul and Mexico City. Japanese cities have done much to face the challenge, with strict regulations enforcing earthquake-proof construction. But cities in less developed countries could suffer catastrophic loss of life if struck by a high magnitude earthquake.

What can be done? Accurate forecasting would, of course, help to save thousands of lives, and there are often warning signs of an earthquake to come. Before the 1976 Tangshan quake in China – the deadliest of the 20th century, leaving 650,000 dead – people reported strange happenings, such as the water level rising and falling abruptly in the city's wells, sometimes several times a day. Slight movements in the Earth's crust, the prelude to a quake, often cause events like these. Scientists can use seismographs to pinpoint the exact location of such tremors, and then check the readings against the normal background level of activity in the area.

The year before the Tangshan quake, it seemed as if they had, indeed, made a breakthrough. When a quake struck another Chinese city, Haicheng, on February 4, 1975, very few people died, because officials, acting on seismic warnings, had already evacuated the city. Since then, however, the results of earthquake forecasting have been mixed – there was no advance warning of the Kashmir or Kobe quakes, for example.

THE RICHTER SCALE

In 1935, Californian seismologists Charles Richter and Beno Gutenberg devised the original Richter scale (since modified) to measure the energy released at the source of an earthquake, based on readings recorded on seismographs. Although the scale does not measure intensity – how much the earth shakes, and so how destructive the quake is, which depends on factors such as geological conditions – this table shows the destructive effects typically associated with quakes of different Richter magnitudes.

MAGNITUDE	EFFECTS	APPROX. FREQUENCY
Less than 3.0	Rarely felt by people, but recorded on seismographs.	Up to 1,000 a day
3.0-3.9	Vibrations similar to the passing of a truck, but rarely causing damage.	49,000 a year
4.0-4.9	Noticeable shaking of dishes, doors and windows. Structural damage unlikely.	6,200 a year
5.0-5.9	Can damage poorly constructed buildings, but slight damage, at worst, to well-constructed buildings.	800 a year
6.0-6.9	Can be destructive in populated areas up to about 100 km (60 miles) across.	120 a year
7.0-7.9	Can cause serious damage over larger areas.	18 a year
8.0-8.9	Can cause serious damage in areas several hundred kilometres across.	1 every year
9.0 or greater	Devastating in areas several thousand kilometres across.	1 every 20 years

Charles Richter, creator of the Richter scale, is reputed to have said, 'Only fools and charlatans try to predict earthquakes.' His words emphasise an uncomfortable truth – there is still no such thing as a global earthquake forecast. What is certain is that shoddily constructed buildings are a major cause of death during quakes. The surest precaution is for countries to enact – and enforce – tougher building regulations.

DANGER ZONE *The San Andreas Fault in California is one of the most active on Earth, triggering hundreds of 'micro-earthquakes' every day.*

SHAKING EARTH

- **An earthquake in the mountains of Kashmir kills at least 75,000**

- **A quake in southern Iran kills more than 26,000 and destroys an architectural treasure**

Kashmir 2005 Nabeel Ahmad was still asleep when an earthquake measuring 7.6 on the Richter scale struck the disputed territory of Kashmir at 8.50 am on October 8, 2005. 'I thought it was a dream at first,' he recalls. 'But when I opened my eyes, I realised the world was shaking.' He was in the city of Mirpur at the time, but his father was in the country outside. 'My father works in a hilly area and said he saw everything become dust. They thought it was the end of the world.'

The quake's epicentre was in mountainous terrain, lying on the edge of Himalayas, in the Pakistani-administered sector of the territory. The official death toll was put at about 75,000 people, but many more are thought to have died during the winter that followed. Hospitals are few and far between in this rugged region, and communications poor. As winter set in, first landslides and then snow cut off countless settlements, making it near-impossible for emergency services and aid agencies to get through.

There were, however, some almost miraculous stories of survival. Most dramatic was that of 40-year-old Naqsha Bibi, believed to have died in the quake when her home collapsed. In December, more than two months later, her family began cleaning up the site. 'We started clearing the debris … ' says Faiz Din, her cousin, 'mainly to pull the iron sheets off the collapsed roof to build ourselves a shelter. But as we cleared one side of the house, some of the debris fell away exposing [a] cavity …' There, incredibly, was Naqsha Bibi – still alive.

By then, she weighed 35 kg – about half the average for a woman of her size – and she was unable to talk or move, having been trapped in a tiny space in the remains of her kitchen for 63 days. When discovered, the space still contained traces of food, and a trickle of water was running over the floor. Without these, she would certainly have perished, like tens of thousands of others.

STRUGGLE FOR SURVIVAL
After the Kashmir earthquake, a homeless woman boils a pan of water amid the ruins of her village.

Bam 2003
Bam in southern Iran was an architectural jewel until an earthquake measuring 6.6 on the Richter scale destroyed it on Boxing Day 2003. The diasaster also killed more than 26,000 people – about a third of the city's population. In modern times, few quakes have caused such loss of life in so small an area. 'The sheer concentration of death is mind-blowing,' said Rob Macgillivray from the charity Save the Children.

Founded more than 2,000 years ago, the fortress city of Bam was the world's largest adobe (mud-brick) structure, standing guard over the Silk Road, an ancient trade route connecting China with the Middle East and Europe. When the quake struck, domed roofs which had stood for centuries shattered, and dust rose in clouds above them. But most people died in the new city, also built of adobe, which had grown up around the walls of the old one. Memories of that terrible day haunt Hamideh Khordoosta, who was staying with friends on the outskirts when the quake hit. 'I was pulling people from the rubble,' she said a few days later, 'but they were dead or dying all around me.' Her own home, inside the new city, collapsed, killing most of her extended family.

While rescuers dug out survivors, one woman, Parisa Damandan, an art historian from Tehran, set about salvaging something of Bam's heritage by hunting for old negatives of the city. 'With my bare hands I started digging at spots where photo shops had been located,' she says. Helpers later joined her, and by the time they had finished nearly three weeks later, they had collected more than 30,000 negatives and prints. Parisa hopes to give some back to surviving relatives. Others will form a record of a world the earthquake swept away.

BEFORE AND AFTER
Until 2003, Bam's citadel (photographed, top, in 1975) had changed little in centuries. The earthquake reduced its defensive walls to piles of dusty rubble.

10 deadliest earthquakes since 1900

Heavily populated regions of China have suffered many of the worst death tolls from high magnitude earthquakes.

	DATE	EPICENTRE	MAGNITUDE	DEATHS	
1	1976	Tangshan, China	7.8	650,000	Official death toll 255,000
2	2004	Sumatra	9.1	280,000	Submarine earthquake triggered giant tsunami
3	1920	Gansu, China	7.8	200,000	Many deaths due to landslides
4	1927	Tsinghai, China	7.9	200,000	
5	1923	Tokyo, Japan	7.9	143,000	Large death toll due to fire
6	1948	Turkmenistan	7.3	110,000	
7	1908	Messina, Italy	7.2	100,000	Deaths from earthquake followed by tsunami
8	2005	Kashmir/Pakistan	7.6	80,000	
9	1932	Gansu, China	7.6	70,000	
10	1935	Quetta, Pakistan	7.5	60,000	City of Quetta destroyed by an earthquake which struck at night

East African Drought

As the world entered the new millenium, the countries of East Africa – Kenya, Ethiopia, Somalia, Sudan, Burundi and Tanzania – were experiencing the worst drought in living memory. Herdsmen, who depend on the rains to provide grazing for their livestock, were the worst affected.

Drought is a fact of life in the region, but its severity in 2005 was unprecedented in recent years. 'I have lived through many droughts but this is the worst,' said Kiteleik Kasale, a 68-year-old Masai tribeswoman. 'First the donkeys died, then the sheep, lastly the cows. We used to have almost 1,000 cattle, but now this place smells of carcasses and there are only two or three left. We are all suffering. Even the young children have nothing to eat. There is a serious shortage of water and what we have been able to find is salty. The animals my son did manage to sell brought nothing – just enough for a 10 kg bag of flour.'

Life in East Africa depends on the rainy season – Africa's equivalent of the monsoon. After months of clear blue skies, rain sweeps in from the Indian Ocean and transforms the bone-dry landscape. Within a few days, fresh grass sprouts, and soon the bare branches of thorn trees grow new leaves. It's a crucial time for farmers, and for millions of wild animals that migrate and breed in step with the changing weather. That, at least, is the normal weather pattern in the region.

Scorched earth

The droughts are caused by natural variations in this pattern, which steers moist air blowing inland from the sea. In 2000, Kenya's 'long rains', which usually fall between March and May, had almost completely failed, leading to a catastrophically low yield of maize – the main crop. In the arid north of the country, nomadic herders were facing their fourth consecutive year without enough water. And in the years that followed, the situation deteriorated further.

LIFE ON THE EDGE *In southern Ethiopia, a woman and a boy herd goats back towards their village at the end of a day on land already badly overgrazed.*

Following several years of poor rains, crops failed and livestock died. By March 2006, 11 million people were affected by drought.

29

In Kenya, 80 per cent of the population are farmers. Many of them are nomadic herdsmen living on the open savannah. Cattle are the key to their survival. A herdsman who loses his cattle has no milk or meat for his family, nothing to trade for flour or water, and nothing to hand on to his children when they take up life on their own. Kaila Nampaso, a Masai herdsman from southern Kenya, describes how the drought affected his clan: 'Everything here was finished [so] I went in search of grass and water. Along the way the animals died. We depend on the cattle for their milk. When the cattle die we have nothing else. My clan used to have 200 cattle, now we are down to just 17.' As the situation deteriorated through 2005, many Masai faced starvation. This strong, proud people were forced to rely on handouts of food to survive. Kimere Nampaso, herself a Masai tribeswoman, helped to co-ordinate the relief effort for ActionAid International in southern Kenya. Although their help was welcomed, for some it had come too late. 'People have died and their animals have died,' she said. 'Life has not been good for us. It has been worse for the very young and very old.'

The drought affected settled communities, too. In the hills of Burundi to the west, crops failed and many people starved. Others, severely weakened by hunger, succumbed to disease. 'Everything here is about hunger and illness,' explained 60-year-old Pelagiya Kabanyiginya. 'I am a widow. I have two sons. We have nothing to eat. It has been like this for the last two seasons. Before, we had a banana and cassava

VITAL SOURCE *After digging a hole in a riverbed, Somalian herdsmen take turns to fill up their water containers while their thirsty animals look on.*

TOO WEAK TO STAND *In a gesture of sympathy mingled with despair, a Masai man strokes the leg of a dying cow shortly before it is slaughtered.*

plantation. We used to drink banana wine and the crops were abundant, but the weather has changed. Because of the sun they have all died.' Twelve-year-old Janette Dusengimana lost her family one by one. 'All my brothers and sisters are dead,' she said. 'I live with my mother. I do not know where my father is.'

The dry north

Lake Turkana straddles the border between northern Kenya and Ethiopia. Nicknamed the 'Jade Sea' after its deep green colour, the 250 km (155 mile) long lake is surrounded by a landscape of extinct volcanoes and blackened lava flows. Even in good times, its windswept shores are blisteringly hot and dry. When drought strikes, the region turns into one of the most hostile inhabited places on Earth.

Nomads live here, dependent on their cattle and goats for survival. Few can read or write, and instead of using dates, they recall past droughts by giving each one a name. Nearly half a century ago, in 1960, the Turkana people were struck by a drought they call Namator, whose name means 'exposed bones'. A decade later came Kimidudu, which means 'the plague that killed humans and livestock'. The latest drought was called Kichutanak, or 'the drought that sweeps everything away'.

Lake Turkana's waters are drinkable, but their high soda content can stoke thirst instead of quenching it, so

> **Everything here was finished so I went in search of grass and water. Along the way the animals died.**
>
> *Kaila Nampaso, Masai herdsman*

A scavenger's banquet

Just as the drought caused hardship for East Africa's people, so it affected many of the region's wild animals. Some species suffered more than others. For hippos, the drought was a double disaster, while scavengers found more than usual to feed on.

Hippos normally spend the day wallowing in muddy water, which protects their delicate skin from the searing tropical sun, and clamber out at dusk to feed on lush plants. But as the drought took hold, pools and rivers dried up and the hippos' food shrivelled away. It was a calamitous situation because, unlike other mammals, they cannot walk off to find food elsewhere.

At the beginning of 2006, Chief Warden Michael Koikai summed up the pitiful state of hippos in Kenya's flagship Masai Mara National Reserve. 'They started dying in mid-December', Koikai told reporters, 'and now we estimate that between 60 and 80 hippos have died.' Dead hippos were drifting down rivers under the horrified gaze of tourists, and carcasses contaminated waterholes, spreading disease.

In a gruesome twist, not all the hippos that died were direct victims of the drought. Crammed into ever-shrinking spaces, mature males instinctively went on the attack, ferociously savaging each other. Bull hippos' canine teeth can measure up to 30 cm long, and this – coupled with a hair-trigger temper – gives them a well-earned reputation for being Africa's most dangerous mammals. With hippos turning on each other, the results were often horrific.

For East Africa's predators, the drought proved a mixed blessing. Weakened by thirst, prey such as antelope were easier for lions and cheetahs to catch, but as water became more scarce, the big cats suffered, too. The only real winners were scavengers, such as hyenas, jackals and vultures. For them, the drought brought a banquet.

GIANTS AT BAY *Trapped in a shrinking pool of mud, hippos watch while a hyena feeds on one of their kin, already reduced to bones.*

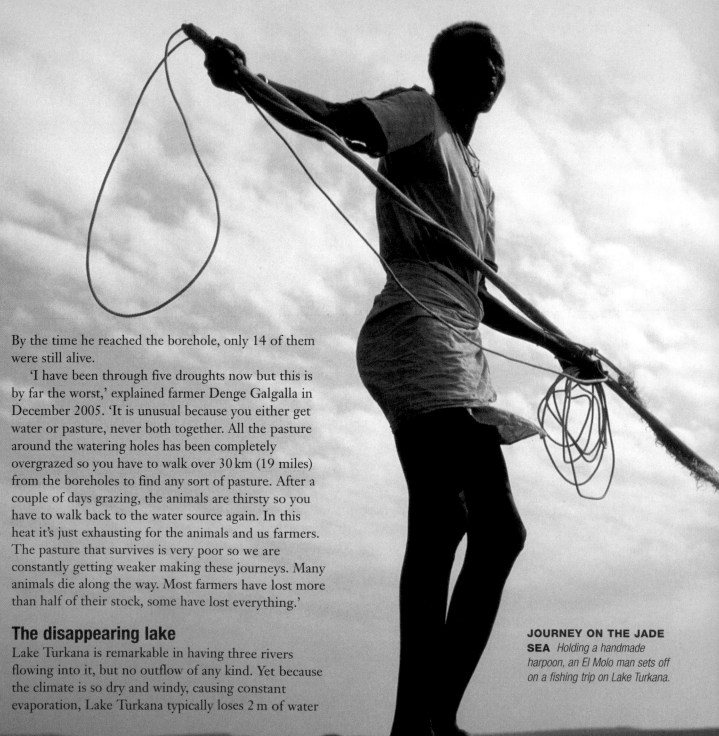

the Turkana people spend a large part of their time searching for fresh water for their animals and themselves. In the flat savannah that stretches east towards Somalia, isolated boreholes attracted herdsmen on a desperate mission to save their animals. One man set off on a 60 km (37 mile) trek towards the settlement of Arbajahan, where a diesel-powered pump was running 24 hours a day. He left with 23 cows – all that remained of more than 80 animals in his original herd.

> **I have been through five droughts now but this is by far the worst ... Some farmers have lost everything.**
>
> *Denge Galgalla, farmer*

By the time he reached the borehole, only 14 of them were still alive.

'I have been through five droughts now but this is by far the worst,' explained farmer Denge Galgalla in December 2005. 'It is unusual because you either get water or pasture, never both together. All the pasture around the watering holes has been completely overgrazed so you have to walk over 30 km (19 miles) from the boreholes to find any sort of pasture. After a couple of days grazing, the animals are thirsty so you have to walk back to the water source again. In this heat it's just exhausting for the animals and us farmers. The pasture that survives is very poor so we are constantly getting weaker making these journeys. Many animals die along the way. Most farmers have lost more than half of their stock, some have lost everything.'

The disappearing lake

Lake Turkana is remarkable in having three rivers flowing into it, but no outflow of any kind. Yet because the climate is so dry and windy, causing constant evaporation, Lake Turkana typically loses 2 m of water

JOURNEY ON THE JADE SEA *Holding a handmade harpoon, an El Molo man sets off on a fishing trip on Lake Turkana.*

ON GUARD *In north-western Kenya, an armed herdsman watches over his goats while they drink, knowing that waterholes attract trouble in dry times.*

a year – one of the highest figures anywhere in the world. In normal times, the lost water is replaced by the rivers, but during droughts the lake slowly shrinks. This has been happening for at least the past half-century, but it is now shrinking faster as a result of recent droughts. Since 1980, the lake's waterline has dropped by more than 10 m.

Lake Turkana's shrinkage has had a far-reaching impact on the El Molo, Kenya's smallest tribe. There are only about 300 El Molo, and most of them live around a bay on the barren south-east shore of the lake. They survive almost entirely by fishing and by hunting crocodiles, a lifestyle that makes them dependent on the lake. But as the lake has shrunk, its water has become more salty, killing fish and making food harder to catch. To make the El Molo's predicament more dangerous, the lake water now contains over seven times the maximum safe level of fluoride. Drinking it is giving the El Molo damaged teeth and deformed bones.

Thirsty camels

Directly east of Lake Turkana is the remote Kenyan town of Wajir. Here even camels found it hard to survive. Aid coordinator Mursal Mohammed was well-used to Kenya's dry north, and had witnessed earlier droughts in the region, but nothing quite like this. 'I vividly remember such a situation in the droughts of 1972, 1984, and 1992,' he said. 'Camels are known to be able to resist severe drought conditions but even they are struggling now.'

Few other large mammals can survive as long without water as a camel. Given enough fresh green food, a camel can go for weeks without drinking; and when it finds water, it can swallow up to 60 litres at a

time. But in the region around Wajir there was not a blade of greenery left and the camels had to feed on dry branches and dead grass. With so little moisture, they lingered close to Wajir's wells. As the locals knew, it was an ominous sign.

Well wars

War-torn Somalia lies less than a day's drive eastwards from Wajir. In a parched landscape scattered with gaunt trees, the drought exacerbated an already tense situation. For decades, these arid borderlands have been notorious cattle-rustling country – the fiefdom of armed bands who do not hesitate to use their weapons when stealing livestock. When the latest drought struck, the bandits found a tempting new target: aid trucks carrying water and food.

A local aid worker described the situation. 'Before I go anywhere in Somalia, I pray. If someone is thirsty, they can shoot you for a glass of water. There's no police to come and no government to say anything.' The man, Sheik Ibrahim Khail, had every right to be anxious. 'In other places they may just want to rob the driver or take the food and sell it. But here they want the water, too.' In a country struck by drought but awash with firearms, control of water became part of the relentless struggle for power.

Wells were often the scene of gun battles as neighbours argued over rapidly diminishing supplies.

> **Before I go anywhere in Somalia I pray. If someone is thirsty, they can shoot you for a glass of water. There's no police to come and no government to say anything.**
>
> *Sheik Ibrahim Khail, aid worker*

Short-lived skirmishes could break out at any time, but sometimes the violence ignited long-running feuds. In the town of Rabdore, a two-year battle broke out over a single waterhole that was claimed by two rival clans. By the time the 'War of the Well' came to an end, in 2005, about 250 men had lost their lives. One of the widows, Fatuma Ali Mahmood, remembers finding her husband's corpse. 'His body was bloodied, swollen and just lying there with the other dead by the well, left in disgrace,' she days. 'The shame. We'd never seen conflict at this level of violence. Thirst forces men to this horror of war.'

Draining the supply

The landscape around Lake Victoria is a world away from the aridity of Somalia and northern Kenya. Here, in the heart of the African tropics, farmers till some of the most fertile land on the continent. The climate is always warm, and in most years enough rain falls to grow crops all year round. The countryside is crowded with productive smallholdings, creating one of the most densely populated rural regions on Earth.

But even in these lush surroundings, the drought had an impact. Lake Victoria normally rises and falls in step with the seasons, but in recent years its water level has only dropped. Unlike Lake Turkana, Lake Victoria has an outlet, the White Nile. For millennia, lake water surged downriver during the rainy season, helping to create the Nile floods used by the farmers of ancient Egypt. In 1954, the lake's outlet was blocked by a vast hydroelectric dam in what is now Uganda, and this age-old cycle came to an end. Lake Victoria became a giant reservoir.

An international agreement between Uganda and Egypt controls the amount of water that Uganda can release from the lake, but some environmentalists suspect that too much water has been released in order to keep Uganda's electricity supply running while river levels are low. Between 2003 and 2006, the lake lost 75 km³ (18 cubic miles) of water, enough to keep a million people in drinking water for about 100,000 years. In places the shore has retreated by 500 m, damaging water supply systems and leaving fishing jetties and landing stages high and dry.

East Africa's human population has increased by more than five times in the last 50 years, creating a huge expansion in cities and towns. All of these need electricity, and much of it comes from hydroelectric dams. Lake Victoria is too big to dry up, but artificial reservoirs are under threat. In Tanzania, the water level in the Mtera reservoir, one of the country's largest, fell so much that by 2006 only a trickle of water kept the turbines turning. Normally, water from this reservoir powers another dam further downstream, so the drought's effects worked like a chain reaction.

To save energy, electricity was cut off in Tanzania's capital from dawn to dusk every day. Hospitals switched on emergency generators, traffic lights went dead and the city struggled to cope without power. Among the few to benefit were the city's frogs. Without electricity to run their filters, swimming pools turned bright green with algae – making them perfect frog habitats at a time when natural pools were hard to find.

The drought breaks – for some

In February 2006, crowds gathered at the Mtera dam and prayed for rain. Those pleas went unanswered, but two months later, storm clouds arrived at last. As the clouds rolled in from the Indian Ocean and lightning flashed across the savannah, they delivered relief and destruction in almost equal measure. Some parts of East Africa were drenched. Others missed the rain completely and remained parched and dry.

Across northern Kenya, aid agencies reported dozens of flash floods, which swept up months of debris and heaped it against bridges like makeshift dams. On hillsides the floods rapidly drained away, but in low-lying regions – such as the border area near Somalia – water and debris gathered in stagnant lakes, blocking roads and contaminating wells.

As the year wore on, aid agencies estimated that at least 70 per cent of cattle had died in the areas affected by the drought, and that several years of good rains were needed for pasture, herds and crops to recover. With much of their livestock gone, nomadic people, in particular, remained dependent on relief supplies of food and water. In autumn 2006, the UN announced that 11 million people in East Africa remained in need of assistance.

FUTURE PROFILE

A warmer, drier world

The severe and increasingly frequent droughts and accompanying famines in East Africa are attributed by environmentalists to a combination of global warming and changes in land use. They are also set to continue unless action is taken to break the cycle.

The world is warming up, and Africa is particularly vulnerable to the effects of this. Nearly three-quarters of the population rely on small-scale, rain-fed agriculture. The extremes of weather, such as droughts and floods, that are triggered by global warming directly threaten their survival.

Global warming is not the only reason that East Africa is drying out. Deforestation and the degradation of wetland areas are also affecting the region's climate. Christian Lambrechts of the UN Environment Programme has pointed out that forests are vital in generating rain. 'Globally, something like 62 per cent of precipitation occurs over land as a result of evapo-transpiration from lakes and wetlands and dense vegetation, in particular

forests pumping water held in the soils, into the air.' Between 2000 and 2003 Kenya lost more than 7,000 hectares (17,300 acres) of forest. In southern Somalia, large areas of woodland are cleared each year to supply the international charcoal trade. The loss of vegetation on such a scale is reducing the environment's ability to produce rain and to recover after periods of drought.

Global warming and deforestation are also threatening the ice cover on the continent's two highest mountains. Kilimanjaro, in Tanzania, has lost more than 80 per cent of its ice cover over the last 80 years, one-third of which has gone in the last 12 years. Mount Kenya has lost 92 per cent over the last 100 years. Environmentalists

predict that both mountains will lose their remaining ice cover within two decades if nothing is done.

The ice fields on the two mountains are important water catchment areas for Kenya, feeding several rivers that are major sources of water and electricity generation. The disappearance of the ice field on Kilimanjaro also affects Tanzania, which has a reduced water level in some rivers that supply villages and hospitals. Tanzania's economy could also be affected as the mountain is a major tourist attraction and major foreign currency earner for the country.

VANISHING SNOWS *Mount Kilimanjaro's ice cap could disappear entirely by 2020 – many experts think that global warming is to blame.*

Freezing rain falls in eastern Canada about a dozen times a year, but most of these storms pass in just a few hours. In January, 1998, exceptional weather conditions produced a storm that lasted for six days and left ice clinging to every surface, from birdtables to the wings of aircraft.

In rural eastern Ontario, Ken Watson watched – and listened – as the storm raged. The falling rain turned to ice, piling up like a glassy jacket on trees and power lines. It was the evening of January 7, three days into Canada's greatest peacetime emergency in over 80 years. As darkness fell the power failed, and the trees around Ken Watson's home succumbed to the storm. 'That night the forest started to come down. For the next two days the forest took on a surreal crystal appearance with branches covered by up to 2 inches of ice. Every 20 seconds or so a crash would resound as another branch, too heavily laden with ice, cracked and fell to the ground, ice shards scattering on impact.'

On the same evening, Pat Drummond, from Manotick near Ottawa, wondered how long her house could survive the onslaught. She noted in her diary that the weather forecast had predicted a further 28 mm of freezing rain. 'I don't see how the trees can take any more, never mind the roof … Again we lost power just as we were finished cooking supper. Again, we lit the fire and candles as the drizzle continued. That night was constant explosions that was hard to sleep through. Each explosion

ICEBOUND *After the ice storm, thousands of servicemen helped in the task of restoring power and clearing roads.*

Nature's Icy Grip

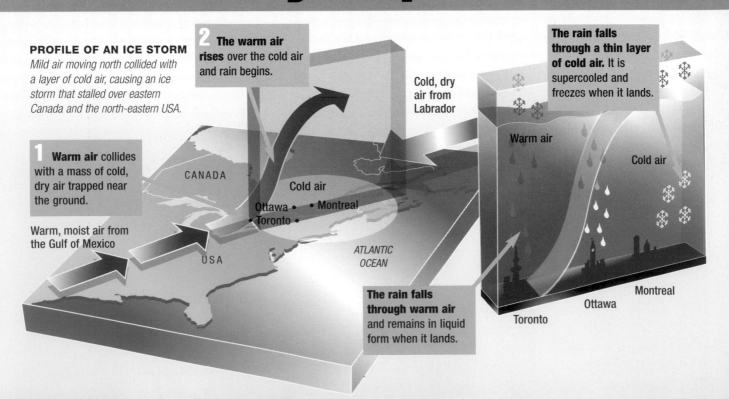

PROFILE OF AN ICE STORM
Mild air moving north collided with a layer of cold air, causing an ice storm that stalled over eastern Canada and the north-eastern USA.

1 **Warm air** collides with a mass of cold, dry air trapped near the ground.

Warm, moist air from the Gulf of Mexico

2 **The warm air rises** over the cold air and rain begins.

Cold, dry air from Labrador

Cold air

Ottawa • • Montreal
• Toronto •

CANADA

USA

ATLANTIC OCEAN

The rain falls through warm air and remains in liquid form when it lands.

The rain falls through a thin layer of cold air. It is supercooled and freezes when it lands.

Warm air

Cold air

Toronto

Ottawa

Montreal

During Canada's worst ice storm, 28 people died and an estimated 4 million were plunged into darkness.

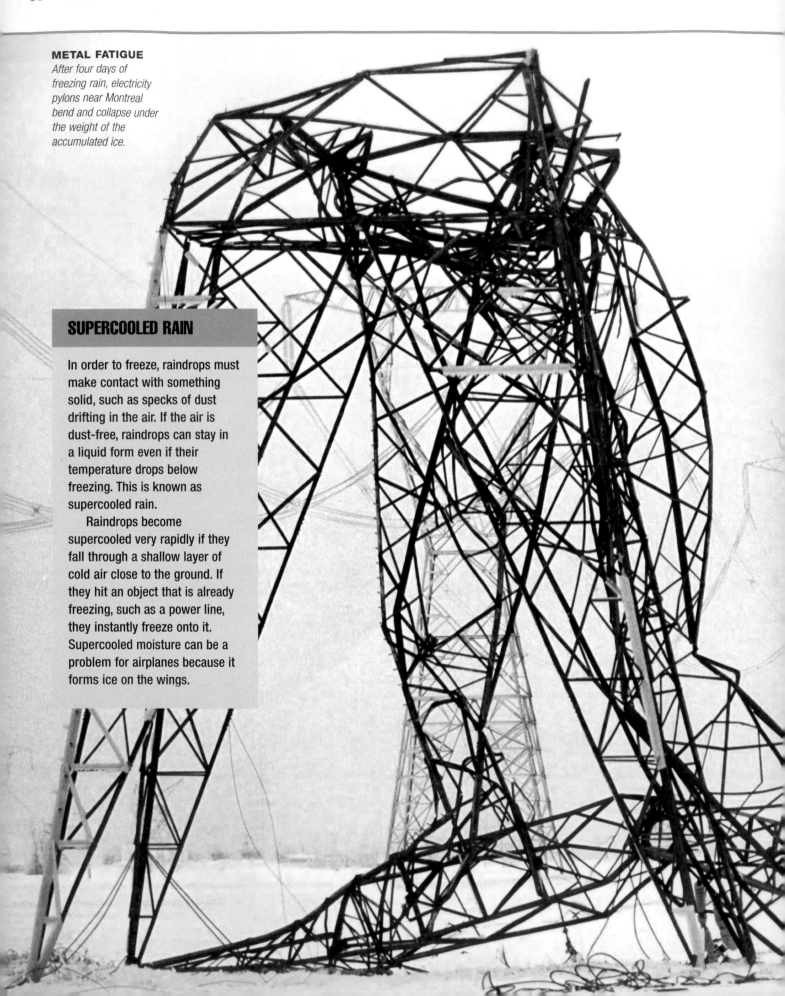

METAL FATIGUE
After four days of freezing rain, electricity pylons near Montreal bend and collapse under the weight of the accumulated ice.

SUPERCOOLED RAIN

In order to freeze, raindrops must make contact with something solid, such as specks of dust drifting in the air. If the air is dust-free, raindrops can stay in a liquid form even if their temperature drops below freezing. This is known as supercooled rain.

Raindrops become supercooled very rapidly if they fall through a shallow layer of cold air close to the ground. If they hit an object that is already freezing, such as a power line, they instantly freeze onto it. Supercooled moisture can be a problem for airplanes because it forms ice on the wings.

was a large branch or tree coming down. It reminded me of movies of those whistling bombs in London during the war, with people waiting for them to hit.'

Throughout eastern Canada, and in neighbouring parts of Vermont and New York State, the story was the same. Hour after hour, day after day, rain fell and froze.

Anatomy of a storm

The storm began like many winter storms. A depression moved across Canada's border with the USA, bringing moist, mild air from the south. In Toronto – the first Canadian city in its path – the thermometer rose and rain fell. As the depression moved east over Ottawa and Montreal, it encountered a wedge of much colder air between it and the ground. Most winter depressions keep moving eastwards, but this time an unseasonally strong high-pressure area in the Atlantic slowed the storm's progress. With the cold air mass also trapped near the ground, freezing rain fell on and off over the region for several days.

The writer Mark Twain was lyrical in his description of ice storms, 'when every bough and twig is strung with ice beads, frozen dewdrops, and the whole tree sparkles, cold and white …' But the effects of the 1998 storm would have dismayed even him. Many specimen trees in Montreal's botanical gardens were badly mutilated, and at Mount Royal, in the city centre, over 75,000 trees were damaged. In the 'triangle de la noirceur', or 'Dark Triangle', to the east of Montreal, an area famous for its cider apples, leafless orchards looked like rows of smashed sticks.

For Hydro-Québec – the region's electricity supplier – the ice storm was nothing short of a nightmare. As the ice built up, the strain on high-voltage power lines and pylons became immense. By the time the storm died out, the maximum ice thickness – recorded at Cornwall, near the US border – was almost 11 cm. Piled up on an outstretched arm, this would weigh at least 3 kg. On a power line suspended between pylons, it could easily weigh several tonnes.

By late afternoon on Tuesday, low-voltage cables were snapping under the strain. The following day, a high-voltage line collapsed, plunging over 100,000 homes into darkness. A Hydro-Québec lineman sent to survey the damage reported: 'All that's still standing here is me.'

As Wednesday wore on, controllers at Hydro-Québec's HQ watched as the grid failed. By the day's end, over a million Canadians were without power – half of them in the 'Dark Triangle'. Thursday brought a brief pause, but by then the ice was doing its worst. Shortly after midday, a string of 28 pylons collapsed on the outskirts of Montreal, shutting down one of the city's main power lines. Reputedly among the strongest in the world, the pylons were now toppled relics. In all, the ice storm brought down over 7,000 km (4,350 miles) of power lines, 1,000 pylons and 28,000 telegraph poles.

Silence in the city

On Friday, crisis managers at Montreal's police department took stock. The freezing rain had begun afresh, threatening what remained of the city's power supply. A section of 38 pylons gave way, and the city's water-filtration plants came to a halt. Without them, Montreal could not function. The mayor, Pierre Bourque, decided to cut the city centre's power supply to release capacity for the water-filtration plants.

Everything powered by electricity, from computers to cash machines, crashed at the same moment. The only light was the muted greyness of the January afternoon. The army was drafted in and, although Montrealers did not know it, an evacuation order was only hours away. But as darkness fell on Friday evening, the weather changed. The thermometer crept above freezing, and at last millions of people heard a welcome sound – the slow, steady drip of melting ice.

Black Blizzard

Sunday, April 14, 1935, dawned bright and clear over the Great Plains in the heart of the American Midwest. But during the afternoon, a mountainous black cloud appeared on the horizon, turning day into night and heralding the worst storm of America's 'Dust Bowl Years'.

During the 1930s, drought, high winds and soil erosion combined to turn the American Midwest into a giant dust bowl.

41

The storm began in the farmlands of eastern Colorado, where years of drought and over-farming had reduced the topsoil to dust. Whipped up by strong winds, millions of tonnes of topsoil were sucked into the air and formed a cloud 3 km (1^3/4 miles) high. Swirling and boiling as it swept over the ground at speeds of up to 95 km/h (60 mph), the dust cloud soon spread to neighbouring Kansas, before moving south across Oklahoma and Texas. Ahead of the storm the sky darkened, the temperature dropped and people fled. 'Everybody tried to get out of there,' remembers Margie Daniels of Hooker, Oklahoma. 'Everybody was scrambling to get out to their vehicles and find their families.' At first there was silence, but suddenly the air filled with the sound of thousands of birds trying to escape the advancing wall of dust.

On the outskirts of Boise City, in the Panhandle region of north-west Oklahoma, people took shelter in any buildings they could find. Cars and trucks stalled as dust

SMOTHERED *The town of Stratford, Texas, is just minutes from being engulfed by a vast cloud of dust, in this picture taken in April 1935.*

clogged their engines, and people on foot lost their way in the eerie darkness. Out on the plains families waited in silence, hoping that their wooden homesteads would withstand the onslaught. 'My dad went into the kitchen when that dirt was blowing the hardest,' recalls J.R. Davison, who was a boy at the time. As the storm hit and the whole structure began to move, his father clutched at the house's wooden framework. 'I can remember my dad … taking hold of those two-by-fours, and his hands would move up and down 5 or 6 inches, this wind was whipping so hard. And I thought to myself, "This thing may blow away." '

In Dodge City, Kansas, complete darkness reigned for more than half an hour, followed by a murky brown half-light that lasted for the rest of the day. Dust was everywhere, forced through gaps in doors and window-frames by the strength of the wind. Asphyxiated cattle lay scattered in the open fields; others sought shelter close to farm buildings or hunched close to the ground. After the storm had subsided, one Nebraska family discovered that their only edible food was a plate of biscuits that had been accidentally left in the oven. Everything else was coated in dust and grit.

A man-made disaster

The Black Sunday storm, as it came to be known, was the most notorious and one of the most intense dust storms that raged across the USA and Canadian Midwest between 1933 and 1936. The storms were part of an ecological catastrophe that destroyed 100 million acres of farmland, brought financial ruin to thousands of the region's farmers and displaced hundreds of

STIFLING DUST
On a Midwest homestead, a young boy covers his nose and mouth as the air fills with fine-grained sand.

> # ❝ A nation that destroys its soil, destroys itself. ❞
>
> *President Franklin D. Roosevelt, 1937*

thousands of people, including an estimated 15 per cent of the population of Oklahoma.

At the heart of the disaster lay the plough. In the late 19th century, thousands of homesteaders arrived in the Midwest and ploughed up large areas of grassland to plant wheat and maize. The Midwest was going through an unusually wet period, although no one realised it at the time, and farmers' yields were high. In any case, many farmers believed that 'rain follows the plough'. This traditional wisdom was to be proved disastrously wrong when, in the 1920s, Nature reverted to type. The climate became drier, with as little as 20 cm of rain a year. In the early 1930s drought set in. Farmers continued to plough and plant, but nothing would grow. As the ground cover that kept the soil in place had gone, the winds that race across the plains from the west blew the soil away. Erosion spread like a disease, with the wind exploiting any break in the surface vegetation.

For the people of the southern Midwest, the impact was particularly catastrophic. Lawrence Svobida had bought land in Kansas before the Dust Bowl years. 'It was breathtaking – hundreds of acres of wheat that were mine. To me it was the most beautiful scene in all the world.' Many of his neighbours felt the same. But when drought struck, followed by the dust storms, Svobida watched all his hard work being blown away. 'When I knew my crop was irrevocably gone, I experienced a deathly feeling which, I hope, can affect a man only once in a life time.'

Defeated on their own land, many farmers packed up their possessions and headed west to the fruit farms of California, where they worked as migrant labourers. Their journey – which inspired John Steinbeck's novel *The Grapes of Wrath* – was long, and the welcome often less than friendly.

Growing awareness

The early dust storms were local calamities, and few people outside the Midwest had any conception of their size and scale. All that changed in May 1934, when a gigantic storm carried dust as far east as New York and Washington DC. Clifford Hope, a representative from Kansas, was in Washington at the time. 'It showered dust on the White House. Some was said to have settled on the President's desk. When I left the Capitol that evening I found my car covered with a film of familiar-looking Kansas soil.' Dust even reached the decks of ships 500 km (310 miles) out to sea. In this one storm, the wind lifted more than 300 million tonnes of once-fertile topsoil from the Great Plains.

One of the lessons of the dust storms was that soil is precious and must be looked after. In 1935, under President Franklin D. Roosevelt's New Deal, Congress passed the Soil Conservation Act to encourage farming methods aimed at keeping the soil in place. As Roosevelt later said: 'A nation that destroys its soil, destroys itself.' Farmers planted trees to create shelter belts, putting a brake on the wind. They also took care to keep the soil covered, sometimes by planting two different crops each year.

Another lesson was that rain could not be guaranteed. Fortunately, the Great Plains turned out to have another water source, hidden under ground. At the end of the last Ice Age, the glaciers that covered much of North America melted and soaked into the ground, forming a vast reservoir – the Ogallala Aquifer – which was first tapped in the early 20th century. During the 1930s, as electricity spread across the Plains, farmers drilled their own boreholes, powered by electric pumps. Today, the heart of the former Dust Bowl is green and productive and – as long as the groundwater lasts – looks certain to stay that way.

MEMORIES OF THE DUSTBOWL

Melt White was tending chickens at his family's Texan farmhouse when the Black Sunday dust storm struck. Although he was a boy at the time, he remembers it as if it happened yesterday.

'And it kept getting worse and worse. And the wind kept blowing harder and harder. It kept getting darker and darker. And the old house is just a-vibratin' like it was gonna blow away. And I started trying to see my hand. And I kept bringing my hand up closer and closer and closer and closer. And I finally touched the end of my nose and I still couldn't see my hand. That's how black it was. A lot of people got out of bed, got their children out of the bed. Got down praying, thought that was it. They thought that was the end of the world.'

The Great Blizzard

Forecasters looked at their weather maps in disbelief. It was March, with typical spring weather, but a winter storm was brewing, promising hurricane winds and heavy snowfall. Most surprising of all, it was heading for Florida.

Snow is not big news in Alaska, or in New England, or even on the streets of New York. But snow in the southern states of Florida and Alabama certainly is. In Roanoke, Alabama, where Don Strength worked for a local radio station, even a scattering of snow is a major news event. So when he heard the forecast of blizzard conditions and temperatures hitting record lows, he was more than a little sceptical. 'I can remember going to bed the night before and thinking, "Boy, the Weather Service must be losing it." If I remember correctly, it was in the low to mid 50s with rain.' For Alabama, the low 50°s Fahrenheit – about 12°C – is fairly normal for March. At around 5 am the phone rang, calling Don in to work. From the moment he arrived at the studio, the world was turned upside down.

Forecasters had watched the storm brewing in the Gulf of Mexico for several days. Usually, such storms fizzle out, but this one didn't. As it tracked north-east, it intensified, lashing the Florida coast with winds over 160 km/h (100 mph). A 2,000 km (1,200 mile) long cold front soon stretched up the entire eastern flank of the USA, causing mountainous seas along the Atlantic seaboard and bringing blizzards to places that had never seen them before. 'The storm was so intense and widespread there were actually seven states that saw more than 40 inches of snow in certain locations,' Paul Kocin at The Weather Channel recalled. Interstate roads were closed, and other roads became impassable. Every major aiport on the east coast was closed at some point.

Michael Leach from Glencoe, Alabama, remembers heavy snow starting at around 6.30 on a Friday evening. Around 8 o'clock, 50-75 mm lay on the ground. 'By about 10, the wind picked up dramatically. I remember looking out my back door and seeing sheets of snow being blown by the wind. I thought the snow would never end ... At about 10.30, ... I saw a flash of lightning and then heard a loud clap of thunder during a period of very heavy snow. It almost scared me to death. About 5 minutes after that, the power went off, and it would not come back on until the following Thursday or Friday. That night, my mom, dad, 3-year-old sister and I slept in the living room in front of the fireplace to stay warm.'

> ❝ **Four-foot snowdrifts in Roanoke, Alabama, are still hard to believe.** ❞
>
> *Don Strength, local radio presenter, Alabama*

Snow in the Deep South

North-east Florida had up to 15 cm of snow – the biggest single fall ever recorded – and over a dozen major tornadoes were reported across the state. Roofs collapsed, or were torn off by the wind, and the sea burst ashore along Florida's east coast. More than 1 m of snow fell in parts of the Carolinas, and in Tennessee deep drifts smothered abandoned cars. In Alabama, the normal radio schedules were scrapped to make way

In 1993, a vicious storm brought heavy snow to the eastern USA, killing 270 people and causing over $3 billion damage in two days.

45

TUMULTUOUS SKIES *Seen from a weather satellite, the 1993 superstorm arcs over the entire eastern seaboard of the USA, from Florida to Maine.*

for emergency messages and storm updates. Many homes were without power, and moving about was difficult and dangerous, because of a lack of snowploughs. In Birmingham, the state capital, the thermometer dropped to –16.5°C, an all-time record for March. After four days, Don Strength finally headed home. 'Four-foot snowdrifts in Roanoke, Alabama. Still hard to believe.'

Apart from blizzards and tornadoes, the 1993 storm front also generated more than 60,000 bolts of lightning, which lit up the snowflakes in lurid shades of green or blue. This phenomenon, known as 'thundersnow', only occurs in the most violent winter storms.

The storm lasted about 48 hours, before heading out into the Atlantic. Across the eastern USA, the damage to property was enormous: power lines were brought down by trees, and buildings were left in ruins. The cost was put at over $3 billion, and 270 people died – from the cold, from blizzard-related accidents or, in Florida particularly, by being swept out to sea.

MOVING OUT *On Interstate 20 outside Atlanta, Georgia, a driver and passenger abandon their car after sliding off the highway.*

Lying just south of the Equator, Leyte Island in the Philippines is one of the rainiest places on Earth. But even by local standards, February 2006 was very wet. The south of the island was drenched by 2 m of rain in just ten days.

Buried Alive

On the morning of February 17, the rain showed no sign of easing. Streams had become raging torrents, and roads and fields were flooded. Mud was everywhere, and minor landslips had closed many roads. In the village of Guinsaugon, near the southern end of the island, farmers stood idle and children arrived at school soaked through. A large number of local women had also gone to the school that morning for a meeting.

A river of mud

At about 9.30 am, catastrophe struck. At the head of a steep valley above the village of Guinsaugon, half a mountainside gave way. Weighed down by the quantity of water that had fallen in recent days, more than 1 million m³ of mud broke away from the underlying rock and surged downhill. It tore trees from the ground and smashed them to pulp as it followed the steepest route towards the valley floor.

Alicia Miravalles was near the bottom of the valley when the landslide began. She felt the ground shaking and realised that something was wrong. 'Moments later I heard a loud explosion, then the sound of many airplanes,' she recalls. 'I looked up to the mountain and I saw the ground and boulders rushing down.' The landslide was moving so fast she had no hope of escaping it by running. Fortunately, it came to a halt before reaching her. 'If the landslide did not stop,' she says, 'I would be dead now.'

Most of Guinsaugon lay directly in the mud's path. The school was one of the first buildings hit. Then the mud moved through the rest of the village, engulfing and flattening houses made of bamboo and palm thatch. By the time it stopped, it had buried nearly 300 ha (740 acres) of land under a layer of mud up to 25 m deep. The school, like most of the village's buildings, had disappeared, with more than 200 children and 100 adults inside.

The mud's impact was so swift and so complete that few eyewitnesses survived. Irenea Velasco was one of the lucky ones;

UNEQUAL STRUGGLE *Despite the overwhelming odds, rescuers try to locate survivors buried under the mud in the village of Guinsaugon.*

In 2006, a mudslide buried an entire Philippine village. More than 1,000 people were killed, and the village school was never found.

despite being swept away, she managed to grab hold of the leg of a billiard table caught up in the slide. The table top was strongly built and it protected her from being crushed by rocks as big as beach balls. Clinging to the table leg, she was carried along with the debris as it overwhelmed Guinsaugon.

Another villager, Florencio Libaton, was at home when his wife Porfiria burst in, shouting that the mountain had collapsed. Libaton's first thoughts were for their children, who were in the school, but his wife told him it was too late. They had to get out themselves. He grabbed her by the arm and they ran as fast as they could, but the landslide advanced on them and swept them off their feet. 'God, is this how we are going to die?' Libaton remembers saying, as the torrent of mud, boulders and broken tree trunks boiled around them.

Despite using all his strength, he lost his grip on his wife and was carried downhill towards what he was sure would be his end.

The buried village

Unlike avalanches or earthquakes, mudslides leave little room for miracle escapes. The weight of the mud crushes most buildings that are not made of concrete or stone. And when the mud stops flowing, it is sticky and hazardous to walk on, especially after incessant rain. If it does dry out, the surface sets in a solid layer, known as a 'pan', that can be far harder than ordinary soil.

In Guinsaugon, soldiers and Red Cross workers were rapidly on the scene, joining local people as they tried to locate survivors. Specialist teams from abroad arrived, but the devastation was so massive that people held out little hope. Rosette Lerias, governor of Southern Leyte, was honest about the struggle ahead.

> **❝I heard a loud explosion ... I looked up to the mountain and I saw the ground and boulders rushing down.❞**
>
> *Alicia Miravalles*

TAKING STOCK *A US Navy helicopter flies around the perimeter of the mudslide, nearly 4 km (2½ miles) across at its widest point on the valley floor.*

THE SEARCH CONTINUES *Filipino soldiers dig through rock-choked mud in a desperate attempt to locate the village school.*

'There are no signs of life, no rooftops, no nothing,' she said. 'I have a glimmer of hope, based on the rule of thumb – within 24 hours you can still find survivors. After that, you move on to the recovery phase.'

Someone claimed to have heard sounds from beneath the mud, and others received SMS text messages from people known to have been in the school. 'We're still in one room, alive,' read one message, sent by a teacher. But as the day wore on, the texts stopped coming.

The mud was too soft for machinery, so soldiers and volunteers tried to dig towards signs of life armed with little more than spades and hands. 'It's very difficult,' explained army captain Edmund Abella. 'The place is so vast and the mud is so thick. When we try to walk, we get stuck in the mud.' Without any landmarks, it was hard even to know where to start. Sniffer dogs were brought in, but the mud worked like a hermetic seal, shutting in any telltale scents.

Meanwhile, under the debris, Florencio Libaton could only wait. He had come to rest on his right side, pinned by a treetrunk against some rocks. Although he could not be seen, he could at least breathe, thanks to cracks in the mud. After several hours he heard familiar voices overhead. One of them was a neighbour who was searching for missing relatives. 'I yelled out, "Help! Help!"' he remembers, 'then they pulled me out after digging with their hands.'

Irenea Velasco was saved by her billiard table, even though she ended up pinned to the mud by one of its

10 biggest landslides since 1900

	DATE	LOCATION	VOLUME	DETAILS
1	1903	Turtle Mountain, Canada	0.03 km^3	Spontaneous landslide partly destroys the town of Frank. About 70 people killed.
2	1911	Soi, Tajikistan	2 km^3	Massive rockslide triggered by earthquake dams river and creates 65 km lake. Few casualties.
3	1920	Ningxia, China	Unknown	Earthquake causes hundreds of separate landslides. About 100,000 people killed.
4	1949	Khait, Tajikistan	Unknown	Landslide triggered by earthquake destroys the city of Khait. About 20,000 casualties.
5	1962	Ancash, Peru	0.013 km^3	Debris slide from Mount Huascarán engulfs the village of Ranrahirca, causing about 4,000 deaths.
6	1963	Vaiont, Italy	0.25 km^3	Spontaneous rockslide plunges into Vaiont reservoir, causing dam to overflow. Several villages are destroyed, causing about 2,000 casualties.
7	1964	Prince William Sound, Alaska	Unknown	Following one of the greatest earthquakes in history, extensive landslide damage occurs in Anchorage and surrounding region.
8	1970	Yungay, Peru	0.05 km^3	The town of Yungay is buried by a volcanic mudslide. About 20,000 deaths.
9	1980	Mt St Helens, Washington State	2.8 km^3	The biggest landslide in recorded history, triggered by the eruption of Mt St Helens. Few casualties.
10	1985	Armero, Colombia	Unknown	Eruption of Nevado del Ruiz destroys the town of Armero, causing 25,000 deaths.

legs. Unable to extricate herself, she waited for people to prise her free. When she and Florencio Libaton spoke from their hospital beds, neither was in a mood for rejoicing. Both had lost their children and spouses, as well as most of their friends and neighbours.

Late on the day of the slide, one of the rescue workers, Dag Navarette, spoke to the BBC. Like everyone, he was stunned by the magnitude of the disaster. 'The mountain rose to about 1,000 m above sea level and it now looks as if about half of the mountain has collapsed onto the village. The area is not yet stable. We had to call off the rescue because the mountain is still crumbling. We hear it rumbling all the time. It sounds like an army of tanks making for us.'

After 24 hours, another rescue worker, Wangyu Abieva, described how it felt to be working in a place where all visible landmarks had been swept away. 'We searched for the school building, but nobody could find the location because most of the houses have been moved about half a kilometre away from their original location by the mud. The village has simply shifted. Some locals said they heard knocking in one place. We tried to dig but the search produced nothing. There are big stones, boulders and rocks getting in our way.'

> **We searched for the school building, but nobody could find the location because most of the houses have been moved ... by the mud.**
>
> *Wangyu Abieva, rescue worker*

The rain continued, threatening more landslides and making rescue work difficult. Abieva found it hard to be positive. 'On the periphery there are people watching and waiting for relatives. It spurs us on. We spent some time desperately knocking on rocks hoping for a response from below. But there were no answers.'

A week after the mudslide, Governor Rosette Lerias announced that the authorities were calling off the recovery operation as there was no possibility of finding more survivors or bodies. The culprit was probably an earthquake, which struck before the slide occurred. It measured 2.6 on the Richter scale – one of hundreds of minor quakes that occur round the Pacific's 'Ring of Fire' every day. Few people on Leyte even noticed it, but even a minor earthquake releases enough energy to liquefy a hillside and turn it into a deadly river of mud.

Ironically, shortly before the disaster, environment department officials in faraway Manila, capital of the Philippines, had been studying the island with concern as they had established that Leyte straddles an active seismic fault. Four-fifths of the island was known to be at risk, and experts were soon due to begin detailed mapping of the south to establish the level of danger. For Guinsaugon, tragically, the assessment came too late.

DEATH IN THE ANDES

• 20,000 buried by a mudslide in the town of Yungay in 1970

Yungay At 3.23 in the afternoon of May 31, 1970, a powerful earthquake measuring 7.9 on the Richter scale shook the seabed off northern Peru. It sent a series of brutal shock waves rippling outwards, some of which hit Peru's coastal province of Ancash, destroying buildings and causing widespread loss of life. Worse still, in just under a minute the shock waves loosened the entire northern face of Mount Huascarán – at 6,768 m above sea level, the fourth-highest peak in South America.

An area of ice and rock nearly 2 km (1¼ miles) long started to move, and then broke into billions of fragments that were funnelled down the mountainside. As the flow reached lower ground, a high ridge of rock split it in two. One arm went on to engulf hundreds of hectares of farmland, while the other surged down a valley towards the town of Yungay, about 5 km (3 miles) away. At the time, many of Yungay's residents were crowded into the town's bars and meeting places to watch the closing minutes of a World Cup football match on television. As the earthquake hit and buildings collapsed, people poured into the streets, only to hear a distant roar from the direction of Huascarán. Many knelt and held hands and prayed in the street, thinking that the end of the world was coming, while others tried to run.

The mudslide, or *huayco*, which was travelling at speeds of up to 300 km/h (185 mph), buried the entire centre of Yungay, along with most of the people trapped there, in moments. Only those who managed to reach high ground survived. As one local child has described it, 'It was a beautiful place with big houses and flowers everywhere. Then the water came pouring down from Mount Huascarán and buried the people.'

The earthquake had filled the air with dust, and it is impossible to guess how many people realised the fate that was about to befall them. An aerial photograph taken shortly after the disaster is marked with a cross to show the Plaza de Armas, Yungay's central square. Above it are the words 'AQUI ESTUVO YUNGAY' – 'Yungay was here'.

TOTAL DESTRUCTION *A high-altitude image taken 24 hours after the mudslide shows the complete obliteration of Yungay.*

White Death

After weeks of exceptionally heavy snowfalls, an avalanche smashed into the Alpine village of Galtür, killing 31 people.

53

On the afternoon of February 23, 1999, a huge slab of snow became detached from the slopes above the Austrian ski resort of Galtür and started plunging down the mountainside towards the village below.

Galtür villager, Georg Walter, remembers the terrifying experience as the avalanche tore into the resort. 'This cloud of snow came down like a steamroller,' he says. 'I saw it rise 40 to 50 metres over that hotel, maybe even higher.' Luggi Salner, a local ski instructor, was also there. 'I saw a huge wave coming towards us. It was like in those films about Hawaii. I thought, "This can't be happening." I was horrified, my eyes widened with fear. Then I screamed, "It's coming!"' Experts have since estimated that the avalanche was travelling at 200 km/h (124 mph).

Smothered with snow

Walter and Salner both survived the onslaught, but others in Galtür were less fortunate. Christa and Helmut Kapellner from Düsseldorf in Germany knew the resort well, having been there on skiing holidays for 20 years. When the avalanche struck, they were walking back to their hotel, videotaping the village, which already lay under a thicker covering of snow than they had seen in all their years of visiting it.

'The avalanche came from behind,' Christa said in an interview with BBC television's *Horizon* series. 'Helmut shouted "Christa!", but I couldn't answer. His legs were pulled from under him by the force and I was hit from behind.' It was the last time she saw her husband alive. 'If we hadn't stopped to take the video,' she admitted, 'then we might have been safe.'

Another tourist, Jason Tait from England, watched the avalanche sweep past the window of his hotel. 'You couldn't see more than a few inches away from the pane of glass,' he says. 'It was like looking into a swirling washing machine.' As soon as the rumbling noise stopped, Tait joined others outside to see what he could do to help. 'We spent seven hours digging to see whether we could get anyone out alive … but the snow had set like concrete. Wherever you went it was solid.'

Despite the difficulties, rescuers dug out many survivors, including Christa Kapellner. She had been buried under 1.5 m of snow. 'I tried to create an air pocket with my hands,' she says, 'and get to the surface, wherever that was. I did not succeed and gave up.' Rescuers uncovered her two hours later, hypothermic and unconscious. After she had been

TRAGEDY ON THE SLOPES
Rescuers search for survivors, using slender poles to feel bodies buried beneath a metre or more of snow.

HELICOPTER RESCUE *With roads impassable, nearly 4,000 holidaymakers had to be airlifted to safety – an operation that took the best part of a week.*

medically treated and come to, her first thought was for her husband. 'I kept asking about my husband, Helmut. It was terrible to find out that he'd died.'

Deadly falls

The avalanche was the result of freak weather, which set in near the end of January 1999 and dropped heavy loads of snow on the Alps. Around Galtür, twice as much snow fell in the first three weeks of February than the region normally gets in an entire winter. 'There was just one area of low pressure after another and no fine weather in between,' explains Manfred Lorenz, manager of the Galtür Avalanche Protection Project, set up after the disaster. As moist air from the Atlantic met cold air over the Alps, the snow piled up to record depths.

By February 23, forecasters had posted avalanche warnings throughout the Alps. In Austria, the warning that day was at 5 – the maximum on the danger scale. But Erhard Berger, a forecaster on Austrian TV, thought this was an understatement. A few days later, he said he would have put the danger level at 6, if it had existed.

The problem, as always with avalanches, was that it was impossible to know when or where one might strike. Avalanches are triggered by an accumulation of local factors. Snow on one slope can be safe and solid, while on another – just a few hundred metres away – it can be on a knife-edge point between stability and collapse. Even in normal years, the Alps experience thousands of minor avalanches, which eat away at the snowpack without causing serious harm. But every so often, weather and topography coincide in a lethal way. Thousands of tonnes of snow build up over a long period, and then suddenly break free. The result is a giant avalanche that sweeps away anything and anyone in its path.

This is what happened at Galtür on February 23. By lunchtime, snow had fallen so thickly that the resort was practically cut off. It was too dangerous for skiers to go out on the slopes; instead, people lingered in the local restaurants and bars, watching the weather from their warm surroundings, little suspecting what it would bring. And still the snow fell. These falls, like the ones in the days before, sat on a melt crust – a smooth layer of ice formed, nearly two weeks earlier, when the snow briefly melted and then refroze. The wind blew strongly, piling up deeper and deeper drifts. Suddenly, at 4.09 pm, high above the ski station, the bond between the new falls and the melt crust gave way. More than 250,000 m³ of snow plummeted towards the village 1,300 m below.

Local hero

Many who survived the avalanche owe their lives to Dr Friedrich Treidl, who was on duty at the Galtür clinic. He recalls his response. 'As quick as possible

I took my rescue bag and went out … At first it was almost unbelievable. I was walking on snow level with the first-floor windows of the houses. You just couldn't recognise the place … Some buildings I used to see – I didn't see them. Others I saw completely destroyed.'

He set up a makeshift clinic in a garage, where he treated victims who had been dug out alive. 'The people we could dig out first had a very good chance of survival,' he says, 'and there were quite a lot of people who were either still conscious or who quickly regained consciousness. But the avalanche was obviously so massive we couldn't begin recovering people from all the places where it had struck.'

In all, 31 people lost their lives – one of the highest death tolls in a European avalanche in the past 50 years. Manfred Lorenz, who lost members of his family, expresses the horror of the experience. 'You expect avalanches,' he says, 'but in a place like Galtür you don't expect avalanches to come right into the village so close to the church. It was astonishing and shocking to see places which historically for centuries had been considered safe suddenly hit. I lost my mother and my daughter-in-law in the avalanche. We lost local people, children, adults and, of course, many tourists who were in Galtür at the time.'

In fact, many people felt angry and betrayed by the events of February 23, because in theory they should have been safe. As a result of the popularity of skiing, many Alpine villages and towns have undergone a construction boom in recent decades. To prevent avalanche damage, local authorities in Austria use a three-tier zoning system, which dictates where buildings can be constructed. The red zone has the highest risk of avalanches, and is strictly off-limits to construction of all kinds. In the yellow zone, the risk is less, but buildings have to be reinforced. In the green zone, the avalanche risk is assessed as minimal, so no special precautions are required. When the 1999 avalanche struck Galtür, however, it smashed its way straight through the zoning map, ploughing into the heart of the village's green zone.

Now, Lorenz works to make sure that such as disaster will never be repeated. His Galtür Avalanche Protection Project has built walls and steel snow barriers on the heights above Galtür to stop avalanches in their tracks. It has also replanted trees, which act as natural barriers, on slopes where they had been felled. Other precautions include re-routing roads, covered with tunnels, in and out of the village and reinforcing buildings. 'We were able to use the building damage to measure the force of the avalanche,' says Jörg Heumader, an engineer who specialises in avalanche protection, 'and we were able to work out more or less what kind of force was necessary to cause this damage to the buildings.' As a result of their work, Galtür today really is among the safest ski resorts in the Alps, and the tourists have returned.

CAUGHT IN AN AVALANCHE

Experienced skiers instinctively check for avalanche risks. For off-piste skiers, safety depends on reading Nature's danger signs. The safest time to ski on suspect snow is in the early morning, after a cloudless night. In these conditions, any wet snow is likely to have refrozen, keeping the snowpack safe. Windy weather or sudden changes in temperature have exactly the opposite effect and are signals to leave the skis indoors.

For anyone caught in an avalanche, wet snow (see page 56) is the most dangerous, because it is heavy and airless and it sets like concrete. People buried by it are often subject to 'crush syndrome', a dangerous condition that squeezes fluid out of their tissues and into their blood. After they are rescued, victims often find that their urine turns as dark as tea – the result of proteins being forced out of their muscles by the sheer weight of snow.

Dry powdery snow generally causes less severe injuries and is easier to dig, allowing victims to scoop out air pockets. Even so, unless help arrives soon, the chances of survival are slim. More than 90 per cent of victims survive if they are dug out in less than 15 minutes, but only one in ten survive after an hour. Depth is also important: having just 1 m of snow overhead is enough to reduce someone's chances of survival to 20 per cent.

This explains the key rule for those who witness an avalanche but are unharmed: do not waste time looking for help – start digging for survivors straight away.

❝ It was almost unbelievable. I was walking on snow level with the first-floor windows of the houses. You just couldn't recognise the place. ❞

Dr Friedrich Treidl

Living with the danger

Snow may be legendary for its softness, but even small avalanches can maim and kill. Faced with these dangers, many mountain communities and ski resorts have active programmes for avalanche control and prevention, ranging from tree planting to the use of artillery.

Every avalanche is different, because no two snowfalls are the same. As the snowpack builds up, the different layers bind to each other in different ways. Large, wet snowflakes adhere particularly well, because their six-pointed crystals melt and refreeze easily, locking into a solid mass. At the other

extreme, small hard pellets of 'dry' snow behave more like a powder. Instead of sticking, they flow over each other like tiny ball bearings, which is why this kind of snow is ideal for skiing. Settled snow – or snowpack – is also affected by other factors, including changes in temperature, orientation and the wind. But for an avalanche to occur, one factor overrides all others: the steepness of the mountain slope.

If the slope is greater than about 50 degrees (roughly, 1 in 2) the chances of a big avalanche are slim. The snow slips off at frequent intervals, so deep snowpack never gets a chance to form. On the other hand, if the slope is less than 30 degrees (1 in 3), the snow settles in a stable mass that gravity cannot shift. Between these two lies a 20-degree danger zone – from 30 to 50 degrees. On this kind of slope, snow can accumulate for days or weeks, but as it piles up, it becomes progressively more unstable. Eventually, it becomes a 'critical system' – one that can be destabilised by the tiniest vibration, triggering a sudden and cataclysmic collapse.

For hundreds of years, Alpine villages have lived with this danger and taken precautions against it. Traditionally, mountainside woods, called *Bannwälder* (literally, 'protective forests'), were left untouched to keep fallen snow in place. They still exist, although not as extensively as in the past. Stone buildings were sometimes constructed with a 'prow' pointing uphill, to part any sliding snow and throw it to either side. Above all, people avoided building on slopes or in gullies where avalanches were known to have struck in the past.

Other, more modern precautions aim to eliminate the possibility of avalanches. High above roads and resorts, steel

barriers help to anchor the snow, while in western Canada, army patrols fire artillery shells into heavy snowpack to break it up before it can cause damage to roads. On the same principle, many ski resorts use 'avalaunchers' – compressed-air cannons that fire heavy projectiles – to prevent build-ups of snow. Avalaunchers are not cheap – at the Jackson Hole resort in Wyoming, the 'artillery' budget is more than $100,000 a year. Even so, this is a small fraction of the cost of the damage an avalanche would cause. More importantly, these pre-emptive strikes help to save lives.

10 deadly avalanches since 1900

An estimated 1 million avalanches occur around the world each year, but chiefly in sparsely populated regions. Most deaths occur when people are buried under the snow and asphyxiated. The number of people dying in avalanches has increased with the growing popularity of skiing.

	DATE	PLACE	DEATHS	
1	May 31, 1970	Mount Huascarán, Peru	17,000	A mud and snowslide, triggered by an earthquake, destroyed the town of Yungay.
2	Dec 13, 1916	Austrian Alps	10,000	During World War I, a series of avalanches, some triggered deliberately by artillery fire, killed at least that number of soldiers.
3	Jan 10, 1962	Mount Huascarán, Peru	2,700	The victims lived in the Andean village of Ranrahirca.
4	Winter 1950-1	European Alps	250	Exceptionally heavy snowfall triggered a series of avalanches, which killed more than 250 people in Austria, Switzerland and Italy.
5	March 1979	Lahaul Valley, India	250	An earthquake dislodged late winter snow falls, killing up to 250 people.
6	Jan 12, 1954	Blons, Austria	200	Two avalanches in one day hit the village of Blons.
7	Sept 20, 2002	North Ossetia, Russia	150	An avalanche from Mount Kazbek buried several Caucasian villages.
8	March 1, 1910	Wellington, Washington, USA	96	Snow buried two passenger trains in the Stevens Pass in the Cascade Mountains.
9	April 4, 1970	Sallanches, France	70	The victims were patients at a tuberculosis sanatorium.
10	Feb 10, 1970	Val d'Isère, France	40	The avalanche struck a youth hostel during breakfast time.

POWDER AVALANCHE
The Hochfugen avalanche was an example of a powder avalanche, when a layer of 'dry' snow breaks free, sending clouds of powdery crystals into the air.

CAUGHT ON FILM *On February 24, 1999 – a day after the Galtür disaster – tourist Georg Mader was standing on the balcony of his hotel in another Austrian ski resort, Hochfugen, when an avalanche struck. He grabbed his camera and recorded what happened. As the avalanche gathered speed, dense clouds of dry powder snow billowed into the air. By the time the avalanche reached the valley floor, the snow's momentum was enough for it to thunder uphill, where it carried on for several hundred metres, finally coming to rest at the edge of a wood. Amazingly, it claimed no victims, although it came perilously close to several buildings.*

Paris in August 2003 felt like a city that was being slowly stifled. With day-time temperatures hitting 40°C, streets and pavements shimmered, tar stuck to car tyres and ice cream melted in seconds. Tourists wearing plastic flip-flops found their footwear disintegrating as they walked.

HEAVY WEATHER *It is early morning in Paris, but the air is already thick with pollution. During the heatwave, pollution figures hit record highs. A cloud of contamination from millions of vehicle exhausts enveloped the city, the hot sun turning the fumes into an acrid and poisonous photochemical smog.*

In shops and offices, on the radio and television, there was only one topic of conversation – *la canicule*, 'the heatwave'. One visitor to Paris, Michel Cannesant, was staying near the centre of the city. He remembers opening a door onto his balcony five floors up. 'It was like walking into a furnace. Normally, you get some breeze in August, but the air was completely still. I was like everyone else – just praying for it to stop.' Even at night, there was no respite. With indoor temperatures hovering above 30°C, people without air conditioning found it difficult to get to sleep. In Paris – a northern city, where air conditioning is rarely fitted in private homes – many were unable to cope.

Chronicle of deaths foretold

The night of Monday, August 11, brought the city's highest night-time minimum temperature since records began – 25.5°C. For the hospitals of Paris, this was the worst possible news. Unlike some disasters, heatwaves are highly selective in their victims, the most vulnerable being the elderly, the poor and people who live alone. In hot conditions, the body's standard mechanisms for staying cool are sweating and pumping blood closer to the skin, but these can break down under the remorseless impact of sustained heat and high atmospheric humidity. Vulnerable people without access to regular medical attention can easily become dehydrated and their body temperatures may reach dangerous levels, leading to fatal damage to vital organs.

Over the previous weekend, doctors had warned that the heat was having deadly effects. Hospitals across the country had seen a surge in emergency admissions.

Heatwave over Europe

'It was like walking into a furnace.
Normally, you get some breeze in
August, but the air was completely
still. I was like everyone else – just
praying for it to stop.'

Michel Cannesant

COOLING OFF *Paris's street-cleaning sprayers offered people a chance to escape the heat.*

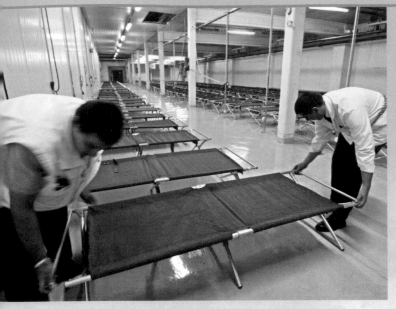

Dr Patrick Pelloux, head of the Emergency Doctors Association, estimated in that Paris alone, in just four days, there had been more than a hundred extra deaths. In the days that followed, the city's mortuaries became so full that the authorities had to find somewhere else to store corpses awaiting formal identification. On the outskirts of Paris, they commandeered a refrigerated warehouse at the city's main fruit and vegetable market. The surroundings were not very '*sympathique*' (pleasant), an official admitted, as refrigeration units hummed in the background. Workmen had installed carpets, curtains and even potted plants, but with the market functioning all around, the atmosphere was hardly serene.

As the fatalities mounted, so did people's anger. In the face of bitter complaints that the authorities were not doing enough to care for those in danger, the health minister attempted to calm the situation with a statement that matters were under control, unwisely issuing it from his holiday home. 'The emergency services are not being swamped,' he insisted. Far from damping down people's rage, his comments were like petrol poured on flames. Patrick Pelloux expressed what many felt. 'The weakest are dropping like flies,' he said. And yet, he went on, the government dared 'to say these deaths are natural. I absolutely do not agree.'

Burning up

A change in weather patterns over the North Atlantic had caused the unremitting heat. In normal summers, a large area of high pressure is centred near the Azores, bringing warm and dry conditions to North Africa and southern Spain. But in 2003, the 'Azores High' drifted north-west, until it stretched over much of Europe, blocking rain-bearing winds and stoking temperatures. In southern Spain, the thermometer reached more than 45°C, and on August 10, in southern England, it touched 38.5°C – an all-time record for the UK.

After months of drought, huge forest fires broke out in many countries, notably Portugal, where they destroyed 40 per cent of the nation's forest cover, killed 18 people and devastated countless farms. The heat and drought also triggered an economic crisis in the countryside. The harvest was at least a month ahead of schedule in many parts of Europe, and often it was so meagre that it was not worth gathering in. Corn shrivelled up, fruit dropped from drought-stricken trees and cattle stood listlessly in bone-dry pasture, kept alive with artificial feed. The worst-affected farm animals were chickens. Without air conditioning, the interiors of industrial poultry farms became like ovens, and millions of birds died.

Many major rivers, meanwhile, were reduced to less than half their normal summer flow. The Danube recorded its lowest level ever, revealing boats and military vehicles hidden on its bed since World War II.

As the blazing heat continued, an alarming new problem arose. With river water in short supply, it was getting more and more difficult to keep nuclear power stations running at a safe temperature – a single nuclear plant sucks up more than 200 million litres of water a day to cool its reactors. In France, engineers watched anxiously as the outer casings of reactors crept towards their 50°C safety limit – the temperature at which they would have had to be shut down. At the beginning of August, with the heatwave reaching it peak, France's oldest working nuclear station, at Fessenheim in Alsace, was within 2°C of the safety limit.

MELTDOWN

The effects of the 2003 heatwave were even felt high up in the Alps. Here, the dry winter followed by an extremely warm summer made glaciers melt at a record rate. In Switzerland, many glaciers lost between 5 and 10 per cent of their volume – a major meltdown for ones already in retreat. As the meltwater surged downhill, it raised the level of many alpine rivers, creating a bizarre contrast with the drought-affected rivers elsewhere in Europe.

Since 2003, some Swiss ski resorts have decided to help their glaciers to withstand the heat. At Andermatt, 3000 m² of the Gurschen glacier is covered in summer with an insulating jacket made of PVC foam. The jacket, which is removed in winter, reflects sunshine off the ice, and helps to prevent heat being absorbed.

SILVER LINING

Hot vintage

Hot, dry summers produce grapes that are rich in flavour and sugars – two ingredients for really fine wines. So what would happen in 2003? Would *la canicule* produce a special vintage, to be savoured with special reverence in years to come? For some of France's vineyards, the answer is a definite yes. In the north of the Rhône valley, 2003 was a truly classic year. Many of the vineyards of Bordeaux, by contrast, were less fortunate – conditions there were so hot that in some places the vines stopped growing, and the grapes were smaller and less juicy than normal.

In fact, the true winners in the vintage lottery lay on the other side of the Channel, in southern England. Here, the budding wine industry had an incredible summer, producing a vintage unlike anything achieved before. As if to underline the point, two years later, during Britain's presidency of the European Union, Prime Minister Tony Blair served English wine at a banquet at Hampton Court Palace for EU leaders. These included President Jacques Chirac of France, a famous lover of fine wine. What the President thought of the English wine, no one knows.

Engineers installed pumps to suck up groundwater, which they sprayed in a fine mist over the reactor's concrete casing. The experiment lasted four days, and reduced the casing's internal temperature by less than a degree. It also caused a backlash from environmentalists. 'When the heat is on,' a Green Party spokesman said, 'they don't know what to do, so they water it. What will they do in winter? Knit woollen sleeves for its pipes?'

The situation was starting to look desperate. Most of Europe's power stations, including non-nuclear ones, were facing similar problems. Hydroelectric turbines, for example, were barely ticking over, and in the slack air, wind turbines were at a standstill. In the event, the heatwave broke just in time. If it had continued for a fortnight longer, energy companies would have had to switch off half of western Europe's electricity supply.

A second spring

The heatwave ended in a spectacular way. As August drew to a close, the Azores High retreated south and cool air pushed its way down from the north. When the cool and warm air masses met, they triggered intense storms, which dropped hailstones the size of grapes. Lightning set tinder-dry woodlands on fire, only for torrential rain to put them out minutes later.

SCORCHED HARVEST *Parched sunflowers droop over a field in south-western France. With irrigation outlawed, many crops produced meagre yields.*

Tomorrow's summers

Just as one swallow does not make a summer, so a single scorching summer does not prove global warming. But many meteorologists think that the summer of 2003 was indicative of things to come. By 2100, according to Britain's Met Office, similar heatwaves might occur every two or three years.

Predicting how the climate will change in the future is notoriously uncertain, but all the signs are that the planet is getting warmer, and that extreme weather events, including heatwaves, will become common. In Europe, such changes would have mixed effects. While the summer of 2003 brought an agricultural crisis in much of southern Europe, in the north many crops produced bumper harvests. Sugar-beet yields, for example, rose by 5 per cent in Denmark and Sweden and 25 per cent in Ireland. Experts predict that climate change could boost productivity on the farms of northern Europe, but that the south faces a bleaker prospect. 'With drier conditions in the south,' says Jørgen Olesen of the Danish Institute of Agricultural Sciences, 'it will be difficult to maintain dairy production … and there will be parts of southern Europe where agricultural production is no longer viable.'

Will the death toll of 2003 be repeated? The World Meteorological Organization warns that heat-related deaths could double by around 2025. On the other hand, governments have learned from 2003. Spain, for example, has measures in place for heatwaves, including a register for those most at risk to sign up for special services.

After months of drought, the scent of damp earth filled the air, and Nature started the process of recovery, although it produced some strange results. During the heatwave, many broadleaved trees had protected themselves by shedding their leaves in a kind of premature autumn. Now, in September, the seasons seemed to be going into reverse. 'It was like a second spring,' recalls François Roumiguières, a farmer from south-west France. 'I'd never seen anything like it – buds bursting in September, and even birds starting to build their nests. But that was only on the surface. Deep down, the soil was still completely dry. It will take years for things to get back to normal. If they ever do.'

It took several months to assess the human impact of the heatwave. France had suffered most, with at least 15,000 people who died from heat-related causes. About 7,000 people died in Germany, and 4,000 each in Spain and Italy. Even in Britain – known for its cool and unpredictable summers – more than 2,000 people died. In total, the heatwave is estimated to have taken at least 35,000 lives, making it one of the worst natural catastrophes ever to hit western Europe.

As life returned to normal, one of the disaster's most poignant legacies came to light – hundreds of bodies which remained unclaimed in mortuaries across Europe. Who knew what tragic stories had led to people dying like this, forgotten and alone? In Paris, the youngest such victim was a homeless man aged 36, who had died on the streets. The oldest was a woman of 97. One elderly victim died in her room in a small hotel – it was seven days before her body was removed. In the end, they were buried in a cemetery in the city's southern suburbs, in the *carré des indigents* – a section, marked by anonymous gravestones, normally reserved for down-and-outs.

Such deaths and those among the elderly caused intense soul-searching in France. One Parisian newspaper had no doubt where the fault lay. It carried the simple headline: 'We're all to blame.'

EMERGENCY COOLING *At Fessenheim nuclear power station, an engineer watches water trickle down the outside of a reactor casing during a desperate attempt to cool it down.*

O

On a freezing winter's night in February 2004, an emergency call was picked up on England's north-west coast. In broken English, the voice said 'sinking … water'. It was the first hint of a tragic accident occurring on one of the world's most treacherous stretches of tidal sands.

The call came from Morecambe Bay, just south of the Lake District in north-west England. The bay covers over 300 km² (115 sq miles), and is famous for fast-running tides, strong currents and a vast expanse of shifting sands and channels. It is also a magnet for coastal birds, which feed among the rich cockle beds.

On a sunny day, Morecambe Bay is one of the most beautiful in England, but on the night of February 4, it wore a different face. In winter, dusk arrives early this far north, and a force 6 wind was blowing in off the sea. The local fishermen had long since gone home, and so had the local cockle-pickers. By 9 pm, the incoming tide was racing landwards and filling up the bay's constantly changing network of channels and

DANGER ZONE *At low tide, Morecambe Bay becomes a vast expanse of empty sands. Every step is a potential trap for the inexperienced or unwary.*

❝ **There is the sound of wind and water and other foreign voices shouting and crying out in the background.** ❞
Emergency services operator

Tak_n by the Tid

muddy creeks. In the dark, areas of quicksand would be impossible to spot, while anyone caught between the fast-filling channels would quickly be trapped. The bay should have been deserted, but out on the sands, faint shouts could be heard in the dark.

The alert

At 9.15 pm Alex Bottomley, a painter and decorator who also worked as a part-time coastguard, received calls on his mobile phone and his pager. A group of cocklers in Morecambe Bay were cut off by the tide. Bottomley knew immediately that there was no time to lose. Even in broad daylight, it takes expert knowledge to find a safe path across the sands. Once the tide turns, it surges in faster than a man can run.

At 9.30 pm, an emergency services operator received a call from someone who seemed to be in acute distress. The caller had difficulty speaking English, and his words were often masked by the sound of the waves and the wind. The operator was unable to make sense of what was said, and within a short time the line went dead. She passed the number to a police emergency operator, who immediately rang it back.

Months later, in court, a transcript of the outgoing call was read out: 'There is the sound of wind and water and other foreign voices shouting and crying out in the background.'

Out on the sands, the speaker seemed to be trying to pass the phone to someone else – someone who could perhaps speak better English. But the only words that could be made out were 'sinking … water'. Shortly afterwards, the line went silent.

As more calls came in – this time from the shore – the police and the rescue services realised that they had a major incident on their hands. Earlier in the day, nearly three dozen Chinese cockle-pickers had arrived on the coast to work. According to eyewitnesses, they had walked past warning signs and had set off towards

WORKING ON THE SANDS
Professional cockle-pickers know exactly when the tide will turn – it is the signal to head back to land.

In 2005, the incoming tide trapped a group of Chinese cockle-pickers on Morecambe Bay's treacherous sands, drowning 21.

SOMBRE MOMENT *Rescue workers carry away the body of a Chinese cockle-picker caught by the tide.*

a sandbank that was slowly emerging more than 3 km (2 miles) out as the tide fell. The afternoon was wearing on, and many local cocklers had stayed at home, knowing that it would be dark before the sandbanks were fully exposed.

The rescue

Three rescue helicopters were launched as coastguards, lifeboat crews and other volunteers began to assemble on the shore. Alex Bottomley was one of the first to arrive. 'When we got down there, the wind was howling in our faces and the tide was flooding. You have only got a short span of time to be able to walk along that beach because then it becomes marshland.'

Another local man, Harry Roberts, was in command of Morecambe's rescue hovercraft – a vessel ideally suited to the bay's constantly shifting sandbanks and shallows. He and his crew had just brought in one of the survivors, and were helping him into an ambulance. 'He was saying "Lots, lots". It was then we realised there were many people out there.'

The hovercraft set off again, sweeping the area where one of the helicopters had picked up a survivor. 'Almost immediately we found a body. As we came back, we came across a patch of eight or nine people, all dead. It looked like a dreadful accident had happened. There were bodies all over the sandbank. We were taking bodies back four at a time to the lifeboat station. This was an extraordinary night. Such a waste of life.'

As the night wore on, Alex Bottomley and other coastguards started a search along the shore, but found no survivors. At first light they resumed the search, and soon found bodies laid out in lines by the tide. Even a man of his experience was shocked at the sight of so many victims.

'We had pulled bodies out of the sea before – one here, one the next year and they are all incidents you don't like going to – but you don't expect to see so many in one spot. It certainly brings it home to you that these are very dangerous places. The bodies had no marks on them. They had shed most of their clothes, I believe because they thought that wearing clothes might weigh them down and not having them on would make it easier to swim to shore, but unfortunately they didn't make it.'

Disaster on trial

On the morning of February 5, the full extent of the Morecambe Bay tragedy became known. Twenty-one people, men and women, all aged between 18 and 45, are known to have died. A further two were missing, presumed dead. As well as the survivors picked up

LIVING SAND AND CLAY

In Old English, 'quick' means alive – a good description for sand that seems to come alive when it is stepped on. Sand is not the only substance that behaves in this way. Quick clay, or Leda clay, contains so much water – up to 80 per cent – that it turns liquid when disturbed. Given a sharp tap, a spadeful of quick clay flows like primeval ooze, eventually dropping off the end of the spade.

Quick clay formed several million years ago. It consists of microscopic particles of sediment that were ground up by glaciers during the Ice Age and then settled in shallow water. Salt in the water helped bind the particles together, forming solid clay. Where the clay was later lifted above sea level, the saltwater drained out and fresh water took its place. Without salt, the clay became much less stable. A sharp shock – from feet, machinery or earthquakes – can make it flow.

Found only in northern countries, such as Canada and Scandinavia, quick clays can cover large areas and have been the underlying cause of many landslides. One took place at Verdalen, Norway, in 1893. The slide covered several km^2 and killed more than 110 people.

The riddle of the sands

Despite its murderous reputation, quicksand does not suck people under and engulf them, although it can hold a person in a tenacious grip. The human body is more buoyant in quicksand than in water, and sooner or later anyone trapped in it will float. But escaping alive is another matter.

Quicksand is a mixture of fine particles of sand and silt that have become oversaturated by water from an underground source. It looks solid, but behaves more like a liquid because water reduces friction between the sand grains.

Unlike most liquids, a quicksand's viscosity, or 'runniness', can suddenly change if it comes under pressure, for example under a human foot. The surface gives way and the victim quickly sinks in up to the knees, surrounded by an area of dense sediment that turns semi-solid around its victim. Releasing the quicksand's grip requires a tremendous amount of force. Without something solid to pull on, people often find that they are stuck fast. Pulling on one leg simply makes the other one sink further.

So how do you escape from a quicksand's clutches? Stay still and call for help. Staying still stops you sinking any further, until – with luck – help arrives on the scene. If no one appears and you need to extract

LIQUID SAND *As water rises through the sand, droplets mix with the sand particles, turning the sand semi-liquid.*

Sand or mud particles | Water droplets

Water source Water comes from the rising tide, or from fresh-water springs.

yourself, gently lie down on your back until your body is floating on the sand. Next, roll over onto your stomach and pull yourself forwards with your hands, so that you gradually 'swim' towards firmer ground. It is a slow and grubby business, but it works.

This technique has one drawback: it goes against a very powerful human instinct. Faced with danger out in the open, nine out of ten people stay on their feet so that they can run away. For someone who is stuck in mud or sand, this can make a bad situation worse, particularly if it is a cold winter's night, with the dark tide rising, thousands of miles from home.

during the night, another 14 were reported to have made it safely to shore.

Police spokesmen were besieged by reporters impatient to learn who the victims were and how they came to be working in such dangerous conditions. For answers, the police turned to the handful of survivors. None of them spoke English, and only one carried any documents. With the help of interpreters, it became clear that all the cocklers were illegal immigrants, most from Fujian province, and were working for a Chinese gangmaster who masterminded the cockle harvest.

On March 4, a police team arrived from China to help with the difficult task of identifying the dead. A criminal investigation began as the police tried to establish who had arranged for the cocklers to travel to Britain, and who had paid them to go onto the sands, in peril of their lives. During a seven-month trial, the prosecution showed that Lin Langren, a Chinese gangmaster, was behind the operation, which exploited illegal immigrants to supply the cockle trade. Convicted on 21 counts of manslaughter, he was given a prison sentence of 14 years.

Russians are used to living in one of the harshest climates on the planet, with bitterly cold winters that helped to repel both Napoleon and the Nazis. But in 2006, even they found the cold hard to endure.

That year, when temperatures plunged below –30ºC for days on end, hundreds of people died. Some of them collapsed after venturing just a few yards down the street, while others froze to death in their own homes after power cuts had left them with no source of heat. The intense cold was a result of freezing Arctic air sweeping west over Russia and even into parts of central Europe from its usual 'home' in Siberia.

American Owen Paun was a postgraduate student in St Petersburg at the time. When walking through the city's congested streets he found he had to get used to breathing air far colder than the inside of a freezer, liberally mixed with car exhaust. 'If you breathe through your nose,' he wrote in his on-line blog, 'the incoming air freezes the inside, literally, and when you exhale, it melts … The cold air chills the blood on its way up into your brain. This is slightly lessened when you breathe through your mouth. Unfortunately, this also has its down side … your gums freeze. There is a sharp, piercing pain at the gum line. So really, you just have to pick your poison. I tend

NON-STARTER *A man inspects his deep-frozen car in St Petersburg. A water pipe ruptured nearby, coating it with water, which turned to ice overnight.*

SILENT CITY *With the thermometer hovering close to –30ºC, and a strong wind blowing, few people linger in the vastness of Moscow's Red Square.*

Russia's Big Freeze

When the chilliest weather since 1927 held Russia in its icy grip for days on end, hundreds of people succumbed to the intense cold.

to breathe through my nose. Mostly because the cars produce so much pollution that I like to filter out whatever little I can.'

Cold front on the march

Antarctica is the coldest continent on Earth, but Russia takes the record for temperature extremes. In 1933, the thermometer fell to –68°C in eastern Siberia – the lowest temperature ever recorded outside Antarctica. With conditions like these, it is not surprising that Siberia has a reputation for being harsh, a place of exile and penetrating cold.

Record-breaking freezes happen about two or three times every century. Siberia's cities are strung out at intervals across its vast landmass, stretching from the

remote fishing port of Magadan in the far east to Yekaterinburg, nearly 4,900 km (3,000 miles) to its west, on the frontier with European Russia. The farther east the cities, the worse the winter cold, because of an anticyclone, a massive block of high pressure, which builds up over eastern Siberia, as bitterly cold, dense Arctic air falls to the ground. If this high-pressure system shifts west, people across the rest of Siberia know to prepare for the worst.

In 2006, the cold front began its advance in mid-January. In Yekaterinburg, radio listeners phoned their local stations to find out if reports of intense cold heading towards them were true. But Nikolai Firyukov, a spokesman for the regional weather service, quashed rumours that anything exceptional was on the way. 'According to our forecasts,' he said, 'the temperature in Yekaterinberg next week is expected to be between –25°C and –27°C.' These temperatures are, in fact, quite normal for the region and a full 15°C above the coldest recorded. Talk of a 'big freeze' seemed overblown. But then no one had anticipated what the weather

A FILIGREE OF FROST
Hoar frost covers trees in Yekaterinburg, to the east of the Ural Mountains. Even in mild years, winter here is five months long.

What −30°C feels like

To anyone who has not experienced the harsh Russian climate, the intense cold of the 2006 winter is almost incomprehensible. When the air is so cold it freezes in your nose, you soon learn to take the weather very seriously, as Californian student Owen Paun discovered in St Petersburg and described in his blog.

'To try and convey what −30°C feels like, here's a brief exercise in absolute value. First, imagine +30°C. We've all felt that. Nice, pleasant, bordering even on a little too warm. Now, compare that to 0°C, freezing. Try to judge the difference between the two, get a good mental feel for that gap. Now reverse it. Imagine a change in temperature of that magnitude, but below zero. Freezing is already pretty cold, we never even get that low in Los Angeles; −30°C is unbelievable.

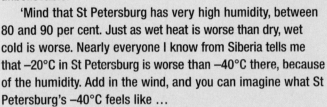

'Mind that St Petersburg has very high humidity, between 80 and 90 per cent. Just as wet heat is worse than dry, wet cold is worse. Nearly everyone I know from Siberia tells me that −20°C in St Petersburg is worse than −40°C there, because of the humidity. Add in the wind, and you can imagine what St Petersburg's −40°C feels like …

'You have to be completely covered up, and I really hate wearing hats. Over here I have a stocking cap, which makes me look like a dockworker. My gloves aren't thick enough –

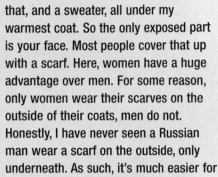

I need to buy new ones. You need long underwear, and I usually end up wearing long underwear, a T-shirt on top of that, and a sweater, all under my warmest coat. So the only exposed part is your face. Most people cover that up with a scarf. Here, women have a huge advantage over men. For some reason, only women wear their scarves on the outside of their coats, men do not. Honestly, I have never seen a Russian man wear a scarf on the outside, only underneath. As such, it's much easier for a woman to use the scarf to cover her face.

'I decided to buck the gender roles, and wore my scarf on the outside a couple of times. Yes, it was nice to have my face covered, but it does present yet another problem. When you breathe out, the breath condenses on the scarf, which gets the area around your mouth wet. When it's windy, this somewhat decreases the utility of this option.

Owen Paun

would do next. Instead of moving westwards and then retreating, as it normally does, the Arctic air continued its advance with unprecedented speed. In Siberia's largest city, Novosibirsk, the air temperature fell from −5°C to −31°C in just 9 hours – remarkable even by Siberian standards. Rinat Yagudin, an official at the city's meteorological office, admitted that he had seen nothing like it in 40 years. On the night of January 11, the temperature near Omsk, the capital of western Siberia, fell to −47°C, and it never rose above −35°C the following day. The cold moved like an invisible invader, freezing everything in its path.

More than 1,700 km (1,056 miles) farther west, in Moscow, the thermometer also started to dive. In January, the average minimum temperature in Moscow is about −16°C. This year Muscovites had to endure something far more extreme. Once the cold front had passed over the city, the temperature dropped well below −30°C, and there it stayed for nearly 10 days.

Soon the cold had reached St Petersburg – Russia's capital in the time of the tsars, and its 'window on the West'. Even here, the front showed no sign of slowing down. It looked as though Russia's western neighbours would be next.

Vodka – a false friend

As the cold deepened, weather forecasters warned people to stay indoors whenever possible, and to put on layers of the thickest winter clothing before venturing outside. Unfortunately, not everyone heeded their advice and many people died from exposure.

One was Elena Agafonov from a town south-east of Moscow. On January 24, she went to a local shop to buy some vodka, carrying her two-year-old child with her. She was wearing just a light coat, because the shop was only minutes away. However, on the way home, disaster struck. She fell over, developed hypothermia and died within 30 m of her own front door. Miraculously, the baby survived. But, as the cold continued, similar tragedies occurred in many cities, often fuelled by vodka – a traditional Russian 'remedy' against the cold. Its reputation is, however, misleading: alcohol may make people feel warm, but it actually increases blood flow to the skin, which makes the body lose more of its heat. In the southern city of Volgograd (formerly Stalingrad), 10 people froze to death in a single day, thanks to the effects of Russia's national drink. After the first week of the big freeze, Moscow's winter death toll from hypothermia climbed to more than 100. Many people took refuge in the capital's spacious metro stations, among the few places that the cold could not reach.

With heating systems working flat out throughout Moscow, electricity consumption began to soar. It soon hit a record high, and the city authorities decided to cut off supplies to many non-essential users, including shops, construction sites and casinos. But while the power suppliers struggled, some Russians – incredibly – insisted on maintaining a centuries-old tradition of taking a ritual outdoor bathe in frozen rivers and lakes on the Orthodox Epiphany, celebrated on January 19. That day, people with chainsaws cut holes in the Moscow river, just as they always do, and several hundred faithful took a brief and intensely bracing dip. Similar scenes took place right across Russia. It sounds suicidal, but although the temperature under the ice was close to freezing, it was up to 30°C warmer than the surrounding air.

Other Russians, known as *morzhi*, or walruses, believe an icy dip has health benefits. Vladimir Grebenkin, a leading Moscow enthusiast, told the news agency Interfax that bathing would take place that year as usual. 'We'll go bathing even if it reaches minus 60,' he said. 'Walrus bathing doesn't stop – the season started at the end of December and it will end as planned in March.' Doctors

WHEN SNOW TURNS DEADLY
On January 31, 2006, the central roof of the International Fair building (below) in Katowice, Poland, gave way under the weight of snow and ice. Firefighters (above) search for bodies amidst the snow and the ruins of the exhibition hall.

take a different view of the practice. Every year, dozens of bathers die of heart attacks from the shock of suddenly immersing their bodies in icy water.

The cold heads west

As predicted, the Arctic air did not stop at Russia's western frontier. It soon spread into the ex-Soviet republics of Belarus and Ukraine, and then into central Europe. Even in faraway Britain, meteorologists monitored the cold front's progress, fearing that it might reach as far as Europe's Atlantic coast.

By January 25, temperatures had dropped below –25°C in Romania and fallen to nearly –30°C in the Czech Republic and southern Germany. Snow even reached as far south as Athens, giving visitors the rare sight of the Acropolis dusted with white flakes. In the Polish city of Katowice, the roof of an exhibition centre collapsed under the weight of snow and ice, killing more than 60 people. In Ukraine, the worst affected country, at least 130 people died of cold, and more than 500 were hospitalised with frostbite and hypothermia.

In the second half of January, the big freeze also began to cast a chill on the international stage. At issue was Siberia's natural gas, used in Ukraine and many other European countries. Before the big freeze, Russia and Ukraine had been involved in a dispute about the price of gas, and on January 1, Russia had abruptly turned off the taps. The two countries reached a compromise, but when the big freeze arrived, the dispute erupted again. For people all over Europe, it was a stark reminder of an awkward fact: when the weather turns really cold, they rely on Russia to keep warm.

Sting in the tail

As January came to a close, the big freeze began to recede, but not before it had delivered a parting series of record lows. In Russia's deep south, tea plantations glistened after sharp overnight frosts, and many of the palm trees in the Black Sea resort of Sochi died. Farther west, in the naval port of Sevastopol, the sea began to freeze for the first time in 60 years. Amazed by this extraordinary spectacle, adults and children risked their lives by walking and skating on the ice.

The severest frosts of all came in the opening days of February, just before the cold released its grip. In Buryatia, one of Siberia's southern republics, night-time temperatures dropped to –50°C. Local television stations reported a sharp upsurge in fire outbreaks, caused by electric heaters overloading faulty wiring. In Russia's far east, Magadan, on the Sea of Okhotsk,

HYPOTHERMIA: CRUEL, COLD KILLER

Hypothermia occurs when the body's core temperature drops below 35°C. Although this is just 3°C below normal body temperature, it can make people drowsy, confused and unable to carry out simple tasks. If someone's temperature drops below 32°C, his or her life is in danger – primarily from a heart attack. Young children and older people (over 60) are at most risk from hypothermia.

Even so, there are many recorded instances of people surviving a sudden and steep fall in body temperature – for example, after being trapped in snow or falling in icy water. In 2001, in Edmonton, Canada, a 13-month-old child, Erika Nordby (below), crawled outdoors unnoticed, wearing only a nappy. After spending several hours at –20°C, she was found, without a heartbeat and clinically dead. However, once in hospital, her heart was restarted and she made an almost full recovery.

experienced lows of nearly –60°C. During the coldest point in the big freeze, one of the port's main power lines fractured. Fortunately, it was repaired in the nick of time – if the break had lasted longer than 48 hours, more than 2,000 people might have frozen to death in their homes.

It was at this point that the Arctic air at last started to retreat. In financial terms, the cost of the big freeze will never be known, but not everyone lost out. Many hotels and bars reported record winter takings, thanks to the number of people who were drawn in by their warmth. Taxi drivers also profited as people found it too cold to walk very far, some increasing their prices by up to 500 per cent.

According to an old Russian proverb, 'It's a hard winter when one wolf eats another.' The winter of 2005-6 was one that few Russians would like to repeat.

Air

Tornado Super Outbreak

Early on April 2, 1974, US meteorologists grew worried. Cold air was spilling down from the Rockies and travelling east, while warm, humid air was drifting north from the Gulf of Mexico. When the two air masses clashed, they would produce violent thunderstorms and tornadoes.

The first tornado hit the ground in Morris, Illinois at 1pm local time. Other outbreaks followed in quick succession in Tennessee, Georgia, Indiana, Ohio, Kentucky and Alabama. Over the next 18 hours, 148 confirmed tornadoes touched down, affecting 13 states and killing more than 300 people.

Hardest hit was Xenia, Ohio, where a tornado funnel 1 km (¹/₂ mile) wide smashed into homes, businesses, schools and university campuses. Freight cars were thrown up from a passing train and hurled across streets. 'People were crying and children were

screaming and the noise was deafening, like a giant airplane right overhead,' said Irene Hale. 'What we saw has never left me since. Everything was gone.'

Meteorologists had seen the storms brewing but had no way of knowing just how devastating they would turn out to be. Computer forecasts predicted that the growing storm system would draw up the warm, humid Gulf air northwards as far as the Ohio valley, causing severe thunderstorms over a huge area of the central and eastern US. The forecasts also revealed that the polar jet-stream winds, which race across the continent several miles overhead, were running very fast over Texas and would boost the intensity of the storms. On the morning of April 3, severe weather warnings were issued for an area stretching from the Mississippi river to the east coast and from the Gulf of Mexico to the Great Lakes, although the forecasters could not give precise locations or times for the severe weather.

Xenia

The first supercell storm erupted in Illinois. As the entire storm system moved east, it grew in intensity over ground that had been heated by scorching sunshine. This intensified the storms, and made the tornadoes more severe. By the time the storm

COLUMN OF DESTRUCTION
The deadliest tornado of the super outbreak ripped through the town of Xenia, Ohio, at about 83 km/h (52 mph). With a damage path of 1 km wide, it left 33 people dead and 1,600 injured.

system reached Xenia, Ohio, at 4.40 pm local time, it spawned a tornado reaching F5 intensity on the Fujita Scale (see page 81).

Xenia locals who saw the storm approaching said that the sky had taken on an unusual appearance. 'The undersides of the clouds resembled cotton balls of a dirty pea-soup colour,' said one eyewitness.

Fireman Homer Ramby was able to watch the tornadoes forming. 'On April 3, 1974 at 4:20 pm, I heard on a fire radio that a tornado had touched down in southern Montgomery County,' he said. 'I noticed a dark cloud hanging down from the storm cloud … we saw a tornado whip up from the ground then it would disappear, then another one would appear then disappear, then one started then it formed two tornadoes side by side, then the two joined together to make the big one that hit Xenia.'

The F5 tornado demolished the local high school just an hour after most pupils had left for the day, although a teacher and class rehearsing for a play fled for their lives seconds before two school buses were launched through the concert hall onto the stage. As it ripped through the town, the tornado gathered a ring of flying debris that some people mistook for a flock of blackbirds circling furiously. The 'birds' were actually roof tiles and other debris ripped up from buildings.

'I saw two small funnel clouds come out of the large cloud and go back into it. It was so close by this time that I saw the debris in it,' said Xenia resident

HIGH-SPEED VIOLENCE
With winds of around 480 km/h (300 mph), the Xenia tornado tossed vehicles into the air and tore buildings to shreds.

1974 STATISTICS

The April 3-4 outbreak was the most extensive ever recorded.

- 148 tornadoes struck in less than 18 hours.
- 13 states were affected: Alabama, Georgia, Illinois, Indiana, Kentucky, Ohio, Michigan, Mississippi, New York, North Carolina, Tennessee, Virginia and West Virginia.
- 6 tornadoes reached F5 on the Fujita Scale; 24 reached F4; 35 reached F3.
- 118 tornadoes had damage paths over 1.6 km (1 mile) long.
- The total damage paths amounted to 4,023 km (2,500 miles).
- 15 tornadoes were on the ground at one time during the outbreak's peak.
- 330 people were killed and 5,484 were injured.

Shirley Stamps. 'I could see through the house to my kitchen window, and it was just white outside. The roar was awful. My little dog was going crazy and of course my daughter was screaming. I could hear glass breaking and something hit my kitchen wall. After that I could smell fresh wood. It was over in what I'm sure was a very short time, but seems like a long time to me ...

The wood smell was coming from my kitchen wall, where a small rafter section from someone's house had been driven through the wall ... Every house behind me was destroyed. The only thing left was where the bathrooms were.'

Another Xenia eyewitness, Irene Hale, described the feeling of disbelief as the storm passed through. 'There

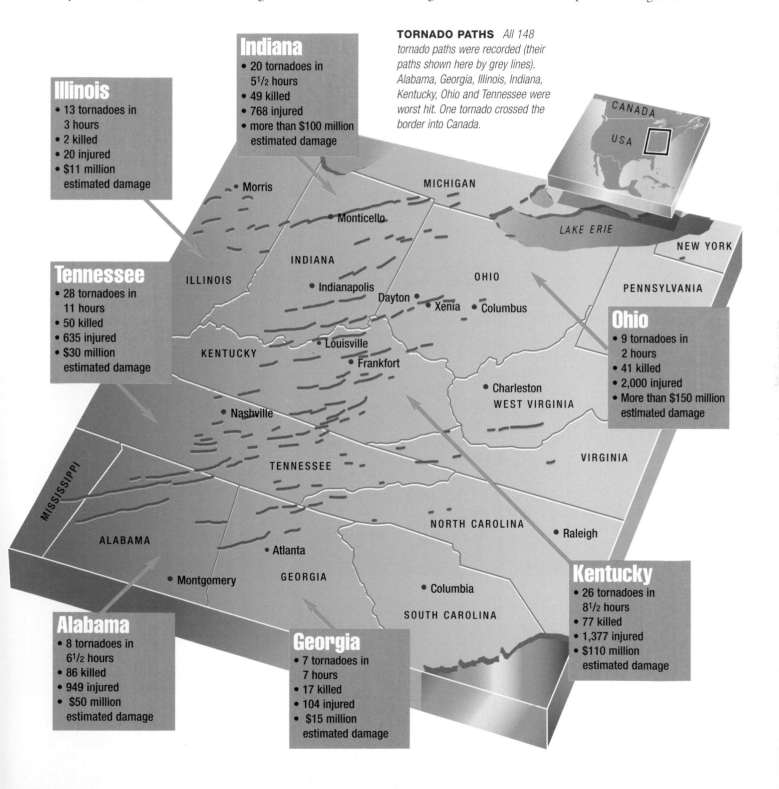

TORNADO PATHS *All 148 tornado paths were recorded (their paths shown here by grey lines). Alabama, Georgia, Illinois, Indiana, Kentucky, Ohio and Tennessee were worst hit. One tornado crossed the border into Canada.*

Illinois
- 13 tornadoes in 3 hours
- 2 killed
- 20 injured
- $11 million estimated damage

Indiana
- 20 tornadoes in 5½ hours
- 49 killed
- 768 injured
- more than $100 million estimated damage

Tennessee
- 28 tornadoes in 11 hours
- 50 killed
- 635 injured
- $30 million estimated damage

Ohio
- 9 tornadoes in 2 hours
- 41 killed
- 2,000 injured
- More than $150 million estimated damage

Kentucky
- 26 tornadoes in 8½ hours
- 77 killed
- 1,377 injured
- $110 million estimated damage

Alabama
- 8 tornadoes in 6½ hours
- 86 killed
- 949 injured
- $50 million estimated damage

Georgia
- 7 tornadoes in 7 hours
- 17 killed
- 104 injured
- $15 million estimated damage

Bird's-eye view

Shortly after 4 pm, a monstrous tornado hit the ground in Kentucky. As the F4 tornado ripped through Louisville with winds exceeding 333 km/h (207 mph), Dick Gilbert, a helicopter pilot and traffic reporter for the radio station WHAS, risked his life to track the tornado's route from the air.

'Well, it's a spectacular sight ... the low clouds, very black, low clouds ... It is swirling around, and it looks like smoke underneath it.

'The power transformers have been blowing regularly in the path of this thing – big, large explosions of blue-white light.

'This tornado touched down right here at the horse barns on the north-south expressway, and it has turned over several cars. And, let's see – one, two, three, four, five, six, seven, eight – I would say eight automobiles have been blown across the road or turned over. There's an ambulance here working in the road.

'Now, the wind damage hit the roof of Freedom Hall and it tore three big holes in the roof. Then it moved over on the eastern end of the building and ripped off about a third of the roof here. The horse barns are no more. It totally wiped out the horse barns. All of the mobile homes and trailers behind the Freedom Hall have been completely torn up. And, over by the ..., I think it's the Twilight Drive-In here, we've had about four trailers completely torn apart. There's fire equipment and emergency equipment in there. Now, be very careful on Crittendon Drive – I see more police cars and emergency equipment heading down toward the trailer park there ... Avoid that north-south expressway – they can only get one or two cars through it at a time.'

Three people were killed in Louisville, but the death toll could have been far higher had it not been for Gilbert's live broadcast, which enabled hundreds of people to escape harm.

On the ground, Weather Service forecaster John Burke at the airport also came dangerously close to the tornado:

'Here comes the wind! We're hitting winds up to – Good gracious sakes alive! ... By golly, the whole thing's going! Hear it? I'm going! Goodbye! ...

'Yes, that storm, we could watch it come right in on the airport here, Glen. There was no funnel in it until it actually got right to the airport, then a funnel developed right in the parking lot, north of the terminal building, and moved on to the east. And, it's moving eastward 45-50 miles per hour. So, this was 10 minutes ago, so that's over in the eastern part of Jefferson County now, moving on eastward. However, Glen, we do have another big storm down south of us, headed east, and it's headed in the direction of Mount Washington, another one about the same size. So, for the next hour or so, the Mount Washington area certainly should be on the alert for developments and take all proper precautions, like we were mentioning earlier.'

Dick Gilbert and John Burke

were people walking in the street, but no one said a word. It was a deafening, numbing silence. Your mind could not accept what you were seeing. It couldn't be – but it was.'

Counting the cost

Tornado damage occurs because of the wind tearing and pushing a building apart; the faster the wind speed, the more damage it does. When flying debris smashes a window, the wind rushes in and often lifts the roof up, causing the supporting walls to collapse. Once debris is airborne, it can be sucked upwards by the tornado's winds and dumped miles away.

Of Xenia's 25,000 residents, 33 people were killed and 1,600 injured. More than 1,400 buildings – about half the buildings in the city – were damaged or destroyed. The total estimated damage exceeded $400 million. Convoys of generators, floodlights, bulldozers and dump trucks arrived overnight from nearby Wright-

Patterson Air Force Base. Xenia was declared a national disaster area, and the American Red Cross, as well as several hundred Ohio National Guard troops, moved in to assist with the rescue and clean up. The Xenia tornado was the deadliest and most damaging of the storms that made up the outbreak.

In 1974, tornado warnings were poor. The forecasters of the National Weather Service (NWS) could see only green blobs on their radar screens and relied on visual confirmation to issue warnings. 'In those days, the NWS did not deem it necessary to outfit each office with state-of-the-art equipment such as Doppler Radar,' says Don Halsey, one of the meteorologists on duty in Dayton, Ohio, that day. The characteristic hook shapes made by tornadoes were difficult to pick out on the radar display. 'But the Meteorologist-in-Charge, Mr Chester Rathfon, played a hunch that what he saw was a hook. He made the decision to issue a warning, and I typed it on the teletype for dissemination to media and emergency management. We called the Greene County sheriff by telephone, since that was the most expedient method of dissemination at the time.' But by then it was too late, and shortly afterwards Xenia was destroyed.

'The picture that amazed me the most was of an automobile rolled up into a near perfect ball. A young lady from Wilberforce drove directly into the path. I still owned a house in Xenia and half of the roof was ripped off cleanly, and diagonally,' remembers Halsey.

One of the most eerie features reported by tornado witnesses is the noise, which sounds like a freight train. The first recording of this roar was made during the Xenia tornado by Thomas Yougen, who had turned on his tape-recorder before the tornado passed over the city.

Setting records

Although most of the tornadoes occurred between 2 pm and 10 pm on April 3, the outbreak continued until the next morning, with the last ones striking in North Carolina at around 9 am. By then, the storms had covered 1,036,000 km² (400,000 sq miles); 15,000 km² (5,800 sq miles) had been directly hit by tornadoes.

Of the 148 tornadoes, 95 were F2 and above, and 30 were exceptionally violent F4s and F5s. Six reached F5

THE FUJITA SCALE

The Fujita Scale is used to rate the intensity of a tornado by examining the damage caused by a tornado after it has passed over a man-made structure. The scale was introduced in 1971 by Dr Ted Fujita of the University of Chicago.

SCALE NUMBER	WIND ESTIMATES*	TYPICAL DAMAGE
F0	64-117 km/h (40-73 mph)	Light damage. Some damage to chimneys; branches broken off trees; shallow-rooted trees pushed over; signboards damaged.
F1	118-180 km/h (74-112 mph)	Moderate damage. Peels surface off roofs; mobile homes pushed off foundations or overturned; moving cars blown off roads.
F2	181-251 km/h (113-156 mph)	Considerable damage. Roofs torn off frame houses; mobile homes demolished; boxcars overturned; large trees snapped or uprooted; light-object missiles generated; cars lifted off ground.
F3	252-330 km/h (157-205 mph)	Severe damage. Roofs and some walls torn off well-constructed houses; trains overturned; most trees in forest uprooted; heavy cars lifted off the ground and thrown.
F4	331-417 km/h (206-259 mph)	Devastating damage. Well-constructed houses levelled; structures with weak foundations blown away some distance; cars thrown and large missiles generated.
F5	418-512 km/h (260-318 mph)	Incredible damage. Strong frame houses levelled off foundations and swept away; automobile-sized missiles fly through the air in excess of 100 m; trees stripped of bark; incredible phenomena will occur.

* The wind speeds are estimates, as they have never been scientifically verified. On February 1, 2007, the Fujita Scale was replaced by the Enhanced Fujita Scale, which accounts for different degrees of damage that occur with different types of structures, as well as damage to things other than structures. Past tornadoes will not be reclassified.

on the Fujita Scale at some point along their paths – about the number normally seen in a decade. Some of them were among the strongest ever recorded. A record 49 were killers. In all, twisters struck 13 states, and one crossed over into Canada from Michigan. Researchers believe that an outbreak of this magnitude only happens once every 500 years. (Surprisingly, the UK could be called the tornado capital of the world, as it has more tornadoes per km² each year than any other country.)

The Xenia mega-twister stayed on the ground for 51 km (32 miles), but that wasn't the record for consecutive length on the ground that April day. An F4 twister that hit Monticello, Indiana, was on the ground

THE WIZARD OF OZ

'The demoniac fury of the cloud was appalling, whirling with most frightful rapidity,' exclaimed a report into a brutal tornado that hit Kansas on May 30, 1879. Even by the standards of the American Midwest, this was an exceptional storm, with houses ripped off their foundations and whirled around like toys. 'It was as though the building had been picked up, violently shaken. The furniture whirled around the room and broke in pieces, and I was whirled around,' described one unfortunate eyewitness. 'Upon rising from the floor I found my clothing torn into shreds, but not a bruise upon my body.'

The tornado left 18 people dead and 60 injured along a path some 160 km (100 miles) long. It also left a particularly deep impression on actor, playwright and newspaperman Frank Baum, who was living in Kansas at the time. Two decades later, he wrote a book inspired by the tornado, in which a house on the Prairies is picked up in a twister and carried away with a girl and her dog inside.

The Wonderful Wizard of Oz was an instant success, made even more famous by the film (1939), with its groundbreaking special effects. To recreate the Kansas tornado was an impressive achievement, using a 10 m muslin stocking suspended from a specially constructed giant gantry and rotated by a motor, with a rod through the tornado base. By moving the gantry and rod in opposite directions, the tornado appeared to snake from side to side, with clouds of dust used to create the turbulence along the ground. The result was the cinema's first realistic artificial tornado.

for an incredible 195 km (121 miles) before dissipating. Along the way, it killed 19 people and injured 362.

Some experts blamed the scale of the outbreak on a La Niña event, when the Pacific off the California coast grows unusually cool, but there is no evidence to support this. It is more likely that a combination of factors encouraged the violent thunderstorms that spawn tornadoes to come together over such a large area.

Improved warnings

In the aftermath of the super outbreak, relief agencies learned valuable lessons in handling natural disasters. Huge improvements were made in communications, warning systems, emergency preparedness and forecast techniques. As a result, longer warning times were given for tornadoes, with better accuracy, greater public awareness and more reliable communications.

John Forsing of the NWS worked as a forecaster that day in Louisville, Kentucky, and helped oversee the weather service's nationwide modernisation effort afterwards. 'What we saw as a green blob on a World War II-vintage radar scope is now depicted in full colour and high resolution detail,' he said. 'With modernised technology such as Doppler radar, weather satellites, and advanced computers, forecasters can now pinpoint tornadoes even before they touch down.'

Joseph Schaefer is director of the NWS Storm Prediction Center in Norman, Oklahoma, which has responsibility for monitoring tornadoes nationwide. 'Since 1974, we have increased the accuracy of severe thunderstorm and tornado watches we issue for the entire country,' Schaefer said. 'Today, more than 95 per cent of the watches we issue subsequently contain severe thunderstorms, compared to about 66 per cent in 1974. Even more importantly, the per cent of F2 or greater tornadoes that occur in areas under tornado watches has doubled in 25 years, leaping from about 40 per cent to 80 per cent.'

Richard Augulis, director of the NWS's Central Region, noted that the 1974 tornadoes helped fund the expansion of the Weather Radio network from about 50 transmitters to 330, with a goal of reaching 70 per cent of the population with storm-warning broadcasts. In 1994, an initiative by Vice-President Gore raised the coverage goal to 95 per cent. 'Weather radios that sound an alarm when severe weather threatens are the public's first line of defence,' Augulis said. 'And certainly, the weather service's modernised capabilities in issuing timely and accurate warnings are a critical part of this defence.'

Storm chasers

Author Priit J. Vesilind accompanied a team of storm chasers in spring 2003, as they hunted tornadoes across the central states of the USA. The group included Tim Samaras, who was depositing probes in the pathways of tornado funnels to measure data such as wind speed and direction.

❝ By June 4 we're in a caravan of four cars barrelling back down to Texas, where we chase a super cell tagged with a tornado warning into Clayton, New Mexico ... And then the world seems to simply disappear. I can see nothing but Tim's red brake lights in front of us. The convoy grinds to a halt as a sandstorm rages, its winds approaching 70 miles an hour, Tim estimates. Somewhere out there a tornado may be brewing. Tim's van begins to rock. Anton's face turns ashen. We can't see the road, only the tops of telephone poles. Twenty minutes pass. Tim finally radios us: his GPS shows a T intersection in the road ahead that we could reach, and so we roll blindly, foot by foot, out of the sandblaster ... We learn later that there was a tornado somewhere in the storm, but we sure as hell couldn't see it.

'Our field time is running out when we caravan into northern Nebraska on June 9 ... A dark anvil lowers in the hurly-burly western sky ... The sky is now rotating majestically, and a confused bird flies into our windshield with a thump, leaving a stain of blood and feathers. And then a triangle of cloud lowers and sharpens into something pointier and leaner. It gathers into a funnel like an elephant's trunk, with the texture of soft grey cotton. It whirls like an apparition, no more than 2 miles from us, looking alien in the landscape, as if a spaceship had landed ...

'The tornado snakes down to the fields, where it's chewing up a maelstrom of soil and vegetation. It seems to stand almost still, and suddenly it's gone! It just lifts up, as if the sky were withdrawing a finger back into its fist. ❞

Priit J. Vesilind, National Geographic Magazine

DEADLY TWISTERS

- **A record-breaking tornado devastates part of Oklahoma City in 1999**

- **In Bangladesh, 1,300 are killed in the deadliest single tornado**

Oklahoma, 1999

On May 3, one of the most powerful tornadoes ever measured carved a path of destruction around Oklahoma City. Its winds reached 511 km/h (318 mph), the fastest measured anywhere in the world. It was also the costliest tornado in US history. More than 10,500 buildings and 47 businesses were destroyed, causing $1.1 billion in damage. Thirty-six people were killed and another 675 injured. The tornado was one of 66 that broke out across Oklahoma, Kansas, Texas and Tennessee over three days.

10 deadliest tornadoes in US history

The American Midwest is the most tornado-prone region in the world, with an average of 1,000 a year. Even so, less than 1 per cent of tornadoes there are violent.

	LOCATION	DATE	DEATHS
1	Tri-State Tornado – Missouri, Illinois, Indiana	March 18, 1925	695
2	Natchez, Mississippi	May 7, 1840	317
3	St Louis, Missouri	May 27, 1896	255
4	Tupelo, Mississippi	April 5, 1936	216
5	Gainesville, Georgia	April 6, 1936	203
6	Woodward, Oklahoma	April 9, 1947	181
7	Amite, Louisiana; Purvis, Mississippi	April 24, 1908	143
8	New Richmond, Wisconsin	June 12, 1899	117
9	Flint, Michigan	June 8, 1953	115
10=	Waco, Texas	May 11, 1953	114
10=	Goliad, Texas	May 18, 1902	114

The May day began warm and sunny, although very humid. But as warm, moist air swept north from the Gulf of Mexico it hit a lid of drier air from the west. The Storm Prediction Center in Norman, Oklahoma, issued a high-risk alert for severe thunderstorms and tornadoes for most of the state of Oklahoma. At 5.41 pm, the centre warned that tornadoes could be heading towards the Oklahoma City Metro area. The threat was raised to a large, damaging tornado emergency at 6.57 pm with dramatic warnings: 'Persons in Moore and south Oklahoma City should take immediate tornado precautions!'

At 7.25 pm the tornado hit south of downtown Oklahoma City and cut through the suburbs of Moore, Del City and Midwest City. By now, it had grown into a cone-shaped cloud 1.6 km (1 mile) across that tore a 130 km (80 mile) gash north-eastwards through a slice of the city and its suburbs. Mobile homes were hurled through the air like tin cans, houses were torn to shreds and showers of sparks cascaded down from exploding electricity transformers and power lines. The air grew thick with a lethal barrage of flying missiles – tree branches, timbers, glass, roof tiles and metal sheeting. Cars were wrapped up into bundles of twisted metal, and a 20 tonne railway carriage was shifted 800 m.

In the suburb of Moore, Scott and Susan Carlin and their two children had been watching the tornado's progress on television. 'It was getting bigger and bigger, and I started noticing that it was heading our way. The tornado was just half a mile away and closing in fast,' explained Susan Carlin. 'The kids were getting really scared at that point because they thought it was basically right there and we weren't going to make it to the shelter in time.' The family ran for their underground tornado shelter in the front yard and slammed the door shut. 'Suddenly you hear this ... it's almost like rolling thunder that just did not want to stop. The walls started vibrating really heavy like an earthquake, you could actually feel it coming,' described Scott. The tornado was making straight for the family's house. 'You could hear it breaking up everything, and all the debris flying around ... glass breaking. We all hugged each other together. The next thing we know the cellar door starts tapping, and then

IN THE LINE OF FIRE
The Oklahoma City tornado cut a clear path of destruction through the suburbs.

DEADLY TWISTERS

boom, it's gone. When that door came off, you could feel your ears pop. And I told my kids, I said, "Hang on." I could hear the destruction, I could hear everything torn up. My kids were just in panic,' said Susan.

With the door of the tornado shelter gone, Scott risked his life for an unforgettable sight: 'I looked up through where the door was, and you could see straight up inside of the tornado. It was a dark grey, tall funnel of cloud reaching up high, I could see debris flying around inside it.'

When the furore died down, the family climbed out of the shelter. 'Everything we'd had for 10 years of being married was trashed,' exclaimed Susan. 'It was like being on another planet, just debris everywhere, not a sign of any house, street, nothing.' Much of

Moore was reduced to a lunar landscape where every recognisable object had been obliterated. Survivors had trouble finding their streets, let alone homes, most of which were reduced to the flat concrete foundations.

The damage was made worse because most houses in the area were wooden-framed buildings easily blasted apart by the tornado. Many collapsed when the winds burst in through windows or garages and lifted off the roof, after which the walls collapsed. The tornado also left some strange sights – streets with houses completely untouched on one side and utter devastation on the other side. Some houses were sliced clean open, revealing the rooms inside, like doll's houses. One kitchen was torn in half down the middle, with crockery intact on one side and the other half

DANGER ZONE *Many people who took shelter under highway overpasses did not survive, although this family did.*

RELIEF WORK *Clothes and toys for tornado survivors are collected in one of Oklahoma City's churches.*

completely missing. Pieces of timber were shot straight through into rooms, and even pine needles were fired into wooden walls like bullets.

Most of the people killed in the tornado were in mobile homes, or were out of doors and were hit by debris shooting through the turbulent air like shrapnel. Others were crushed inside their homes or cars. Few had proper tornado shelters – underground metal bunkers designed to withstand even the most powerful tornadoes. Several people tried to shelter under a highway overpass, believing they would be safe under the concrete bridge. Not so: they were blown over and suffered serious injuries. Three of them died.

Bangladesh, 1989 and 1996

Outside the USA and Canada, Bangladesh suffers some of the most violent tornadoes in the world. At the beginning of the monsoon season, usually in April to May, deep masses of hot, humid tropical air collide with much cooler, dry air spilling over the Himalayas, producing thunderstorms that spawn tornadoes over large distances.

In April 1989, the country was in the throes of a chronic drought, and on the 28th President Hussain Mohammad Ershad ordered nationwide prayers for rains. Even he must have been shocked at the sudden turn of events only hours later when a thunderstorm struck the district of Manikganj, 60 km (37 miles) outside the capital,

Dhaka. As the storm bore down with torrents of rain, it unleashed a giant tornado that tore a path 16 km (10 miles) long and 1.6 km (1 mile) wide. Everything in its path was destroyed – buildings, trees, crops, livestock – creating a disaster zone that covered 6 km² (2¼ sq miles). Even for a nation used to violent weather, this was an exceptional tornado, possibly an F5.

The town of Shaturia was flattened, and about 80,000 people were made homeless. Villages were reduced to rubble, and rescue workers took weeks to recover the bodies. As many as 1,300 people were thought to have been killed and 12,000 injured. This is the world's highest number of fatalities from a single tornado, although accurate numbers of deaths and injuries are hard to come by.

On May 13, 1996, a tornado event struck near Tangail, only about 50 km (30 miles) from the scene of the 1989 tornado. Thunderstorms bore down on western Bangladesh with violent winds that killed up to 1,000 people, injured more than 30,000 and left 100,000 homeless. 'The whole village has been made into a huge grave,' observed a police officer in the village of Barabhita.

At Bashial, nearly 120 people were killed, many of them students at a school that collapsed. The twisted damage to many trees indicated that some of the windstorms had tornadoes embedded in them, and this was supported by reports that people and animals were hurled over long distances. Homes, buildings and trees were tossed around like feathers, and the air became filled with loose sheet metal that cut like blades of an enormous blender. 'Buses and trucks frantically ferried the injured to hospitals in Tangail and the nearby town of Mymensingh; others were carried on shoulders or carts', one report described. Of those injured, one clinic reported that almost all had multiple injuries caused by flying corrugated iron sheets from buildings.

Although Bangladesh suffers far fewer tornadoes than the USA, casualties are much higher. While the USA recorded an average of 65 tornado fatalities per year between 1974 and 2003, the annual average in Bangladesh is 179 deaths, the highest tornado death toll anywhere in the world. Bangladesh's population density is so high that a tornado strike just about anywhere is almost certain to cause death and destruction.

Forecasting and warnings are almost non-existent. And buildings are generally poorly constructed, with many people living in shacks made of mud, straw, bamboo or corrugated steel. Tornadoes rip these apart and turn the debris into airborne missiles.

Clouds of Sand

Every spring, giant plumes of sand are carried by the wind hundreds of kilometres across northern China as desert areas in the north-west expand under pressure from overgrazing, deforestation and drought. Each year, the deserts creep closer and closer to Beijing.

On April 17, 2006, Beijing was subjected to its eighth sandstorm of the year, and the worst for five years. Residents were told to wear masks out of doors and children had to stay inside. Hospitals reported a sudden rise in respiratory problems. Beijing resident Francisco Little described the experience: 'The sand was everywhere, covering the city like dirty talcum powder. It choked, clogged and floated its way into the lives of Beijing residents. You felt it in your eyes, hair, teeth and worst of all you had to breathe this wind-borne menace.'

From February to June each year, Beijing is plagued by dust storms that feel like a biblical curse. A fine grit stains the sky an eerie yellow and coats absolutely everything. People battle against the dusty wind, trying in vain to cover their faces, which are pasted yellow. Cyclists and pedestrians have to lean into the wind and dust to move forwards, their heads wrapped in scarves, towels and jackets. 'Suddenly the sky is very dark – even at home, with all your windows closed, your air is full of dust,' remarked environmentalist and Beijing resident, Dai Qing. The air slowly asphyxiates its victims, leaving them gasping for breath, and hospitals become overwhelmed by people suffering from chronic respiratory problems. In April 2006, the number of outpatients in two of the city's hospitals rose by 30 per cent.

The sandstorms carry more than dust. The cities of China are increasingly blanketed in pollution, including sulphur, particles of soot from diesel engines and coal fires, toxic gases and metals, as well as pesticides carried off farmland. Beijing is now one of the most polluted cities in the world, even without its notorious dust storms, and 'Beijing fogs' are growing more frequent and more intense, as the sky grows murkier and the Sun weaker behind a veil of pollution. That pollution is swept up in the sandstorms, adding to the health hazard. Beijing reported grade V pollution, the most serious level, during the April 17 storm.

Apart from the human suffering, the sandstorms force airports and schools to close, crops wither and die and hundreds of kilometres of roads and railways are blocked by sand. Official reports estimate that the sandstorms cost China up to $3 billion each year.

Deserts on the move

The storms usually strike in the spring, when the climate over Asia is ripe for the creation of a massive dust bowl. In the deserts of Mongolia and north-western China, the frozen ground thaws after the bitter cold of winter. Rasping winds race down from the interior of Mongolia and rake up monstrous clouds of dust. These are carried high into the sky and blown eastwards by the prevailing winds towards Beijing and beyond. The dust clouds often spread out over thousands of kilometres.

The storms are nothing new. The great military tactician Sun Tzu wrote in his war manual, *Art of War*, how a tiny Chinese army 2,500 years ago routed a barbarian force using a sandstorm as cover. 'They are many and we are few, but in the midst of

'You felt it in your eyes, hair, teeth and worst of all you had to breathe this wind-borne menace.'

Francisco Little, Beijing resident

As the deserts of northern China expand, spring dust storms are becoming more frequent and more damaging.

89

WIND AND DUST
Residents of Hohhot, Inner Mongolia, veil their faces against strong winds and choking sand during the April 17 storm.

SUPER-STORM *In April 2001, a dust storm measuring up to 1,800 km (1,200 miles) across, and carrying millions of tonnes of topsoil, travelled from Inner Mongolia to the USA.*

April 6 Sandstorms in Inner Mongolia

April 7 Dust cloud arrives in China

RUSSIA

April 12 Leading edge reaches North America

Beijing

CHINA

PACIFIC OCEAN

USA

April 12 Dust cloud over Pacific

April 8 Dust cloud begins to leave China

SLOW BURIAL *The village of Langtou Gou 130 km (80 miles) from Beijing is gradually being covered by sand from the Gobi desert. The fields beyond the village are already destroyed.*

this sandstorm our numbers will not be discernible; victory will go to the strenuous fighter, and the wind will be our best ally.' The difference now is that more of north-west China is turning to sand as old deserts expand and new ones form; the number of sandstorms has also increased.

In the 1950s, there were only a few storms in the entire decade, but over the past two decades several have struck each year, with a total of 11 in 2006. The April 17 storm was a monster. For the first time, the wind was laden with sand grains ten times larger than the usual dust particles. Over 330,000 tonnes of sand fell on the city in four days, enough to fill 820 jumbo jets. 'It was as if the desert has crawled to Beijing overnight,' said resident Zhang Rui, which was fitting, because Beijing is truly being swallowed up by deserts as

the northern territories turn into a giant dust bowl. Sand dunes are now only 70 km (43 miles) away from the capital and drift closer each year. At this rate, they will reach the outskirts of the city by 2040, and Beijing will become the world's first modern city to disappear under the desert. In May 2000, the premier of China, Zhu Rongji, was forced to admit the unthinkable – that the Chinese capital may eventually be forced to move from Beijing.

The impact of the growing deserts is already clear as they swallow up land in the surrounding region. The village of Longbaoshan lies about 100 km (60 miles) from Beijing, and its houses and fields are vanishing under vast banks of sand. Digging has become a way of life for the villagers, such as Li Ming Jiang, a farmer. 'The dune was way off over there,' he said, pointing to a sand hill nearby. 'But just in the last few years, it has begun to move towards us, very quickly.' The dune is

SWEEPING UP *A city worker clears sand from the streets of Beijing.*

moving by 20 m every year, and the villagers can only wait and watch as the silent invader swallows up their homes. They say that they do not know where they will go or how they will live once their houses are buried.

Land laid bare

China has one of the fastest-deteriorating environments in the world. In the 1950s, the deserts were expanding at around 1,560 km² (602 sq miles) each year; the figure has doubled in recent years. 'China is one of the countries in the world with the highest soil erosion rates anywhere,' explains desertification expert Juergen Voegele at the World Bank. 'One quarter of the total land area in the country is in the process of active desertification, and a large portion of that is actually irreversible.' Nearly 20 per cent of the country's

FIGHTBACK *Farmers plant trees as part of the 'Great Green Wall' being created across north-west China to try to halt the spread of the deserts.*

landmass is now desert, making it one of the largest desert regions in the world, and an estimated 110 million people are suffering the impact.

As its population has grown, China has industrialised at breathtaking speed. Fast-developing cities are eating up farmland and water resources, while construction and furniture industries are consuming forests for timber. On the plains of northern China, shrubs and trees have been cut down, leaving bare soil exposed to the elements. The land that is used for cultivating crops has been over-farmed, and farmers have pushed further into the fragile grasslands that border the desert regions in the west of the country. Those grasses protected the fine, sandy soil, but as herds of livestock overgrazed the area, they exposed the soil to the elements.

Climate change is another driving force behind the sandstorms. The northern half of China, which is growing warmer and drier, is gripped by increasingly chronic and prolonged droughts. Crops and pastures are withering and, as the soil dries out and crumbles to fine dust, it blows away easily on strong winds.

A spreading menace

In recent years the dust storms have become so severe that they spread far beyond China's borders. Clouds of dust regularly choke Korea and Japan and often sweep far out into the Pacific. One super-storm, in April 2001, reached record-breaking proportions. The winter had been unusually dry, and a monstrous wind swept down from the Gobi and Taklimakan deserts with a million tonnes of dust that brought apocalyptic scenes to Beijing and the rest of northern China. A thick yellow cloud blotted out the Sun and created a choking fog so dense that people could hardly see their way in the streets. Schools and offices were forced to close, flights were cancelled and public life ground to a halt. Strangest of all, the static electricity generated by the rushing particles of dust created sheets of lightning that lit up Beijing's dark skies, followed by earth-shattering thunder, although there was no rain.

From space, satellite pictures revealed that the cloud of dust was nearly 2,000 km (1,200 miles) long as it swept out of China, over North Korea and Japan, and out across the Pacific Ocean. Meteorologists watched the satellite pictures in awe as the yellow cloud advanced towards North America. Six days later, on April 12, the cloud's leading edge reached the US west coast. 'In Seattle we had one of the worst days of the year,' Dan Jaffe, professor of atmospheric sciences at

WASHING AWAY THE DUST

In a bid to combat sandstorms, the Chinese have invested in the challenging science of rainmaking. Across China, artificial rain is made using around 30 aircraft, 4,000 rocket launchers, 7,000 artillery pieces and 37,000 workers. This huge operation is designed to launch silver iodide powder into clouds to encourage raindrops to form. The silver iodide imitates the natural specks of salt or other floating particles that 'seed' clouds, encouraging moisture in the air to condense into water droplets.

China has the largest rain-seeding programme in the world, and proponents claim that the extra rain washes down dust from the air, as well as easing droughts. But it is extremely difficult to establish how much impact cloud-seeding has – or even if it works at all. 'It's very hard to quantify how much rain falls because of the seeding, and how much is natural,' admits Zhang Qiang, head of the Beijing Weather Modification Office. And even if the technique does work, some people fear that it 'steals' rain from other regions.

the University of Washington, remembers. 'I looked up in the sky and saw milky, washed-out blue. My first thought was of a volcanic eruption.'

The cloud eventually stretched across North America from Alaska to Florida, raining dust over the continent. It looked like a white haze in the sky as sunlight was scattered by the dust particles; in places, cars were blanketed in a fine yellow powder. 'You couldn't miss it,' said Duane Hilton, a resident of Bishop, California. 'We usually have 50 miles visibility, but at one point you could see dust in the air just 8 to 10 feet away.' The million-tonne dust cloud was unlike anything seen before. 'In terms of area covered, this was the largest dust storm we've observed in the Northern Hemisphere' said Jay Herman, at NASA's satellite observation department. 'I think it's a good example of how we're all tied together. Things that happen in Tokyo and Beijing and New York affect people on other continents in very surprising ways.' Two days later, the dust cloud crossed the east coast of North America. By the time it disappeared from satellite images on April 24, the cloud had crossed two-thirds of the Atlantic.

The 'Great Green Wall'

The Chinese government has been fighting back against the advancing deserts. In 1978, it initiated the greatest tree-planting project in the world, at an estimated cost of $6-8 billion. So far, 35 billion trees have been planted in an attempt to halt the spread of the deserts and protect the northern cities from being engulfed in sand. The scheme, known as the 'Great Green Wall', aims to plant a total of 35 million hectares (86 million acres) of trees by 2050, mostly in the margins of the Taklimakan desert in north-west China, and in Inner Mongolia.

Two decades of tree-planting have failed to halt the spread of the deserts. The tide of sand keeps moving, and some experts say that the project is a waste of effort and possibly harmful to the environment. Professor Hong Jiang, at the University of Madison in Wisconsin, said that large-scale tree-planting was not necessarily the answer. 'As a dry land, the environment doesn't really support such a massive planting – especially of tree species that use up a lot of groundwater. So I have seen a lot of planting, but I have also seen a lot of failures.'

Other schemes are also being tried, such as planting grasses and shrubs, or using chemicals to fix the sand. But despite these measures, rampant agriculture, industrialisation and climate change continue to take their toll on the land.

Feeding the oceans

There is one possible benefit to China's dust storms. The Asian dust contains minerals, especially iron, that are important nutrients for phytoplankton, microscopic algae that inhabit the oceans. As the dust drifts over the Pacific Ocean, the iron in it converts into a soluble form that can be taken up by the phytoplankton.

In April 2002, NASA satellites tracked an Asian dust storm spreading out over the North Pacific. As the storm passed over the ocean, it kicked up waves and also dumped large quantities of iron-rich dust onto the sea surface. Floating buoys in the sea measured a doubling in the mass of phytoplankton as they fed off the dust, creating a bloom so immense it turned the sea green with chlorophyll.

Through photosynthesis phytoplankton absorb carbon dioxide, one of the main greenhouse gases driving global warming, from the atmosphere. Some scientists believe that artificial fertilising of the oceans with iron particles to stimulate phytoplankton growth could increase carbon dioxide absorption and slow global warming.

SILVER LINING

When Hurricane Katrina tore through Florida, slammed across the Louisiana and Mississippi coastlines and swamped New Orleans in August 2005, it inflicted North America's worst natural catastrophe in 100 years.

ALL IS LOST *A resident of Biloxi, Mississippi, weeps as she surveys the damage. A storm surge up to 9 m high left much of the coastal city in ruins.*

In 5 hours of mayhem, Katrina devastated major Gulf Coast cities, including New Orleans, one of the USA's biggest seaports, and wrecked an area of 234,000 km² (90,347 sq miles) – the size of Britain – along 240 km (149 miles) of heavily populated shoreline. It destroyed more than 500,000 homes and displaced almost 2 million people in the nation's largest exodus since the Civil War. An estimated 1,836 people died and at least 1,840 went missing – dead bodies were still being discovered several months after the disaster.

Faced with this disaster, politicians and some relief agencies seemed paralysed with shock. They were grappling with a catastrophe of extraordinary proportions – caused by the third-strongest hurricane ever to strike the USA, the sixth-strongest Atlantic hurricane ever recorded, during the worst hurricane season since records began. The fact that many in authority had clearly been negligent, ignoring repeated warnings that a crisis like this was bound to happen sooner or later, did not help. It would prove to be the world's costliest natural disaster, with damage estimated at over $100 billion – a clear demonstration of the power of Nature to wreak havoc with modern civilisation.

A stunning aberration

The most deadly aspect of the hurricane was not its high winds, but the storm surges it generated. Although the winds were terrifying as Katrina tore down on the coasts of Louisiana and Mississippi, they were actually weakening by that time. They and the incredibly low atmospheric pressure, however, had created a ferocious battering ram of high water, topped by wild waves. It was this lethal wall of water that did most of the damage. As it hit the shallow coastline, it reared up onto the land, crushing everything in its path, and because the shore is so flat and riddled with rivers and canals, its surges thrust deep inland. Author Douglas Brinkley saw one surge on the Mississippi: 'I witnessed a stunning aberration. Just below me, the white-capped Mississippi river was roaring backward, northward, due to Hurricane Katrina's wrath.'

Downriver from New Orleans, a surge up to 7.6 m high overtopped embankments called levees – from the French *lever*, 'to raise' – built to protect the low-lying city, while a 4.6 m surge bulldozed up the Intracoastal Waterway, used by shipping. From that, it funnelled right into the heart of New Orleans along the drainage canals that crisscross the city. The power of the water pouring into the canals seemed uncontrollable. As it washed over the tops of levees, it also began to scour away the bases of some of them, until they collapsed, and floodwaters came pouring into the metropolis, deluging particularly the poor, working-class areas of eastern New Orleans. 'There was essentially a lot more momentum in the water then there was in the wind,' explains Elizabeth English at Louisiana State University.

> **We knew on Saturday night that this was going to be the big one. That it was going to sink New Orleans.**
>
> *Ivor van Heerden, Louisiana State University*

D stroy d by Wind and Wav

TRAIL OF CHAOS *Canal Street in New Orleans' Central Business District is a scene of devastation, with toppled palm trees and tangled power lines, after Katrina's rampage through the city.*

Towering walls of water – storm surges – decimated New Orleans and surrounding areas when Hurricane Katrina struck in 2005.

For the city's inhabitants, the events of that Monday, August 29, were truly terrifying. The New Orleans Police Department received harrowing calls telling of roofs ripped off, water spilling over levees, sewers backing up and houses filling with water. One was from a police officer, Chris Abbott, trapped in his house: 'The water is rising. I'm trying to get out. It's up to my neck.' In the end, he used his gun to blast his way out through the roof of his attic. Many others were less fortunate. They had no means of escape and drowned horrifically in their own homes.

THE SAFFIR-SIMPSON HURRICANE SCALE

Americans Herbert Saffir and Bob Simpson devised their scale in 1969 to classify Western Hemisphere hurricanes according to the intensity of their sustained wind speeds. Two other classifications exist: tropical depressions, with winds blowing up to 62.7 km/h (38 mph); and tropical storms, with wind speeds of 62.8-119.0 km/h (39-73 mph).

CATEGORY	SUSTAINED WIND SPEED	STORM SURGE	WIND DAMAGE
1	119.1-154.4 km/h (74-95 mph)	1.2-1.7 m	Little damage to buildings. Some damage to trees and shrubs.
2	154.5-178.5 km/h (96-110 mph)	1.8-2.6 m	Some damage to roofs, doors and windows. Some smaller trees blown down.
3	178.6-210.7 km/h (111-130 mph)	2.7-3.9 m	Some structural damage to small buildings. Some larger trees blown down.
4	210.8-250.0 km/h (131-155 mph)	4.0-5.4 m	Extensive damage to roofs, doors and windows. Large numbers of trees blown down.
5	251.1 km/h (156 mph) and over	5.5 m +	Severe damage to buildings. All trees blown down.

Birth of a monster

Katrina began on Tuesday, August 23, 2005, as a fairly unremarkable tropical depression skirting The Bahamas. But this was an embryonic monster, feeding on unusually warm sub-tropical Atlantic seas and growing at an astonishing speed. By the next day, it had become a tropical storm, and that evening the National Hurricane Center (NHC) in Florida warned that it 'could intensify a little more than anticipated'.

Only a few hours later, it struck Florida just north of Miami as a Category 1 hurricane on the Saffir-Simpson scale (see box, left). It deluged south-east Florida with up to 350 mm of rain in just 24 hours – more than triple the region's normal rainfall for August. Eleven people were reported killed, and damage was estimated at $2 billion. That alone would have made Katrina a disaster, but far worse was to come.

Starved of its warm sea-water fuel supply, Katrina weakened as it swept across Florida and was downgraded to a tropical storm. But the storm still kept its swirling shape, and only 7 hours later, in the early hours of Friday, August 26, it re-emerged on the far side of the state. Forecasters had dreaded this scenario: the storm recharged itself on the warm waters of the Gulf of Mexico and in only an hour Katrina was reborn as a Category 1 hurricane.

Initially, the forecasters predicted that it would swing north into Alabama and northern Florida. But high pressure in the atmosphere above steered the hurricane farther west into the Gulf of Mexico, giving it more time to refuel over the warm waters there. It also started to take aim at New Orleans. 'I just don't see any reason why this will not become a very, very powerful hurricane before it's all over,' warned NHC director Max Mayfield.

At 10 am on Saturday, August 27, the NHC issued a hurricane warning for metropolitan New Orleans and the surrounding region, predicting that the storm would make landfall just east of the city. Max Mayfield was so concerned that he phoned the governors of

A DISASTER UNFORETOLD?

In the chaos of Katrina and the recriminations that came afterwards, it was clear that two federal agencies had done their job correctly: the National Weather Service and the National Hurricane Center. They forecast with remarkable accuracy both the path of the storm and the potential for devastation. This called into question White House claims that Katrina was a catastrophe no one had envisaged – experts had frequently and insistently warned of precisely such a crisis.

The disaster also raised questions about agencies' ability to cope with emergencies within the USA. Ironically, a year earlier, in July 2004, officials had organised a one-week exercise in case of a flood in New Orleans. Called Hurricane Pam, it had assumed that a Category 3 hurricane would pass close to the city, flooding it and leaving 60,000 dead. Some 200 people attended from local, state and federal agencies, including the Federal Emergency Management Agency (FEMA) and representatives from the White House. Among the plans tested were search-and-rescue and evacuation procedures, but at the end of the exercise these were left 'to be determined at a later date' – revealing attitudes that would become only too apparent when Katrina struck.

AT A STANDSTILL *As the hurricane drew near, huge traffic jams built up on the interstate highways out of New Orleans.*

Louisiana and Mississippi and the mayor of New Orleans to express his alarm. 'I wanted to leave the hurricane center that night … knowing that I had done everything that I could do,' he later recalled. The next day, he reinforced his message during a video conference with President George W. Bush.

As Katrina charged across the Gulf of Mexico, it fed on an intensely warm body of water called The Loop – a deep whorl of sea water that surges between Mexico's Yucatán Peninsula and Cuba each year, feeding through into the Gulf Stream. Often, storms weaken as they churn up cooler waters below the sea surface, but in The Loop even the deep waters are warm. As the storm traversed this region, it was like adding high-octane fuel to a fire. On the night of August 27-28, in a matter of 9 hours, Katrina exploded from a Category 3 to Category 5 hurricane, a truly monstrous tempest.

At Louisiana State University, civil engineer Ivor van Heerden and his hurricane team forecast a catastrophic flood in New Orleans, based on a computer model of hurricane storm surges. Van Heerden made the news public and sent email after email to officials in charge. 'We knew on Saturday night that this was going to be the big one,' he recalled, 'that it was going to sink New Orleans – and so we tried to get the word out as much as possible.'

Unheeded warnings

For years, meteorologists and engineers had warned of the disaster if a big storm flooded New Orleans. The city spreads out over a bowl in the ground, or rather five individual bowls, lying largely below sea level – as much as 3 m below in places. It is surrounded by water, including the massive 780 km^2 (301 sq mile) Lake Pontchartrain to the north and the 1 km (0.6 mile) wide Mississippi. A network of levees keep the city dry, as well as canals and pumps. But experts had repeatedly warned that these defences were not enough and a hurricane could easily overwhelm them.

At 10 am on Sunday, August 28, the National Weather Service issued a warning, which was almost biblical in its language. It predicted a 'most powerful hurricane with unprecedented strength ... Power outages will last for weeks, water shortages will make human suffering incredible by modern standards.' At the same time, New Orleans Mayor Ray Nagin was holding a news conference. 'We are facing a storm that most of us have long feared,' he declared. He ordered an immediate evacuation of the city. But the order was about a day later than for most other cities and counties

CONTINUED ON PAGE 100 »

A chronicle of devastation

Katrina devastated a society as well as a physical region. It triggered a diaspora of nearly 2 million people from Louisiana, Mississippi and Alabama across all 50 states of the USA. Of the 900,000 who fled New Orleans, only 200,000 returned to live there.

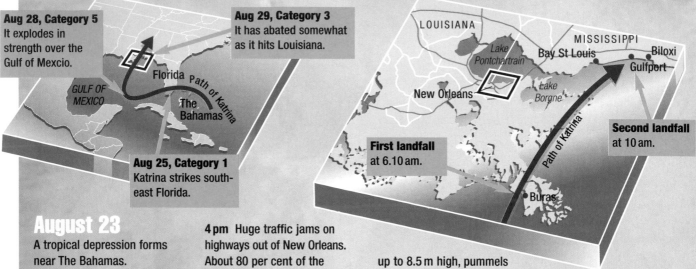

Aug 28, Category 5
It explodes in strength over the Gulf of Mexcio.

Aug 29, Category 3
It has abated somewhat as it hits Louisiana.

GULF OF MEXICO

Florida Path of Katrina

The Bahamas

Aug 25, Category 1
Katrina strikes south-east Florida.

LOUISIANA

MISSISSIPPI

Lake Pontchartrain

Bay St Louis

Biloxi

Gulfport

New Orleans

Lake Borgne

First landfall at 6.10 am.

Path of Katrina

Second landfall at 10 am.

Buras

August 23
A tropical depression forms near The Bahamas.

August 24
The depression is upgraded to Tropical Storm Katrina.

August 25
Katrina hits south-east Florida as a Category 1 hurricane.

August 26
Katrina re-emerges from the west coast of Florida and enters the Gulf of Mexico.

August 27
5 am Katrina reaches Category 3.
1 pm Airlines begin closing down operations at New Orleans airport.
10 pm Forecasters warn that entire central Gulf Coast is in serious danger.

August 28
0.40 am Katrina reaches Category 4.
6.15 am Katrina reaches Category 5.

4 pm Huge traffic jams on highways out of New Orleans. About 80 per cent of the inner city's population of 485,000 have evacuated.
5 pm It starts to rain on the Louisiana coast – the first sign of the approaching hurricane.
8.30 pm The last train leaves New Orleans, mostly empty.
9 pm The first rains hit New Orleans.

August 29
0.00 am A storm surge starts to push into the Mississippi coastline. The New Orleans Superdome is opened as a 'refuge of last resort'.
4.30 am The first breaches of canals in New Orleans.
5 am Levees along the MR-GO waterway start to crumble.
6.10 am Katrina hits the coastline as a Category 3 hurricane at Buras.
7.45 am Levee breaches in the Industrial Canal send a wall of water into New Orleans' Lower Ninth Ward.
8.30 am Another storm surge,

up to 8.5 m high, pummels the Mississippi coastline.
10 am Katrina hits the coast again at the Louisiana/Mississippi border.
12 pm Katrina is downgraded to Category 2 as it passes over land and loses power.
1 pm Looting breaks out in New Orleans. Rescue operations with boats begin.
2 pm Many eastern districts of New Orleans are reported to be under 1.8 m of water. Local television stations show footage of looting. Katrina, by now far inland, is downgraded to Category 1.
6.45 pm The US Coast Guard launches a search-and-rescue operation.

August 30
10 am Efforts to stem the breaches in the canals fail. Looting is now widespread.
11.30 am Across Louisiana and Mississippi, 1.1 million homes and buildings are without power.

12 pm Fires break out in New Orleans.
1.30 pm New Orleans airport reopens for relief efforts.

August 31
11.30 am President Bush flies over the Gulf Coast disaster area.
12 pm Floodwaters stop rising in New Orleans as levels in the city and lakes Pontchartrain and Borgne are equal.
2 pm The first evacuations of the Superdome begin.
7 pm Mayor Nagin declares martial law in New Orleans to control looting and other lawlessness.

September 1
2 am The first evacuees arrive in Houston, Texas. An estimated 4,000 people, many of them elderly and sick, are still stranded on an overpass on the Interstate 10 highway.

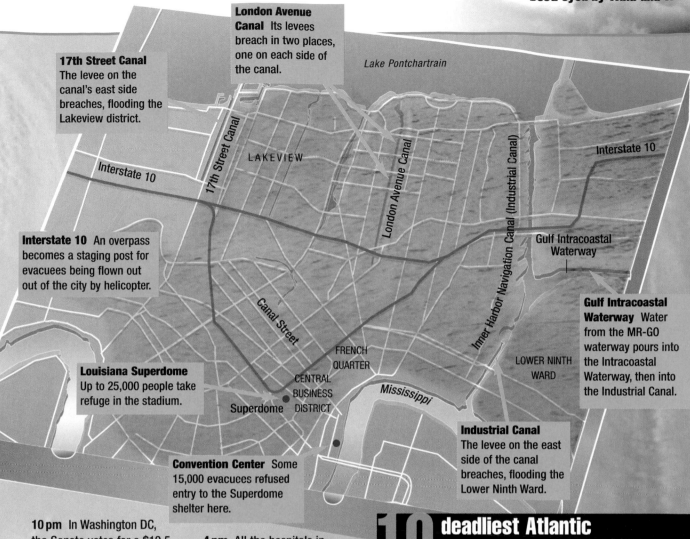

17th Street Canal The levee on the canal's east side breaches, flooding the Lakeview district.

London Avenue Canal Its levees breach in two places, one on each side of the canal.

Lake Pontchartrain

Interstate 10

LAKEVIEW

17th Street Canal

London Avenue Canal

Inner Harbor Navigation Canal (Industrial Canal)

Interstate 10

Interstate 10 An overpass becomes a staging post for evacuees being flown out out of the city by helicopter.

Canal Street

Gulf Intracoastal Waterway

Gulf Intracoastal Waterway Water from the MR-GO waterway pours into the Intracoastal Waterway, then into the Industrial Canal.

FRENCH QUARTER

LOWER NINTH WARD

Louisiana Superdome Up to 25,000 people take refuge in the stadium.

CENTRAL BUSINESS DISTRICT

Mississippi

Superdome

Industrial Canal The levee on the east side of the canal breaches, flooding the Lower Ninth Ward.

Convention Center Some 15,000 evacuees refused entry to the Superdome shelter here.

10 pm In Washington DC, the Senate votes for a $10.5 billion emergency relief package for the disaster zone. Because of oil refineries closed in Louisiana, the price of petrol in the USA has soared to over $3 per gallon.

September 2

9 am Around 1,000 National Guard troops storm the Convention Center to take control of anarchic conditions there. They bring 200,000 meals with them.
10.35 am President Bush starts a tour of the Gulf Coast.
12 pm Convoys of army trucks deliver supplies to New Orleans.
2.05 pm The United Nations announces plans to send aid to the Gulf Coast. Many countries have started their own relief efforts.

4 pm All the hospitals in New Orleans have finally been evacuated.
8.30 pm Amtrak trains start taking evacuees out of New Orleans.

September 3

2.15 am Evacuation of the Superdome is almost complete, but buses stop coming and 2,000 people are left behind.
12 pm Evacuation of the Convention Center begins.
1.45 pm Helicopters evacuate the last people stranded on the Interstate 10 overpass.
5.45 pm The last people are evacuated from the Superdome.
9.50 pm The last people are evacuated from the Convention Center.

10 deadliest Atlantic hurricanes since 1900

The deadliest Atlantic hurricane ever recorded struck the eastern Caribbean islands of Barbados, Martinique and Sint Eustatius in October 1780, leaving an estimated 20-22,000 people dead. Hurricanes have been officially named only since the 1950s.

	NAME	DATE	PLACES MOST AFFECTED	ESTIMATED DEATHS
1	Mitch	1998	Honduras, Nicaragua, El Salvador, Guatemala, Belize	9,000-18,000
2		1900	Galveston, Texas	8,000-12,000
3	Fifi	1974	Honduras	8,000-10,000
4		1930	Dominican Republic	2,000-8,000
5	Flora	1963	Haiti, Cuba	7,000-8,000
6		1928	Leeward Islands, Puerto Rico, Bahamas, Florida	4,000
7		1928	Martinique, Guadeloupe, Puerto Rico, Turks and Caicos, Florida	3,375-4,075
8		1932	Cayman Islands, Jamaica, Cuba	2,500-3,107
9		1934	El Salvador, Honduras	2,000-3,006
10		1931	Belize	1,500-2,500

along the Gulf Coast. There were already vast traffic jams, even though lanes on both sides of the interstate highways had been turned over to outward traffic the previous afternoon – nine lanes heading north.

The order also failed to take into account those who had no transport of their own or who were too ill or infirm to move – and New Orleans had a higher proportion of poor and elderly people than many US cities of a similar size. Public transport, meanwhile, had

ARE HURRICANES GETTING WORSE?

Although there is no evidence that the number of hurricanes is increasing, the damage they cause is getting worse. This is partly because populations are growing in hurricane-prone regions. Some experts, however, believe that the storms themselves are becoming more intense, as global warming makes the oceans warmer, increasing the energy supply for tropical storms. The Atlantic hurricane season of 2005, for example, was phenomenal, with a record 28 tropical storms and hurricanes, four of which – Emily, Katrina, Rita and Wilma – reached Category 5 on the Saffir-Simpson scale. On the other hand, hurricanes do naturally wax and wane in number over decades, as the salt content and temperature in the Atlantic's deep ocean currents vary over a cycle of 40-60 years.

Kevin Trenberth and Dennis Shea of the US National Center for Atmospheric Research have tried to untangle the natural variations from more unusual factors. They found that there were record sea-surface temperatures during the 2005 season. Across the so-called Hurricane Alley – the tropical belt of the Atlantic where hurricanes are spawned and grow – the readings were 0.9°C higher than averages going back a century. Trenberth and Shea believe that half of that extra heat was from global warming, while natural cycles were much less important.

Other recent studies reveal that over the past 30 years major tropical storms in the Atlantic and Pacific have increased in duration and intensity by about 50 per cent, tying in with rising sea and air temperatures. Some experts, however, argue that sea temperature is only one factor involved in breeding monstrous tropical storms. And so the debate continues. Unfortunately, we will probably not know for sure whether climate change is the driving force behind the recent hurricanes until many more storms such as Katrina have blown up.

SAVED FROM ABOVE *A helicopter rescues New Orleans' residents who had taken refuge on their rooftop. Strewn debris surrounds wrecked houses (opposite). Katrina destroyed more than half a million homes in Louisiana and Mississippi.*

been suspended, and there were shortages of rental cars and fuel. That afternoon, Delta Airlines cancelled all flights from New Orleans.

At 1 pm, Katrina reached its frenetic climax, the atmospheric pressure at its heart plunging to 902 millibars and the winds reaching sustained speeds of 280 km/h (174 mph). It charged through many of the oil and gas fields of the Gulf of Mexico, then headed for the coasts of Louisiana and Mississippi.

In New Orleans, 430,000 cars had left the city and its suburbs by evening, and the highways were at last clear of jams. But as many as 100,000 inner-city residents, along with many tourists, were stranded, because they were unable to leave. In fact, 550 city buses could have been used to ferry out 22,000 people on each trip. Trains, too, could have picked up thousands of evacuees. But the mayor gave no order to use them.

At midnight, as a 'refuge of last resort' for residents unable to get transport out of the city, he opened the

70,000-seat Superdome, home of the New Orleans Saints American football team. Priority was given to the elderly – they had to bring enough food, water and medicine to last up to five days.

Making landfall

At 3 am on Monday, August 29, a buoy 80 km (50 miles) east of the mouth of the Mississippi registered waves towering 12 m high. At 6.10 am, Katrina made landfall as a strong Category 3 hurricane near the small town of Buras, Louisiana, only 24 km (15 miles) from the place where forecasters said it would strike. In less than an hour, Buras was virtually wiped off the map. All 1,146 of its homes were obliterated – fortunately, the entire population of around 3,000 people had been evacuated.

At that point, Katrina was a swirling mass of wind, rain and clouds, 740 km (460 miles) across. Over the next few hours, it swept across the Mississippi Delta, back out over the sea in the Mississippi Sound and then, at 10 am, struck the Mississippi coast between Bay St Louis and Gulfport. Biloxi, Mississippi, some 40 km (25 miles) to the east, was just one place to suffer massive devastation. A storm surge crashed into the city, and in the local hospital, seriously ill patients had to be moved up to the second storey as the waters rushed in below. 'We had fish swimming around the first floor,' said one nurse. The staff also saw crabs and snakes in the corridors, and a large snapping turtle invaded the emergency room. But, in spite of all that, they kept the hospital going. Making do without painkillers, oxygen tanks, food, electricity or other essential supplies, they treated 800 people in three days.

All in all, Katrina left 238 people dead in Mississippi state, 67 missing and billions of dollars of damage. Officials calculated that 90 per cent of buildings within 0.8 km (half a mile) of the state's shoreline were completely destroyed. It also spawned 11 tornadoes, which ripped up trees and power lines. Farther east, big storm surges and violent winds hit the Alabama coastline and the Florida Panhandle. Four tornadoes were reported in Alabama, and at least 18 spun off farther north in Georgia. Strangely, the hurricane swept through so rapidly that people reported their ears popping as the barometric pressure suddenly rose again.

A city spared?

New Orleans, meanwhile, had been spared a direct hit. The eye of the storm had been aiming straight at the city, until at the last moment it veered eastwards. Initially, there was relief, and many media reports early that Monday morning declared that New Orleans had mostly 'dodged the bullet'. Tall buildings had been hardest hit, as winds were faster higher up than on the ground. In the Hyatt Regency Hotel, windows were blown out and beds were seen flying out into the sky. The Superdome had a large section of its

roof ripped off and rain blew inside. At 5 am, the power failed in the city.

It was chaos, as rain slammed down and the winds blew, but at least the all-important defensive levees seemed to be holding – or so it was thought. Later, however, jubilation gave way to shock, when TV crews showed large areas under water, with hundreds of people stranded on roofs, highway overpasses – anywhere that was still dry. Storm surges, rushing up from the Gulf of Mexico, had burst through some levees, notably on the Industrial Canal on the east side of the downtown area. The US Army Corps of Engineers, responsible for them, had no external monitoring equipment, so most of the initial surges had gone unnoticed – the engineers relied on the media and calls from local people for information.

Around 9 am, at St Rita's Nursing Home in the south-eastern suburbs, staff and residents heard an ominous rumbling sound – the water of a surge. The owners had not evacuated, thinking that the storm would not be as bad as forecast. It proved a fatal decision. Within 20 minutes the single-storey building was flooded to the ceilings. 'People were screaming like somebody

KEEPING BABY SAFE *A New Orleans father places his baby beyond the reach of the floodwaters. The couple had to abandon their car after it started to float.*

was murdering them,' said Gene Alonzo, who was visiting the home. Frantic efforts were made to float residents out on mattresses through windows or the roof, but it became increasingly difficult and 35 elderly residents died. The owners were later indicted for negligent homicide.

And more was to come. After 10 am, when Katrina made its second landfall, on the Mississippi coast, a 8.5 m surge heading west drove another wave of water into the city. Four hours later, the Army engineers finally checked on reported damage to the canals downtown. They were stopped in their tracks – the levees on the 17th Street and London Avenue Canals had burst in three places. This meant that water from Lake Pontchartrain was pouring into the city. By 3 pm,

water was bursting through the levees in 28 separate places, and some 383 km² (148 sq miles) of urban landscape were flooding.

Michael Brown lived in Chalmette, also in the south-eastern suburbs. 'All of a sudden, water was everywhere,' he said. 'As far as the eye could see, there was nothing but black water.' He and his family moved up to the first floor of their house, where they remained for the next two days. But being marooned in floodwaters without food or drinking water was only one of the hazards. 'I looked and saw this movement in the water. We had water moccasins [poisonous snakes] on the ground floor. They were everywhere.'

Another danger was pollution. Chalmette and the neighbouring area of Meraux were inundated with crude oil leaking from a tank that had floated away from an oil depot. More than 25,100 barrels of crude oil spilled out.

New Orleans was filling up like a bowl, exactly as experts had warned for years that it would do. Only a few places escaped the flooding, such as the French Quarter, the historic heart of the city, which stands on higher ground than most districts.

Trapped

By Monday evening, news teams were reporting not a miraculous escape but a catastrophe. People wandered the flooded streets with nowhere to go. Debris, including dead bodies, floated everywhere. Temperatures were sweltering, and a large part of the city stank. There was no clean water or electricity, and some hotels and

Design disaster

Katrina's storm surges revealed just how inadequate New Orleans' flood defences were. The water simply bulldozed levees, whose designers had taken no account of extreme storms – they were built to withstand Category 2 hurricanes at the worst – and had often used poor materials.

New Orleans has two types of levee. Its earliest earthen levees were built in the 18th century, while more recent concrete and steel floodwalls form part of a scheme authorised by Congress after Hurricane Betsy swamped parts of the city in 1965. The system was expected to take 13 years to complete at a cost of $85 million. But when Katrina hit, the project was still not finished and had cost $738 million. To make matters worse, the foundations of many of the levees were far too weak; the soil under the embankments was unstable, and the steel sheets reinforcing them were driven in too shallowly. Some levees did hold up, especially along the Mississippi, but these are giants – 90 m wide at the base, 30 m wide at the top and rising 7.6 m above sea level.

Another problem was shipping canals, including the Mississippi River-Gulf Outlet (MR-GO). Built to provide an express route for ships between New Orleans and the Gulf, this also acts as an express route for storm surges. 'The federal powers had designed an excellent storm-surge delivery system, to bring a mass of water with tremendous load right into the middle of New Orleans,' commented Ivor van Heerden of Louisiana State University. This is what happened on August 29, when a 5 m surge tore up the MR-GO and was funnelled into a tight channel with inadequate levees. At 6.30 am, it pushed over the funnel's levees, feeding into other canals. At 7.45 am, a stretch of levee along one canal collapsed and water exploded into the city's Lower Ninth Ward.

OVERWHELMED *Water pours through a broken levee. Storm surges scoured out many of New Orleans' levees, which had been poorly designed and built with inadequate foundations.*

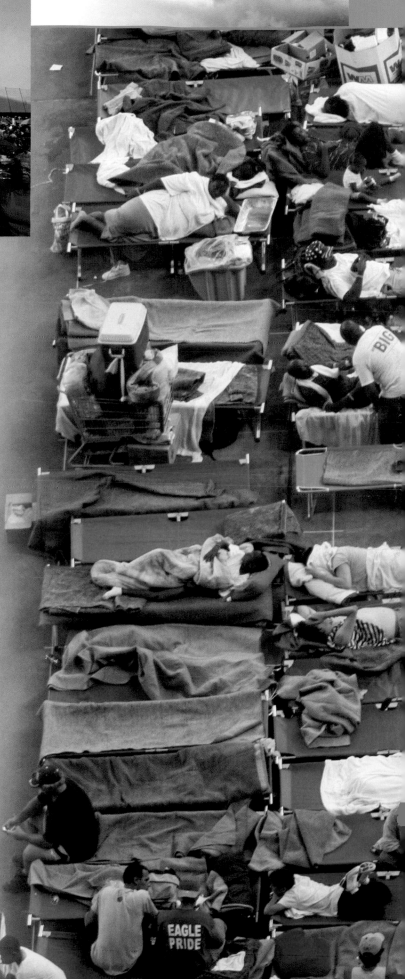

WAITING FOR RESCUE *Survivors wait to be evacuated from the Superdome (above). Many were taken to Houston, Texas, where they ended up camping in the city's Astrodome (right).*

hospitals reported diesel fuel shortages. Emergency care was almost non-existent.

In the Superdome, conditions were becoming unbearable. There was no water, food, power, sanitation or medication. Instead, evacuees had to endure stench, heat, looting and menacing by thugs. It had also reached saturation point, and that night it was closed to further evacuees. New arrivals were left outside in the streets – many broke into the New Orleans Convention Center.

As dawn broke on Tuesday, August 30, water covered some 75 per cent of Greater New Orleans, and it was still pouring in. Around 50,000-70,000 people remained stranded in the city, and two-thirds of those were in severe danger – on the verge of drowning or trapped on rooftops or in attics. 'The devastation is worse than our worst fears,' said Kathleen Blanco, Louisiana's Governor. 'Pray for patience, pray for courage.'

Journalist Jaqui Goddard of the London *Times* was one of many foreigners in the city. 'The tens of thousands of us trapped in New Orleans are witnessing scenes that we never thought we would see in the 21st century in a major western city,' she reported. 'There is no electricity or running water. Telephone lines are down. The mobile phone system has crashed. Outside my downtown hotel … there is a knee-high soup of brown water swirling with debris – lethal shards of glass, road signs, sheets of metal, tree branches and lampposts.'

Nor was there any sign of outside help, from the Red Cross, the Federal Emergency Management Agency (FEMA) or the National Guard. The only organised rescue efforts came from boatmen of the Louisiana Department of Wildlife and Fisheries and the US Coast Guard. The boatmen pulled people out of the water and muck, assisted by a growing flotilla of anglers

> ❝ **People sleeping in the street. People lying in the gutter. Dead people. People chanting, "Help, help, help."** ❞
>
> *Tony Zumbado, NBC News*

in their own small boats. Overhead, Coast Guard helicopter pilots hovered above the rooftops, plucking off survivors in rescue baskets. Over the 10 days following Katrina, the Coast Guard worked round the clock, evacuating more than 33,500 people.

By Wednesday, August 31, the statistics of New Orleans' humanitarian crisis were frightening: around 25,000 people trapped in the Superdome, 15,000 in the Convention Center, 1,700 in hospitals and 2,430 children separated from their families. In and around the Convention Center, there were scenes of almost hellish deprivation. Guns abounded and crime went unchecked, while in the streets outside people died from neglect.

Nobody coming for us?

News reporter Tony Zumbado of NBC News described what he saw: 'People sleeping in the street. People lying in the gutter. Dead people. People chanting, "Help, help, help." Kids crying. Dogs running around. Trash all over the place.' In the words of one victim, it 'was as if all us were already pronounced dead. As if somebody already had the body bags. Wasn't nobody coming for us?'

New Orleans' airport, meanwhile, had become a makeshift medical centre for treating patients, evacuated by helicopters and ambulances from flooded hospitals. It also had evacuees from convalescent homes and nursing homes, people rescued from rooftops and many more who had made their way there independently.

The rest of the world looked on in horror, wondering why help was not getting through. Reporters and cameramen seemed to be able to move in and out of the city, even with large vehicles. FEMA, meanwhile,

CLEARING UP *Rescue worker Jeff Gottbreht surveys the damage in a house near the 17th Street Canal. He had come from Lincoln, Nebraska, to help the local emergency services.*

Defences for the future

Since the Katrina disaster, low-lying coastal regions around the world have reviewed their defences against storm surges. There are many options, but one key element is coastal wetlands. Experts argue that these need to be maintained and restored to act as a buffer between land and sea.

The devastation caused by Katrina alerted other places vulnerable to storm surges to the potential danger they were in. Residents of northern California, for example, looked at deteriorating levees along the Sacramento and San Joaquin rivers, where a collapse would flood the Central Valley and foul the state's water supplies. Cities facing similar dangers include Miami, Rotterdam, London and Shanghai, left vulnerable as their foundations subside and sea levels rise.

An effective strategy against surges uses many forms of defence, including systems of dams and floodgates, improved pumps for removing water and even raising parts of cities above flood level – as was done in Galveston, Texas, after a hurricane smashed through it in 1900. Another defence, increasingly favoured by experts, is the restoration of coastal wetlands. These are a highly effective protection against storm surges, acting like sponges to soak up the incoming water. But they are disappearing at an alarming rate. Between 1930 and 2005, 4,000 km^2 (1,544 sq miles) of wetland were lost in southern Louisiana alone.

Paradoxically, the building of flood defence levees is partly to blame. Before they were built along the Mississippi, the river flooded each spring and carried tonnes of silt to the sea, replenishing the wetlands along the coast – now, they are being starved of new soil. At the same time, they have been drained for development, creating another problem – as the reclaimed land dries out, it shrinks, sinking New Orleans even further below sea level. Stands of cypress trees, which once acted as natural windbreaks during hurricanes, have also been chopped down.

Restoring wetlands is an expensive and long-term option – one project, Coast 2050, which aims to restore marshes and swamps in Louisiana, would cost about $14 billion over 30 years. But, experts argue, it needs to be done. To keep out rising seas, engineers are prepared to sacrifice dry land to the sea – a measure that would once have been unthinkable.

promised buses, food, water and medicine, yet these did not even begin to materialise until Thursday, September 1. Essential supplies, supposed to have been in place outside the Gulf Coast area, proved to be non-existent. As a result, FEMA officials had to scrabble around the country for what was needed.

On Friday, September 2, Terry Ebbert, Homeland Security Director for New Orleans, described the situation as 'a national disgrace'. FEMA had finally arrived. 'Yet,' Ebbert said, 'there is no command and control. We can send massive amounts of aid to tsunami victims, but we can't bail out the city of New Orleans.' In fact, food, water and extra personnel did finally arrive that day. By then, too, relief organisations had found suitable places for relocating refugees. Many were being bussed to the cities of Houston, San Antonio and Dallas in Texas and farther afield, where they were housed in old air force bases, parks and stadiums.

As the first week of the disaster came to a close on Sunday, September 4, an astonishing 1.7 million people had left New Orleans and its suburbs and were now scattered throughout the USA. On September 6, Mayor Nagin ordered a forced evacuation of everyone still in the city who was not involved in clean-up work. It was not just an attempt to restore law and order; there were fears that diseases such as cholera and typhoid might break out. Eviction efforts escalated three days later, when door-to-door searches were conducted. Despite this, a number of residents defied the eviction order, and National Guard troops eventually began to remove residents by force.

By Monday, September 5, the Army Corps of Engineers had managed to close some of the major breaches of the levees and had got the city's great drainage pumps working again. Within weeks the city was drained. But when the waters had receded, New Orleans was a wasteland with miles of devastated buildings covered in filth and debris. Though the job of rebuilding the city could begin, in many people's minds the soul of the city had been lost forever.

The storm of 1987 was England's most devastating natural catastrophe for more than 250 years. On the night of October 15-16, winds reached speeds of over 160 km/h (100 mph), killing 19 people, blacking out some 3 million households and businesses and flattening 15 million trees.

There had been warnings days before that a storm was brewing, but the UK Met Office believed the worst winds would strike northern France. On the evening of October 15, BBC TV forecaster Michael Fish announced on a weather bulletin: 'Earlier on today a lady rang the BBC and said she'd heard that there was a hurricane on the way. Well, don't worry if you're watching, there isn't.' He qualified that, however, by saying it would be windy and wet later that night. 'I did broadcast saying, "Batten down the hatches, there's some really stormy weather on the way", but the media took it out of context,' he later remarked. In the event, the storm – not technically a hurricane (see box, page 96), but with hurricane-force winds – left an insurance bill of about £1.5 billion, making it the most expensive single natural disaster in the world until that time.

A night of devastation

The weather was certainly strange that evening in southern England. An unusually warm breeze blew across the region, becoming hotter as the night wore on. At Heathrow airport, near London, the temperature was a fairly normal 9°C at 6 pm, but by midnight it had reached 17°C; the temperature in Farnborough, Hampshire, soared 8.5°C in only 20 minutes. The heat was a warning sign that hot, subtropical air was sweeping in at the leading edge of a storm. By 9 pm, moderate winds were blowing. An hour later, they had strengthened and spread northwards, with powerful gusts. Shortly after midnight, the eye of the storm smashed into Plymouth on the south Devon coast.

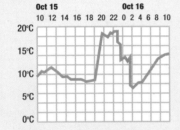

TEMPERATURE SWINGS
Hot subtropical air hitting cold Arctic air sent temperatures fluctuating wildly in the 24 hours from 10 am on October 15.

England's Great Storm

COMMUNICATIONS CUT
Toppling trees blocked roads and railway lines and even knocked over phone boxes, as seen here in Brighton.

A BATTLEFIELD *The trail of uprooted trees was partly due to weeks of wet weather before the storm. In the face of the wind's violents blasts, trees collapsed because the soil around their roots was too loose and damp to hold them upright.*

Hurricane-force winds rampaged across southern England in October 1987, leaving an insurance bill of some £1.5 billion.

Soon afterwards the Met Office issued a severe weather warning for southern England, but it was far too late and very few people were awake to hear it.

In the English Channel, meanwhile, the sea was whipping itself into a frenzy. Waves grew into monstrous peaks, 12 m high, their crests licked by the howling wind into almost horizontal sheets of spray. Hundreds of small boats were smashed to pieces along the Channel coast, even in protected river moorings and marinas. The 16,000 tonne freighter *Sumnia* sank as it tried to get into Dover harbour, and two cross-Channel ferries struggled to stay afloat. One was the *St Christopher*, which spent several terrifying hours tossed about in the violent seas before finally docking at 2 pm the next day. The wind and waves had buckled the steel doors of her upper car deck, and lorries had toppled over and crushed cars.

Her sister ship, the *Hengist*, suffered a still worse fate. The wind broke her moorings in Folkestone harbour,

forcing Captain Sid Bridgewater to put to sea to prevent the ship from being smashed onto the harbour walls. Soon after leaving harbour, however, she lost power and started drifting helplessly. 'I thought we were going to capsize,' the captain recalled. 'It was a hopeless situation, thrown around in the sea in the dark without engines, risking the lives of the 25 crew members.' They sent out Mayday calls, but before help could arrive, the *Hengist* struck a concrete embankment on the coast, which ripped open a gash in the hull as large as a double-decker bus. Fortunately, it was high tide and the waves drove her up the shore onto a relatively flat beach. When the tide withdrew, she was left high and dry – and everyone on board survived.

All along the South Coast, meanwhile, winds equivalent to those of a Category 2 Atlantic hurricane (see page 96) had battered the shoreline. Journalist Fiona Baird-Murray was in the seaside town of Worthing, West Sussex: 'Upturned fishing boats bounced along

BEFORE AND AFTER
The storm also pummelled the Channel Islands. It sent most of the avenue of trees along this street in Jersey (left) crashing to the ground, leaving a scene of havoc after the tempest (below).

the beach,' she reported later. 'Windows were wrenched out of sea-front shops. Brick walls had crumbled, trees lay resting, and iron railings and road signs had buckled under pressure from the elements.'

By 5 am, the storm had reached eastern England. Here, the winds pushed back the oncoming tide, exposing mudflats and shorelines which would normally be under deep water. At the port of Harwich, a former ferry, used to house refugees seeking asylum in the UK, broke from its moorings and began to drift. No one was injured, but there was a public outcry afterwards that so many lives had been endangered, and the ship was withdrawn from that use. Across southern and eastern England, caravans were flung around like toys, light aircraft were flipped upside down,

> **Upturned fishing boats bounced along the beach. Windows were wrenched out of sea-front shops.**
>
> *Fiona Baird-Murray*

roofs were ripped off, their tiles hurled through the air like missiles, and glasshouses were shattered. Trees, which were still in full leaf, caught the full force of the wind. Because the ground was wet from weeks of heavy rain, they collapsed in swathes and many were uprooted. Conditions on the roads, meanwhile, were lethal. Many of the fatalities that night happened when vehicles overturned or were crushed by falling trees. To add to the terror, electricity cables crashed to the ground or sent up showers of sparks as debris caught the cables and short-circuited them.

There were some almost miraculous escapes. At Merrow in Surrey, the Reverend Harry Fordham and his wife underwent an astonishing ordeal. 'There was a huge crash and I woke up on the ground floor instead of the bedroom upstairs, covered in rubble,' Fordham recalled. The floor beneath their bed had collapsed. 'Amazingly, I was lying next to the 'phone, so I called for an ambulance and immediately afterwards the line went dead.' Luckily, his message got through and an ambulance took the Fordhams to hospital shortly before the roads were blocked by fallen trees.

On the South Downs above Brighton, a pair of windmills called Jack and Jill were at serious risk. Their sails had been locked using large brakes to prevent them spinning, but Jill's sails broke the brakes and the friction as they spun wildly round and round set the building's timbers ablaze. Local enthusiasts rushed to the rescue, dragging buckets of water from a nearby house. 'The wind was so strong I couldn't stand up, and had to crawl up the hill on my hands and knees,' remembered Simon Potts. 'When I got inside the mill, it was shaking backwards and forwards, like being on board a ship.'

GROUNDED *Huge waves hurled the Sealink ferry Hengist onto the shore, where it remained stranded for a week after the storm. All on board were rescued.*

Eventually, he and the other rescuers managed to put the fire out and jam the sails' brakes with grit.

A coincidence of events

Exactly what detonated a storm of such fury is still not fully understood. It had begun innocuously enough in the mid-Atlantic and had travelled east, reaching the Bay of Biscay at around midday on October 15. It remained there for a short while, then suddenly exploded into a monstrous tempest. Much of this energy was drawn from the clash between humid, hot air sweeping up from North Africa and cold, dry air from the Arctic. The contrast between the two air masses created the storm conditions, but does not explain why the storm turned so violent so rapidly. One possibility is that the remains of Hurricane Floyd, which had just battered the coast of Florida, injected a burst of energy into the jet stream, a ribbon of fast winds several kilometres high in the atmosphere. This jet streak may have intensified the storm while steering it towards England.

Another phenomenon, which scientists have only recently discovered, may also have played a part. Satellite pictures reveal an unusual, clear path carved straight through the storm clouds, where a burst of very dry, cold air some 5 km (3 miles) high plunged down through them. Snow and ice in the cloudtops would have made the air even colder. Rather like an avalanche rushing down a mountainside, this dense, cold air would have accelerated downwards until it crashed into the ground with winds reaching speeds of up to 160 km/h (100 mph).

SILVER LINING

A wildlife boom

The October 1987 storm seemed to have inflicted catastrophic damage on woodlands, leaving many ancient and valuable trees smashed and fallen. But the next spring brought a sensational boom in wildlife. Most animals survived surprisingly well, and thanks to the plentiful supply of wood-feeding insects gorging themselves on the fallen timber, populations of birds and bats flourished. Even larger mammals, such as deer, thrived on the protection the fallen logs gave them.

In some places, heavy machinery used to clear fallen logs damaged the topsoil, leading to erosion, and conifer plantations were also a problem, faring less well than other woodlands. Many failed to regrow, highlighting the danger of growing tree species out of their normal habitat and in regimented patterns. Elsewhere, however, trees regenerated far better than anyone expected. Trees that had lost their crowns regrew well, and even trunks snapped close to the ground sprouted new growth. Woodland floors were opened up to daylight, allowing seeds buried in the ground to sprout into new saplings. When spring came, the open glades hosted a spectacular burst of primroses, bluebells, lesser celandine and other woodland flowers.

The perfect storm

When three different weather systems collided off the east coast of the USA in October 1991, they gave birth to a storm of gigantic proportions. It was a freak of meteorology, when the atmosphere seemed to go beserk in ways that weather experts had never seen before.

Sebastian Junger's book, *The Perfect Storm*, made the tempest famous and was later turned into a movie starring George Clooney. It told the story of a doomed fishing boat, the *Andrea Gail*, and its six crew members, who were hunting swordfish 800 km (500 miles) out to sea when the storm struck. It was a tale of immense bravery as rescue boats fought against all odds to reach the *Andrea Gail*, but the storm was too powerful and the fishing boat and her crew were lost.

The storm built up over a week, between October 26 and 31. It began with an unremarkable depression over the Great Lakes, passing from Chicago to Maine and over Nova Scotia. On the way, it collided with a bitterly cold high-pressure system drifting down from Canada. The two systems combined forces in a storm off the Nova Scotia coast. Even this was not remarkable until a third element arrived – the remains of Hurricane Grace sweeping hot, humid tropical air up from the south. On October 29, the storm exploded with colossal force, feeding off the temperature difference between the cold, dry air off Nova Scotia and the warmth and humidity from Hurricane Grace. On satellite pictures the resulting tempest looked like a giant white whirlpool 3,200 km (2,000 miles) wide, stretching from Jamaica to the coast of Labrador.

The storm tore across the Atlantic with winds of more than 160 km/h (100 mph) and waves up to 30 m high, the height of a ten-storey building. It lasted almost five days, and even though its centre never reached the US coast, it generated enough mayhem to tear seawalls and coastal houses apart, rip beaches away and cause massive damage. It brought 9 m waves onto beaches from North Carolina to Nova Scotia, and the ocean swell even reached the Dominican Republic in the Caribbean. According to David Vallee, a US forecaster who tracked the storm, 'This was truly an awesome example of Nature taking advantage of everything she's got available.'

The phenomenon is called a 'sting jet' and is thought to be responsible for other devastating Atlantic storms.

Dawn the next day revealed the extent of the damage. Many railways and roads were virtually impassable. In some places, it would take three weeks before electricity was restored. To make matters worse, heavy rains fell a day later, pouring through holes in damaged buildings. Bizarrely, people far inland found sea salt encrusted on south-facing windows and trees, glinting like frost – the wind had carried it up to 65 km (40 miles) from the sea. At Highdown Hill on the South Downs, trees blown over in the storm had human bones tangled in their roots. At first, people feared that it was the scene of a macabre crime, but the site was later identified as an Anglo-Saxon burial ground.

In the aftermath of the storm, the question everyone asked was why there had not been better warnings. There was widespread criticism of the Met Office, which led to a government enquiry. In fact, this found that forecasters were only partly to blame. As the storm sped north from the Bay of Biscay on the evening of October 15, its deepening core of low pressure drew the winds into an ever-tightening spiral which largely bypassed shipping in the English Channel. Without regular reports from ships at sea, the Met Office had no information about its intensity. Furthermore, financial cuts had forced the withdrawal of weather ships dedicated to collecting sea and weather information in the Atlantic. One of the scrapped ships had been based off Finisterre, Spain's most westerly point – the exact spot from where the storm came and where weather readings would have provided plenty of advance warning.

At the time of the October 1987 storm, experts commented that events like it were rare, occurring only once every 200 years or so. But on January 25-26, 1990, an equally powerful storm struck Britain. The Met Office forecast it correctly this time, but it still left 47 people dead. The second storm gave rise to a new concern – were two big storms in such a short period a warning sign of climate change? Unusually warm sea temperatures around the UK were a feature of both storms, and may have fuelled the ferocious winds. Scientists fear that as global warming increases, Atlantic storms may grow more powerful.

CAPSIZED *The Ferris Flotel, a floating hotel, lies on its side in Pusan harbour after being tipped over by Typhoon Maemi.*

The north-west Pacific is the most dangerous region in the world for tropical storms. The most ferocious are classed as typhoons, and they threaten half a billion people living along the coastlines of the Philippines, China, the Korean peninsula, Japan and other Pacific Ocean countries.

Typhoon Havoc

On the night of September 10, 2003, a typhoon bulldozed into the tiny Japanese island of Miyako, south-west of Okinawa, with winds gusting to 333 km/h (207 mph) – faster than the Japanese bullet train. Torrents of rain lashed down, reaching 465 mm, a new record for the island. Hundreds of power lines collapsed, bringing widespread failures and leaving most of the island's population of 58,000 in the dark. All seven of the island's wind-turbine generators were wrecked, and the airport was put out of action when the roof of the control tower collapsed and the building flooded with rain. The sugarcane crop was flattened, roofs were ripped off buildings and windows blown in, sending shards of glass flying like shrapnel.

A farmer, Yoshitaka Sunagawa, spent a fearful time that night as the windows of his house smashed in and rain flooded the ground floor. 'We felt the house being shaken by gusts as the wind screamed,' he said. There were 700 casualties on Miyako,

including one woman who was injured when a window smashed, and who died of a heart attack.

Five days earlier, satellite pictures had picked up a tropical disturbance forming near Guam, a remote island in the north-west Pacific. A mass of thunderstorms had merged into one large one, but this was not unusual. Depressions often brew up during the rainy season in this part of the Pacific, only to fizzle out at sea. But this disturbance had taken a more sinister turn when the winds within it began to whirl around a central core in a steadily accelerating vortex – the start of what meteorologists call a tropical depression.

The following day, September 6, winds in the depression had reached more than 74 km/h (46 mph) – strong enough for it to be upgraded to a tropical storm. It was a beast serious enough to warrant its own name, Maemi, the Korean word for 'cicada'. Shipping was warned to avoid the area. Maemi was still far out in the Pacific and too remote to worry most people, but it was gaining power at an alarming rate. By September 7, with winds blasting at 111 km/h (69 mph), it had developed into a full-blown typhoon and was steaming west towards Okinawa, one of the southernmost islands of Japan. On September 8, Maemi's winds escalated to 139 km/h (86 mph), and satellite pictures revealed the clear eye in the storm's centre surrounded by raging winds and rain. Within 24 hours, the wind speed had

DAMAGE STATISTICS

- 117 people killed; another 13 reported missing and never found.
- 774 roads, 27 bridges and 17,400 ha (43,000 acres) of farmland flooded.
- More than 5,000 houses wrecked and a further 13,000 damaged; 25,000 people homeless.
- Nearly 40,000 cars damaged.
- 282 ships sunk or damaged.
- Total economic loss estimated at $4.1 billion.

In 2003, Typhoon Maemi exploded into life in the warm waters of the Pacific and raged for three days, leaving havoc in its path.

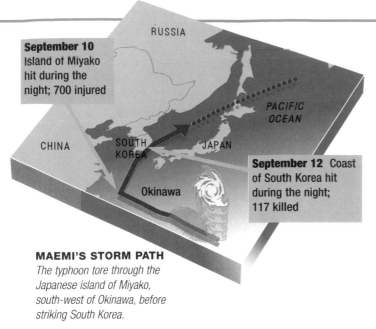

September 10
Island of Miyako hit during the night; 700 injured

September 12 Coast of South Korea hit during the night; 117 killed

RUSSIA

PACIFIC OCEAN

CHINA

SOUTH KOREA

JAPAN

Okinawa

MAEMI'S STORM PATH
The typhoon tore through the Japanese island of Miyako, south-west of Okinawa, before striking South Korea.

exploded from 165 km/h to 278 km/h (103 to 173 mph), in a burst of power that catapulted Maemi from Category 2 to Category 5 on the Saffir-Simpson Scale of hurricane intensity (see box, page 96). Escalation as rapid as this is rare, seen only once in several years, and was detonated by an eddy of unusually warm water 700 km (435 miles) wide. This was fuelling Maemi into a super typhoon, a terrifying mega-storm even in the tempestuous Pacific. By the time Maemi hit Myako, with its monumental winds and atmospheric pressure that had sunk to 912.0 millibars, it was the fourth most powerful typhoon ever recorded in Japan.

Catastrophe in South Korea

The fate of Miyako was a warning of far worse to come. On September 11, Maemi lurched northwards and put on an extra spurt of speed as it took aim at the Korean peninsula. The only hope of reprieve came when the winds eased slightly, to 222 km/h (138 mph), and Maemi lost its super-typhoon status, but it remained a wild and furious tempest.

On the night of September 12, with winds blasting up to 216 km/h

(134 mph) and rainfall reaching 450 mm, Maemi smashed into the southern coast of South Korea. 'Maemi was by far the most powerful typhoon since we began compiling weather records in 1904,' Yoon Seok-hwan at the Korea Meteorological Administration reported to news agencies.

Waves off the coast reached a height of 8 m. To add to its devastating power, Maemi rode into the coast on a high tide, piling up a 3 m storm surge that tore into the shoreline along the most industrialised area of Korea, which includes the major cities Pusan, Masan and Ulsan. About 282 ships were either sunk or wrecked, many having been ripped from their moorings. Some were heaved up onto beaches by the brute force of the surging sea waters.

South Korea's largest port, Pusan, which normally handles 80 per cent of the country's container shipping, received the full brunt of the storm. Huge waves battered the harbour, sending ships crashing into each other or into quays. Shipping containers 6 m long were tossed through the air in the screaming winds, and 11 industrial cranes used for lifting cargo containers – each weighing about 1,000 tonnes – crashed to the ground, reduced to mangled pieces of steel. A floating hotel that was moored alongside the docks was flipped over and capsized. Fortunately, the guests and crew had all been evacuated just before the typhoon struck.

CLEAN-UP *South Korean soldiers clear mud and debris from a building in Pusan after the flood waters subsided. Wind, floods and mudslides caused $4.1 billion of damage.*

SUPER TYPHOON TIP

The greatest storm ever recorded was Super Typhoon Tip, which formed in the western Pacific on October 5, 1979. It grew to a monstrous 2,170 km (1,350 miles) wide, about five times greater than a typical Atlantic hurricane. At its peak on October 12, the air pressure fell to a world-record low of 870 millibars, the lowest atmospheric pressure ever measured at sea level, and winds around the eye were estimated at 320 km/h (200 mph). The eye wall reached 17 km (11 miles) high, where the temperature was -92°C. Tip then slowly weakened as it headed towards Japan. It made landfall on Honshu on October 19 as a minimal typhoon, but largely missed land. Nonetheless, it was responsible for 68 deaths, most due to flooding, and caused millions of dollars of damage to Japan's agricultural and fishing industries.

Across the south-eastern corner of the country, the typhoon sent trees and cables crashing down and caused widespread flooding. Some 25,000 people were evacuated from their homes. 'Water poured into my house in a minute, I couldn't get anything out except myself,' Choi Joong-kwon, a resident of Taegu city, told YTN television. 'Winds were chaotic: my apartment building was noticeably swaying with each burst. Windows were literally sucked out of my girlfriend's apartment, frames and all. I was simply hoping the glass of windows wouldn't implode upon me,' reported Devon Rowcliffe in Pusan. 'A five-star hotel had its roof peeled off and deposited on the roof of the building that I was in, which is actually taller by four floors. The noise of the howling wind was similar to that of avalanches,' reported John Quirk in Ch'angwon.

'Our windows shook and shook and made noises like you could never imagine. The building swayed and shuddered,' described Grace Morris in Ulsan.

The storm shut down five of the nation's nuclear power plants after their main transformers or power lines were damaged, and left 1.4 million people without power. Fortunately, no radiation leaks were reported.

The city of Masan suffered massive damage from the storm surge. The flood defences there were inadequate and provided no protection against tidal waves. Reclaimed land along the coast had slowly subsided over time, which made the situation worse. In one case, floodwaters engulfed a building, drowning 20 people trapped in the basement. Navy divers were called in to search flooded areas for victims, and soldiers were reduced to using buckets to scoop out water from flooded basements.

The sudden and huge rainfalls triggered flash floods. Mudslides swept away roads, and a landslide in the central province of Ch'ungch'ong-Bukto derailed an express train bound for Seoul, injuring 28 on board. Part of the 1 km (½ mile) Gupo bridge over the Nakdong river in Pusan collapsed in the raging floodwaters.

In the port of Ulsan, 9 m high waves were recorded. A 200,000 tonne offshore oil rig being built by the world's largest shipbuilder, Hyundai Heavy Industries, was swept away and smashed into a 37,000 tonne petrochemicals ship in the dockyards, causing immense damage to both. Road signs were uprooted and thrown onto vehicles. Cars were seen floating down streets that were turned into raging torrents, and many roads were blocked by landslides or washed away.

At the height of the storm, electric signs showered sparks over pedestrians hunched under blown-out umbrellas on flooded streets. Many of the 117 deaths that night were caused by landslides, drowning or electrocution from fallen power lines. The death toll could have been far worse had it not been the Chuseok holiday (harvest festival), a time when families get together, and most people were indoors.

As Maemi pushed further inland, it was no longer fuelled by the warm sea water. It swept across the south-eastern region of Korea in only 6 hours and by the evening of September 12 it was running out of steam. The devastating, whirling circulation of the once-powerful storm began to fall apart, and it slowly died. By September 14, it was just an insignificant gale blowing past the Kamchatka Peninsula in Russia.

deadliest western Pacific tropical cyclones

The western Pacific is the most active place in the world for tropical cyclone activity. China and the Philippines receive the most storms and typhoons that make landfall.

	DATE	NAME	PLACE	DEATHS
1	1991	Thelma	Philippines	6,000
2	1984	Ike	Philippines, China	1,363-3,000
3	1960	Lucille	Philippines	300
4	1990	Mike	Philippines, China	250
5	2003	Maemi	Ryukyu Islands, Japan	117
6	2004	Rananim	China	115
7	2002	Rusa	Korea	113

The waters of the Indian Ocean are a notorious breeding ground for tropical cyclones, which feed off the warm sea and are sent spinning northwards into the Bay of Bengal. The ferocious storms then funnel into the Bangladesh coast and the largest delta in the world.

In the dead of night on November 12, 1970, Cyclone Bhola approached the coast of Bangladesh (which was East Pakistan at the time). It had been building up for some days far out to sea. Winds gusting to over 220 km/h (137 mph) raged in a frenzy around the eye of the storm and, as it headed towards land, it pushed up the surface water into a large storm surge that rode in on an exceptionally high tide. The result was a wall of water up to 10 m high that thrust into the heart of the low-lying, densely populated Ganges delta region while most people slept.

Many were drowned in their beds. Survivors described waking up to find themselves afloat, their houses swept away. Tens of thousands of sea and river fishermen, who work at night, died as their boats were swamped. Many made futile attempts to escape, but were dragged under the raging torrents that surged over the land. There were miraculous escapes, too. Some people managed to cling to the tops of banana or coconut trees. Others used toppled trees and coconuts, which are buoyant, as floats.

UNICEF official, Francis Smethwick, who was inspecting water systems on islands in the delta region, was in a brick bungalow when the storm struck. 'I was holding on to a door up to my knees in water, praying. The noise of the wind was crashing, worse than a torpedo hitting

A D_adly Storm Surg

GRIEF-STRICKEN *A man sobs after losing his entire family in the floods.*

In 1970, Cyclone Bhola swept a 10 m high storm surge deep into Bangladesh's delta region, killing an estimated half million people.

a ship, so loud you couldn't hear anyone shouting. Buckets, pans, anything loose was flying around the bungalow. Water was swirling around. Then the strangest thing, the rain and wind suddenly subsided, there was just water sloshing around. It was the eye of the storm passing over.' He owed his life to the strong brickwork of the bungalow. Most people on the islands lived in flimsy wooden shacks and had no protection.

Smethwick emerged the next day to a scene of utter devastation. 'Trees were down, houses flattened, very few people were alive. A sand bank on a stream opposite was just full of bodies.' Word got out that he was alive and a day later he was picked up by one of the few working boats, crowded with survivors. 'I was looking at thousands of bodies floating past our boat. For three days and nights all we saw were human bodies and the remains of livestock, houses, trees. Everything was washed away. We had very little food or water.'

Cyclone Bhola was the worst weather disaster of the 20th century anywhere in the world, and the deadliest cyclonic storm ever recorded. An estimated 500,000 people were killed, but some estimates put the figure at 1 million. The scale of the disaster was so vast that the

WASHED AWAY *Crops and livestock were destroyed on Urir Island in the Bay of Bengal, but human casualties were low as cyclone shelters were available.*

true figure will never be known. The coastline and islands in the delta were the worst affected areas. Some 8,000 km² (3,100 sq miles) of land was devastated, towns and villages were swept away, virtually all crops were destroyed and more than 1 million cattle were lost. So comprehensive was the annihilation that the region resembled a second Hiroshima.

Ikram Sehgal, who flew over the area, recalls the scale of the disaster. 'The rivers flowing into the ocean seemed clogged by the carcasses of animals and debris. Nobody believed us when we said these were corpses of human beings, in their thousands and thousands. The islands of ... Bhola and Manpura ... were swept almost clean of humans, animals and houses ... Except for the odd cement structure and the occasional tree, a giant lawn-mower cum road-roller seemed to have wiped the area clean.'

Shifting land

Cyclones strike Bangladesh in two seasons each year: as the Indian monsoon advances, from April to June, and then retreats, from September to November. The howling winds and torrential rain are punishing enough, but, as most of the country barely rises above sea level, the greatest threat comes from the storm surge caused by high winds pushing at the ocean surface. As a storm sweeps up the Bay of Bengal, the funnel-shaped coastline squeezes the bulge of sea water even higher, often up to 6 m, in a heaving mass of waves that smash

into the coast. If a surge coincides with high tide, the resulting storm tide floods deep into the delta, can sweep away entire islands and large parts of the coast.

The delta itself is a patchwork of islands criss-crossed by waterways that often change course. The Brahmaputra and Ganges rivers carry around 2.4 billion tonnes of fertile silt each year, much of which is unloaded in the delta, where it forms sandbars that gradually develop into islands. These emerge, move and disappear again with the annual monsoon floods. The silt creates land so lush that it can yield three rice harvests a year, with plenty of irrigation provided by rivers and monsoon rains.

Islands with vegetation on them are known as chars. Government regulations say that if a char has not been eroded after four years, it can be used for settlement or cultivation. But Bangladesh has the densest population in the world, with more than 1,000 people per km² (2,600 per sq mile). Every patch of land is used to its maximum potential, and as overcrowding has grown more acute, landless farmers have been forced farther out into the delta and closer to the sea, rushing to settle on new chars as soon as they appear, even though the islands can easily be washed away in floods.

The relief effort

For almost 72 hours after Cyclone Bhola struck, the full extent of the disaster was unclear to the outside world. East Pakistan's governor, Vice Admiral Syed Mohammad Ahsan, claimed that only 16,000 people had been killed. It was a grotesque underestimate, and some 10 million survivors were left in desperate need of shelter, food, medicine and drinkable water.

When the true scale of the tragedy was realised, the international response was swift. Pledges of aid came in from over 40 countries, and the Red Cross was the first to get supplies flown into the airport at Dacca (now Dhaka), the capital of East Pakistan. Distributing that aid was extremely difficult, though, given the challenges of the terrain, with few roads and airstrips, and waterways clogged with debris.

Relief was also severely hampered by the lack of boats and heavily blocked rivers and waterways. Helicopters were sent in by the US, British, French, West German and Saudi Arabian air forces, and thousands of tonnes of relief supplies were airlifted, or dropped by parachute from light aircraft. But by the time relief supplies arrived, survivors were crazed with hunger and thirst. One American helicopter was almost ransacked by desperate crowds when it delivered sacks of food and was forced to make an emergency take-off.

FOOD DROP *The US army drops supplies. The relief effort relied on helicopters and boats to reach the delta region.*

A four-ship British task force anchored off the coast brought in food, clothing, medicine and water purification pills to remote coastal areas. Volunteer lifeboat crews from Britain used inflatable motor boats, which can navigate narrow water channels. A fortnight after the cyclone, they arrived at the coast. 'We saw breached sea walls, large boats swept inland and bodies of men, women, children, cows and goats were piled up.'

Yet despite obstacles, the relief effort succeeded in averting an even greater humanitarian catastrophe from starvation and diseases such as cholera.

Unheeded warnings

The death toll and level of destruction need not have been so high. Although weather satellites were in their infancy, pictures from a satellite over the Bay of Bengal clearly showed the approaching storm, and cyclone warnings were broadcast over the radio. But a crucial code indicating the force of the cyclone was omitted from the warning, and the public were unclear about how severe the storm would be.

Many people had also grown sceptical of cyclone warnings. Previous storms had been weaker than anticipated, and people assumed the same this time. 'I don't know what the Disaster Warning Systems really mean ... We often hear announcements of possible disasters, but later we find them to be false alarms,' explained Muhammad Bulu Mia.

Yet some older people had suspected a powerful storm was brewing when they noticed unusual signs in the natural world. A muddy smell was reported on the wind, crabs came into houses and courtyards, dogs were howling, cattle became restless, pond and river water became warmer and black rolls of cloud swept across the sky. 'A strong wind was blowing. The atmosphere warmed up alarmingly. Dogs were wailing without any break. I felt some flood or cyclone was going to hit us. At around 2 in the night, the water started flooding into my place,' reported Shahinur Begam. People largely ignored the signs, however, regarding traditional weather folklore as old-fashioned and superstitious. And elderly people did not want to spread alarm, or look foolish if they were proved wrong.

Political fallout

Recovery from the disaster was swift. The shortage of land in Bangladesh is so chronic that survivors reoccupied the disaster zone within two months of the cyclone. The government, shaken by criticism of its handling of the crisis, overhauled its cyclone preparedness. Within a year, the authorities had constructed 238 concrete cyclone shelters. Up to three storeys high, they provided secure accommodation during floods and storms. Earth embankments were improved and extended, and improved weather warnings were instigated.

Perhaps the biggest consequence of the 1970 cyclone disaster was the political storm it fuelled. At the time, Pakistan was divided into East and West,

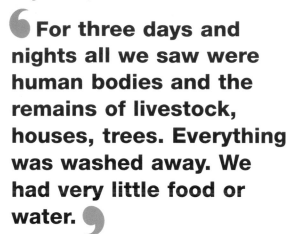

For three days and nights all we saw were human bodies and the remains of livestock, houses, trees. Everything was washed away. We had very little food or water.

Francis Smethwick, UNICEF official

separated by an enormous swathe of northern India. The country was ruled from Islamabad in West Pakistan, but the government seemed paralysed by the disaster. The navy was not ordered to search for survivors, some 500,000 tonnes of grain remained locked in warehouses in East Pakistan and the air force fleet of some 40 helicopters stayed on their airfields in West Pakistan. Help from neighbouring India was refused because of the enmity between the two governments, and when Indian aircraft loaded with relief supplies did try to land in East Pakistan, they were turned away because they did not have the necessary visas.

Long before the cyclone, many politicians in East Pakistan had been agitating for more autonomy or outright independence from West Pakistan. In the aftermath of the cyclone disaster, that discontent grew and by March 1971 the political situation deteriorated so badly that war broke out. The fighting lasted around nine months and eventually gave East Pakistan independence, after which it was renamed Bangladesh, while West Pakistan became Pakistan.

5 top storm surges

Several factors affect the height of a storm surge, such as the area of sea covered by a storm, the strength of the wind and the shape of the coastline. Storm surges combined with a high tide are the most destructive as they can reach areas usually safe from flooding.

Worldwide storm-surge data is sparse, and measurements from before modern times must be viewed with some scepticism. The storms listed below caused very high surges.

	DATE	HEIGHT	STORM	LOCATION
1	1899	14.6 m	Cyclone Mahina	Bathurst Bay, Australia
2	1905	14 m	Strong typhoon	Marshall Islands, Pacific
3	1970	12.2 m	Cyclone Bhola	Hatia Island, Bangladesh
4	2005	9 m	Hurricane Katrina	Bay St Louis, Mississippi
5	1969	7.4 m	Hurricane Camille	Mississippi coast

Rising sea levels

Cyclones will always plague Bangladesh. During 1980-2000, about 60 per cent of all deaths in the world from tropical cyclones occurred there. The problem is growing worse as the country faces rising sea levels caused by global warming, with the increased threat of storm surges and flooding.

According to Sir John Houghton, a former director of the UK Met Office, a sea-level rise of 50 cm could sweep away or make uninhabitable about 10 per cent of the habitable land of Bangladesh, where at least 6 million people live. Added to that, the delta region is subsiding, partly because groundwater is being abstracted for agriculture to feed the nation's 140 million people. By 2050, waters could have risen by 1 m, claiming 20 per cent of Bangladesh and displacing 15 million people. By 2100, the ocean may have encroached upriver almost as far as Dhaka, one of the world's fastest-growing cities, and across the Indian border to the edge of Calcutta.

Added to that, the population is growing at a rapid rate, having doubled since 1961 to 165 million, and this has led to an increasing number of people living in the areas most at risk from the storm surges that are whipped up by cyclones. When a large storm surge comes in on a high tide, it can flood deep into the low-lying delta area, not only drowning thousands of people, but also washing away whole islands and sections of coastline.

VULNERABLE COASTLINE
The warm waters of the Indian Ocean are a prime breeding ground for tropical cyclones. Storms that travel northwards into the Bay of Bengal are funnelled straight into the Bangladesh coast.

Repeat performances

The programme of cyclone shelter building begun after the 1970 disaster gradually fizzled out until the next major storm disaster, in May 1985, when 4,200 people were killed. A UN resolution called for more cyclone shelters, and the Bangladeshi government planned to construct another 3,000, but the programme again ground to a halt. However, around 3,600 km (2,200 miles) of embankments were built in the delta by 1989.

Yet again the improved defences proved inadequate when another catastrophic cyclone struck in the middle of the night on April 29, 1991. Winds reaching 225 km/h (140 mph) during a high tide produced a storm surge up to 7 m high.

'At about midnight the wind ripped the roof off the house. The wind was howling from all around. It was blisteringly hot. When it turned round to reach the sea, the water came with a booming sound. A giant wave lifted us up and we grabbed hold of the branch of a tree,' said one survivor.

Another who escaped was a 15-year old boy, Mesbahur Rahman. 'Waves crashed into each other and soared upwards. The water sounded like cannons firing. My two sisters and my mother hung onto a branch of the same tree but the branch broke. I saw them taken away by the wind and fall into the swirling water. Whoever could not keep hold fell into the eddy and drowned.'

In 1991, more than 130,000 people were killed and half a million injured. More than 860,000 houses were destroyed, 440,000 cattle were drowned and huge swathes of farmland were contaminated by saltwater. The storm surge tore down 434 km (270 miles) of earth or concrete embankments and badly damaged another 858 km (533 miles). Damage was estimated at $1.5 billion (at 1991 values), and 10 million people were affected.

A Noxious Cloud of Gas

Lake Nyos is a beautiful body of water in the remote volcanic highlands of Cameroon, West Africa. But the people of the region say that bad spirits lurk deep in its crystal-blue waters. Outsiders used to dismiss this as superstition – until a terrifying incident made them think again.

> ❛The thing was white, white like cloth. It didn't go up in the air; it mostly went down near the ground❜
>
> *Papa Nyako*

On the moonlit night of August 21-22, 1986, the spirits of Nyos awoke. The lake, surrounded by fertile land ideal for the local small-scale farmers, lies in the crater of an extinct volcano. At around 9 pm, it gave forth a rumbling sound and a strange cloud emerged from its depths. 'We heard a loud sound just like an explosion,' recalled one survivor, David Chia Wambong. 'I went outside and saw all my cows lying on the ground. I went back inside and saw my wife and daughter had fallen to the floor.'

The monster of Nyos went stealthily about its work. 'The thing was white, white like cloth. It didn't go up in the air; it mostly went down near the ground,' said Papa Nyako, another lucky survivor. The lake had also turned from its usual deep blue to brick red, as if something had churned up the mud on its bed.

The next day, silence hung over the area. The few survivors awoke to find a ghost settlement, where almost all people, livestock and wildlife were dead. In the village of Nyos, only four people had come out of that horrific night alive; other villages lower down the mountain had also suffered. Ahadji Abdou cycled through the district on his way to his farm. 'I stopped my bicycle and I stood still,' he remembers. 'I saw dead people all over the road. I knew something terrible had happened here.' Many corpses were clustered around fires and tables, where they had dropped dead on the spot. Other people had tried to flee and their corpses were found still clasping their hands over their noses and mouths. A total of 1,800 had died.

The mystery of Nyos

Once news of the slaughter at Nyos reached the outside world, it galvanised an international relief effort, but getting supplies to the area was hugely difficult. Heavy rain had turned the dirt roads to mud, and it was a struggle to get vehicles and equipment over the steep mountain passes. When the first rescuers arrived, they were shocked and baffled by what they saw. For up to 27 km (17 miles) around the lake, trees, plants and buildings appeared untouched, yet nearly every human or animal lay dead.

Scientists from around the world tried to solve the mystery. At first, many thought that a contagious disease had suddenly swept across the area, and 20,000 people were evacuated accordingly. But autopsies of the corpses ruled out a deadly infection. Instead, they showed signs of poisoning from a gas. Geologists suspected that the long-dormant volcano under Lake Nyos had re-awoken and erupted with toxic sulphur or chlorine gases. But there was no sign of an eruption. The truth that emerged was far more puzzling – the dead appeared to have been killed by lethal quantities of carbon dioxide.

BEFORE AND AFTER *The gas eruption stirred up mud from the bottom of the lake, turning it from its usual crystal blue to murky brown.*

ANIMAL DEATH TOLL *The carbon dioxide released from the lake killed 1,800 people and thousands of animals, including cattle near the village of Wum.*

In August 1986, lethal quantities of carbon dioxide erupted from the depths of Lake Nyos in West Africa, leaving 1,800 people dead.

Normally, this is a harmless gas, which we breathe out. Levels of carbon dioxide in the air are usually very low, a mere trace, but at higher concentrations the gas can cause choking, asphyxiation and eventually unconsciousness and death. Yet to overwhelm so large an area so rapidly would have taken a huge eruption of carbon dioxide. And where did it come from?

In fact, the answer had already been discovered, just two years previously in a neighbouring lake – but the warnings had been ignored. Lake Monoun is another volcanic lake which lies only 30 km (19 miles) from Nyos. In the middle of the night of August 15-16, 1984, it had burst with a toxic agent that killed 37 people in the surrounding villages. Because the carnage at Monoun had struck when everyone was asleep, there had been no eyewitnesses of what happened. Scientists suspected that the volcanoes in the region might be responsible.

SILVER LINING

Economic bonus

Cameroon's gas-filled volcanic lakes are not alone in Africa. Lake Kivu, between Rwanda and the Democratic Republic of Congo, has the potential to cause a catastrophe of apocalyptic proportions. It is 2,000 times larger than Nyos, and contains 1,000 times more gas, threatening around a million people living along its shores. Rightly exploited, however, this lake's time bomb could be a source of virtually free energy.

Kivu contains both carbon dioxide and methane, a poisonous and highly explosive gas. If the methane erupted, it could ignite a giant fireball, followed by a cloud of carbon dioxide, creating a disaster that would dwarf Nyos and Monoun. There were fears of an explosion in 2002, when the nearby Mount Nyiragongo erupted and lava spilled into the lake (see pages 146-149).

But methane is also a valuable energy source, and pumping the gas from the lake could supply Rwanda's electricity needs for hundreds of years. This would ease the pressure on deforestation, since the country currently gets 90 per cent of its energy from burning wood. A pilot project was begun in August 2006 when a pipe was sunk and gas piped back to shore. It is the first phase of a £48 million project which will build a power plant near the lake to turn methane into electricity.

One of these scientists, the Iceland-born volcanologist Haraldur Sigurdsson from the University of Rhode Island in the USA, searched the lake for signs of a recent volcanic eruption, such as unusually warm water or emissions of chlorine and sulphur gases. He started by going out in a boat, lowering bottles into the water and hauling up samples. He was amazed by what he found. 'There was no evidence of chlorine, sulphur, or any other volcanic gases in the lake water, and no temperature increase either,' he explained. 'But as soon as the sample bottles were raised up from the floor of the lake, the water in the bottles was bursting with gas bubbles, and then fountains of gas. It was incredible.' Sigurdsson was so concerned that he and his helpers fled immediately in case the lake exploded.

The gas Sigurdsson collected was odourless and colourless, and he suspected carbon dioxide, which was later confirmed by laboratory analysis. 'Carbon dioxide often seeps out from the flanks of volcanoes, and it is coming out of the crust of the Earth in that part of Africa,' he said. 'Usually it escapes easily into the air, but at Lake Monoun it became trapped in the waters.' It is carbon dioxide that gives the fizz to sparkling mineral water, and normally it bubbles to the top. But in Monoun, the sheer weight of water lying above it was trapping the gas in the lake's bottom layers.

As a result, the lake had become a giant gas bomb. Carbon dioxide was steadily building up at the bottom as it seeped up from the lake bed into the water. The slightest landslide, earth tremor or even a heavy rainfall would be enough to trigger an explosion. 'The lake is rather like a bottle of soda,' Sigurdsson noted. 'If the pressure was suddenly released, the gas could explode out of the top.' As the gas erupted from the depths, it would churn up the mud on the lake bottom, changing the colour of the water from blue to muddy brown. Then, because carbon dioxide is heavier than air, it would sweep up out of the lake and along the ground on either side of it, overwhelming anyone unlucky enough to be caught there.

Gas explosion

It was a unique theory – nothing like it had ever been documented before – and despite the wealth of evidence, many scientists were scathing of Sigurdsson's results. After the eruption of Nyos, however, they changed their minds. They now reckon that the pressure from the gas at Nyos had grown so great that 1 billion m³ of carbon dioxide finally burst up out of the lake in a jet soaring 80 m high. A cloud of the gas then swept along the ground and into the surrounding valleys at speeds of up to 50 km/h (30 mph), too fast to outrun.

Worryingly, tests on Nyos revealed that the gas was still accumulating at the bottom, and at an alarming rate. Lake Monoun was in an even more dangerous state, with an even higher concentration of carbon dioxide. In a race against time, scientists considered ways to relieve the pent-up gas in the two lakes before either could erupt again. In the end, they decided to run a pipe from their depths to the surface to siphon off the carbon dioxide and release it gradually and harmlessly into the air – after several years the lakes would be safe. In January 2001, they sank a plastic pipe into Lake Nyos, and almost immediately, a 45 m high geyser shot into the air. Lake Monoun received the same treatment.

There is a snag, however. With only one pipe, it will take more than 30 years to make Lake Nyos safe. Five pipes might do the job in five or six years, but so far funding for extra pipes has not materialised. People, meanwhile, are drifting back into the nearby areas, despite official bans. 'You can't keep people out forever,' says Greg Tanyileke of Cameroon's Institute for Geological and Mining Research. 'We need to go faster.'

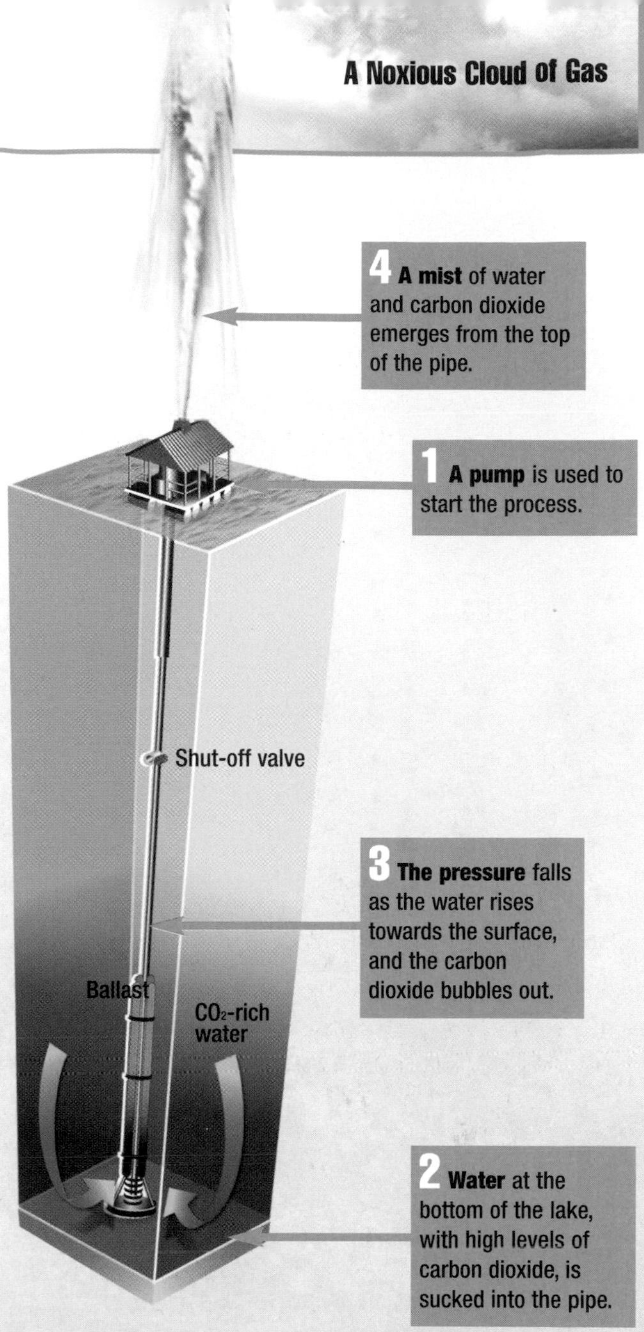

4 **A mist** of water and carbon dioxide emerges from the top of the pipe.

1 **A pump** is used to start the process.

Shut-off valve

3 **The pressure** falls as the water rises towards the surface, and the carbon dioxide bubbles out.

Ballast

CO_2-rich water

2 **Water** at the bottom of the lake, with high levels of carbon dioxide, is sucked into the pipe.

STILL DANGEROUS
A lone figure walks along the shore of Lake Nyos, with the geyser from the de-gassing pipe spouting in the background.

PIPING GAS *As with siphoning, some water has to be pumped up the pipe initially. But once started, the process becomes self-sustaining.*

London's Great Smog

London was always famous for its fogs, but in December 1952 an unprecedented darkness gripped the city for five horrific days – a deadly miasma of fog combined with soot, tar and acid from coal smoke.

Strangely, it all began with gloriously sunny conditions. Friday, December 5, was a crisp day with hardly a breeze, and a relief after weeks of thoroughly wet weather. But there was also a cold nip in the air, which spurred Londoners to pile coal onto their fires to keep warm. As this combined with the coal smoke already billowing from factories, power stations and railways, gradually a thin brown haze built up in the sky, although it was nothing out of the ordinary for a winter's day.

That night, however, a monster descended. As the sun set, temperatures plunged and bitterly cold air sank to the ground. The freezing temperatures turned the moisture on the ground into fog, which rapidly soaked up the coal smoke in the air to form a mass of thick, black smog. When pubs and cinemas emptied that night, the crowds found themselves lost in a frightening world, where once familiar streets had vanished into a gloom so deep that streetlights could barely penetrate a few feet. Traffic ground to a crawl and an eerie silence descended as the blanket of smog grew thicker and more claustrophobic. 'The smog hit us like a wall,' remembered Barbara Fewster, a dancer who had been out for dinner with her fiancé. At the end of the evening, they tried to get back across London by car. 'It was a terrifying journey. The only thing to do was for me to walk in front of the car and guide my fiancé, who was driving, and who was hanging out of the window.' By the time they reached Kingston upon Thames, their 'faces were black, our noses were black and everything was filthy'.

Temperature inversion

When people woke up the next morning, there was no sign of daylight – they faced a weekend of black gloom. A high pressure system, centred over southern England, was giving calm weather, which allowed a lid of warmer air to trap the smoggy, cold air on the ground, in what is called a 'temperature inversion'. The winter sunshine was too weak to break the stranglehold of the warm air above and release the smog; nor was there any wind to blow it away. Geography was another factor – the low hills that ring London helped to enclose the smog. To make matters worse, with the stagnant air still bitterly cold, Londoners piled more and more coal onto their fires. A million chimneys billowed out smoke into the choking atmosphere, which grew still more toxic.

Curiously, the smoggy layer was shallow – just 100 m above the ground in places. People living on the hills around London were amazed to be basking in a clear sunny morning, while below them the metropolis had disappeared under what looked like a blanket of black cotton wool. In fact, visibility on the high ground was so good that people on Hampstead Heath in north London could see all the way across to the hills of Surrey, on the southern outskirts of London.

In the metropolis below, meanwhile, the smog's dark embrace brought chaos. Drivers abandoned their cars,

LONDON VANISHED *Five days of continuous smog blotted out Piccadilly Circus and other familiar London sights.*

> **Our faces were black, our noses were black and everything was filthy.**
>
> *Barbara Fewster*

Thousands died after a five-day smog descended on London in 1952, the worst episode of continuous air pollution ever recorded.

KEW GREEN

TRANSPORT PARALYSED *The smog was so thick that buses got lost in the gloom and had to be guided using flares.*

Even pedestrians had to grope their way through the murk. 'I lost myself in a street ... which I knew like the back of my hand. I couldn't see anything, had no idea where I was, and had to go to a wall and feel my way,' remembered Sir Donald Acheson, formerly Chief Medical Officer. Nor were buildings immune. Maureen Scholes was a nurse at the Royal London Hospital. 'You couldn't see along the corridor that you walked in when you came on duty,' she recalled. 'You couldn't see, actually, from one end of the ward to the other, and it's not that enormous a length.' Cinemas closed when audiences could no longer see the screens and at the Sadler's Wells theatre a performance of Verdi's opera *La Traviata* had to be cut short after the first act.

Trains stopped, and Heathrow airport closed after visibility dropped to less than 10 m. Horse racing, football matches and just about all other outdoor sporting fixtures were called off. At the annual Smithfield Show for agriculture, held at the Earls Court exhibition centre, prize livestock collapsed and died. Interestingly, animals on dirty bedding survived, possibly because the ammonia in the straw neutralised the acid in the air around them.

or crashed into other cars, trees or streetlamps. 'We got on a bus but the journey was very hazardous,' recalled one South London resident, Betty Crowhurst. 'The conductor walked in front ... but we ended up in a side turning by mistake and nearly turned over.' In the East End, brewery employee Peter Prentice remembered the mayhem. 'The smog was so bad that you couldn't see your hand in front of your face. Drivers could see even less; all they could do was follow the lights of the vehicle in front. One of our dray lorries, with the drayman guiding it through the smog, turned into the brewery – unfortunately all the traffic in Commercial Road, including double-decker buses, followed it into the yard. The following morning it took hours to free the deadlock.'

> **The smog was so bad that you couldn't see your hand in front of your face. Drivers could see even less; all they could do was follow the lights of the vehicle in front.**

Peter Prentice

A London particular

Despite the horrific conditions, most people considered the December 1952 smog as quite normal. London had experienced such events for centuries. As early as 1272, King Edward I tried to ban coal burning in London because of the foul air over the city. By the 19th century, the Industrial Revolution had brought factories that pumped out even more smoke day in, day out, and the frequent smogs became known as 'peasoupers' for their greeny, yellow-brown colour. They featured in novels, such as Charles Dickens' *Bleak House* (1852), where he used another term for them – a 'London particular'. In Arthur Conan Doyle's Sherlock Holmes stories, Dr Watson, the narrator, describes how he and Holmes, pushed 'back our chairs from breakfast … [and] saw the greasy, heavy brown swirl still drifting past us and condensing in oily drops upon the window panes.'

But the peasouper of December 1952 was far worse than any previous London smog and its effects were far reaching. Instead of lasting a day or two, it continued for the best part of a week and choked the capital with increasing virulence as the hours and days went by, growing into a terrifying cloud of poisons. Air filters designed to protect the artworks at the National Gallery trapped 56 times the normal levels of smoke particles for a December day.

For nearly five days, London suffered the worst episode of continuous air pollution that has ever been recorded. The most lethal of the various pollutants was sulphur, and its high levels were due, indirectly, to a political decision. The government had ordered the nation's high-quality coal to be exported, to earn desperately needed foreign currency to pay off debts following World War II. The only supplies left for domestic use were cheap, low-grade coals full of sulphur, which burned poorly and gave off clouds of sulphur dioxide. This reacted with the water droplets in the fog to form sulphuric acid. The smog developed an acidity of around pH2, the same level as in a car battery.

When people breathed in these fine droplets, the acid inflamed their bronchial tubes and lungs, causing bronchitis, emphysema and pneumonia. The result was a health crisis across the capital. Some people collapsed dead at home, choked by the smog. Others, who made it to the hospitals, rapidly filled up the wards. Donald Acheson was then working at the Middlesex Hospital: 'The morticians ran out of space in the mortuary and in the chapel of rest, and we had to use the anatomy department's dissecting room in another building.'

Yet, despite the crowded wards, many doctors were unaware that a crisis was unfolding, because the symptoms of the smog victims were typical for a cold winter, consisting largely of respiratory and heart cases. 'There weren't bodies lying around in the street,' observed Dr Robert Waller, who was working at St Bartholomew's Hospital at the time, 'and no one really noticed that more people were dying.' But some were aware of the rising death toll.

Funeral directors knew well enough that winter smogs brought considerable business, but in December 1952 there were so many funerals that undertakers ran out of coffins and florists had no more wreaths. Coroners, pathologists and registrars of deaths at local council offices were inundated with work.

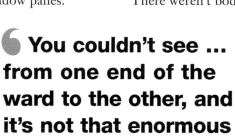

> **You couldn't see … from one end of the ward to the other, and it's not that enormous a length.**
>
> *Maureen Scholes*

NURSE SCHOLES *The smog even invaded buildings, including the Royal London Hospital where Maureen Scholes was working.*

End of the ordeal

On Tuesday, December 9, the smog suddenly vanished, as quickly as it had appeared. A strong wind blew the lid off the temperature inversion and swept the whole filthy mess out to sea. The smog had lasted continuously for 4 days 18 hours, a new world record for a smog caused by coal smoke. The smog had stayed so long because the persistent anticyclone, or area of high pressure, which had centred itself over the south of England had brought an almost complete absence of wind.

The Great Smog is remembered as the world's most lethal episode of air pollution. When the mortality statistics emerged, it was estimated that 4,000 people had died – a death toll not seen since the flu epidemic of 1918 or the cholera epidemic of 1854. But this figure counted only those who died during the five days of the smog and the two weeks after it. A recent reassessment of the statistics reveals a more alarming picture. The death rate remained abnormally high throughout that winter, into spring and even into the summer, long after the smog had vanished. Using this much longer time frame, the final death toll is now estimated at 12,000 – and this may well be an underestimate.

At the time, many assumed that the smog victims were only the old and sick. In fact, although two-thirds of the victims were over 65, the death rate among other age groups also rose. Among 45-64 year olds it leapt three times higher than normal, and twice the usual number of babies died.

For about a century, some doctors had suspected that smogs killed people, but until then they had lacked convincing proof that it was air pollution that caused the deaths – the effects of smog were very similar to

Great Smog statistics

The statistics for London's Great Smog of 1952 were extraordinary. It is estimated that the poison cloud which enveloped the capital contained:

- 2,000 tonnes of carbon dioxide.
- 1,000 tonnes of smoke particles.
- 370 tonnes of sulphur dioxide.
- 140 tonnes of hydrochloric acid.
- 14 tonnes of fluorine compounds.

those caused by lung disease. The Great Smog of 1952 helped to provide that proof. And yet, although it should have been a wake-up call to tackle air pollution, there was much foot-dragging in official circles, where the initial response was to deny that the government had any responsibility in the matter or that there was any need for legislation. As local government minister Harold Macmillan, later prime minister, complained: 'Today everybody expects the government to solve every problem. It is a symptom of the welfare state. For some reason or another "smog" has captured the imagination of the press and people ... I would suggest we form a committee. We cannot do very much, but we can seem to be very busy.'

Ministers even tried to blame the deaths on a flu epidemic, although there was no evidence for this. One explanation for their attitude was their preoccupation with rebuilding Britain after the devastation of World War II. With a virtually bankrupt economy, the government was under huge pressure to increase industrial productivity, boost exports and build new homes. Among many individual members of parliament, however, the smog prompted unease. Jolted into action by a popular private member's bill, the government finally gave way and announced an inquiry.

In the end, the inquiry committee called for the total ban on coal fires. Somewhat reluctantly, the government brought in a Clean Air Act in 1956, authorising local authorities to force people to burn smokeless fuel in their areas. Another clean air law was passed in 1968, tightening up the smokeless coal regulations. By then, however, the age of coal was drawing to an end. Industry was using it less and less; railway steam engines were being scrapped to make way for diesel or electric trains, and people were switching to gas, oil or electricity for heating their homes.

SILVER LINING

Transformed!

The Clean Air Acts of 1956 and 1968 were milestones in legislating against pollution. They allowed local authorities across the country to declare 'smoke control areas', where the burning of coal and other smoke-emitting fuels was banned in homes. Smoke emissions from factories and other industrial premises were also controlled. The results were startling, especially in visibility and the hours of daily sunshine. In the early part of the 20th century, central London averaged just 38 hours of sunshine in November; by the end of the 20th century that had almost doubled to over 70 hours' sunshine. The corrosive effect of smogs on buildings and metalwork became largely a thing of the past. Urban buildings stood out sparkling clean after the layers of black soot were scrubbed from them, and vegetation such as lichens, which are particularly sensitive to air pollution, recolonised London and other cities.

21st-century smogs

Coal smogs are mostly a thing of the past, but lethal smog of a different kind still regularly chokes the world's cities under a cloak of brownish haze. This is mostly caused by traffic emissions, which release minute soot particles and react with sunlight to form photochemical pollutants.

In these modern-day smogs, trucks are the main culprit. Although they make up 5 per cent of traffic, they are responsible for 63 per cent of fine particle emissions, which can lodge deep inside the lungs when breathed in. They also contribute 30 per cent of nitrogen oxide gases. These irritate the respiratory system and may increase susceptibility to infections. In sunlight, they react with hydrocarbons to produce photochemical pollutants, such as ground-level ozone, a cause of breathing problems. Levels of nitrogen oxides rise dangerously when anticyclones bring calm conditions over urban areas and the air becomes stagnant with fumes. The problem is most acute in cities, including London, Los Angeles and Mexico City, where surrounding hills help to trap the air.

This modern form of pollution can be as lethal as many coal smogs of the past. A study in 2005 estimated that 500,000 people die worldwide each year from air pollution. More people die in London from traffic emissions than from road accidents – in 1997, an estimated 380 people died there from air pollution, compared with 230 from road accidents. The problem will only improve when vehicles using non-polluting fuels are more widely and cheaply available. Meanwhile, cities tackle it in different ways. Roads in Paris and Milan are often closed to high-polluting traffic when pollution is expected to rise to dangerous levels. In Los Angeles, tough emission standards are enforced on vehicles to try to cut down the sources of the pollution.

TRAFFIC FUMES *The brown haze of pollution hangs over a traffic-choked Paris boulevard.*

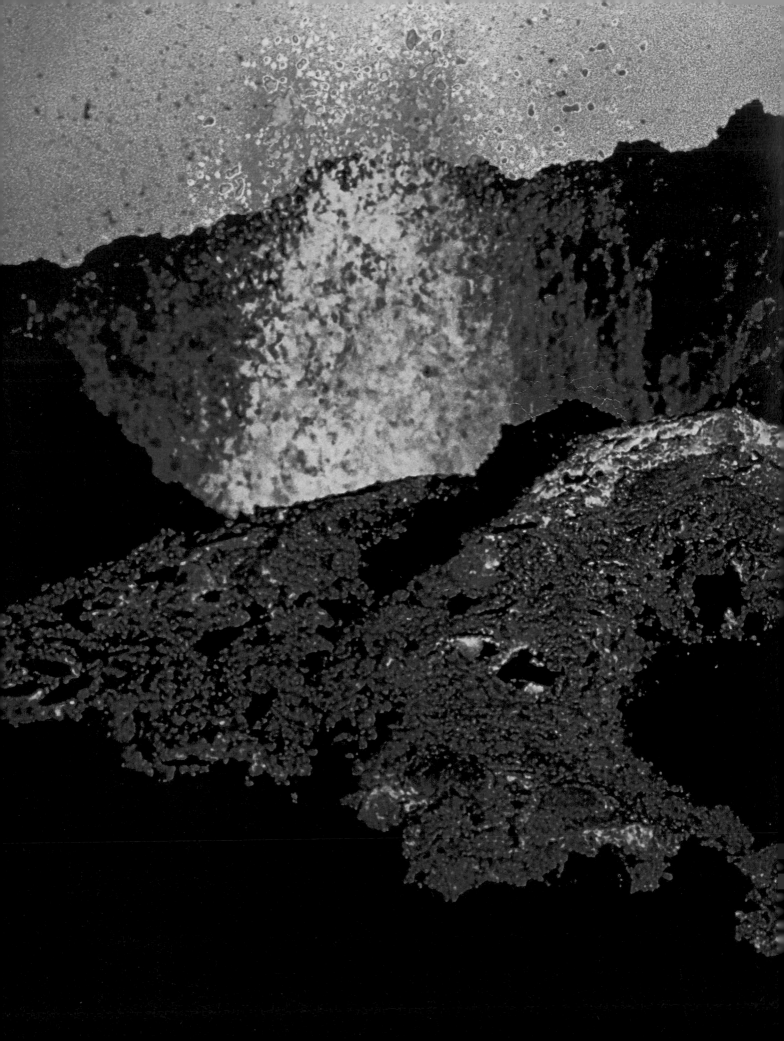

Fire

The world was watching when Mount St Helens exploded in May 1980. The eruption followed two months of rumblings on the mountain, which had drawn numerous camera crews and crowds of tourists to Skamania county in south-west Washington State.

There was a festival atmosphere as people waited around the volcano, hoping to witness one of the great spectacles of nature. As the mountain let off occasional puffs of smoke, some were even impatient and complained that the small steam explosions were not dramatic enough.

Then at 8.32 on the morning of May 18, the party came to an abrupt end. With a blast that had the energy of 500 atomic bombs, Mount St Helens erupted. The largest landslide in recorded history headed down the mountain, followed by fiery pyroclastic flows of hot ash, pumice and deadly gases reaching temperatures of 700°C. The intense heat rapidly melted the snow and ice on the mountain peak, creating boiling mudslides, called lahars, which carried ash, boulders and debris down river valleys. Trees were uprooted and swept away, roads and bridges destroyed and 57 people killed. The mountain was left 400 m shorter and an area of 600 km² (230 sq miles) lay devastated. It turned out to be the deadliest, most destructive eruption in the history of the United States, costing more than $1 billion.

The Mount Fuji of the West

Before the eruption, Mount St Helens was picture-postcard beautiful – a majestic snow-capped cone, rising some 2,950 m above sea level. Its symmetrical shape had earned it the name of the 'Mount Fuji of the West', but Native American Indians know it by a different name. They call it Loo-Wit, or 'Keeper of the Fire', and with good reason. The 40,000-year-old volcano is young in geological terms and the most active in the entire Cascade mountain range, which runs along North America's west coast from northern California as far as British Columbia in Canada. The mountain has been especially active over the past 4,000 years, erupting roughly once every 100 years.

Keeper of the Fire

EXPLODING MOUNTAIN
Mount St Helens hurled 1.1 km³ (0.26 cubic miles) of ash into the atmosphere. Within a few days, this had been distributed over an area of some 57,000 km² (22,000 sq miles).

The eruption of Mount St Helens on May 18, 1980, was the deadliest in US history, leaving 57 dead and damage estimated at over $1 billion.

VOLCANOES JARGONBUSTER

Volcanology, like all other sciences, has special terms for particular phenomena. Here are a few key terms:

CALDERA A large, crater-like depression formed by the collapse of a volcano, sometimes because of the violence of a past eruption.

DOME A steep-sided mount that forms when high-viscosity lava seeps from a vent.

EXPLOSIVE ERUPTION A violent eruption that shoots debris high into the air. Contrasts with an 'effusive eruption', characterised by an outpouring of low-viscosity lava.

FUMAROLE A vent that releases volcanic gases and steam.

HARMONIC TREMORS Continuous rhythmic earth tremors, associated with the movement of magma underground, which often precede or accompany volcanic eruptions.

LAHAR Also called a 'mudflow'. A flow of water-saturated volcanic rock debris moving down the slopes of a mountain. Originally an Indonesian word.

LAVA Magma that has been erupted onto the Earth's surface.

MAGMA Molten rock within the upper part of the Earth's mantle and crust.

PHREATIC ERUPTION An explosion of super-heated steam, water, mud and other material, which typically occurs when rising hot magma comes into contact with groundwater or the snow and ice in a volcanic mountain's ice cap.

PYROCLASTIC FLOW A mixture of hot gases, volcanic fragments, ash, pumice and other material that forms during an eruption, reaching high temperatures (300-800°C) and moving away from the volcano at high speeds. Also called a *nuée ardente*, 'glowing cloud' in French.

STRATOVOLCANO Also called a 'composite volcano'. A steep-sided volcano built up in layers over centuries by successive eruptions of high-viscosity lava and ash. Contrasts with a 'shield volcano', which has more gently sloping sides (like an upturned warrior's shield), built up by runnier lava flows.

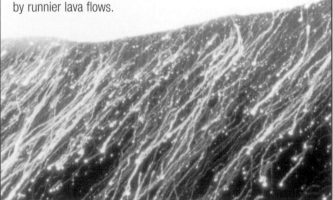

After 123 years in which Mount St Helens had lain dormant, the May 1980 eruption was overdue. Signs that the volcano was stirring had been evident since March 20, when geologists detected an earthquake measuring 4.1 on the Richter scale. At first, they were unsure what the activity indicated, but then on March 27 a small explosion of super-heated steam scattered ash on the summit and left a 76 m crater. It was a phreatic explosion (see box, left), the result of groundwater being heated above a rising plug of hot magma within the volcano's core. At this point, officials decided to evacuate hundreds of loggers, campers and residents from the mountain and set up a 24 km (15 mile) exclusion zone.

But keeping people out of the danger zone was next to impossible. Over the following few weeks, small explosions began to generate tall grey columns of ash above the crater, and people thronged to see them. They did not fully appreciate the danger they were in. 'No one would listen,' Skamania County Sheriff Bill Closner told *The Columbian*'s Pat Moser. 'It didn't matter what we did. People were going around, through and over the barricades. As you know, people were climbing right up to the rim of the crater.'

A pressure cooker ready to blow

By the end of April, a bulge could be seen on the north face of the mountain. It was about 2.5 km (1.5 miles) wide and protruded by at least 80 m – and it was growing at a rate of around 1.5 m a day. The bulge was rising as the pressure of hot gases and magma increased beneath it. Mount St Helens was a pressure cooker ready to blow. But when? Even though geologists were monitoring the mountain intensively with portable seismometers, gravity meters, tiltmeters, infra-red photography and gas sensors, they could not answer this question. They knew that something was about to happen, but the exact timing and severity remained unknown – such is the nature of volcanoes.

In the second week of May, the volcano appeared to quieten and the small steam explosions stopped. For some of the 2,000 residents who had been evacuated from their homes, the wait was proving too much. Threatening to withhold their taxes, residents demanded to be let back in to take away some of their belongings. Washington Governor Dixie Lee Ray relented.

Nancy Ashutz was one of the residents who returned. 'On Saturday, May 17, the geologists and the Governor of Washington declared the mountain to be the safest it had been since becoming active,' she told *The Columbian*. 'We went with a caravan of cabin owners, state patrolmen

and news media to visit our homes and retrieve some belongings … Randy, my husband, was very anxious and wanted to pack up a few things and get out of there. He declared the air and animals too still … I pooh-poohed him and we stayed until about 5 pm. The state patrol said they would make another trip up the next morning on May 18 at 10 am. Randy said, "No way, we are not coming back!" Boy, was he perceptive. The next morning his Mom called at 8.30 am and told us to look out the window. The mountain blew!

'We hurried to the mouth of the Toutle River … We watched in awe, all day until dark, as huge walls of trees, mud, cars and even houses passed by us. There will never be words to express the sheer awesome power of nature.'

On the right side of the mountain

For people who were on the mountain that day, their chances of survival depended on which side they were on – and whether they could move out of the way fast enough. Strangely, too, because of the topography of the mountain and the way sound is reflected, many people close to the mountain did not hear the explosion, while others hundreds of miles away did.

Kran Kilpatrick was part of a tree-planting crew at work at its foot, only 4.8 km (3 miles) from the summit. Luckily, he was on the 'right' side, the south side. Even so, like most people on that side, he did not hear the blast, as he told *National Geographic*'s Rowe Findley: 'There was no sound to it, not a sound – it was like a silent movie, and we were all in it. First the ash cloud shot out to the east, then to the west, then some lighter stuff started shooting straight up. At the same time the ash curtain started coming right down the south slope toward us. I could see boulders – they must have been huge – being hurled out of the leading edge, and then being swept up again in the advancing cloud.'

He and the rest of the crew immediately jumped into their trucks and made a frantic dash for safety over mountain roads. Kilpatrick later realised just how lucky they had been. Only the day before, they had been working on the north-east side of the mountain, now a scene of lifeless, grey, mangled desolation.

Mike Moore, his wife and two children were camping in the Green River area when the eruption happened.

CONTINUED ON PAGE 142 »

HIGH WATER *Lahars left mudlines on trees along the Toutle River. A 6 ft tall USGS geologist provides a sense of scale.*

Countdown to eruption

The first clear signal of the impending eruption of Mount St Helens came just under two months earlier, with an earthquake in March 1980. Explosions of super-heated steam followed, then rhythmic earth tremors. Finally, a bulge formed on the mountainside, heralding the explosion to come.

March 20 A lone seismometer on the western flank of Mount St Helens sends a message to seismic recorders at the University of Washington, Seattle, revealing that a large earthquake – 4.1 on the Richter scale – has occurred on the mountain.

March 27 The first explosion of super-heated steam scatters ash on the mountain top and creates a 76 m wide crater. Geologists begin to think that the mountain may be ready to erupt. The steam explosions continue sporadically until May 14. The spectacle draws hundreds of tourists and media professionals to the foot of the mountain, although a 24 km (15 mile) exclusion zone has been set up to keep them off it.

April 3 Geologists detect harmonic tremors coming from Mount St Helens. This rhythmic pattern of seismic activity is distinct from the sharp jolts associated with earthquakes; it indicates that magma is on the move within the mountain.

April 27 A bulge has formed on the mountain's north flank. Like other volcanoes along the Pacific Ocean's Ring of Fire, Mount St Helens contains magma rich in silica. This viscous magma tends to solidify near the surface, forming domes and plugs that seal off the chambers through which molten magma is rising. When the surrounding rock can no longer hold the expanding magma, the result is an explosive eruption.

May 10 Aerial infra-red photographs show several hot spots in the crater. The bulge on the north flank, now more than 90 m high, continues to grow at a rate of 1.5 m a day. It is weakening the north side of the mountain.

May 17 A group of residents are escorted back into the exclusion zone so that they can retrieve some of their possessions.

May 18 At 8.32 am an earthquake measuring 5.1 on the Richter scale sends the weakened northern slope crashing down the mountain in a massive landslide. As this slips down the mountain, pressure is released from the gases and magma within the volcano and about 30 seconds later they blast outwards. Witnesses on Mount Baker describe how the debris from the blast overtakes the avalanche. Pyroclastic flows of magma and gases follow, moving at speeds of up to 130 km/h (80 mph). The heat of these flows melts glaciers on the mountain, creating lahars (mudslides) that flow down river valleys. The lahars destroy 27 bridges and 200 homes. Countless animals perish, including 7,000 deer, elk and bear. At a distance of 16 km (10 miles) from the mountain, ash and pumice lie 25 cm deep on the ground; at 97 km (60 miles), 2.5 cm, and at 480 km (300 miles), 1.3 cm.

Before 18 May 1980

The attractive snow-capped peak of Mount St Helens rose some 2,950 m above sea level. It was a popular destination for hikers, campers and nature lovers.

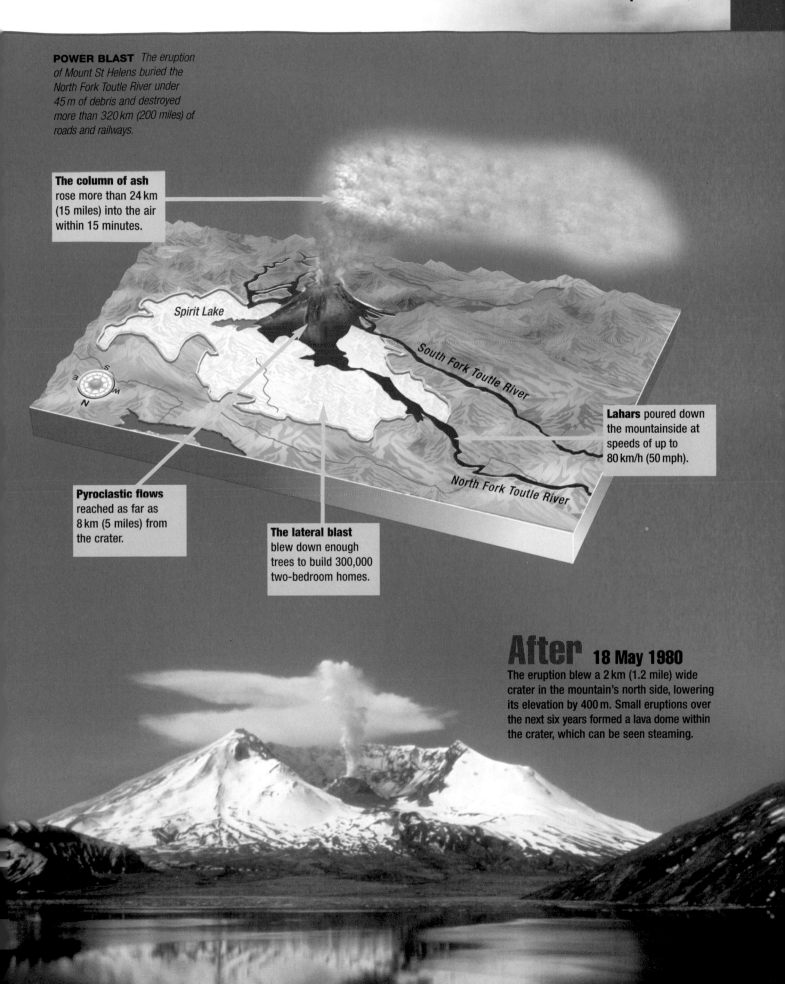

POWER BLAST *The eruption of Mount St Helens buried the North Fork Toutle River under 45 m of debris and destroyed more than 320 km (200 miles) of roads and railways.*

The column of ash rose more than 24 km (15 miles) into the air within 15 minutes.

Spirit Lake

South Fork Toutle River

North Fork Toutle River

Lahars poured down the mountainside at speeds of up to 80 km/h (50 mph).

Pyroclastic flows reached as far as 8 km (5 miles) from the crater.

The lateral blast blew down enough trees to build 300,000 two-bedroom homes.

After 18 May 1980

The eruption blew a 2 km (1.2 mile) wide crater in the mountain's north side, lowering its elevation by 400 m. Small eruptions over the next six years formed a lava dome within the crater, which can be seen steaming.

DANGER IN THE CASCADES

Mount St Helens is by no means a solitary phenomenon. The Cascade range, which skirts North America's Pacific coast, has several active volcanoes. It sits above the zone where the Juan de Fuca and related oceanic plates slip beneath the continental plate of North America. It is part of the Ring of Fire, which encircles the Pacific and contains two-thirds of the world's active volcanoes.

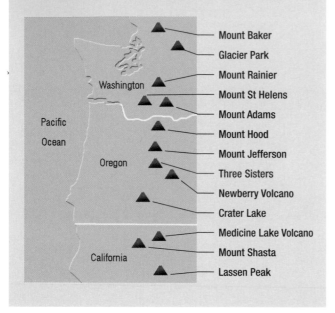

Their campground lay about 24 km (15 miles) to the north of Mount St Helens, but was sheltered from it by Black Mountain and a ridge in front. Mike described events to Oregon Public Broadcasting: 'We didn't hear an explosion but ... a rumbling sound like an aircraft way up high ... that was in trouble. And we also felt the ground shake. Almost immediately after that the air began to compress around our bodies, squeezing us like you were coming off the high pass at a thousand miles an hour ... At this point I'm beginning to put two and two together. It's coming towards us.'

The family's car was parked about 4 km (2.5 miles) away. Mike knew that they would not be able to get back to it before the ash arrived, so they headed for an old shack nearby and waited. 'We had no choice but to hunker down and fairly quickly the light dropped to zero. And when I say zero, I mean zero. While we were in there, there was a tremendous thunderstorm.' Although he could hear the thunder, the cloud of ash prevented him from seeing the lightning. Many witnesses further away did see lightning flashes. Some reported frightening

red bolts, while others spoke of strange balls of lightning which appeared to bounce and roll along the ground.

Mike waited 20 minutes for the thunderstorm to subside, before deciding it was safe for the family to head for the car. Holding wet handkerchiefs to their faces so that they would not inhale the ash still in the air, they stepped out of the cabin. Even though Black Mountain and the ridge had deflected the full force of the blast, a torn-up, near-impenetrable landscape of strewn rocks and fallen trees spread out around them. They were forced to camp another night. When they did eventually reach their car the following day, they found that it had been crushed by four fallen trees. Fortunately, a National Guard helicopter soon lifted them to safety.

Mike Moore's description of a rumbling sound rather than a percussive blast corresponded with many accounts from people closer to the mountain. By contrast, Dave Miller, a resident of Newport, Oregon, some 225 km (140 miles) to the south-west of Mount St Helens, told the BBC how he heard it: 'Our family was eating breakfast when we heard what sounded like blasting in the hills north of the town: "Boom ... Ba ba boom ... Ba boom." My immediate reaction was "Mount St Helens!" Like everyone else I had been following the news ... The booms continued for about 15 minutes ... Our first reaction was great horror – if we could hear it from 140 miles away, in our imagination, all of south-west Washington must now be a smouldering crater.' In fact, the sound of the explosions had bounced off the stratosphere, allowing people like Miller to hear it.

When day became night

Within 15 minutes of the eruption, a thick column of ash was towering 24 km (15 miles) above the volcano, sending towns into darkness as it travelled north-eastwards on prevailing winds. It was carrying 540 million tonnes of ash, which were distributed over an area of 57,000 km² (22,000 sq miles) – a little under half the size of England. Much of the gritty volcanic ash fell on eastern Washington, northern Idaho and the west of Montana.

J. Marc Johnson and his two daughters from Lewiston, Idaho, were at an air force base open day near Spokane in western Washington State when the news came that Mount St Helens had erupted. It had been a beautiful sunny day until a dark cloud headed towards them from the south-west.

Johnson told *The Columbian* of his journey home: 'The light grey dust you see in all the pictures does not do justice to the absolute and total blackness that slowly fell over us as we drove towards home. It was the middle

Staying on the mountain

Some who lost their lives in the Mount St Helens eruption were volcano enthusiasts who had volunteered to be there. These people were monitoring and measuring the event even as it consumed them. One – David Johnston – recognised more than most the level of danger he faced.

At the time of the eruption Johnston, a survey volcanologist, was camping on Coldwater Ridge, 8 km (5 miles) north of the volcano, and reporting his findings to the US Geological Survey (USGS) in the city of Vancouver in southern Washington State. He must have been the first to detect the explosion, because at 8.32 am he sent a radio message: 'Vancouver, Vancouver, this is it!' And then he was gone, a victim of the mountain.

Further north, at Coldwater Peak, volunteer volcano watcher Gerald Martin also saw the eruption. He radioed that he had seen the blast of hot ash overtake Johnston's car, then said: 'It's going to get me too.' It did.

There were also journalists, such as photographer Reid Turner Blackburn. He was found dead in his car, parked on a ridge above Coldwater. He died of asphyxiation from the hot, caustic ash. Did he know that his chances of survival were slim as he placed his camera deep in his back pack? We will never know. He took four pictures, but they were destroyed by the heat of the blast and we can only imagine what that wall of ash, rocks and debris looked like as it came rushing towards him, burying his car.

UP CLOSE *David A. Johnston at Coldwater II observation station on May 17, 1980. He did not survive the next day's eruption.*

One local resident became famous in the days before the eruption, because he refused point-blank to leave his lodge by Spirit Lake, north of Mount St Helens. Harry R. Truman, 84, was a colourful character, who told Rowe Findley of *National Geographic* what happened when officials placed a steel gate across the highway, barring outsiders and locking him in. His response was robust, as was the language he used: 'I said block the **** road, and don't let anyone through till Christmas ten years ago. I'm havin' a hell of a time livin' my life alone. I'm king of all I survey, I got plenty whiskey, I got food enough for 15 years, and I'm settin' high on the **** hog.' He had run the lodge with his wife since 1928. She had died three years earlier and he now lived alone – apart from 16 cats. 'I'm going to stay right here because,

I'll tell you why, my home and my **** life's here. My wife and I, we both vowed … that we'd never leave Spirit Lake.' Harry stayed and indeed became part of his beloved mountain. His lodge now lies buried some 60 m beneath Spirit Lake.

Cameraman David Crockett was a lucky survivor. He was at the base of the mountain when it blew. He narrowly escaped being engulfed in a mudslide, but carried on filming for 6 terrifying minutes. 'Oh dear God, this is hell,' he reported. 'I just can't describe it – it's pitch black, this hell on earth I'm walking through … at this moment I honest-to-God believe I'm dead.'

FINAL SHOTS *Photographer Reid Turner Blackburn was found buried in his car on a ridge above Coldwater Creek.*

of the afternoon and all the lights were on everywhere. I stopped once and turned off the car's lights. If it wasn't for the spots of lights from the houses, it would have been as black as an underground cave … My daughters were spending most of their time under a blanket. The dust boiled around inside the car … By this time there was a couple inches of dust on the ground and it was falling faster than ever.'

When they reached Colfax, Washington, they found the State Police had set up a road block and that they would have to spend the night in a nearby school. 'The small town of Colfax, however, has a big heart … People came down and gave blankets, cots, food, and a strong showing of real concern … Because I had my two young daughters with me, a complete stranger came up to me and offered me and my daughters supper and a place to spend the night. It was a gesture of kindness that I will never forget.'

Better monitoring

SILVER LINING

Huge advances have been made in the monitoring of volcanoes since 1980 – with the potential to save thousands of lives in future eruptions. Suites of portable surface monitors, for example, were successfully used to predict the eruption of Mount Pinatubo in 1991 (see pages 158-163).

Then, in 2006, British and US scientists unveiled a new approach, which involves analysing tiny droplets of silicate glass trapped inside crystals in magma erupted from an active volcano. These were once liquid and preserve the chemical composition of the liquid portion of the magma as it was far underground. By studying the droplets, geologists can learn much about the temperature, pressure and chemical composition of the magma.

The water content is especially important. 'If the magma is stored at high pressure,' explains Professor Jon Blundy of Bristol University, 'it can contain quite a lot of water and has the potential to form a lot of bubbles – more bubbles, a more explosive eruption.' It is like the release of pressure when a champagne bottle is shaken and the top knocked off.

Blundy and his colleagues hope to combine their observations with those of surface monitors to provide more accurate insights into the activity beneath a volcano, improving their predictions of if and when it is likely to erupt explosively.

A transformed landscape

When journalist Rowe Findley flew over the mountain the day after the blast, he saw a scene of devastation that stretched for miles. 'Dozens of houses inundated or swept away,' he reported, '… rail lines wiped out and railcars swept away … Through Kelso-Longview the silt-heavy Cowlitz [river] carries a miles-long jumble of logs.'

'The whole world was a spectrum of greys,' he added later, 'powder light when dry, almost black when water soaked, with many shades between. In the vast debris flow that floored the valley lay chunks of ice from the glaciers, a few as big as boxcars. They were melting and creating wet circles like grief-darkened eyes.'

Yet amongst this tangle of uprooted trees, tossed boulders and thick grey mud, people had somehow survived. It took brave souls like Jess Hagerman, a Washington Army National Guard helicopter pilot, to fetch them to safety. Hagerman was one of the first to enter the blast zone around Mount St Helens. Ash filled the air and visibility was poor, so he needed all his years of experience as a Vietnam veteran and ex-Marine to manoeuvre his helicopter.

Among those Hagerman saved were loggers Jim Scymanky and Leonty Skorohodoff. Hagerman and his crew chief, Randy Fantz, found the two survivors after spotting a truck and footprints in the ash leading away from it. Following the footprints, they found the men, lying injured on the road. But there was nowhere for the helicopter to land and that is when Fantz made a quick decision to jump down into the mudflow. Risking his life, because the mud could still have been boiling hot, he helped the men reach a point where Hagerman could bring his helicopter down. Scymanky's face and 50 per cent of his body were covered in burns – his gloves had melted onto his hands. Skorohodoff was in even worse shape and died 10 days later.

Hagerman and Fantz spent the next two days flying on and off the mountain, searching for survivors. 'You'd find little pieces of the puzzle,' Hagerman recalled, 'but you couldn't put the whole picture together, where the survivors might be.' In all, they rescued seven people, including the Moore family from the Green River area. Thereafter, the mission took on a darker dimension, as they searched for bodies rather than survivors.

The people they rescued during those dreadful days after the eruption will always remember them. For Hagerman, some 25 years after the blast, the memory was as clear as if it happened yesterday. 'Something like that – it just kind of ingrains indelibly on your mind.'

Who would be a volcanologist?

There may be old volcanologists, or bold volcanologists – but there are no old, bold volcanologists. When dealing with one of Nature's most capricious forces, it pays to be cautious. Such is the philosophy of Catherine Hickson, senior research volcanologist with the Geological Survey of Canada.

SENSIBLE APPROACH *Dr Catherine Hickson treats her subject with respect, working mostly on long dormant volcanoes.*

DANGEROUS PURSUIT *A heat-resistant suit offers protection when investigating a lava lake, as here in Erta Ale volcano in Ethiopia.*

Dr Hickson's attitude is born of experience, since she was one of the people near the slopes of Mount St Helens when it exploded and lived to tell the tale. 'When I'm out in the field on an active volcano, I am so much more cautious than many of my colleagues,' she says. 'It's simply because I have witnessed, I have lived first-hand, what I guess you would call a death-defying experience. As a result I have a lot more respect for volcanoes.'

She was a geology student in 1980 and like many others she had been drawn to the slopes of the rumbling volcano out of curiosity. Fortunately she was 14 km (8.7 miles) off the east flank when the mountain blew.

Yet the average day for a volcanologist is not nearly so dramatic. 'Ninety per cent of the work of volcanologists is on non-erupting volcanoes,' says Dr Hickson. 'We go out and tramp around in the field with backpack and camera in hand and try to look at where the flows went.' But there are still occasions when a volcanologist will be required to venture onto an active volcano, to collect molten lava, for example. They use 'long spoonlike things, about 3 m long, to collect it. You can get very close to basaltic lava. I have been within a metre or so of active flows in Hawaii. It's hot and I singed the hair on my arms. You have to be extremely careful because lava crusts over very

quickly and its hard to tell cool but still liquid lava from solid lava.'

Being acquainted with the ferocity of volcanoes means that volcanologists tend not to take chances. But there have been some daredevil experts who flouted such caution, the most famous being Katia and Maurice Kraft. The French couple made a living out of taking close-up photographs of active volcanoes. They produced some stunning images but paid with their lives. 'Maurice was a risk-taker,' says Dr Hickson. 'He'd do things that were not considered very prudent by other volcanologists and unfortunately both he and his wife met their deaths at Mount Unzen in Japan in 1991.'

A

A river of lava seethes across the landscape. At a temperature of 1,000°C, it incinerates everything. Vegetation burns, buildings are engulfed and it moves so quickly – over 40 km/h (25 mph) – no one can outrun it. For anyone in its path, death is almost inevitable.

It is the stuff of nightmares, yet on the morning of Thursday, January 17, 2002, that was reality for people living on the higher slopes of Mount Nyiragongo, a volcano in the far east of the Democratic Republic of the Congo (DRC), close to the border with Rwanda. Three huge flows of lava moved down the heavily populated mountainside, sending fiery streams coursing through banana plantations, consuming 14 villages and sliding a 500 m wedge through the heart of Goma, a city of some 400,000 inhabitants, 18 km (11 miles) to the south.

Within a few days, the mountain had spewed out an estimated 20 million m³ of magma (enough to fill 8,000 Olympic-sized swimming pools), killing more than 100 people and leaving 100,000 homeless. For the region's inhabitants, it was as if the fates were conspiring against them. They had already endured appalling human-inflicted suffering, as a result of the 1994 genocide in Rwanda, which sent refugees pouring into the DRC, and their own country's civil war. Now Nature was adding to their woes.

Like flowing water

Mount Nyiragongo consists of a huge crater, 1.2 km (0.75 miles) across and 800 m deep, with a lake of molten lava at its centre. It is doubly dangerous, because its lava has a low silica content. This gives it a very low viscosity, so that it runs like water. When the sides of the crater crack, the lava pours out. This is what happened on an earlier occasion, on January 10, 1977, when the crater cracked and the lava inside it drained out in the space of an hour, killing at least 700 people.

Then, in 2001, the whole vicious cycle started up again. In February, geologists detected increased seismic activity in the Nyiragongo region. On October 7, they picked up a strong tectonic earthquake of magnitude 3.5-4. When experts inspected the summit crater, the ground temperature, normally 5-9°C, had risen to 28°C. At the beginning of January 2002, witnesses reported rumbling sounds coming from the volcano and dark smoke rising above it. Between January 4 and 16, seismic activity increased again, and then the mountain went ominously quiet for 8 hours.

CHOKING AIR *A thick lava flow drove a wedge through Goma. Ash and smoke particulates hung in the air for days, leading to an increase in respiratory disorders.*

Rivers of Lava

Lava poured through a city, consumed 14 villages and killed more than 100 people when Mount Nyiragongo erupted in January 2002.

UNSTOPPABLE FORCE
The fiery lava crossed the runway at Goma's airport, igniting fuel tanks as it went.

At 8.25 the next morning, the volcano burst into life. A fracture opened in the wall of Shaheru crater – 2 km (1.2 miles) south of the summit crater – and lava started to drain down Nyiragongo's south-eastern slopes. As the morning wore on, further fractures cracked open on the southern flank of the Shaheru cone, and others developed on Nyiragongo's north-western flank. More lava spurted out, and still the fractures opened, until they formed a deadly line stretching south-east of the village of Munigi; by 2pm they had reached the outskirts of Goma. Meanwhile, lava from the vents higher up the volcano was also surging towards the city.

The people living within the monster's grasp could only snatch up whatever they were able to carry and run. Awete Emilie lost her house to the lava. 'It came this way and kept coming,' she said. 'We ran for our lives when it was coming for us.' She was lucky – she escaped. It is thought that most of the 45 people who died in the first 24 hours of the disaster did so as they tried to retrieve possessions from their homes. Those too old or handicapped to run had to be left behind.

By the time the lava reached Goma's main street, it had slowed to a crawl. But at 500 m wide and 2 m deep, the fiery flood was still an unstoppable force. On its journey down the mountain, it had already poured over the runway of Goma's airport, igniting fuel tanks there. It went on to destroy 20 per cent of the city, before finally making its way towards Lake Kivu to the south.

As it neared Kivu, the possibility of a fresh disaster loomed. Geologists feared that when the lava entered the lake, it might disturb poisonous gases dissolved in its deeper waters (see also page 126). Mercifully, this did not happen. That night, when the lava flow started slipping into the lake waters, it released noxious gases, but not in the catastrophic quantities feared.

On the move

In the initial aftermath of the eruption, Goma became a ghost town as its population fled. Most headed east to the lakeside town of Gisenyi, just across the border in Rwanda; about 100,000 went west towards the town of

RIFT ACTIVITY

Nyiragongo is one of eight volcanoes in the Virunga mountain chain, which runs along the borders of the Democratic Republic of Congo, Rwanda and Uganda, between Lake Edward in the north and Lake Kivu in the south. With its neighbour Mount Nyamuragira, Nyiragongo accounts for around 40 per cent of all eruptions in Africa. But because of the low viscosity of their lava, neither volcano explodes with blasts of rock and debris. Instead, the lava oozes out of a network of cracks and smaller craters around the mountains.

The volcanoes' activity arises from their location on the western flank of the Great Rift Valley, which extends more than 4,000 km (2,500 miles) from Syria to Mozambique. The rift has formed as the two African continental plates and the Arabian plate all move away from each other. As the Earth's crust is stretched and pulled, fissures form through which lava can emerge.

Sake near Lake Kivu's northernmost tip or took boats across the lake to the city of Bukavu to the south. The lava was still flowing, meanwhile, and earth tremors, sometimes coming as frequently as one an hour, could be felt as far away as Bukavu. In Gisenyi, they were strong enough to crack walls.

Accommodating the victims and getting aid to them were fraught with problems. The Rwandan government set up two camps near Gisenyi, and several aid agencies were already based in the region because of the 1994 genocide and the DRC's civil war. But many of their local headquarters had been destroyed in the eruption. The region sank into chaos. Refugees scavenged for food and water; criminals looted abandoned houses and shops; burns victims overwhelmed the hospitals.

Then people started flooding back into Goma. Three days after the eruption, earthquakes were still shaking the land – around 250 had been recorded on Saturday, January 19. Yet people would not stay away, especially those who had fled into Rwanda. Richard Mwambo, a local teacher, voiced the views of many: 'If we are to die, it is better to die in Congo, not Rwanda.'

Guardian reporter James Astill took a helicopter ride over the city on Monday, January 21. 'Goma was a scene of Pompeii-style devastation,' he said. 'The middle of the town, north to south, was buried under a black-brown slick of cooling lava, scattered with orange pools where it still oozed.' The steaming lava had made many routes impassable, but people desperate to get back to their homes just went across the lava, running so as not

to burn their feet. Oxfam's Rob Wilkinson, warned how dangerous this was: 'Lava is like ice – a crust forms on top, but if it cracks, then people fall through, and it can cause horrific injuries or even kill.'

And lives were still being lost in other ways, too. On January 21, a few people were trying to siphon fuel from tanks at a petrol station in eastern Goma, when some of the petrol spilled onto the molten lava, igniting a 60 m fireball. This in turn lit barrels of fuel in the station's storeroom, which continued to explode for hours, sending up 30 m flames. Between 30 and 50 people died in the accident.

The next day, a further series of earthquakes shook Nyiragongo, and its main summit crater collapsed. Four hours of explosive activity followed, and huge clouds of ash went billowing into the sky. Soon after, hot ash covered the village of Rusaya, 8 km (5 miles) south-west of the summit, in a 10 cm thick layer.

Nonetheless, the situation was slowly coming under control. On Wednesday, January 23, the World Food Programme began to distribute food, medical supplies and other relief goods from sites in Sake and Goma. By Friday, January 25, 50 per cent of the water supply was working again.

As the days went by, the rumblings from the mountain gradually subsided and life returned to a semblance of normality. When the lava hardened, people simply rebuilt their homes and shops on top of it; businesses reopened and the bustle of everyday life resumed. But some reminders of the trauma could not be erased so easily. Three years later, in summer 2005, a wall of hardened black lava still divided the city, while around it stood the ruins of burnt buildings, including the eerie skeleton of the city's former Catholic cathedral.

HOME TREASURES *Within a few days of the eruption, refugees who had fled Goma were back, desperate to retrieve what they could of their personal possessions.*

The 20th century's deadliest volcanic eruption occurred on the Caribbean island of Martinique on Ascension Day, May 8, 1902. With a blinding flash and a terrible roar, Mont Pelée at the northern end of the island let forth an incandescent cloud of boiling ash, fumes and rocks.

Martinique was then a French colony, and Saint-Pierre, its capital, at the foot of Mont Pelée, was a thriving city, trading in sugar, coffee, rum and cocoa. In the space of 2 minutes, the cloud had rushed down the mountainside, wiping out both the city and its 30,000 inhabitants.

The mountain had of course issued warnings, but geologists of the time did not understand them. They did not know, for example, that Mont Pelée is part of the Lesser Antilles volcanic arc, formed by the subduction of the North American continental plate under the Caribbean plate – plate tectonics were not understood until the 1960s.

One clear signal had come two weeks earlier, when Mont Pelée shot a column of steam into the air. Earth tremors shook Saint-Pierre over the next few days, accompanied by falls of ash and clouds of choking sulphurous gas from the summit above. Then hoards of insects started invading mountainside villages, driven from the summit by venting toxic fumes. More deadly were venomous fer de lance snakes, also fleeing their normal habitats – in a few days, at least 50 people died from snakebites.

On May 5, the Blanche River, which flows down Mont Pelée, suddenly became a torrent of scalding hot, muddy water – rising magma beneath the mountain had heated groundwater, forcing it to boil up to the surface and swell the river. As it thundered down the mountainside, the hot water mixed with mud and debris creating a mudflow, or lahar, 35m high. It deluged a rum distillery at Le Prêcheur, north of Saint-Pierre, killing the owner's son and daughter-in-law and 30 other people.

PATH OF DESTRUCTION
The nuée ardent *was travelling at 190 km/h (120 mph) when it hit Saint-Pierre. The billowing cloud roared through the city for three minutes, turning it into a pile of rubble. The intense heat set fire to buildings and ignited barrels of rum, creating a firestorm that burned for three days.*

An entire city, Saint-Pierre, was destroyed, along with its 30,000 inhabitants, when Mont Pelée erupted in May 1902.

151

Shortly afterwards, in Saint-Pierre, the sea abruptly receded, leaving 50 m of its harbour floor bare. Then it rushed back in again, flooding the waterfront. It was a tsunami, created as the lahar smashed into the open sea. By this time, people were becoming anxious, but officials, including the island's governor, told them not to be alarmed – the governor would soon be among the 30,000 dead.

Then, at 8.02am on May 8, Mont Pelée let rip. In the town of Le Morne Rouge, to the east, a Catholic priest, Father Mary, was preparing to celebrate the religious feast of Ascension Day. He reported that he saw 'black vapour from the side of the mountain. Looking down … it seemed to me as if all Martinique was sliding into the sea … Only the towers of the Cathedral of St Pierre remained untouched, and they only for a brief moment, for the fiery mass enveloped them too.'

Sudden death

For most people in Saint-Pierre, death was instantaneous. Clouds containing molten particles of volcanic glass, scalding ash, steam, mud and boulders raced through the city, knocking down some buildings and burying others. Fires broke out, fanned by strong winds, and turned into firestorms. Even when the pyroclastic flow reached the sea, it blasted on, boiling the water and destroying all but one of the ships moored in the bay.

When rescue workers ventured into the city the next day, they found horrific scenes. Bodies were stacked in doorways, where people had sought refuge, only to be crushed as the buildings collapsed; in the street were the corpses of people who had been knocked down by the blast, their bodies contorting grotesquely as they burned. One charred victim still held a silk handkerchief to her lips.

Only two people came out alive – a cobbler called Léon Compère-Léandre, who miraculously survived in his house, and Louis-Auguste Cyparis, a criminal in solitary confinement in Saint-Pierre's prison. Cyparis, who had been protected from the worst of the pyroclastic flow by his prison's thick, stone walls, received the most publicity. 'Everybody was screaming, "Help! Help! I'm burning. I'm dying",' he recalled. 'Five minutes later, nobody was crying out any more – except me. Then, a cloud of smoke gushed [in]… It burnt me so much that I was dancing up and down, left and right – everywhere – to get out of its way.' He spent the next few days trapped in his cell, until May 11, when his cries for help were heard and he was rescued.

> **It burnt me so much that I was dancing up and down, left and right – everywhere – to get out of its way.**

OUT OF THE FIRE *The thick walls of the city prison (below) helped Louis-Auguste Cyparis to survive. Some time later, he received a pardon.*

The deadliest eruptions are not necessarily the largest. Never was this more clearly seen than in November 1985, when the relatively small eruption of Nevado del Ruiz, a volcano in the Cordillera Central region of the Andes in Colombia, sent 25,000 people to their deaths.

On the evening of November 13, the mountain spewed forth pyroclastic flows – hot gases, rock, ash and pumice – which melted vast quantities of ice at the summit. The meltwater mingled with the rock and other debris to create torrents of mud, called lahars, which cascaded downwards at an average speed of 60 km/h (37 mph), picking up more loose soil and boulders and stripping valley sides of vegetation. All the time, they increased in size, so that in some narrow valleys, they grew to be as deep as 50 m.

The fatal onslaught

Within just 4 hours, the lahars had travelled 100 km (62 miles), destroying more than 5,000 homes in the valleys of the Chinchiná, Gualí and Lagunillas rivers. Hardest hit was the coffee-growing town of Armero, 60 km (37 miles) from the volcano, at the mouth of a canyon in the Lagunillas valley. Mud deluged the town, killing 20,000 of its inhabitants and injuring another 5,000. Tragically, many, if not all, of those people could have been saved, if the authorities had taken emergency action sooner.

One of the lucky survivors was geology student José Luis Restrepo, who was staying in a hotel in Armero on a field trip. At 11.25 pm, when the mudflows on Nevado del Ruiz's eastern side started pouring into the town, he and some other people were listening to a local radio staton. 'Suddenly it went off the air,' he recalls. 'Electric power went out and that's when we started hearing the noise in the air, like something toppling, falling, and we didn't hear anything else, no alarm.'

> **❛ There were people buried, calling out, calling for help, and if you tried to go to them, you would sink into the mud. ❜**
>
> *José Luis Restrepo*

Deadly Mudflows

SMOKING GUN *The crater of Nevado del Ruiz was still smouldering on November 17, 1985, three days after the eruption that destroyed the town of Armero at its base.*

SEA OF GREY *On the morning after the eruption, rescuers began to pull people from the thick mud of the lahars. Roads had been destroyed, so many survivors had to wait for helicopters to carry them to safety.*

Mudflows poured down Nevado del Ruiz in Colombia when it erupted in 1985, wiping out the town of Armero and most of its inhabitants.

1 **3.05 pm** A steam eruption sends ash shooting into the air.

2 **9 pm** The volcano explodes twice in an hour. Fiery pyroclastic flows melt its ice cap, creating deadly rivers of mud (lahars).

5 **11.25 pm** Mudflows begin to swamp Armero. The final death toll here is 20,000.

FATAL INACTION Areas at risk from mudflows had been clearly identified before the eruption, but tragically officials failed to act in time to save the people of Armero.

4 **10 pm** Mudflows sweep down the Chinchiná valley into the town of Chinchiná, killing 2,000 people.

3 **9.45 pm** Pumice and ash fall on the town of Murillo.

Guali River

Lagunillas River

Azufrado River

Chinchiná River

Nevado del Ruiz

Armero

• El Libano

• Murillo

Recio River

He and his companions went out into the streets. Without electricity, there was no light, except from cars' headlights. They were running along a street and had nearly reached a corner, when they saw a 'river of water' coming towards them. Immediately, they 'turned around screaming, toward the hotel, because already the waters were dragging beds along, overturning cars, sweeping people away.'

They went into the hotel. 'Suddenly I heard blows, and looking towards the rear of the hotel I saw [something] like foam, coming down in the darkness … it was [a wall of] mud … and sure enough it crashed against the rear of the hotel and started crushing walls … and then the ceiling slab fractured … the entire building was destroyed and broken into pieces.'

Raining ash

Nevado del Ruiz had started exploding at 3.05 that afternoon, when a steam eruption sent a black column of ash shooting into the air. In Armero, people were becoming worried by 4 pm, when ash and debris began falling on the town. Shortly afterwards, it started to rain heavily, the rainwater saturating the ash. At 6 pm, with ash and rain still falling, the local priest told Armero's residents to keep calm and stay indoors. An hour later, a severe thunderstorm whipped up over the town, masking any sounds from the volcano.

Ironically, while this was happening, the members of a regional emergency committee were meeting in Ibagué, capital of the department (region) of Tolima, which includes Armero. The top item on their agenda was to

MUD COVERING *Farm buildings on higher ground near Armero have survived the mudflows, which submerged the surrounding fields.*

scrutinise a hazard map, which had been published the day before, anticipating the consequences if Nevado del Ruiz erupted and outlining emergency measures. They wound up their meeting at 7 pm, having agreed that the Red Cross should prepare Armero for evacuation, along with the towns of Mariquita and Honda to its north. It is not certain that this news ever reached Armero.

By now, night had fallen. Then, at 9.09 pm, a witness some 9 km (5.6 miles) from Nevado del Ruiz heard the mountain roar. Two explosions were followed by hot pyroclastic flows. Another explosion at 9.37 pm sent a plume of ash and rocks shooting thousands of metres above the volcano. Glowing rocks fell to earth like bombs several miles from the vent. At 9.45 pm, pumice and ash began falling on Murillo, 17 km (10.5 miles) east of the volcano. Around the same time, the regional civil defence director in Ibagué tried to radio Armero to order an evacuation, but could not make contact. There are reports that others also tried, but failed, to get in touch by radio.

By 10 pm, heavy rain was lashing El Líbano, 32 km (20 miles) east of the volcano, while ash and rain continued to deluge Armero. Half an hour later, mudflows were hurtling down the Molinos and Las Nereidas valleys on the mountain's western slopes. They joined forces in the Chinchiná valley, sweeping through the town of Chinchiná, where they killed 2,000 people and destroyed hundreds of homes.

A deluge of mud

In Armero, the initial onslaught was more watery than muddy. The flow was cool and shallow, but still strong enough to drag cars along.

By that time, people could have escaped to higher ground – some did, in fact, alerted by telephone calls from concerned relatives, but these were the minority. A few others survived by standing on the roof of the town's hospital. Most, however, trusted the official advice to 'stay calm'. They remained in their houses, which soon became their tombs.

'A torrent of mud ... came with a horrible noise. It dragged houses, cattle, tree stumps and gigantic rocks.'

Marina Franco de Huez

The deadly tide turned hotter and much thicker, pouring through the town with a roaring sound, in waves up to 6 m deep. Survivors later described how it seemed to flow in waves or surges. This is because bridges along the route of the flow temporarily held it back, only to release it as they gave way to the extreme force. The first pulse, which destroyed most of the town, lasted 20 minutes. A second started at 11.50 pm and lasted 30 minutes. Intermittent pulses continued after that.

'At 4.30 am or 5 am, more or less,' José Luis Restrepo remembers, 'the noise increased again, then we thought that another mudflow was coming. And, sure enough, towards the side you could see something shining that was moving ... And [then] it started to be light, and that's when we lost control, because we saw that horrible sea of mud which was so gigantic.' The mud carried a gruesome human cargo along with it: 'there were people buried, calling out, calling for help, and if you tried to go to them, you would sink into the mud.'

Fatal delays

The eruption's fatal consequences could have been avoided – or at least mitigated – had the authorities ordered an early evacuation. The threat was known.

Nevado del Ruiz, rising 5,400 m above sea level, is one of seven stratovolcanoes (see box, page 138) in the Cordillera Central – the region's volcanic activity is a result of the eastward subduction of the Nazca oceanic plate beneath the South American continental plate. What makes Nevado del Ruiz potentially lethal in an eruption, as the 1985 events so tragically demonstrated, is the huge mass of snow and ice at its summit – an icy layer, some 10-30 m deep, covering an area of around 19 km² (7 sq miles). As pyroclastic flows cross this, they melt the ice, mix with the meltwater and send terrifying tides of mud crashing down the mountain's steep flanks

It had happened before. One eruption, in 1595, killed 636 people as thick mud torrents rushed down the Gualí and Lagunillas valleys. In 1845, an earthquake triggered another immense mudflow, which flooded the upper Lagunillas valley, leaving 1,000 people dead. The mud was channelled down the river before spreading out across the floodplain at the foot of the mountains. Ominously, this is where Armero was built in 1895, directly over deposits from the 1595 and 1845 flows.

The first signals that Nevado del Ruiz was getting restless again had come a full year before the 1985 disaster, when earthquakes were recorded near the summit in November 1984. More tremors and small earthquakes followed, and in March 1985 John Tomblin, a seismologist from the UN Disaster Relief Organisation, arrived to inspect the volcano. He concluded that the activity was typical of events that precede an eruption 'of magnitude'. Colombia's Geology and Mines Bureau (INGEOMINAS) should monitor the volcano closely, he said, and immediately prepare a hazard map. After a field trip later on in March, however, INGEOMINAS concluded that the activity was 'normal' for an active volcano. Danger was 'not imminent', they announced, and they did not produce a hazard map.

Months of disorganisation followed, as the mountain rumbled on. Monitoring was haphazard and inefficient, and local and international bodies failed to communicate information to each other. Then, on September 11, the mountain called everyone's attention with a phreatic or steam eruption (see box, page 138), which lasted 7 hours, raining ash and rocks from the summit crater. Ash fell on the municipalities of Manizales and Chinchiná, both about 25 km (16 miles) from Nevado del Ruiz. Later

5 most deadly eruptions since 1900

Many factors other than 'explosivity' influence the number of people who die as a result of an eruption – the density of the local population, for example. This table compares the deadliness of volcanoes with their place in the volcanic explosivity index (VEI) – used to measure an eruption's size, on a scale of 0 to 8 of increasing explosivity.

	VOLCANO	YEAR	DEATHS	VEI	MAIN CAUSE
1	Mont Pelée, Martinique	1902	30,000	4	Pyroclastic flows
2	Nevado del Ruiz, Colombia	1985	25,000	3	Mudflows
3	Santa Maria, Guatemala	1902	6,000	6	Mudflows
4	Kelut, Indonesia	1919	5,000	4	Mudflows
5	El Chichón, Mexico	1982	3,500	5	Pyroclastic flows

CLINGING TO LIFE *Many Armero residents stayed in their homes, rather than seeking refuge elsewhere. Efraín Gomez was one of the lucky few who survived.*

that evening a mudflow, travelling 20 km (12 miles) down the upper Azufrado valley, gave a taste of things to come.

Only then did the authorities acknowledge the threat of an eruption. Work at last began on a hazard map, a preliminary version of which was issued in October, and the Colombian authorities now acknowledged that there was a '100 per cent chance of mudflows' associated with an eruption. Even so, they issued no clear guidance about what to do if, or when, such a thing occurred. In a magazine article the mayor of Armero said that the local emergency committee 'did not have the necessary information or financial resources to do anything in the event of a catastrophe … For this reason, the people have lost confidence in the veracity of the information and have commended their fate to God.' In fact, the government rejected the map as 'too alarming' and ordered a revision, due for publication on November 12.

Wiped off the map

A few days later, the headline in a local newspaper, *El Campo*, said it all: 'Armero wiped off the map'. In the space of a few hours, the town had disappeared. In its place was a sea of grey mud, wrecked buildings and here and there a survivor clinging on to life. As dawn broke on November 14, rescue workers had begun to arrive. Many of those they saved had horrific tales to tell. 'I heard my son screaming, "Papa, papa, come back and save me! The river is taking me away!"' one man told reporters, sobbing as he spoke. 'I saved him, but when I got back all my other children were dead.' Another, Edeliberto Nieto, had lost all his family. 'I think it was past 11 o'clock last night when we heard a frightening noise, and then a blast of wind hit us and we saw fire falling from the sky. It was horrible, so horrible. My wife was killed. My mother was killed. My little girl who would have been four years old tomorrow died.'

Marina Franco de Huez was luckier. 'At around 10 o'clock at night the ash rain increased and the whole world began to scream. I woke up my daughter and we ran out to one of the streets around the cemetery. We were able to stay out of danger until they rescued us.' The cemetery, on higher ground, was one of the few areas of Armero not to be swamped in mud. She added: 'More than half of the population was buried under a torrent of mud that came with a horrible noise. It dragged houses, cattle, tree stumps and gigantic rocks. There was no time for anything. The church was buried, the school, the theatre.'

In the midst of such tragedy, the human spirit often emerges stronger than ever. Felix Rojas lost his father and seven brothers and sisters, but that did not deter him from putting his all into the rescue efforts. It helped to ease the pain, he said. 'Yesterday we saved a family of nine. We saved another woman named Ofelia whose leg was trapped underneath a concrete post. She had a machete and was trying to cut her own leg free but we got to her.' Soon, however, only dead bodies were being removed from the solidifying mud. Around 4,000 were recovered on the first day.

Many volcanic disasters come from an inability to predict an eruption or the resulting disaster, but this was not the case with Nevado del Ruiz. Responsibility for this tragedy rested firmly with officials who refused to act on accumulating evidence that an eruption was imminent. As for its effects on the survivors, José Luis Restrepo summed it up: 'now [we] must start counting time as before Armero, and after Armero … it's like living and being born again.'

Angry Mountain

For the Aeta people of the Philippines, Mount Pinatubo is a sacred place, the home of their supreme deity, Apo Namalyari. On June 15, 1991, after 500 years of silence, the sacred mountain spoke – in the second-largest volcanic eruption of the 20th century.

Shooting more than 5 km³ (1.2 cubic miles) of magma into the air, the explosion created a stupendous ash column, up to 35 km (22 miles) high and 18 km (11 miles) wide. Fiery pyroclastic flows of ash, gas and pumice rushed 16 km (10 miles) down the mountainside, travelling at speeds of up to 80 km/h (50 mph) and filling valleys with deposits up to 200 m deep. In the 20th century, only Novarupta (Katmai), in a sparsely populated region of Alaska, erupted more violently, in 1912.

Journalist Susan Kreifels was in Angeles City, to the east of Mount Pinatubo, when it happened. She described in *The Honolulu Star-Bulletin* how day turned to night and ash and rocks began to fall. 'Although we couldn't see Pinatubo, we heard it booming and felt it shaking. Eerie orange flashes ignited the black skies. We didn't know what the volcano would do next.'

But the story of Pinatubo is not one of complete disaster. Before the eruption, there were almost a million people living on the mountain and around its base, yet when it finally blew its top only 300 lives were lost. Thanks to a timely response by geologists at the Philippine Institute of Volcanology and Seismology (PHIVOLCS), working in close cooperation with the US Geological Survey (USGS), the eruption and its likely impact were predicted. Philippine officials had enough time to evacuate people from the danger zones and thousands of lives were saved.

> ❛Although we couldn't see Pinatubo, we heard it booming and felt it shaking. Eerie orange flashes ignited the black skies.❜

Prompt government action saved thousands of lives when Mount Pinatubo erupted in June 1991, but a deadly legacy remained.

159

WAVE OF ASH *Photographer Albert Garcia took this famous shot of the eruption as he was fleeing for his life. His van was in the middle of a convoy of three.*

ASH AFFECTS THE WORLD CLIMATE

The eruption of Pinatubo also had a global effect. By pumping huge amounts of ash and gases into the atmosphere, it affected the entire world climate – for example, during the 15 months following the eruption, the average global temperature fell by 0.5°C. The amount of ash ejected was extraordinary – at least 5 km³ (1.2 cubic miles) of magma. The amount of sulphur dioxide was estimated at 20 million tonnes. Using satellite monitoring, NASA scientists were able to study the movement of both as they travelled around the globe. They observed that as the sulphur dioxide moved up through the troposphere into the stratosphere, it reacted with water to form a layer of aerosols, tiny particles of liquid (in this case, sulphuric acid) suspended in the atmosphere. Aerosols scatter and absorb incoming sunlight and therefore exert a cooling effect on the Earth – this produced the 0.5°C drop in temperature. The gases also weakened the ozone layer for more than a year and altered regional weather patterns, including wind patterns in the North Atlantic. One result, despite the period of overall global cooling, was that Europe had a warmer than average winter in 1991/2.

AEROSOL LAYER
Satellite images from before the eruption, immediately after it and a month later show how aerosols spread through the stratosphere. Blue indicates low levels and red the highest.

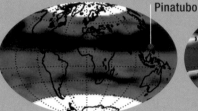

Pinatubo

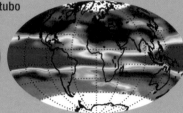

April/May 1991   June/July 1991   August/September 1991

The sleeping giant wakes

It all began a little more than two months earlier. At that time, Mount Pinatubo, which is part of the Zambales mountain range on Luzon, the main island of the Philippine archipelago, hardly even looked like a volcano. It was somewhat eroded, with a rich covering of vegetation. It had last erupted around 1500, and many local people had forgotten the mountain's deadly secret.

That changed at the beginning of April, when small steam explosions (see box, page 138) from vents (or fumaroles) to the north of Pinatubo's summit dome created a line of new craters and dusted villages 10 km (6 miles) away with ash. Over the weeks that followed, volcanic activity continued as a series of earthquakes shook the mountain, sometimes more than 1,000 times a day, and more and more ash spewed from its mouth.

Small though the April explosions were, officials responded promptly. Aeta villagers – ethnically distinct from most other Filipinos and possibly descended from the first people to settle the Philippines 30,000 years ago – lived closest to Pinatubo's summit. The authorities evacuated some 5,000 of them from their homes within a 10 km (6 mile) radius of the peak.

At the same time, geologists from PHIVOLCS installed portable seismographs on the mountain. At that stage, they were recording 40-140 small earthquakes a day. On April 23, USGS scientists arrived with more

portable monitoring equipment. Forming a joint US-Philippine team with their PHIVOLCS counterparts, they installed seven seismometers on Pinatubo, which were linked to powerful computers at the US Clark Air Base, 40 km (25 miles) away to the east.

Hundreds of small earthquakes continued throughout May, and by May 13 vents on the mountain were emitting around 500 tonnes of sulphur dioxide gas a day. By May 28, this had risen over tenfold to more than 5,000 tonnes a day. It indicated that magma inside the volcano was rising – as magma rises, it releases the volatile gases dissolved within it. PHIVOLCS started telling locals about its alert system to make them aware of the danger. At that stage, the volcano was at Alert Level 2 – warning of moderate earthquakes and rising magma, as indicated by the escaping sulphur dioxide.

Rising pressure

By June 1, the sulphur dioxide emissions had fallen, while the earthquakes were concentrated 5 km (3 miles) below the surface. Geologists surmised that the magma was being blocked and that pressure was rising within the mountain, increasing the likelihood of an explosive eruption. On June 3, there was a small explosion, followed by increasing seismic unrest and ash emissions. Harmonic tremors (see box, page 138) were detected – a sign that the magma was on the move.

Two days later, the volcano was bulging outwards due to an influx of magma, and PHIVOLCS issued a Level 3 alert – an eruption was possible within two weeks.

On June 7, the geologists recorded 1,500 earthquakes in one day. A steam explosion sent a column of ash shooting 8 km (5 miles) into the air. The alert was raised to Level 4 – an eruption possible within 24 hrs. The evacuation zone was extended to 20 km (12 miles) – by the time this had been enforced, 25,000 people had been removed from the danger area. Two days later, the first pyroclastic flows hurtled down the mountain, and the alert was raised to Level 5 – an eruption in progress. The day after, some 14,000 non-essential US military personnel and their families were transferred from Clark Air Base to Subic Bay Naval Station, lying at a safer 75 km (47 miles) from the volcano, to its south-west.

The first major eruption came at 8.51 am on June 12, shooting up a 19 km (12 mile) column of ash and steam. Explosions continued sporadically that day, and the remaining military personnel at Clark Air Base were evacuated, as was everyone within a 30 km (19 mile) radius of Pinatubo. At the same time, in the seas off the island of Samar in the eastern Philippines, Typhoon Yunya was forming, which would play a part in intensifying the disaster to come.

The mountain roars

Pinatubo made its last, ferocious roar with the cataclysmic explosion of June 15. This final phase of the eruption began at 1.40 that afternoon, by which time most of the seismometers on the mountain had been destroyed by volcanic activity. At Clark Air Base, the remaining PHIVOLCS staff had to evacuate their station; elsewhere, panic swept those who had not already been moved to safety.

By 2.30 pm, the sky was as dark as night. The volcano was spewing out golfball-sized pieces of pumice and grit, and a sour stench of sulphur filled the air. No one

LINGERING ASH *Even a year after the eruption, residents faced the task of sweeping up heavy ash deposits, which the wind regularly dumped in their streets.*

knew how far Pinatubo's fiery hands would reach, and it became a race against time to get as far away as possible.

As the journalist Susan Kreifels tried to drive away from Angeles City with her Filipino assistant, Virgilio Herrera, the roads were choked with fleeing people. Kreifels recalled how 'panicked villagers were fleeing the city with baskets on their heads, children in arms and carabao [domesticated water buffalo] running behind them. Roads were jammed. Our headlights showed the terror in their faces.' A desperate Filipino man handed over his baby to her, begged her to take the child to safety, then disappeared into the darkness. Kreifels later left the child with a local woman in the hope that she might eventually be able to reunite it with its father.

The eruption lasted 9 hours, and in a supreme case of bad timing, it coincided with the arrival of Typhoon Yunya, which swept by at this point 80 km (50 miles) north of Pinatubo. Its cyclonic winds distributed volcanic ash in all directions – satellite images reveal that it spread outwards in an umbrella shape more than 200 km (124 miles) from Pinatubo. This left most of Luzon in darkness and a 5 cm covering of ash across an area of 1,544 sq miles (4,000 km²) – a little larger than the English county of Suffolk.

To add to the devastation, the typhoon also brought heavy rainfall, which created lethal lahars (mudslides)

out of the ash and debris. A Catholic woman, Beby Tolentino, told a *New York Times* reporter how she had repeatedly crossed herself and prayed as she watched a mudslide carry off her local church. 'People think that maybe God was trying to punish us,' she said, her face and hands coated deathly white with volcanic ash. The punishment, if it was such a thing, did not end there.

Fatal legacy

By around 10.30 pm, the eruption had run its course. It had brought a major upheaval to the region, including the destruction of 8,000 homes and, in the preceding weeks, the evacuation of 20,000 Aeta villagers and a further 200,000 people from the mountain's lower slopes.

But in the end the real curse was the ash it spewed forth. Susan Kreifels described the ghostly appearance of the landscape the next day: 'The rich, green rice paddies had turned into grey-white dust, like nuclear wastelands seen in bad movies. Lines of traumatised refugees trudged nowhere through hot, dusty ash, a half-foot thick or more… Roofs had collapsed under the weight of ash, mudflows had taken down bridges, and cars had overturned in riverbeds.' In fact, the ash had caused most of the deaths. It becomes as heavy as concrete when wet, and most of those who died did so when the roofs of buildings buckled under its weight.

And there was more to come. The eruption of Pinatubo left another fatal legacy, one the authorities could do little about and which would recur year after year – further mudflows, called 'secondary lahars', as a result of the Philippines' annual monsoon and typhoon rains. These torrential rains come between May and October, and as much as 50 mm can fall in the space of an hour. Year after year following the eruption, they lifted the remaining ash and pumice deposits from the mountain and carried them down onto the surrounding floodplains, where most people live, in thick torrents.

These had the consistency of wet cement. The largest were up to 100 m wide and 10 m thick, and the fastest travelled at more than 30 km/h (19 mph). In the first five years after the eruption, the mudslides covered more than 400 km² (154 sq miles) of land, and by 1997 they had destroyed more than 100,000 homes.

Caught in the mudflows

Scott Bryan, senior lecturer in volcanology at Kingston University in London, visited Pinatubo in 1995. Soon after the eruption, people had started returning to the mountain, but try as they might to re-establish their lives, they faced the yearly onslaught of the mudflows. 'Houses would be buried in sand and mud,' Bryan said, 'and without services like fresh water, sewerage and electricity, these towns were pretty inhospitable places, especially in the middle of a tropical summer. Many locals wouldn't or couldn't move and the authorities couldn't make them move as they had nowhere else to go.'

It seemed like a never-ending struggle. 'A lahar would deposit a metre or two metres of sand and mud across their town; the villagers would then start rebuilding their homes on the roof of their buried houses. Those with money could afford to jack up their houses 2-3 m at a time to keep above the flood levels.' But even this measure was not really sustainable. 'At 2-3,000 euros a time, this was pretty costly…'

Everyone suffered, but hardest hit were the Aeta villagers who had lived near the summit of Pinatubo. They lost more than their homes in the eruption and subsequent mudslides; the explosion of their sacred mountain had also devastated their centuries-old way of life. Tubag Hagatan, who had been evacuated to a resettlement site on the lowlands before the eruption, expressed their yearning to recover what they had lost. 'I want to rebuild what we had in Mount Pinatubo. There land is plentiful and we can move freely. Here all lands are owned by somebody else.' The prompt action of the Philippine authorities in 1991 had saved thousands, but for Tubag Hagatan and others like him rebuilding their lives would prove a lasting challenge.

STUNNING SUNSETS
Astronauts on board the space shuttle Endeavour *took this photograph of the Sun through clouds of Pinatubo's ash, still circling in the Earth's atmosphere over a year after the eruption.*

Super-eruptions

The long-term effects of Pinatubo were felt worldwide, yet they pale when compared with the effects of a volcanic cataclysm that geologists now believe must happen some time – somewhere – as it has happened in the past.

Super-eruptions are the eruptions of exceptionally large volcanoes, called super-volcanoes. There is evidence that a number of these occurred during our planet's prehistory, with effects similar to those caused by the impact of a 1.5 km (1 mile) diameter asteroid. The crucial difference is that an asteroid impact of that size happens around every 400,000-500,000 years, whereas super-eruptions occur roughly every 100,000 years.

One such explosion was the super-eruption of Toba in Sumatra, Indonesia, 74,000 years ago. This released an estimated $2,500\,km^3$ (600 cubic miles) of magma into the atmosphere, depositing a layer of ash about 15 cm thick over India and much of south-east Asia. An eruption of that severity would have killed millions of people, and recent DNA evidence supports this theory, suggesting that the Toba eruption reduced the number of early humans on the planet to just a few thousand.

Ash and gases

The most significant threat from super-eruptions is the massive release of ash and gases into the atmosphere. This would have a major impact on the world's climate and weather. As a means of comparison, geologists have measured the effects of three eruptions in the past 200 years: Pinatubo; Krakatau in Sumatra, Indonesia, in 1883; and Tambora, also in Indonesia, in 1815.

Tambora released $50\,km^3$ (12 cubic miles) of magma into the atmosphere, and the next year was dubbed the 'year without a summer'. New York State had frosts in June; in Europe, storms brought

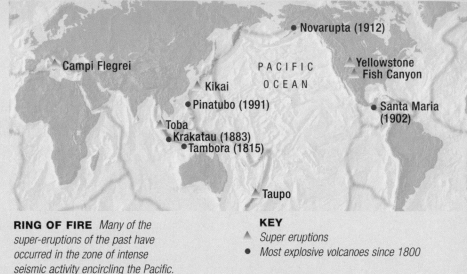

RING OF FIRE *Many of the super-eruptions of the past have occurred in the zone of intense seismic activity encircling the Pacific.*

KEY
▲ *Super eruptions*
● *Most explosive volcanoes since 1800*

severe flooding and crops failed – an estimated 200,000 Europeans died of famine, in the flooding or from other causes related to the bad weather. The explosion of Krakatau released $12\,km^3$ (3 cubic miles) of magma and again created wintry conditions. The four years after the eruption were unusually cold and record snowfalls fell worldwide.

A super-eruption would be hundreds of times larger than these more recent events, and scientists surmise that the consequences would be correspondingly severe. A covering of just 1 cm of ash, for example, would be enough to disrupt agriculture. The ash would also pollute water supplies, disrupt transport systems and interfere with communication equipment.

A growing awareness

In March 2005, the Geological Society of London published a report, explaining the potential super-volcano hazard.

It used a dramatic imaginary scenario to convey the likely impact of such an event. 'A super-eruption in Trafalgar Square, London, yielding $300\,km^3$ of magma would produce enough volcanic (pyroclastic flow) deposits to bury all of Greater London to a depth of about 210 m.' Ashfall deposits, meanwhile, could cover an area greater than Europe.

The report concluded that it was only a matter of time before a super-eruption occurred, and around 40 likely candidates have already been identified. They are located where the conditions needed to create a super-eruption already exist – where thick, viscous magma rises at plate boundaries. They include Lake Taupo on New Zealand's North Island and the Yellowstone caldera in the USA, both on the Ring of Fire around the Pacific Ocean, and the Campi Flegrei (Phlegrean Fields) caldera, west of Naples in Italy.

A BBC *Horizon* programme in 2005 explained what might happen if the Yellowstone caldera erupted today. Since super-eruptions occur at Yellowstone roughly every 600,000 years – past eruptions happened 2.1 million, 1.3 million and 640,000 years ago – it could well be that one is overdue. The documentary suggested that it would cause more than 25 million deaths in the first week alone. Eighty per cent of the USA would be covered in volcanic ash, and 20 per cent would be uninhabitable. Ash and sulphur dioxide emissions would lower global temperatures by up to 15°C.

The good news is that scientists should, in theory, have some warning of a super-eruption. It is thought that 10,000 m³ of magma would need to build up beneath the volcano and this would cause a swelling of the Earth visible from space. But this is little consolation as, at present, no one knows how the world could escape the eruption's potentially apocalyptic power.

5 super-eruptions

The super-eruptions of prehistory dwarfed even the worst eruptions of the past 200 years. Tambora in 1815 came closest, ejecting 50 km³ (12 cubic miles) of magma. By comparison, Krakatau in 1883 and Pinatubo in 1991 were modest events, ejecting 12 km³ (2.9 cubic miles) and 5 km³ (1.2 cubic miles), respectively. The volcanic explosivity index is a measure of the size of an eruption (see box, page 156).

ERUPTION	WHEN	VOLCANIC EXPLOSIVITY INDEX	VOLUME OF MAGMA ERUPTED (KM³)
1 Fish Canyon, USA	28 million years ago	8	5,000
2 Toba, Sumatra	74,000 years ago	8	2,500
3 Taupo, New Zealand	26,000 years ago	8	400
4 Campi Flegrei, Italy	35,000 years ago	7	300
5 Kikai, Ryukyu Islands, Japan	6,000 years ago	7	100

DISASTER ZONE *Comparing the relatively tiny ashfall of Mount St Helens with the widespread deposits of previous North American eruptions demonstrates just how devastating a super-eruption could be. Yellowstone's most recent eruption deposited ash well over 1,600 km from the volcano.*

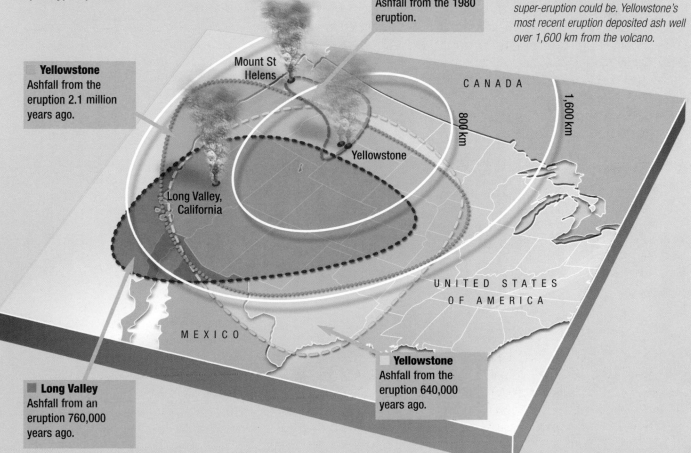

Mount St Helens
Ashfall from the 1980 eruption.

Yellowstone
Ashfall from the eruption 2.1 million years ago.

Long Valley
Ashfall from an eruption 760,000 years ago.

Yellowstone
Ashfall from the eruption 640,000 years ago.

A Bolt from the Blue

The wrath of God or a force of Nature – call it what you will, lightning is a killer. Approximately 3 million lightning flashes occur around the world every single day, and every year it accounts for more deaths than floods, tornadoes or hurricanes.

Travelling at about 22,500 km/h (14,000 mph) towards the ground, and carrying 300,000 volts of electricity, a lightning bolt heats the air around it to 28,000°C – almost five times hotter than the surface of the Sun. If you happen to be standing in the way, you could be in for a nasty shock.

On June 21, 2003, Jennifer from Pensacola, Florida, was on the telephone. Her husband was outside, when there was a huge flash of lightning and a thunderclap that sounded 'like a cannon going off'. Hurrying into the house, he discovered that, somehow, the lightning had struck Jennifer. She described the sensation of this strange phenomenon: 'Lightning running through my body and out the front of my legs. I was on our cordless phone when lightning entered through my left ear, travelled down my body and out the front of my legs. The lightning formed a big orb around my legs and then dissipated into the floor. The phone was shot out of my hand and into the pot on the back burner of the stove.'

When lightning flows over the body in this way, it is known as an external flashover. It can also flow through the body, causing internal damage. In Jennifer's case, the damage appeared to be external. 'I had discoloration to both fronts of my lower leg area and bruising, however no burns, and only one blister. The phone ironically still works, however the charge was drained out of it.'

But, as is often the case with lightning victims, Jennifer did not feel the worst of the effects immediately. 'On the way to the hospital I started twitching slightly and feeling cold from the inside out. I went into seizures approximately 30 minutes after the strike and they lasted about three hours. I spent a couple of days in the hospital. I was left unable to walk on my own, but could move all my muscles. My vision was blurry for weeks … Everything in my body was shaking for weeks and I was cold continually.' It was six weeks before Jennifer could feel warmth in her body. The lasting legacy of her brush with lightning included memory loss, vision problems, hypersensitive hearing, numbness and all-over weakness. But

> ❝ **Lightning entered through my left ear, travelled down my body and out the front of my legs.** ❞
>
> *Jennifer, Florida, USA*

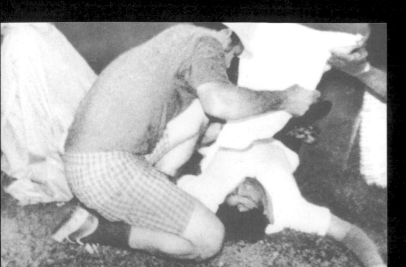

UNLUCKY FOR SOME *In 1975 American golfer Lee Trevino narrowly escaped death when he was struck by lightning at the 13th hole in the Western Open, Oakbrook, Illinois.*

SUPERSTORM *Spectacular thunderstorms regularly light up the sky during the Arizona monsoon in late summer, raining down lightning strikes on heavily populated areas.*

Lightning has a powerful beauty, but every year it kills about 10,000 people around the world and injures another 100,000.

LIGHTNING FACTS

- Lightning can strike up to 16 km (10 miles) away from the storm that created it.
- It is a myth that wearing rubber-soled shoes prevents injury from lightning.
- An average lightning flash could light a 100-watt light bulb for three months.
- On average, lightning bolts are 9 km (6 miles) long.
- Lightning does not always strike the tallest object. It is attracted towards an object that will allow a good flow of electrical current.

through it all, Jennifer remained positive: 'I am so thankful to be alive and know that I am blessed to still be here.'

Staying out of strike range

At any one time there are around 2,000 thunderstorms taking place around the world, producing about 100 lightning strikes per second. According to the UK Met Office, around 100,000 people are injured and 10,000 killed by lightning around the globe each year. So how do you avoid becoming a lightning statistic?

The first thing to consider is location. The saying that lightning never strikes in the same place twice is not strictly true. Lightning hits the 450 m tall Empire State Building in New York more than 20 times each year. And there are certain regions in the world where

> ❝ My hair and eyebrows were burnt, my zipper blown open, my shoes had been blown off, a hole in the ground marking the spot. ❞

lightning happens more frequently than others. Using optical sensors on satellites, NASA has been able to produce a map showing the global distribution of lightning. This shows that it is most attracted to central Africa, while Florida is a hotspot in the USA; in England, the place to avoid is Kent.

Commonsense precautions include the obvious maxim, 'Don't go out in a storm'. Perhaps it is a testament to how much golfers love their game that a large number of lightning strikes occur on golf courses. Mike was taking part in a charity tournament on a Cape Cod golf course when he was struck. The starter had told Mike and his friends, Bill, Dick and Jimmy, that there were thunderstorms in the area, but they wanted to play on. 'We had played four holes, none of them very well, by the time we came to number 10 … As we approached the green, the storm clouds off in the distance were filled with the sounds of thunder and the occasional flash of lightning. It was right about here that Bill asked Dick if we were walking up to the highest place on the course. Being familiar with the course, Dick thought it was either the highest or the second highest.'

A short while later, they heard the emergency horn warning golfers to leave the course, but it was too late. 'Dick said let's get out of here, Jimmy dropped the putt, I put the flag back in the hole and was about 10 steps behind the guys as we hurried off the green. Just then they heard a loud bang, "the loudest sound I ever heard", according to Dick, an ex-major in the marines, who has heard some loud bangs in his life. They turned to see me stumble to the ground, smoke coming from my body. When they reached me, I was lying in a lifeless heap, similar to a broken doll. My hair and eyebrows were burnt, my zipper blown open, my shoes had been blown off, a hole in the ground marking the spot. At this point I had suffered cardiac arrest, had

SILVER LINING

Restored sight

There are occasions when a lightning strike can have a clearly beneficial effect. In 1971, Edwin E. Robinson, a truck driver from Falmouth, Maine, suffered head injuries in a road accident and lost most of his sight and hearing. In June 1980, he was struck by lightning in his backyard. 'It was like somebody cracked a whip over my head,' he told reporters. 'I fell right on the ground, face forward.'

Curiously, Edwin's health improved after the strike. It seems that the electric shock reversed the effects of the 1971 accident so that his hearing and sight returned. Some eye specialists have speculated whether the original blindness was down to hysteria on Edwin's part, but Edwin isn't worried. He gives the credit to God.

STRUCK LUCKY *Edwin Robinson was happy to see his granddaughters after a lightning strike restored his vision.*

survivors are neurological, and include headaches, insomnia, depression and memory loss.

How lightning happens

Lightning is a form of electrical discharge. It occurs because clouds contain differentially charged ice particles. As a thundercloud grows, small, positively charged ice particles collect at the top, and larger, negatively charged particles collect at the bottom. The separation of the charge creates a large electrical potential within the cloud, and between the bottom of the cloud and the ground, which is positively charged. As opposites attract, negative sparks, or electrons, begin moving downwards from the bottom of the cloud, creating a path known as a stepped leader. As this approaches the ground, positive sparks stream up to connect with it. This completes the discharge channel, and electrons rush down the channel to the ground, lighting up the lower part of the channel. As electrons from higher up rush down, they light up the upper part. The whole process takes about half a second. When a stepped leader starts forming between cloud and ground, electrons often branch out along several different paths, rather like a river delta, producing forked lightning.

In its rush to make contact with the ground, the stepped leader travels towards any grounded object in its vicinity, so tall or isolated objects, such as buildings, trees, steeples and people, are vulnerable to a strike. Metals allow a free flow of electricity, so metal objects that are in contact with the ground are particularly attractive.

Some people have reported seeing small luminous spheres that hover in the air, move around and then dissipate. Vivienne Coyne from Essex will never forget the day when she saw what she describes as ball lightning enter her kitchen. 'The afternoon had been muggy, with thick, dark thunderclouds. I was standing with my hands in the sink when I noticed it – a floating white-hot ball of electricity. It was making a popping sound and there was a smell of ozone. I was terrified. I thought that was my lot. Then with a sizzle it was

ATTRACTIVE TARGET
Metals are good conductors of electricity, so pylons are prime targets for a lightning strike.

no pulse and my chances for survival were something between slim and nil.' Fortunately, Dick knew how to give CPR (cardiopulmonary resuscitation) and Mike lived to tell the tale.

Cardiac arrest is the most common cause of death after a lightning strike, and most deaths happen within an hour. On the positive side, most victims (90 per cent) survive a lightning strike, although 70 per cent of survivors suffer long-term psychological or physical effects. Most problems experienced by gone.' Though many people, from occultist Aleister Crowley to Russian scientist Georg Richmann, claim to have seen ball lightning, scientists disagree about whether this phenomenon exists.

Perhaps the strangest form of lightning is St Elmo's fire. It appears as a bluish or greenish-tinged light around elevated objects, such as weather vanes and ships' masts. It occurs when the electrical field concentrated around such sharp projections has become large enough to produce glowing ions in the air. St Elmo is the patron saint of sailors, who believed that his fire would protect them from storms.

Lightning strikes on aircraft

A lightning strike on an aircraft is a spectacular sight, and many witnesses believed that lightning caused an Air France plane to skid off the runway and into a ravine as it attempted to land at Toronto's Pearson airport on August 2, 2005. A violent thunderstorm was raging as the aircraft came in to land. Passengers spoke of the lights suddenly going out, and suspected that lightning had hit the plane. Fortunately, all 309 people on board were evacuated safely, just minutes before the plane burst into flames.

Lauren, from nearby Mississauga, witnessed the accident. 'I saw it happen from my office window ... it looked to me like a huge bolt of lightning hit the plane before it crashed.' Other witnesses were similarly convinced that lightning had hit the plane, but later investigations found no evidence of this,

although officials did concede that the atrocious weather conditions had been a contributing factor.

Commercial planes are hit by lightning once every 3,000 hours in the air, roughly once or twice a year. Yet, according to the Aviation Safety Network, there have been only 14 accidents due to lightning since 1951, with 12 resulting in loss of life. The most famous was PAN AM flight 214 in 1963. The Boeing 707 fell from the sky when its fuel tank was struck by lightning. All

LIGHTNING SAFETY

The UK Met Office gives the following tips for keeping safe during a thunderstorm:

- Avoid using the telephone as telephone lines can conduct electricity.
- Avoid using taps and sinks as metal pipes can conduct electricity.
- Never shelter under tall trees during a storm. You are safer in your car.
- If you are out of doors, avoid water and find a low-lying, open place that is a safe distance from tall structures such as trees, poles or metal objects.
- Avoid activities such as golf, rod-fishing or boating on a lake.
- If you are in an exposed location, you could squat close to the ground, with hands on knees and your head tucked between them. Try to touch as little of the ground with your body as possible. Do not lie down on the ground.

81 people on board were killed – a record death toll for a single lightning strike.

Although the potential exists for damage to a plane's structure, or to electronic and fuel systems, planes rarely crash as a result of lightning. They have an outer skin made of aluminium, which is a good conductor of electricity. Usually, lightning travels though this and exits again, leaving no more damage than burn marks.

EASY TARGET *Lightning hits a C-130 at Balad airbase, Iraq. Strikes on aircraft are seldom fatal.*

LONG REACH *During a storm over Oklahoma, one discharge travels outwards, redressing the balance between the cloud and the surrounding air.*

Yellowstone National Park, straddling the borders of Montana, Wyoming and Idaho, is a landscape shaped by fire. It is part of a gigantic volcano system, manifested in occasional tremors and boiling springs, such as the Old Faithful geyser.

> **'These are conditions that we haven't seen in the recorded history of Yellowstone.'**
>
> *Joan Anzelmo, park spokeswoman*

Every summer, wildfires sparked by lightning burn sections of the park, clearing out dead and diseased trees and stimulating new growth. Ecologists accept the fires as part of the forest's natural cycle. But events in 1988 challenged that way of thinking when ancient lodgepole pines lit up like torches as intense wind-driven fires swept through their crowns, sending thick plumes of smoke thousands of feet into the air. Small fires in different parts of the park joined up and gained momentum, forming giant firestorms with 100 m tall sheets of flame. Even with the help of the military, firefighters were unable to contain the larger fires, and by the end of the summer more than a third of the 890,000 ha (2.2 million acre) park had been destroyed. Yet this raging inferno had very ordinary beginnings.

The wildfire season began, much as it always did, in May. The first fires were allowed to burn, and 11 of the 20 early fires burned themselves out. Since 1972, Yellowstone, like many other US national parks, had operated a policy of 'natural burn', whereby fires that started naturally, such as those caused by lightning, were allowed to run their course. But in the summer of 1988, the whole western USA experienced a severe drought. Thunderstorms produced lightning without rain – as many as 2,000 strikes on some days. In Yellowstone, at least a third of the trees were over 250 years old and at the most flammable stage of their life cycle.

At the beginning of July, it became apparent that the fires were not behaving as expected; instead of burning themselves out, they expanded and became stronger. On July 2, the Fan fire, which burned for a week in the north-western corner of the park, made a run of 746 ha (1,843 acres) in one day. 'These are conditions

Yellowstone Ablaze

HIGH-SPEED CHASE *A crown fire races through the tops of the trees along Mirror Plateau. Crown fires move at incredible speeds and are impossible to stop.*

HIGH-LEVEL INFERNO *Violent indrafts of air formed at ground level as oxygen was sucked upwards to feed the flames.*

In summer 1988, firestorms destroyed almost 6,000 km² (2,000 sq miles) of forest – an expanse a third of the size of Wales.

that we haven't seen in the recorded history of Yellowstone,' Joan Anzelmo, a park spokeswoman, told *The Washington Post.* 'It's a fire that's exhibiting what fire officials call extreme behaviour, which is difficult to predict.'

By the third week in July, more than 16,000 ha (39,000 acres) of the Greater Yellowstone area had burned. With more weeks of drought promised and the fires threatening communities on the borders of the park, the decision was made to fight all fires aggressively. But it was a frustrating task. Firefighters would make small gains, only to lose them again. Firefighter Danny Bungarz told the *LA Times:* 'This fire is kicking our ass. We put our lines in, mop up, patrol and then two weeks later the wind comes and pushes it back over what we did.' But the worst was yet to come.

Black Saturday

On August 20, 'The Daily Park Briefing', a telephone information service for park personnel, predicted 'warm and windy' weather, and warned that fighting the fires 'will be difficult at least'. As the day wore on, that would turn out to be something of an understatement. With wind speeds of up to 128 km/h (80 mph), already enormous fires were fanned into firestorms. By the end of the day, 66,000 ha (165,000

LIFE GOES ON *Deer flee the fast-moving flames. Although many animals were killed by the fires, the majority survived.*

acres) would be lost, and the day would forever be remembered as Black Saturday.

That morning, Phil Perkins, Yellowstone's assistant fire management officer, came in early to prepare the park briefing and to fly over the fires with the chief ranger to check on their progress. 'We had three large fires around us that day. Clover Mist, Storm Creek and another fire in the north-west.' At 9 am, he was surprised to see how lively the fires were. 'Normally, fires get active at about midday when things heat up. It's extremely unusual for them to be active so early in the morning, but within about 15 minutes all three fires were sending up smoke columns. I've seen it a few times, but not very often.' The strong, dry winds had breathed new life into the fires, and the flames were standing twice the height of the trees while smoke columns rose 6,000 m into the air. 'I knew we were in for a very hard day,' said Phil.

The fires grew so large that they created their own wind. The Storm Creek fire made a 16 km (10 mile) run. Another fire to the north of the park, the appropriately named Hellroaring fire, was eating up the forest at an estimated 1.5 km (1 mile) an hour.

Every fire in the park spread that day due to the prevailing gale-force winds. One reporter from *The Billings Gazette* watched the terrifying North Fork firestorm approaching: 'As it nears, a wildfire creates much of the sensation as an approaching train. First you hear – almost feel – a distinct rumble. Puffs of black smoke appear in the columns of grey – a sign of greater burning intensity – and the sound of the fire increases. Then whiffs of air hit the back of your neck as you face the fire, evidence that the fire is creating its own wind, sucking oxygen from around the ground to sustain itself, then blowing it thousands of feet into the air in a boiling column of smoke. As the inferno nears, it roars like a jet engine as the blaze sucks more and more in. You can feel the heat of the flames half a mile away. Thick smoke occasionally obscures the blaze and noise dissipates for a moment as the flames gasp momentarily for air before making the next leap.'

It was clear that the firefighters were not going to win this battle on their own. On August 22, after a brief course in firefighting, more than 1,000 army troops were flown in to give a hand. In September, several hundred Marines would follow. But with thick smoke and ash filling the sky, firefighting aircraft and helicopters were often grounded, and the fires had grown so intense and so massive that no one could get

CONTINUED ON PAGE 178 »

The fight for the Old Faithful Inn

O n the morning of September 7, the North Fork fire was spreading towards the Old Faithful complex and the historic inn at its heart. Built in 1904, the inn was made of timber and there seemed little hope of saving it. National Park Service ranger Jeff Henry watched firefighters battle to preserve it.

'From where I was on top of the inn it looked as though the buildings of the area were about to be incorporated into the firestorm and that a lot of people probably were going to die.' Many visitors remained in the area as Jeff left his vantage point. He watched firefighters dowse the inn with water.

'Those brave firefighters, some of whom had even stationed themselves perilously on the flat roofs ... of the inn, deserve great credit ... Without their efforts to keep the walls and roofs of the inn wet, the building certainly would have ignited in the fiery holocaust that blew in that afternoon. Indeed, the very air seemed to be on fire. Several times that day I saw isolated bits of fuel, things like upturned stumps in the geyser basins or fallen logs on islands in the parking lot, burst into flame in seemingly spontaneous ignition, as though exhaled upon by some fire-breathing dragon. In addition to the ground blizzard of sparks and embers that swirled around our ankles and calves, larger embers showered down upon the inn like fiery ejecta from an erupting volcano.'

Some of the wooden shingles on the roof did catch fire, but they were quickly put out. Then came news that the fire had been spotted at Observation Point, above Geyser Hill on the other side of the river. It seems that the barren geyser plains and wide expanse of concrete surrounding the wooden building acted as a firebreak.

'Slowly, it became safe to believe that the Old Faithful Inn and the other major buildings of the area were going to survive and that no one would be killed or seriously injured in the afternoon's conflagration.'

Jeff Henry, a National Park Service ranger

Life and death of the Yellowstone fires

The park, which covers 890ha (2.2 million acres), was experiencing a severe drought – the summer proved to be the driest on record. Thunderstorms produced lightning without rain, and a number of fires touched off. In the beginning, the fires were left to burn themselves out.

Yellowstone Park

4 **Clover** and **Mist** fires caused by lightning July 9-Oct 10 129,325 ha (319,570 acres)

1 **Storm Creek** fire caused by lightning June 14-Sept 17 38,445 ha (95,000 acres)

Targhee National Forest

• Norris

• Old Faithful

Shoshone Lake

Yellowstone Lake

• Grant Village

2 **Shoshone** and **Red** fires caused by lightning June 23-Sept 19 69,615 ha (172,025 acres)

3 **Fan** fire caused by lightning June 25-Sept 19 8,455 ha (20,900 acres)

6 **North Fork** fire caused by cigarette July 22-Nov 18 206,390 ha (510,000 acres) – nearly a quarter of the park

5 **Mink Creek** fire caused by lightning July 11-Sept 18 47,075 ha (116,325 acres)

June 14 Lightning sparks off a fire at Storm Creek on the north-east border of the park.

June 23 Lightning ignites a fire near Shoshone Lake at the southern end of the park. Two days later, lightning starts the Fan fire in the north-west corner. On July 1, the Red fire begins near Shoshone. There is no sense of alarm, and the fires are allowed to burn.

July 9 Lightning strikes set off the Clover and Mist fires in the north-west. Two days later, the Mink Creek fire ignites in the south.

July 14 7,385 ha (18,250 acres) have burned in the Yellowstone area.

July 21 A total of 17,480 ha (43,195 acres) have burned in the Greater Yellowstone area, and the

long-range forecast promises more dry weather. The fires are growing very rapidly despite efforts to suppress them, and a decision is made to fight all fires aggressively.

July 22 A carelessly tossed cigarette starts the North Fork fire in the Targhee National Forest. This would turn out to be the largest and

most destructive fire, burning 206,390 ha (510,000 acres).

July 23 The Snake Complex, comprising the Shoshone, Red and Falls fires, has burned 4,450 ha (11,000 acres). Residents of Grant Village are evacuated. The Clover and Mist fires join up with several smaller fires.

July 28 The fires have encompassed almost 52,610 ha (130,000 acres).

Aug 15 In the north of the park a camp fire is left untended and grows into Hellroaring fire.

August 18 The fires are almost out of control. The Clover Mist fire covers 44,110 ha (109,000 acres); eight firefighting crews plus air support are continuing a direct attack along the east and north-west flanks. Winds in the Gibbon River valley have spread the North Fork fire across 26,300 ha (65,000 acres); the campground and facilities at Norris Junction have been evacuated. Seven crews with air support are fighting the Red and Shoshone fires, which have now burned 20,755 ha (51,285 acres).

August 20 On 'Black Saturday', sustained winds of up to 128 km/h (80 mph) fan the flames and 66,775 ha (165,000 acres) are lost to

7 Hellroaring fire caused by campfire Aug 15-Sept 11 27,000 ha (66,725 acres)

MONTANA

• Norris

IDAHO

• Old Faithful

• Grant Village

WYOMING

FIGHTING THE FLAMES *More than 100 aircraft were deployed, dropping over 6.4 million litres of fire retardant. In total, more than 25,000 firefighters took part.*

ANIMAL VICTIMS *Bison were seen roaming the park during the fires. Most avoided the flames, but carcasses were found near long fire fronts.*

20 km — 20 miles
10 km — 10 miles
0 km — 0 miles

the fires – the largest area in a single day. Huck fire starts when a tree falls on a power line.

8 Huck fire caused by tree falling on power line Aug 20-Sept 18 45,000 ha (111,200 acres)

September 7 The
North Fork fire heads for Old Faithful Inn, but firefighters save the historic building by dowsing it in water.

September 10
With wildfires still rampaging out of control, officials close the entire park to the public.

September 11
The first autumn snowfall damps down the fires. Firefighters begin to leave the park, and residents return home.

November 15
The last flames are put out and the summer of fire is over.

close enough to fight them. In the end, the only option was to concentrate efforts on evacuating areas in the path of the fire to ensure that at least no lives were lost. Only two people died as a result of the fires, both outside the park itself: a pilot died when his helicopter crashed, and a firefighter was killed by a falling tree during the clean-up.

On August 22, when the fires were at their worst, firefighter Norm Beul, who had been on the lines for four weeks without a day off, told *The Washington Post*: 'The only thing that is going to put these fires out is heavy snows this winter. I've seen them crown where the wall of fire went 300 ft into the sky and they were moving faster than you can run.' He was right – the fires continued to rage until finally Nature showed mercy. On September 11, a thin covering of snow dampened the flames and the nightmare was finally over.

Although hundreds of animals died in the fires, this was a small percentage of the overall population. Larger animals are good at finding a way around hotspots, and smaller ones retreat underground. Nearly 400 large animals perished, including 333 elk (from an estimated 40,000-50,000), nine bison and six deer. The majority

PROTECTIVE COATING *A fire crew covers a building in foam to prevent it catching fire.*

of carcasses were found in places where the fire front had exceeded 2 km (1¹/4 mile) in breadth and had advanced at a rate of 4 km/h (2¹/2 mph) or more. Most had died from smoke inhalation. Thousands more elk perished in the following winter due to lack of food.

Surprisingly, throughout the Yellowstone fires most of the park stayed open – and tourists continued to visit, even in August, when the fires were blazing strongly and the air was filled with smoke. Joan Anzelmo told *The LA Times*: 'Some people are

SILVER LINING

Out of the ashes

The fires of 1988 were so devastating and so extensive, it seemed impossible that Yellowstone would ever recover. Lush swathes of forest had been reduced to charcoal, the skeletal remains of trees standing among the debris like burnt matchsticks. But all was not lost. For a start, not all of the forest had burned, and there were areas of partial burns that would provide new habitats for plants and animals. Even in areas where fire had razed everything to the ground, fire-tolerant seeds in the soil prepared to emerge.

In the spring, and for several years after, ash-enriched soil produced spectacular displays of wildflowers. 'It was beautiful – the best spring flowers the park has seen,' said Phil Perkins, Yellowstone National Park's fire warden. 'But there were already areas of green, where the grass was growing back, in the autumn after the fires,' he added.

Areas of cleared ground, open to the sunshine, were soon colonised by lodgepole pine, whose seeds are activated by fire. But the regeneration of a forest takes time. In 1998, 10 years after the fires, National Public Radio's Alex Chadwick visited Yellowstone and spoke to Don Despain, a US National Park forester when the fires broke out. He was not concerned by the devastation. 'Fire is a natural part of the system,' he said. 'Apparently, fire's been a part of the wood environment as long as there's been plants on the Earth. The lodgepole pines are 3¹/2 or 4 ft to 8 ft tall. They're growing 16 in to 18 in a year. The ground cover is back to what it was before the fire, and it's a ten-year-old forest that's well on its way to recreating the forest that was here in 1988.'

A large fire occurs every 200 years or so in Yellowstone. Old and diseased trees are destroyed and the nutrients in the soil from the ash enable saplings to get a good start. Today many of the old trees that were standing after the fire have fallen and will form habitats for insects. As they decay, they will impart nutrients into the forest floor. Young trees are growing in the clearings, competing for light; some will die, others will make it to maturity. And some, in time, will succumb to the wildfires that still burn through the park each summer.

❝beautiful ... the best spring flowers the park has seen❞

Phil Perkins, assistant fire management officer, Yellowstone National Park

coming in specifically to see the wildfires and firefighters at work. There are firefighters alongside the road who have had their pictures taken as much as Old Faithful this summer.'

In places where wildfires could break out, authorities issue reports on current fire conditions. Visitors should check bulletin boards for information and weather reports, and look out for warning signs. Smoke will first be visible at the horizon. If the volume of smoke increases, head in another direction. Trees and thickets provide fuel for fires and should be avoided. Roads and paths can provide escape routes; gravel or asphalt areas and large rock outcrops can also provide places to escape a fire. It is dangerous to get uphill of a fire: heat rises, and fire travelling uphill can outstrip a person.

Business as usual

Frank Markley from Ohio, who often holidayed at Yellowstone in August, feared he would have to cancel his trip. But when he checked his reservation, he found that the Old Faithful Inn was still open for business. Arriving on August 30 via the east entrance, he noticed that visibility was poor. 'Great columns of white smoke arose in the distance across Yellowstone Lake, the largest coming from the Old Faithful area and widening in the sky overhead as it passed into the hazy east.' As he went deeper into the park, he began to see the stark aftermath of the fires. 'I saw charred standing and fallen trees lining the roadside. In some places, red plastic ribbon was stretched across pulloffs to protect curious motorists from the dangers of often-hidden smouldering areas or falling snags.'

That evening at the Old Faithful Inn, activities seemed strangely unaffected by events playing out in the surrounding landscape. 'Here, on this late summer evening, there is no apparent fear or anxiety caused by the fire which burns in a valley just a few miles away. Many of us here have gone outside and looked toward the west to see if we can really see flames or a glow from the North Fork fire … But on this evening and at this location we see no flames and no glow. The haze of the air obscures visibility and the geographical placement of the fire hides all but its unmistakable smoke.'

Frank stayed at the Old Faithful Inn until September 6, the night before it came so perilously close to being burned to the ground.

GLOBAL INFERNOS

- **75 killed in Australian bush fires on Ash Wednesday, 1983**

- **240,000 ha (593,000 acres) of Portugal scorched and 30,000 homes destroyed in 2005**

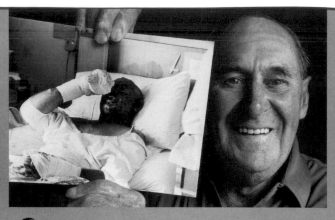

6 This is what I looked like when I came in, and if I can do it, you can do it too. 9

Ranald Webster

Australia 1983

The eucalyptus forests of south-eastern Australia are among the most fire-prone environments on the planet. Drought during the hot, dry summers creates perfect conditions for fires, while strong winds fan the flames and spread them with terrifying speed. This is what happened on February 16, Ash Wednesday, 1983, when more than 100 bush fires raced across the states of Victoria and South Australia. The fires consumed an area of more than 200,000 ha (494,000 acres), killed 75 people and injured hundreds more.

The bushfire season had started in the previous November, and by mid-February several large fires had occurred in Victoria and South Australia. Victoria, in particular, had been in the grip of a prolonged drought for ten months, and extensive areas of scrub were ready to burst into flames.

On the morning of February 16, Melbourne, the capital of Victoria, recorded temperatures of 43°C, with a relative humidity of just 6 per cent (the normal level in summer is 43 per cent). A hot, dry, northerly wind gusted to over 100 km/h (60 mph). Fires ignited at Branxholme and Cudgee to the south-west of Melbourne, and in the Dandenong Ranges to the east. At one point 54 fires encircled the city. Across the border in South Australia, the Mount Lofty Ranges to the east of Adelaide were also ablaze.

Fanned by the northerly wind, the fires marched southwards in long, thin lines. Then, in the early evening, the wind suddenly swung into the west, driving the flames eastwards; many of the fires merged with others. What had previously been narrow ribbons of flame spreading south became long fronts travelling east and impossible to control. It was in the hour after the wind changed that most property was destroyed and lives lost.

Fireman Ranald Webster from Narnargoon Country Fire Authority was fighting blazes in the Dandenongs when the wind changed, sending flames shooting towards him and a colleague. The two men jumped into their van. 'We just had to get out,' said Webster. 'We hared off in the van. There was a sheet of flame across the road. The van crashed and rolled. When it came to a stop there was fire all around us … I couldn't see anything because of the flames.'

By the time the fires had burned themselves out, Webster's colleague was dead and Webster himself was suffering head-to-toe burns. When he was admitted to the Royal Melbourne Hospital, his face was swollen and charred, and the skin on his hands had been burnt away entirely. Doctors gave him only a 4 per cent chance of survival. But Webster had a fighting spirit and, although his body was scarred, his mind stayed strong. Most of the scarring vanished after four years, and only his hands needed skin grafts.

Twenty years later Mr Webster could still be seen in the burns unit – talking to other victims. Visiting once a month and during crises such as the Bali bombing in 2002, he was an inspiration: 'I will show them the photos and I'll say, "Well, this is what I looked like when I came in, and if I can do it, you can do it too." '

Portugal 2005

In the summer of 2005, all of southern Europe sizzled under a blanket of hot African air. After a winter of lower-than-average rainfall, Spain and Portugal were enduring their worst drought for 60 years, while temperatures soared to 41°C. Fires flared in Portugal, in particular, and by July they had devastated large parts of the country's northern and central regions. By mid-August, thousands of firefighters had been deployed, tackling up to 50 fires.

BBC reporter Paul Henley visited the central district of Santarém. 'By all accounts, it is the speed and unpredictability of the forest blazes that once again seem to have defeated the authorities here,' he wrote. 'Huge blackened swathes of withered eucalyptus, pine and olive trees are left, as if a burning motorway has been run through the landscape. Actual roads are no barrier – the flames jump from one side to the other without problem.'

Wildfires are common in the arid climate of Portugal, but the sheer scale of these fires and the shortage of personnel to deal with them were taking their toll. 'I've been many times near the fires – fires that we have here every year. But nothing compared to this year,' said Elder Silvano, a volunteer firefighter in the Santarém district of Abrantes. 'This is something never seen before here. It is like a monster that comes towards us … We have about 750 km² of terrain in this municipality – half of that burned in three days. It is just something unimaginable.'

At the end of August, a cool spell brought some respite. 'We can now claim victory,' said Paulo Tavares, coordinator of the volunteer firefighters in the town of Coja in Coimbra, to the north of Santarém. 'At this moment everything is under control – if it remains cool, this will remain under control.' More than 240,000 ha (593,000 acres) of forest had burned across Portugal, affecting 12 of the country's 18 districts. Fifteen people died – 10 of them firefighters.

REPEAT PERFORMANCE
Residents watch a forest fire near the village of Figueiro Dos Vinhos, central Portugal, on October 5. After a relatively quiet September, hot, dry winds had fanned the fires into life again.

Smog over South-east Asia

At the end of September, 1997, the Malaysian state of Sarawak, on Borneo, found itself at the epicentre of an environmental catastrophe. Since July, hundreds of forest fires had been burning out of control in neighbouring Kalimantan and Sumatra (Indonesia).

Smoke and ash from the fires in Indonesia spread across Sarawak, trapping traffic exhaust fumes and industrial pollution at ground level and cloaking Sarawak's towns and cities in a thick, choking haze. On September 18, the Air Pollution Index (API), which measures levels of sulphur dioxide, nitrous oxide, carbon dioxide, lead and dust, reached 400 (a level of 300-500 is classified as 'hazardous'), and all schools were closed. Next day the Index reached 600, and Sarawak declared a Haze Emergency that was to last for 10 days. Offices and factories were shut down, and flights to peninsular Malaysia were halted; food stores and hospitals were allowed to stay open. The government advised residents to stay indoors, and to wear masks if they needed to go outside.

Dark days

In Kuching, the capital of Sarawak, the smog was so thick that visibility in some places was reduced to just a few metres. Hatta Morsidi said she and her family 'closed all the windows and doors', and described how the dense haze made her

THAILAND

VIETNAM

MALAYSIA

Smoke is carried northwards by the prevailing winds.

Singapore

Sumatra (INDONESIA)

Sarawak (MALAYSIA)

INDONESIA

Kalimantan (INDONESIA)

Forest fires rage out of control in Sumatra and Kalimantan.

CARRIED ON THE WIND
Smoke from hundreds of forest fires in the Indonesian states of Sumatra and Kalimantan spread northwards across much of South-east Asia.

A poisonous smog cloaked large areas of South-east Asia, blocking out the Sun and threatening the health of millions.

183

neighbourhood unrecognisable: 'Even from across the road we couldn't see the house.' Some 19 km (12 miles) outside the city, Hadiah binti Nasir and her family had to go to a nearby clinic to seek medical treatment because 'tears were running down our cheeks' due to the smog. 'We kept all the children inside the house,' she added. At one point, pollution in Kuching reached a record level of 839 – double the hazardous level.

While Sarawak was the worst hit by pollution, swathes of South-east Asia were affected as the prevailing winds carried smoke northwards as far as Thailand and the Philippines. Tens of thousands of people rushed to hospitals and health centres as the choking yellow haze aggravated heart and respiratory conditions and caused skin and eye irritations. In all, up to 70 million people in six countries were affected.

> **❛You feel very sleepy in class and you can smell the smoke when you breathe, and your eyes smart.❜**
> *Khavita Kaur, Singapore*

In Singapore, high-school student Khavita Kaur complained that the thick smog caused 'a headache and you feel very sleepy in class and you can smell the smoke when you breathe, and your eyes smart.'

In the Malaysian capital, Kuala Lumpur, *New York Times* reporter Seth Mydans wrote on September 24: 'On the bad days, a milky twilight settles over the city at noon, tall buildings become ghostly shadows and people hurry along the streets with surgical masks covering their mouths and noses.'

Two days later, an airbus crashed when it tried to land on Sumatra, claiming the lives of all 234 people on board, and a collision between two merchant ships in the Straits of Malacca, between Sumatra and peninsular Malaysia, left 29 dead. Both accidents were blamed on poor visibility. Air-pollution levels rocketed, and at least two deaths in Indonesia were officially attributed directly to the choking haze.

JAMBI SUFFOCATES
Residents could not escape the smog in the Indonesian town. Breathing its toxic air was likened to smoking 80 cigarettes a day.

In the Philippines, officials announced that the haze had spread to the southern island of Palawan, and could reach Manila within three days.

Burning out of control

Forest burning in Indonesia takes place annually during the dry season as it is a cheap yet illegal way to clear land for crops such as palm oil and rubber. Rain forests are among the wettest places on Earth, and the fires are usually controllable. But in 1997, the 20th century's most severe El Niño event caused a very long dry spell (see pages 224-5): no rain fell in some parts of Borneo for several weeks. The drought conditions fanned the fires, allowing them to spread fast and get out of control.

In Kuching, the dense smog eased on September 28, although meteorologists attributed this to changing wind patterns rather than to any abatement in the fires in Indonesia. On September 29, Sarawak's Haze Emergency ended. In Kuching, foodstall-owner Vincent Wee revelled in the novelty of glimpsing his own shadow – something he hadn't been able to see for weeks – and added: 'Last night I looked up and saw the stars.'

On the night of September 27, 2003, a giant fireball streaked across the heavens over the state of Orissa in eastern India. Lighting up the sky as it went, the fireball fragmented with a series of explosions, and burning pieces fell to Earth over a large area.

As it travelled along a trajectory from north-west to south-east, the fireball was witnessed by people in several districts in Orissa's coastal region, and caused widespread panic. 'When I saw the huge fireball with so much bright light I first mistook it for a crashing aircraft,' said local resident Bandita Das. 'For about 10 seconds, the evening on Saturday got lighted up. I panicked and took my kids inside the house.'

Turning night into day

According to local reports, the red, dish-shaped meteorite with a greenish tail – from which a blue light emanated – appeared at around 6.30 pm, about half an hour after sunset. The celestial spectacular lasted for nearly a minute and was followed by a series of loud explosions. 'It was all there for just a few seconds but it was like daylight everywhere', said one Orissa resident.

Numerous witnesses desperate for information made frantic calls to newspaper offices and the Doordarshan TV station. 'Incidents of this kind are a rare phenomenon in this region,' explained Dr Jayadev Kar of Pathani Samant Planetarium. 'Such occurrences are common in space but not visible to the naked eye.' 'Such explosions take place regularly ten times every hour in the Universe,' added expert, Subhendu Patnaik. 'But this is a rare occurrence in Orissa.'

The affected area stretched from Kaptipada in Mayurbhanj district to Suniti in Kendrapara district – a distance of over 120 km (75 miles). 'It was seen by people in seven or eight districts, covering about 14,000 to 15,000 sq km,' said Bishwa Bhushan Harichandan, a minister in Orissa's state government.

Fragments from the fireball gutted a thatched house in the village of Surusuria in the Mayurbhanj district. About 120 km (75 miles) south-east of Surusuria, the fireball broke up with a noise resembling a series of explosions and several pieces landed in the estuary area of Kendrapara district. One fragment landed in the village of Subarnapur, where it created a nearly cyclindrical pit in the wet ground 11 cm in diameter and 27 cm deep. Two pieces were found in the Suniti area. One, weighing 5.7 kg, fell in the backyard of a thatched house in West Suniti. The other fell about 1.5 km (1 mile) away on the banks of a pond in the village of Suniti. It weighed 5.4 kg and created an irregular cylindrical pit 13 cm wide, 37 cm deep and 20 cm long. The meteorite pieces had a smooth dark crust. Broken surfaces were a greyish-white with traces of metals visible. A few smaller fragments were recovered from other sites in Kendrapara district.

Three people in the area passed out from shock and suffered significant injuries, although initial reports had suggested that more than 20 people were affected as

> **❝ I first mistook it for a crashing aircraft. For about 10 seconds the evening sky got lighted up. ❞**
>
> *Local resident Bandita Das*

Fire from the Sky

METEOR STORM *On November 18, 1999, up to 1,500 meteors per hour flashed through the night sky over the Middle East and Europe as dust particles trailing behind the comet Tempel-Tuttle burned up on entering the Earth's atmosphere.*

Most rock debris from space burns up when it enters the atmosphere; a few pieces survive the journey and crash to Earth.

pieces of the meteorite landed. The shock reportedly killed one elderly man.

There have been 12 previous recorded incidents of meteorite showers in India, two of them in Orissa. Eyewitness accounts of this event and the fact that there were two main groups of impact sites suggest that the fireball broke up in two stages during its flight. The first fragmentation probably happened over Surusuria, with most of the pieces burning up at that point, and the second one over Suniti. 'I have never seen a meteor covering such a large area with a huge fireball and roaring sound,' said Basant Kumar Mohanty, senior director of the Geological Survey of India. Witnesses in Orissa said that windows rattled as it passed overhead.

Shooting stars

Meteorites should not be confused with meteors, which are dust particles or minute fragments of rock that burn up when they enter the Earth's atmosphere, usually at altitudes of 95-130 km (60-80 miles) above the ground. These fast-moving streaks of light are rarely seen for more than a few seconds, and are often referred to as 'falling stars' or 'shooting stars'. Many are random, appearing out of the blue and travelling in various

6 I have never seen a meteor covering such a large area with a huge fireball and roaring sound. 9

Basant Kumar Mohanty, Geological Survey of India

directions. On a clear night you may see about ten shooting stars per hour. More spectacular are the meteor showers that occur when Earth passes through the trail of dust and debris left by a comet (see box below left). They vary in intensity, depending on where the comet is on its orbit. The comet Tempel-Tuttle is responsible for the annual Leonids shower in November. As its orbit through space takes 33 years, approximately every 33 years the meteor shower is particularly intense.

Fragments of the Solar System

The fragments that landed in Orissa – and caused such panic – were meteorites, lumps of rock or metal from space that survive friction in the atmosphere and reach the Earth's surface. Some meteorites arrive intact, others break apart as they travel through the atmosphere, producing a shower of fragments that hit the Earth together.

When pieces of rock enter the atmosphere, they are usually travelling at speeds of 36,000-252,000 km/h (22,000-156,000 mph). Smaller fragments are slowed by friction as they travel through the atmosphere, and hit the Earth with a similar impact as if dropped from a tall building. The rare pieces that are larger than a few hundred tonnes are not slowed down, and cause huge damage on impact.

As the rock fragment travels through the atmosphere, its outermost surface heats up and melts, producing a bright fireball – typically white or blue, although yellow, orange, green and red fireballs have been reported. Scientists think that these differences are caused by the speed at which the object is travelling, not its composition.

Most meteorites are fragments from collisions between asteroids, and date back some 4.6 billion years to the birth of the Solar System, although some are known to have come from Mars or the Moon. Those that are around 98 per cent metal are known as 'irons'. 'Stony-irons' are a mixture of metal and rock. The

METEOR WATCHING

As comets orbit the Sun, they leave a trail of dust and debris. When the Earth crosses this trail, the fragments burn up in the atmosphere and we see them as shooting stars (meteors). Since the Earth always follows the same path around the Sun, it always crosses the trail of a particular comet at the same point in its own orbit. This has enabled astronomers to draw up a meteor-shower calendar, and amateur stargazers can plan their celestial viewing. The showers are named after the constellation from which they appear to emanate.

WHEN TO SEE IT	SHOWER	HEMISPHERE
January	Quadrantids	Northern
April	Lyrids	Northern
May	Eta Aquarids	Southern
July and August	Perseids	Northern
October	Orionids	Both
November	Leonids	Both
December	Geminids	Both

COLLISION COURSE
Many people witnessed fragments of the Peekskill meteorite speeding through the sky over the north-eastern USA.

most common meteorites are 'stones', which look much like ordinary rocks from Earth. The meteorite pieces recovered from sites around Orissa were stony meteorites, a type that often breaks apart in the atmosphere.

Meteorite hazards

Every day, around 100 tonnes of extraterrestrial material falls to Earth. Most arrives as dust grains less than 1 mm across. Larger meteorites arrive only occasionally – about 1,000 meteorites, weighing between 1 and 100 kg, each year. The risk of being hit, let alone killed, by a meteorite is very small. The only recorded fatality was a dog unlucky enough to be in the wrong place at the wrong time when, in 1911, the Nakhla meteorite fell as a shower of stones in Egypt.

In October 1992, a brilliant fireball startled fans at a high-school football game in Peekskill, New York. The sight was followed by a terrific crash as a rock the size of a bowling ball plummeted onto a parked Chevy Malibu, burning through the boot and denting the driveway beneath. When it was found, the meteorite smelt strongly of sulphur.

Larger meteorites, though rarer, pose a greater hazard. Over the last 200 years, records indicate that a 100 kg meteorite hits Earth roughly every four years, and a 1,000 kg meteorite every 50 years. Yet even meteorites this size reach a maximum width of only about 100 cm, and do not form significant craters. The largest meteorite ever found is the Hoba meteorite, which weighs 60 tonnes. Discovered in 1920 near Grootfontein in Namibia, it hit the Earth 80,000 years ago.

Meteorite showers have aroused awe and fear in the human race for thousands of years. Egyptians used a hieroglyphic symbol to depict iron meteorites, which

FINAL IMPACT *On October 9, 1992, a meteorite smashed through the boot of a car in the Peekskill suburbs of New York City, and left a crater underneath.*

they called 'iron of heaven'. In the West, few scientists before 1800 believed that rocks fell to Earth from space. Research into a series of dramatic meteorite showers across Europe and the USA in the early 1800s convinced sceptics that these unusual rocks did indeed have extraterrestrial origins. Since then, the study of meteorites has provided information on the beginnings of the Solar System, how planets and asteroids formed and on the history of our own world.

Something extraordinary happened in the skies over a remote Siberian region of forests and swamps on June 30, 1908. It was around 7.15 am, and local resident Semen Semenov was sitting on his porch in the trading station of Vanavara, on the Stoney Tunguska river.

The sky 'was split in two and high above the forest the whole northern part of the sky appeared to be covered with fire. At that moment I felt great heat as if my shirt had caught fire … I wanted to pull off my shirt and throw it away, but then there was a bang in the sky, and a mighty crash was heard. I was thrown to the ground a few metres from the porch and for a moment I lost consciousness … The crash was followed by noise like stones falling from the sky, or guns firing. The earth trembled, and when I lay on the ground I covered my head because I was afraid that stones might hit it.'

Like a second Sun
Even today, this is Russia's most thinly populated region, and apart from Semenov and some nomadic reindeer herders of the local Evenki people, there were few witnesses of the terrifying event when a massive fireball streaked through the sky, leaving a long

A FOREST FELLED *Trees flattened by the blast wave lay splayed outwards from the centre of the site. Only a few near the centre remained standing.*

Impact from Outer Space

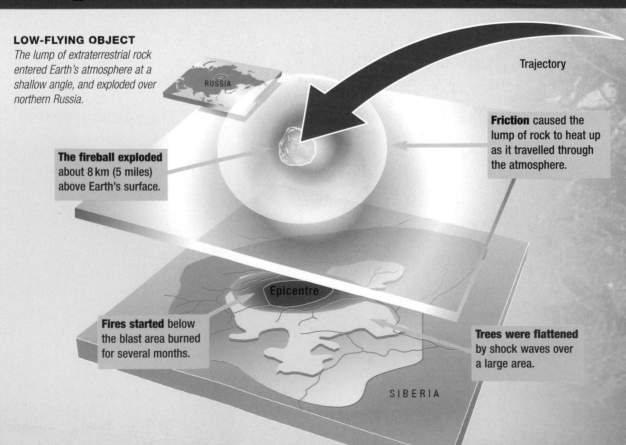

LOW-FLYING OBJECT
The lump of extraterrestrial rock entered Earth's atmosphere at a shallow angle, and exploded over northern Russia.

RUSSIA

Trajectory

Friction caused the lump of rock to heat up as it travelled through the atmosphere.

The fireball exploded about 8 km (5 miles) above Earth's surface.

Epicentre

Fires started below the blast area burned for several months.

Trees were flattened by shock waves over a large area.

SIBERIA

> **At that moment I felt great heat as if my shirt had caught fire ... There was a bang in the sky ... The earth trembled.**
>
> *Local resident*
> *Semen Semenov*

trail of light as it went. Travelling from south-east to north-west, its intensity increased as it neared Earth, setting trees ablaze. Then it exploded, at a height of about 8 km (5 miles) above Earth's surface. One Evenki herdsman, called Chuchan, described what he witnessed: 'I saw a wonder: trees were falling, the branches were on fire, it became mighty bright, how can I say this, as if there was a second Sun, my eyes were hurting, I even closed them.'

The fireball was a large lump of extraterrestrial rock, called a bolide, heading for Earth at a speed of around 11,500 km/h (7,145 mph). Scientists have calculated that the energy from the mid-air explosion was equivalent to around 20 million tonnes of TNT – or 1,000 times the power of the Hiroshima atom bomb. Seismographs in Russia, Germany and England recorded tremors, and barographs picked up changes in air pressure, the result of shock waves from the blast. For several days afterwards, the skies glowed orange long after sunset for thousands of miles around. The glow was so bright that people in western Europe could read without the help of a light.

It was nearly 20 years before the Soviet government sent a scientific expedition to the region to investigate the event. Even then, in 1927, the devastation was still

In 1908, 2,000 km² of remote forest in northern Russia was destroyed when a fireball exploded high above Earth's surface.

PERFECT CIRCLE *Wolfe Creek Crater, Australia, is about 880 m wide and was formed by a 50,000 kg meteorite.*

apparent. After an arduous journey, the expedition members looked across a scene of utter desolation – fallen, charred trees spreading as far as the eye could see over a vast area of more than 2,000 km² (770 sq miles). 'The results of even a cursory examination exceeded all the tales of eyewitnesses and my wildest expectations,' wrote the expedition's leader, geologist Leonid Kulik. In 1960, when mathematician Wilhelm Fast took part in an expedition to the area, he was similarly struck by the devastation. 'The first time I saw the fallen trees, I was in awe,' he remembered.

The alignment of the trees suggested that they had been blown over by the shock waves. Most scientists agree that the object which wrought this havoc was at least 50 m in diameter, although whether it came from an asteroid or a comet is still a subject of debate. No crater has been found, only a roughly circular area of swamp at the centre of the ravaged area. As for the orange glow in the night skies, one theory is that the force generated by the blast sent huge amounts of dust shooting high into the upper atmosphere, where it reflected light from the Sun.

Asteroids that break free

At the time of the 1927 Tunguska expedition, the study of asteroids (large bodies of rock and iron that orbit the Sun like minor planets) was in its infancy, and the notion that they have the potential to crash into Earth was relatively new. The main asteroid belt between Mars and Jupiter had been identified by the end of the 18th century, but only by the 1920s were scientists beginning to realise that some asteroids break free – and that some of these head towards Earth.

The Tunguska bolide burned up in mid-air, but other extraterrestrial rocks survive the fiery journey through the atmosphere and plough into the planet's surface. Known as meteorites (see page 186), these leave a telltale crater. One of the first to be identified was Barringer Crater (or Meteor Crater) in the Arizona desert, USA. Scientists believe that about 50,000 years ago a 40 m wide meteorite dug this pit, which is 1 km (just over ½ mile) wide and 200 m deep.

Currently, there are 170 known impact craters, some so large that the impact would have had a catastrophic global effect. One is believed to have brought about the mass extinction of the dinosaurs 65 million years ago. Geologists came to this conclusion when they found that the layer of rock corresponding to the time of the extinction contained a higher than expected amount of iridium – this was consistent throughout the world. Iridium is rare on Earth but relatively common in meteorites. The concentration of the metal pointed to a massive asteroid impact, which dispersed vaporised iridium all over the planet. Scientists calculated that the asteroid would have been enormous – roughly 10 km (6 miles) wide – and would have left a crater more than 160 km (100 miles) in diameter. They began looking for a suitably large crater

10 largest impact craters

Spotting impact craters has not always been easy, because the Earth's surface is constantly changing. They may be eroded, covered with vegetation or destroyed through the movements of tectonic plates. Now, thanks to aerial photography and satellite imaging, we can appreciate the density and size of the impacts.

	CRATER	LOCATION	AGE (YEARS)	DIAMETER (KM)
1	Vredefort	South Africa	< 2 billion	300
2	Sudbury	Canada	1.85 billion	250
3	Chicxulub	Mexico	65 million	170
4	Manicouagan	Canada	214 million	100
5	Popigay	Russia	35 million	100
6	Acraman	Australia	450 million	90
7	Chesapeake Bay	USA	35.5 million	90
8	Puchezh-Katunki	Russia	175 million	80
9	Morokweng	South Africa	145 million	70
10	Kara	Russia	73 million	65

Could we be hit again?

The asteroid that dug the Chicxulub crater was 10 km (6 miles) across, but an asteroid only 1 km (¹/₂ mile) wide would be enough to have global consequences. On impact, it would flatten an area the size of England, killing millions.

According to Kevin Yates, Space Communications Manager at the UK's National Space Centre, it is not a question of whether Earth will collide with an asteroid, but when. 'The likelihood is 100 per cent,' he says. 'But in terms of the timescale, it is difficult to put a number on it, and it depends on the size of asteroid you are talking about. Something that is 100 m across hits the Earth roughly every 800–1,000 years, while an asteroid of 1 km diameter makes an impact every few hundred thousand years. Something like the event in Chicxulub happens every 100 million years.'

Although the chances of being hit by an asteroid big enough to cause a global catastrophe remain slight, there are plenty of smaller asteroids. If one of these hits Earth it could cause utter devastation on a national or local scale.

To combat the threat, astronomers are keeping their telescopes trained on the skies, looking for rogue asteroids whose paths may bring them uncomfortably close to Earth. By May 2006, they had recorded more than 4,000 Near Earth Objects (NEOs), and around 55 new ones are being discovered every month.

The ultimate aim is to spot a potentially devastating asteroid before it comes close, allowing us to deflect it from its course. But we would need to identify it decades in advance, because the technology to deflect an asteroid is still in its infancy.

Even with thousands of telescopes searching the sky, there is a chance that we will not see the big one when it comes. Kevin Yates says: 'If it comes from the direction of the Sun, no telescope on Earth would spot it.' In 2002, an asteroid called 2002MN did just that. It came incredibly close to Earth from the direction of the Sun, and no one had the slightest idea. 'We did not know about it until three days later,' says Kevin. '2002MN was within the Moon's orbit, and at 100 m across, if it had hit us it would have caused a Tunguska-scale event.'

of the right age, and found it in 1990, in Mexico's Yucatán peninsula. The Chicxulub crater is buried, but geological surveys estimate that it is 180 km (110 miles) across.

The impact creating such an enormous hole would have released energy equivalent to around a billion tonnes of TNT. It is thought that 100 trillion tonnes of the Earth's crust would have been smashed and sent flying into the air. Besides the immediate destruction from rocks falling like bombs from the sky, the heat of the impact would have ignited massive forest fires and its force would have caused earthquakes and tsunamis over thousands of miles. The sky would have darkened from the mass of dust and debris, leading to a rapid global drop in temperature. The whole world would have been affected, and it is not surprising that many species, including the dinosaurs, did not survive.

Near misses

The past 100 years have brought some near misses by asteroids, although all were far smaller than the one which created Chicxulub. In 1937, an 800 m wide asteroid known as Hermes sped past Earth at a distance not much farther away than the Moon. In March 1989, an asteroid called 4581 Asclepius, approximately 400 m wide, passed by just 650,000 km (400,000 miles) away – again, little farther off than the Moon. On March 18, 2004, the 30 m wide 2004FH made the closest known approach by an asteroid, speeding past at a distance of just 43,000 km (26,720 miles) – not much more than the circumference of the Earth.

On December 24, 2004, NASA's Near Earth Object Program gave another asteroid a 1-in-37 chance of hitting the Earth. Asteroid 2004MN4 is 400 m in diameter and could have caused serious damage had it struck. Astronomers are still watching 2004MN4. Now known as 99942 Apophis, it is on course for another fly-by on April 13, 2029, when it will come so close to Earth that its orbit will be changed by our planet's gravity. Astronomers calculate that if by chance it passes through a narrow patch of space, known as a 'gravitational keyhole', its orbit will change in a way that will make it hit Earth in 2036.

Water

Boxing Day Tsunami

Morning prayers were over in the Sumatran coastal town of Banda Aceh, and the mosque had emptied. It was 7.55 am, but there was no rush to work or school. It was, after all, Sunday, December 26, the day after Christmas.

In his house in the east of the town, Jusuf Umar and his family were having breakfast. As they sat around the table, the crockery started to shake. Suddenly, the whole fabric of the house was creaking and pictures were falling off the walls. Jusuf jumped to his feet and stumbled as the ground moved beneath him. He had felt earthquakes before, but nothing like this. Could it be a tsunami (from the Japanese word for harbour wave)? He had to get the family to high ground. Grabbing his wife by the arm, he pulled her towards the front door and shouted at his two sons to follow. 'We have got to get out of here! Get on the bike!' All around, people were streaming from their homes. Although the ground was still shaking periodically, everybody was trying to get inland as fast as they could and by any means possible. With his wife riding pillion and his two sons perched precariously on the motorbike, Jusuf roared down the street. Another tremor threw the bike into a wobble. Soon they reached the edge of town. Ahead, across a narrow plain covered with rice paddies, the land rose towards forested hills.

They quickly reached the hills and started to climb. Jusuf glanced back. The tide seemed to have gone out farther than ever before, and new islands of sand had appeared where water had previously been. He stopped, but kept the engine running. The tremors had ended but there was a new noise – a distant roar. Looking over the town, he saw a line on the horizon getting ever bigger. The tsunami was coming. They had to get higher.

A minute later they were nearing the top of the hill. But now they could not go higher or farther inland without driving downhill first, and they simply would not have time. Jusuf stopped the bike, and they all watched as a wall of water engulfed the seaward edge of the town. It was vast – twice the height of the tallest coconut palms. Below them, the plain filled with people fleeing as the town disappeared. Behind the wave front a surge of water swamped everything as it poured inland. A bus on the outskirts of the town was tossed up and swept away like a toy. All the time the roar was getting louder, accompanied by the sound of snapping treetrunks.

An hour passed and the water retreated out to sea. Jusuf scanned the town and the plain and saw utter devastation. The main mosque

7 hours that shook the world

00.58 GMT
EARTHQUAKE An undersea earthquake measuring 9.3 on the Richter Scale occurs off Indonesia. Fifteen minutes later, scientists in Hawaii issue a bulletin recording the quake.

+15 minutes
SUMATRA IS HIT The Indonesian island of Sumatra, close to the epicentre of the quake, is hit by the full force of the tsunami. Many towns and villages in Aceh province on the western tip of the island are completely washed away, and the capital, Banda Aceh, is destroyed. Some villages lose as many as 70 per cent of their inhabitants.

+30 minutes
ANDAMAN ISLANDS STRUCK Lying only 100 km (60 miles) from the epicentre of the earthquake, the remote Andamans are next to be hit. At least 1,900 people die. A year later 5,500, mainly from Katchall island, are still missing.

THE FIRST SURGE
People turn and start to run as the first wave of the tsunami smashes into beach huts along the coast of Thailand.

On December 26, 2004, a giant tsunami hit the coastlines all round the Indian Ocean, leaving over 250,000 people dead.

the beach. From the balcony of their second-floor hotel room, his wife Beverley looked on in horror.

'The second wave was the largest,' she recalls. 'I'd say it was about 15 ft. The water just smashed everything in its path. It came up over the beach, over the road running along the beach front, behind the main part of the hotel, and swept away four-wheel-drive vehicles.

'Water surged into the hotel lobby of our wing, on the other side of the road, and smashed the windows of shops fronting the street.'

SWEEPING ALL BEFORE IT *The first wave hits the Sheraton Grande Laguna Resort in Phuket, Thailand. Within seconds, the hotel grounds are inundated. As the water continues to rise, a local man clings to a tree to avoid being carried away.*

was still standing, but most other buildings had gone. Wrecked fishing boats lay where houses once stood, and bodies were strewn everywhere.

Next in line

An hour after it hit Sumatra, the tsunami reached Thailand. It had lessened slightly in height and power but still struck the Thai coast with incredible force. Canadian Don Howie was snorkelling off the resort island of Phuket when the waves hit. He could feel the water being sucked out from under him.

'The sea surged out for about 200 m,' he says. 'There was nothing left but sand. Luckily, I was standing on the rocks where I had been looking at the fish and coral. Anyone swimming in line with the middle of the beach must have been dragged well out to sea.'

Before he could react, the first giant wave bowled him over. Don suffered cuts and scratches as he was dragged over the rocks and coral, but managed to pull his head above water and ride the surge up and along

Before the second wave struck, Howie and other survivors from the beach managed to scramble up a hill behind the sea front, guided by hotel staff. This almost certainly saved their lives; thousands along Thailand's west coast were not so lucky.

Paradise lost

The tsunami was caused by movement along a fault line running through the seabed of the Indian Ocean. As the fault runs north-south, the waves travelled out across the ocean in mainly easterly and westerly directions. Coastlines to the north of the fault line, such as that of Bangladesh, were affected far less than those to the east and west.

One of the worst-hit places was Sri Lanka, which lay almost directly west of the earthquake's epicentre. Although the waves had travelled more than 1,000 km (620 miles) across the ocean, they had lost little of their devastating power and in places surged several kilometres inland.

Most people who witnessed the tsunami were on land when it hit, but Warren Lavender and his wife experienced the terrifying power of the waves from a totally different perspective.

'We were about 20 m down, scuba-diving off the shore of Sri Lanka, when the first wave hit,' Lavender remembers. 'All of a sudden the current became unbelievable. Everyone held onto coral or whatever they could to prevent themselves from being swept away.

'As we surfaced, the boat, which had been tied to a buoy, was still intact. We headed back to the dive centre, but as we neared it we saw that the beach had simply disappeared. We could see the hotels in a

CONTINUED ON PAGE 200 »

+1.30 hours
WAVE HITS THAILAND
The packed resorts of Phuket and Krabi lie directly in the path of the tsunami and both are struck. Farther south, the tsunami has less impact as the shielding land mass of Sumatra blocks some of its energy, but it still causes great devastation. Just under 5,400 people die in Thailand, half of them tourists. Thousands more are injured and nearly 3,000 go missing.

+2.00 hours
SRI LANKA STRUCK
With nothing between it and the epicentre of the earthquake but open ocean, Sri Lanka bears the full brunt of the tsunami. Tens of thousands of lives are lost here – more than in any country other than Indonesia. The island's coast is mostly low-lying, and in many places water sweeps for miles inland.

+3.30 hours
WAVE HITS MALDIVES
With no continental shelf to lift the tsunami's waves as they near shore, the Maldives gets off relatively lightly. The capital, Malé, suffers little significant damage, and fewer than 110 people out of a population, including tourists, of around 300,000 lose their lives.

+7.00 hours
WAVE HITS SOMALIA
AND THE EAST AFRICAN COAST Having travelled across the Indian Ocean, the tsunami finally strikes Africa. Despite the time lapse it arrives unexpectedly, and hundreds of people are killed. In Somalia, 142 people are drowned. The most distant casualties occur in Tanzania, more than 4,000 km (2,500 miles) from the epicentre of the quake.

TRAIL OF DEBRIS *After peaking, the surge water recedes out to sea, depositing the wreckage as it goes.*

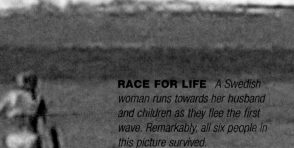

RACE FOR LIFE *A Swedish woman runs towards her husband and children as they flee the first wave. Remarkably, all six people in this picture survived.*

Anatomy of the Boxing Day tsunami

The waves that ravaged the coasts around the Indian Ocean on December 26 were giant ripples caused by a cataclysmic tectonic event 6 km (3³/₄ miles) below the sea. Along a fault line two sections of the Earth's crust juddered and shifted as one slid beneath the other.

The plates that make up the Earth's crust are constantly moving, and the lines where they meet are areas of intense seismic and volcanic activity. Along the fault line where the tsunami began, the plate that forms part of the floor of the Indian Ocean is continually being pushed towards and under the plate that carries Sumatra and the landmass of South-east Asia.

Friction prevents the plates sliding past one another, and large forces build up. When these forces become great enough to overcome the friction, the plates slip suddenly with a jolt or series of judders, which we experience as an

earthquake. Measuring 9.3 on the Richter Scale, the earthquake that caused the Asian tsunami was one of the largest on record and the biggest anywhere on the planet for 40 years.

As the two plates jolted past each other, the seabed along the fault line cracked and buckled. On the eastern side, it was forced upwards several metres, displacing hundreds of km² of water. This water bulged upwards and then fell back in on itself, causing waves that moved out from the fault line at speed.

In the open ocean, the wave fronts travelled at around 800 km/h (500 mph).

They were so low and far apart that they went unnoticed. As the wave fronts neared a coastline and the water got progressively shallower, the waves slowed down and merged, and the wave height increased.

Survivors reported first seeing the sea go out, as if drawn back by some sudden, very low tide. This was due to the trough that preceded each wave. The waves arrived at intervals of between 5 and 40 minutes. Each took minutes to pass, washing over the land like water might slosh over the edge of a bathtub. Most coastlines experienced several waves in succession.

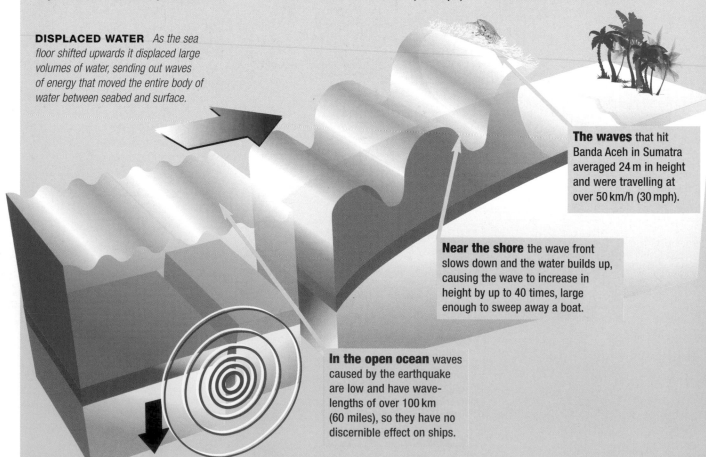

DISPLACED WATER *As the sea floor shifted upwards it displaced large volumes of water, sending out waves of energy that moved the entire body of water between seabed and surface.*

The waves that hit Banda Aceh in Sumatra averaged 24 m in height and were travelling at over 50 km/h (30 mph).

Near the shore the wave front slows down and the water builds up, causing the wave to increase in height by up to 40 times, large enough to sweep away a boat.

In the open ocean waves caused by the earthquake are low and have wavelengths of over 100 km (60 miles), so they have no discernible effect on ships.

ALL QUIET *This low-level satellite image shows the resort town of Kalutara, Sri Lanka, minutes before the tsunami arrived. Small waves break gently along the beach and everything seems normal.*

RECEDING SURF *As the front of the tsunami surge slows and the back builds up, water is drawn away from the coast. Unaware why this was happening, curious onlookers followed the retreating water, putting themselves in danger.*

PATHS OF DESTRUCTION
The tsunami travelled at great speed and covered huge distances, causing casualties as far away as Africa, thousands of kilometres from where it began.

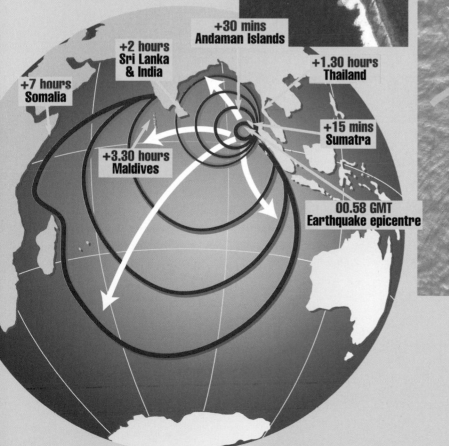

+30 mins
Andaman Islands

+2 hours
Sri Lanka & India

+1.30 hours
Thailand

+7 hours
Somalia

+15 mins
Sumatra

+3.30 hours
Maldives

00.58 GMT
Earthquake epicentre

SWEPT AWAY *One of several tsunami waves comes swirling into Kalutara, which is already under water.*

shambles – some of them collapsing – and tonnes of debris in the water. Somehow we landed and then we saw another wave heading for us. We ran for our lives.'

The aftermath

The Asian tsunami left chaos behind it. Where hours before there had been towns, villages and beach resorts bustling with life, now there was rubble, debris and dead bodies. Those who had survived stumbled through the twisted wreckage of what they had once known. Some were crying, searching frantically for lost loved ones. Others were silent, bewildered and dazed.

'The whole town was destroyed,' recalls Deepa from Galle in southern Sri Lanka. 'It was like a dream. I had never seen anything like it.'

Even in a war zone many buildings are spared, but the tsunami missed nothing. Everything in its path was destroyed, badly damaged or just swept away. 'The second wave carried a car right past me,' says Les Boardman, an Australian who was on holiday in the Thai resort island of Phuket. As the waves receded, he says, 'you could see bodies going out with the water.'

In Patong Beach, on Phuket, there were similar scenes. 'I just couldn't believe what was happening before my eyes,' says Boree Carlsson, a Swedish worker in a neighbouring hotel. 'As I was standing there, a car actually floated into the lobby and overturned because the current was so strong.'

LOST LIVELIHOODS *In the Indian state of Tamil Nadu, fishing boats wrecked by the tsunami are left piled high.*

10 worst tsunamis

The Boxing Day tsunami of 2004 was by far the most destructive tsunami on record, and caused more fatalities than any other natural disaster since the Tangshan earthquake of 1976. Many past tsunamis have also caused great loss of life.

	DATE	PLACE	ESTIMATED DEATHS
1	2004	Indian Ocean	250,000
2	1782	South China Sea	40,000
3	1883	Krakatoa (Sunda Strait, Indonesia)	36,000
4	1707	Japan	30,000
5	1826	Japan	27,000
6	1868	Chile	25,674
7	1896	Japan	22,070
8	1792	Japan	15,030
9	1771	Japan	13,486
10	1703	Japan	5,233

Tens of thousands had been killed by the tsunami, but an even greater number – half a million across all the areas hit – were injured, and the task of seeing to their needs fell on anyone who could help.

'We heard coughing from the debris of a collapsed building,' remembers Neil, a Briton who was on holiday on Thailand's Koh Phi Phi islands. 'We followed the sounds and found a young Thai girl who had taken in a lot of water. I remember thinking how difficult it was to carry her. She was only small, but being virtually unconscious made her a dead weight.'

Others recalled harrowing details of their rescue. Fiona from London was on a daytrip to a small island near Krabi, Thailand, the morning the tsunami struck. She saved herself by clinging to a mangrove tree when the first wave hit, then lost consciousness. When she came round, she saw that her right leg was badly

quarter of a million people were killed by the tsunami. Around 40 per cent of those are still officially listed as missing, their bodies having been swept out to sea.

The worst-hit region by far was Aceh at the northern tip of Sumatra, which was around 1,000 km (620 miles) from the epicentre of the earthquake. In the short time the waves lasted, 167,000 people in Aceh and on the nearby island of Nias were drowned. In the town of Banda Aceh, three-quarters of the population were killed in just 15 minutes. The coastline was destroyed beyond recognition, virtually scoured clean of buildings and trees. Elsewhere in Indonesia, a further 69,000 people lost their lives, most of them on the island of Sumatra.

Sri Lanka suffered the second-highest death toll. In total, 35,000 people there were reported missing or killed – at least 800 died when a train was swept off the tracks near Telwatta. In addition, half a million Sri

broken. 'My foot was at an angle that wouldn't normally have been possible,' she says. 'At that point I saw Simon, my boyfriend, about 10 ft away ... With the help of a Norwegian man who then appeared, Simon managed to pull me out of the mangrove trees. That was when we realised that my leg was in a much worse state than we had originally thought. The tibia was snapped completely, like a twig, and all the skin on my lower leg seemed to have sloughed away.'

Within a few hours Fiona was on a boat back to Krabi, where she was taken to hospital. Four days later, she was moved to a hospital in Bangkok, where her leg was amputated. Despite everything she is thankful to be alive. 'We later found out that 20 people died on the island that day,' she says. 'Without Simon and the others who helped, I don't think I would be here today.'

After the sea had withdrawn and the injured had been rescued, the grim business of counting and identifying the dead began. The process took days, and many bodies remained unclaimed. In total, over a

A GEOGRAPHY LESSON SAVES LIVES

The Asian tsunami caught thousands of people by surprise, but not ten-year-old English schoolgirl Tilly Smith, who was on holiday with her family in Phuket, Thailand. As the sea began to churn and retreat, exposing the seabed, Tilly recognised the first signs of a tsunami, which she had recently learnt about in school. 'I noticed that when we went down to the sea, it was all frothy like on the top of a beer. It was bubbling,' she says. 'I was having visions from the Hawaiian videos that I had seen two weeks before.' She told her mother, Penny, who took no notice until Tilly became hysterical. Penny told her husband, who explained the danger to a security guard. The message spread and the beach began to clear. Minutes later, the tsunami struck.

LIFE-SAVER *Thanks to Tilly, no one who had been on her beach was killed or seriously injured.*

Lankans were made homeless. The south and east coasts of the island were the worst hit, with the waves surging well over 1 km (1/2 mile) inland.

Most other casualties were in Thailand and India. Just under 5,400 people were confirmed dead in Thailand, around 2,400 of them foreigners from 36 different countries. Another 2,800 Thais and foreign tourists are still officially recorded as missing. India lost some 16,000 people, almost half of them from the

Andaman and Nicobar Islands in the southern part of the Bay of Bengal. People were also killed in Myanmar (Burma), Bangladesh, Malaysia, the Maldives, the Seychelles, Somalia, Kenya and Tanzania.

Tsunami triggers a flood of kindness

The worst natural disaster of the 21st century – so far – produced the greatest-ever international humanitarian response. A year after the event, a review showed that charities and private individuals had given more than

HUMAN COST *A man holds the hand of his dead son, killed by the tsunami in Cuddalore, southern India.*

TWISTED METAL *One of the single greatest losses of life occurred near Telwatta, Sri Lanka, where a packed train was ripped off the tracks by a 9 m wave. At least 800 – and possibly as many as 1,500 – people were killed. The force of the wave was so great that the tracks were uprooted and twisted out of shape.*

US$4 billion in humanitarian aid to places hit by the tsunami. That represented 67 per cent of all the money spent, dwarfing even the largest official government donation – US$500 million pledged and delivered by the government of Japan.

In the UK, leading charities under the auspices of the Disasters Emergency Committee raised more than £420 million (US$735 million), the equivalent of £7 (over US$12) for every person in the country. Much more was raised by smaller charities and committed individuals. In total, the UK's charitable contribution made up over one-eighth of all the humanitarian aid for the disaster given by charities and governments worldwide.

In many other European countries and in the USA record amounts were donated to the tsunami relief funds. The level of the response was so great that some charities were almost overwhelmed. UNICEF, for example, received almost twice the global donations it had anticipated. The financial response from the public has made a huge difference to the speed and scope of reconstruction, improving the lives and futures of millions of people.

A year after the disaster, the US government had given US$133 million of the US$350 million it had pledged. Canada had delivered all of its US$100 million in aid. The British, Chinese, Italian and Australian governments had given well over 80 per cent of what they had promised. But despite the cash that poured in from every corner of the world, in the first days after the disaster it seemed hard to imagine that the region would ever be the same again.

A new beginning

For many, a return to normality meant starting again and rebuilding the fabric of their lives. As well as money, humanitarian organisations and overseas volunteers contributed valuable skills and enthusiasm. But it was the survivors who drove the process. Far from giving up or moving away, they were determined to regain what they had lost. In most cases, they succeeded. A year after it had been reduced to rubble, Banda Aceh was largely rebuilt. The town had regained its vitality, and people were settling down and even making plans for the future.

The same signs of recovery are evident in all the countries hit by the tsunami. In Thailand, for instance, the hotels have been repaired and refurbished, and other resort facilities rebuilt. In 2005, almost as many foreign holidaymakers visited Thailand as had done in the year before the tsunami. For a region where tourism underpins the economy this was important, speeding up the recovery. Many tourists were pleased to help by spending their money where it was needed.

Surviving the tsunami

Jerome Kerr-Jarrett and his girlfriend Felix, holidaying on the south coast of Sri Lanka outside Galle, narrowly escaped death when their beachfront cabana – raised on stilts just 10 m from the shoreline – was torn apart by the tsunami.

'I was in the bathroom when I realised something was wrong. I could hear the sound of water swirling beneath it and the sea was unusually noisy.

'As I turned to walk back into the main room a jet of water shot up through the toilet and I could hear Felix in the main room shouting that water was coming into the hut.

'I recall trying to calm the situation by saying not to worry, as it must be a very high tide. When I opened the front door I could see swirls of sea frothing white all around us.

'The second time I opened it I let the waves in and the water broke through the front wall. I was thrown against the concrete back wall of the cabana and became trapped when a wardrobe fell on me. Felix stumbled through the floating debris and managed to pull me out.

'We then made our way out of the cabana though the broken-down front wall but became separated as Felix was pulled beneath the cabana structure and trapped, underwater, against the main floor frame. I lost her at this point amongst the waves and force of the current. It was not until a break in the current that she was able to get her head above water.

'I remember saying very little, except shouting to Felix that she needed to follow me. I let go of the cabana structure and was immediately taken about 20 ft to the right of the hut, treading water over what was once another open-air hut, used for relaxing.

'I kept my focus on Felix, who, having just emerged from under water, was still holding on to a support pillar on the cabana. I was shouting to her to swim. Eventually, she let go and together we managed to reach a tree, which was sticking up out of the water opposite the beach bar.

'We were still treading in deep water and just behind us was the first floor balcony of the bar's rooms. We could have swum to our left to an outside staircase that would have led us to safety. However, it meant going over what was once the bar's parking lot and I feared we would either be injured by the floating wood and debris or get bashed against what we could not see under the water, such as cars, my motorbike that had been parked there and most certainly a couple of three-wheeled tuk-tuks. My thoughts were that what we could not see could hurt us and in fact were safer holding to the tree.

'The whole experience lasted about 20 minutes, and we received cuts and lacerations to our bodies but thankfully we escaped without any serious injury. We remained holding on to the tree until the water receded. Once we could touch the ground we walked out to safety.

Jerome Kerr-Jarrett

Atlantic tsunami

Following a volcanic eruption in 1949 on the island of La Palma in the Canaries, a 2 km (1¼ mile) long rupture opened up on the volcano's western side. A future eruption could trigger a landslide into the Atlantic Ocean, creating a tsunami even more devastating than the Asian one.

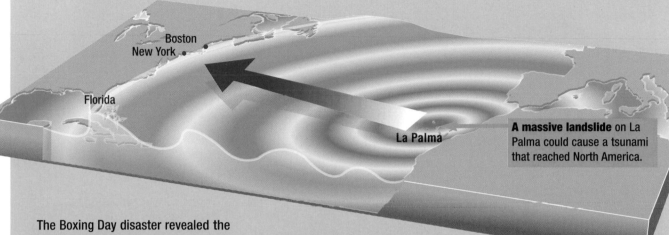

A massive landslide on La Palma could cause a tsunami that reached North America.

The Boxing Day disaster revealed the potential threat tsunamis pose across the world. But long before the Asian tsunami, scientists were already warning that a similar disaster could happen in the Atlantic, and that the east coast of North America was directly at risk. At the time, although it was not entirely ignored, the warnings set few alarm bells ringing.

Now, in the wake of the tragedy that befell Asia, American scientists are re-examining the potential for an Atlantic tsunami. And these days, rather than 'what if?', the question has become 'when?'.

The culprit for such a disaster is the volcanic island of La Palma, situated on the eastern side of the Atlantic, at the north-western end of the Canary Islands. The volcanoes on La Palma are currently quiet, but far from dead. In 1949, Cumbre Vieja erupted, opening up a crack in its western half.

Volcanologists say that Cumbre Vieja will erupt again and the crack will open further. It may take just one eruption or several, but eventually this fault line will become critically weakened. Then the entire western half of the volcano – some 500 km² (200 sq miles), or half a trillion tonnes of rock – will plunge into the ocean, causing a tsunami of catastrophic proportions. Near its starting point this wall of water could be as much as 650 m high, although it would lose height and power as it travelled westwards across the Atlantic. Some researchers believe it would strike the eastern seaboard of the USA as a giant surge some 50 m high, with enough force to plough on and cause havoc as far as 20 km (12 miles) inland.

As well as Cumbre Vieja, there is always the danger that a tsunami may result from an as-yet unidentified threat. After all, no one predicted the Boxing Day tsunami, and people living in coastal regions anywhere around the world could be affected.

In the Pacific Ocean, where tsunamis are relatively common, seismic activity and sea levels are constantly monitored so that giant waves can be detected long before they reach land. The Asian tsunami was particularly deadly because nobody knew it was coming.

In the wake of the disaster, the United Nations is setting up an Indian Ocean early-warning system. The UN says that the Indian Ocean system will be the first part of a global system for detecting tsunamis, to provide better protection for coastal communities around the world. The urgency of the task was underlined on March 28, 2005, when a magnitude 8.7 earthquake occurred between the islands of Nias and Simelue, off the west coast of Sumatra. The earthquake did not cause a tsunami, but it highlighted the potential for another in the future.

Th Black Dragon Roars

Every year, on the 18th day of the eighth month in China's lunar calendar, tourists from all over the country gather in the small eastern town of Yanguan. They come to witness the world's largest tidal bore – an enormous wave that roars up the Qiantang river from the East China Sea.

Funnelled by the river's trumpet-shaped mouth, the Black Dragon, as it is sometimes known, surges up the river at speeds of more than 30 km/h (20 mph), rising higher and higher as it goes, until it towers up to 9 m high, the size of a two-storey building.

In 1993, the eighth lunar month coincided with August in the Western calendar, and on August 18 people were preparing for the annual tide-watching festival all along the lower reaches of the Qiantang. Yanguan on the shores of its estuary is the best place to watch the Black Dragon and, as ever, it drew the biggest crowds. As the sun rose over the town, flags were raised and the smell of freshly baked moon cakes filled the air. On top of the 400-year-old Zhan'ao Pagoda, a huge battery of fireworks was primed for a celebratory display that evening.

Waiting for the wave

As morning turned to afternoon, anticipation mounted among the spectators jostling each other on Yanguan's stone-paved sea wall. Those who had been there before had come prepared with waterproof clothing and sporting umbrellas – spray from the bore is liable to wet everyone. Among the crowds, word spread that the wave was likely to be even larger than usual this year, as a typhoon had whipped up the waters offshore.

As always, the bore began its rise silently, travelling some distance up the estuary before it was visible. Gradually, with the main wave still far behind, the white caps along its leading edge started to merge, forming a snaking line from one bank of the estuary to the other. Opposite Yanguan, the water level rose visibly and then the thunder of the main wave made itself heard. Finally, a great wall of white water came into sight. Some locals who had joined the throng became nervous and backed away from the river banks as they noticed the wave's size. Most people, however, stood where they were, trusting that the concrete defences would protect them. Standing stock still, they stared, awestruck, into the face of the wave.

It hit Yanguan with terrifying ferocity, the sudden deluge washing away everything in its path. As the combined forces of tide and river poured over the banks, people on the sea wall were tossed away. Farther back, some were able to flee to safety, but many were too slow and were also caught up in the torrent.

TIDE-WATCHERS *Tourists crowd the banks of the Qiantang river in China to watch the world's largest tidal bore. This picture was taken in 2005, 12 years after the disaster that swept dozens to their deaths.*

In August 1993, 87 people died when the largest tidal bore ever recorded surged up China's Qiantang river.

Yanguan
In 1993, most people were swept away at this point.

CHINA

Hangzhou Bay
At its mouth, the bay is 100 km (60 miles) wide.

Wave height:
1–2 m

Wave height:
9.14 m

Wave height:
4–6 m

Qiantang river

Ganpu
The bay narrows to 22 km (14 miles), forcing the bore to rise.

BREEDING A DRAGON
The largest bores occur when the incoming tide collides with river water swelled by months of rain.

By the time the bore had passed, dozens in Yanguan were dead, and the destruction continued as the wave rushed upstream, taking more lives. When evening came, 87 people had been killed and over 100 injured. It had been the largest tidal bore ever recorded anywhere in the world. At one stage, the wave was 9.14 m from trough to peak and it had travelled at around 40 km/h (25 mph).

The Everest in surfing

The thrill of watching the Black Dragon has a long history – the earliest references are from the 4th century BC. The wave has always brought death, with past bores killing as many as 10,000 people at a time, dwarfing the 1993 disaster. Yet still the visitors come, hoping to see for themselves the drama and spectacle of this natural phenomenon, despite the perennial danger. One thing that has always impressed people is the thunder of the approaching wave. In the words of one Chinese poet, Li Kuo, it was as 'loud as a million marching men', while to Shi Yushan it was like 'ten thousand mountains crashing down in a landslide'.

Nowadays, it also tempts adventurers. In September 1988, a team of English 'bore riders', surfers who relish the danger of riding tidal bores, made an attempt on the Black Dragon. 'It must be the ultimate challenge, the Everest in surfing,' said team-member Stuart Matthews. 'We saw a

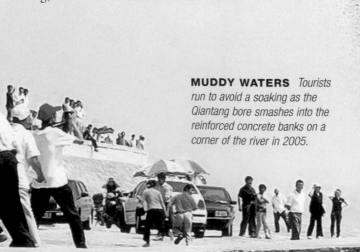

MUDDY WATERS *Tourists run to avoid a soaking as the Qiantang bore smashes into the reinforced concrete banks on a corner of the river in 2005.*

10 ft wave out there and that's the small one,' he went on. 'Behind that it was 15 ft and there was an enormous hole. The size of the wave matters in increments of fear ...' In the end, Matthews rode the bore twice when it reached a height of 8m. Other people try to race the bore in their cars, tearing along roads on the river banks.

Killing the god of the tides

There have been a number of attempts to tame the bore's destructive powers. According to legend, one Chinese king, Qian Lu (AD 852-932), tried to build dykes along the river banks to restrain it, but the god of the tides, who was believed to cause the bore, repeatedly thwarted his efforts. Eventually, the king ordered his archers to fire 10,000 arrows into the wave to kill the deity. The attack was apparently successful and after that the king was able to build permanent dykes. Today, the river bears his name: Qiantang literally means 'Qian's dykes'.

10 tidal bores

Although the Qiantang bore is the world's highest tidal bore, it is far from unique. Others exist on rivers and estuaries all around the world:

Canal do Norte Pororoca, Brazil The Amazonian *pororoca* (meaning 'mighty noise') can reach a height of 3 m in the river's northern mouth.

Gironde Mascaret, France This *mascaret* (bore) in south-western France is a favourite with 'bore riders'.

Hugli Bore, India A barrage across the Ganges, built in the 1970s, lessened the impact of the Hugli bore.

Lupar Benak, Malaysia In 1949, writer Somerset Maugham nearly drowned in the *benak* in Sarawak.

Petitcodiac Bore, Canada This is one of a number of bores on rivers flowing into Canada's Bay of Fundy.

Seine Mascaret, France This rivalled the Qiantang bore, until tamed by dredging in the Seine estuary.

Severn Bore, England Britain's most famous bore can reach as far inland as Gloucester and a height of 2 m.

Shubenacadie Bore, Canada This bore occurs twice a day on another river flowing into the Bay of Fundy.

Turnagain Arm Bore, USA The bore forms in the dramatic setting of a fjord off Cook Inlet in Alaska, overlooked by the Chugach Range.

Wager Bay Bore, Canada The most northerly recorded bore forms in an inlet off Hudson Bay. Its wave front regularly crests at 4.5 m.

In reality, the bore is largely a result of the Qiantang's geography, particularly the funnel shape of Hangzhou Bay into which it flows. At its mouth, the bay is about 100 km (60 miles) across, but 89 km (55 miles) upstream at Ganpu it narrows to just 22 km (14 miles). The bottleneck causes a huge increase in the tidal range as the incoming water is forced up the sides of the bay. As a result, spring tides (the highest of the month, shortly after each Full and New Moon) are exceptionally high at Ganpu. Upstream, the river also contains a large sandbar, which deforms the incoming tidal surge, causing it to break as a wave front.

The bores vary in height during the year, depending in part on the size of the tides. But the river itself also plays a part. In August and early September, when the largest bores tend to form, the Qiantang is full to the brim with the run-off from five months of rain. The collision between the mass of water flowing downstream and the surge of the tide flowing up creates a strong wave front. In addition, stormy seas and easterly winds can drive spring tides even higher. When this occurs, as it did in August 1993, the bore can force the swollen river over its banks with unprecedented force.

Most years, a few people who come for the tide-watching festival ignore warnings and are swept to their deaths. But the closest Yanguan has come to the 1993 disaster was on September 9, 2002. With a bore almost as high as in 1993, the town was again inundated – but this time, miraculously, nobody was killed.

ON BOARD A BORE *A surfer riding the Pororoca bore on the Amazon's Canal do Norte. Unlike coastal waves, tidal bores continue breaking, often for miles. The Qiantang bore has never been ridden successfully over any significant distance.*

Hard Rain in Mumbai

On the morning of July 27, 2005, the world's third-largest and India's most populous city was under water. The monsoon brings rain to the parched Indian subcontinent every summer, but that year's downpour in Mumbai was so intense that it set a new global record.

> **The road outside our office was flowing like a river. But the flood of people walking eclipsed the floods themselves.**
>
> *Ganesh Nadar*

In previous summers, even the heaviest downpours soon drained away. This time the rain collected so that streets resembled rivers. People died in their hundreds, and thousands more were trapped in vehicles, homes and schools. Many residents blamed the city planners for their predicament. Mumbai, capital of the state of Maharashtra, is on the coast, and storm drains that snapped shut to keep out high tidewater were instead keeping the rainwater in. But the real cause of the disaster could not have been predicted. Over a period of 24 hours, Mumbai received 944.2 mm of rain, more than had ever been recorded for one day in any city anywhere in the world, and about the same amount as Chicago receives in a year. Even by monsoon standards, this downpour was extreme. The previous daily record for Mumbai was 575.6 mm, set on July 5, 1974. The 2005 deluge not only exceeded that, but it set a new record for the whole of India, surpassing the previous high of 838.2 mm that had fallen on Cherrapunji on July 12, 1910.

A submerged city

Although heavy rain had been falling periodically during the previous week, the real downpour began on the night of July 25. As the people of Mumbai woke the next morning, many streets had begun to flood. Temporary flooding in some areas during the monsoon is common, so few people took particular notice of the ankle-deep water. Children were sent to school and adults walked or drove to work as normal. But the heavy rain continued without respite and the flood waters steadily rose. By the time people began to realise the seriousness of the situation, many of them were

CONTINUED ON PAGE 213 »

FERRYING ESSENTIALS
A human chain relays packs of food and drinking water into one of the worst-affected areas. Many people were trapped in buildings without any supplies.

A SEA OF UMBRELLAS
As streets all over the huge city flooded, traffic came to a halt and people waded through the floods to get home.

In July 2005, 24 hours of rain overwhelmed Mumbai, India's commercial and entertainment capital.

A MONSOON VORTEX

The monsoon is a wind pattern that occurs because land heats up and cools down more quickly than the ocean. As the landmass of India warms up in summer, air over the land rises. This creates an area of low pressure that draws in moisture-laden air – the monsoon – from the Indian Ocean. Different parts of the Indian subcontinent heat up at different rates, and the path of the monsoon follows this pattern. It arrives in the far south around the beginning of June, moves north, then westwards, and reaches the border of Pakistan in the first or second week of July.

Meteorologists think that in July 2005 a series of vortices developed within the prevailing monsoon trough. Monsoon vortices cause very heavy downpours over small areas about 30 km (18 miles) wide. They are rare, unpredictable and difficult to forecast.

A STATE-WIDE DISASTER
Much of western Maharashtra's farmland was flooded, and 20,000 ha (50,000 acres) of land had its topsoil completely washed away, preventing farmers from replanting.

3 Low pressure forms as the wind rotates upwards, producing a localised cloudburst.

Mumbai (Bombay)

INDIA

MAHARASHTRA

Western Ghats

2 The monsoon wind is blocked by the mountains, and begins to rotate around its own axis.

Normal course of winds

GOA

1 Moisture-laden monsoon wind blasts in strongly from the Arabian Sea and meets the Western Ghats mountain range.

ARABIAN SEA

Monsoon vortices can cause exceptional but localised downpours along the coastal plain between the Western Ghats and the Arabian Sea.

THE CLEAN-UP BEGINS
A woman throws disinfectant powder onto the streets. The city's drains and sewers had flooded, raising the threat of water-borne diseases.

already trapped in their homes and offices. Streets that normally escaped flooding began to disappear under water and before long, a third of this city of 15 million people had been inundated.

Everywhere, traffic ground to a halt as roads became impassable. 'My wife phoned late yesterday morning and told me the floods in the suburbs were getting worse,' said Sanjay Shah from his office in the city centre the following day. 'She thought I should come home but I ignored her advice. I wish I hadn't – I have been stuck here the whole night.'

The floods had pushed the city into chaos. Those who had left work early probably wished they had stayed where they were. Many drivers were forced to abandon their cars as the flood waters continued rising. Those who took public transport fared little better. Buses, like cars, were caught in jams, and parts of the rail network were out of action as the tracks became flooded. Many passengers spent the night where they were. In some parts of the city people couldn't even walk home. 'It seemed as if the entire population was out on the streets,' said Sunita Masani. Some found themselves wading up to their necks in water.

'The road outside our office was flowing like a river,' said Ganesh Nadar. 'But the flood of people walking eclipsed the floods themselves. There were young men on the streets keeping people away from potholes and gutters. Children were floating on inflated

> ❝ **Before I could do anything my car was afloat ... I tried to balance it by moving from one seat to another.** ❞
>
> *Kiran Joshi*

car tyres, and one man was talking on his mobile phone, ignoring the rain completely. The rains may have paralysed the city, but they had not paralysed the spirit of the people.'

Most of Mumbai's population is used to occasional hardship and, across the city, the floods seemed to bring out the best in people, rather than causing despair. 'What I saw on the streets was remarkable,' said Bharat Mahajan. 'People were handing out food and water to strangers, and opening their homes to them.' Akshay Khatri agreed: 'The people have been so strong and cooperative. I did not see a single fight, no religious clashes. Many people on the streets were singing songs.'

SILVER LINING

India's season to be jolly

Although the monsoon can bring death and destruction, to most people in most years it signals hope and new life. Every summer, after months of dry heat, the monsoon brings rain to the parched lands of India. Its arrival is a cause for celebration and relief as the rain clears the air and washes away months of dust, fills wells and reservoirs, and waters freshly sown crops. Although floods and landslides are common during the monsoon season, the damage is usually far outweighed by the benefits of the rain. India is home to over a billion people, around one-sixth of the world's population. In a normal year, the monsoon may kill dozens of people, but it ensures the survival of countless more.

While most tales associated with that extraordinary day are of good humour, friendliness or occasional heroism, the floods also left a trail of destruction and death. In the northern suburb of Saki Naka the torrential rain caused a landslide, destroying homes and killing more than 60 people. 'I was scared the hill could fall,' sobbed Aslam Khan. 'I kept telling my cousin "let's leave", but he wouldn't listen. Now it's too late.'

Elsewhere, many were caught by the quickly rising floodwater and drowned, or were electrocuted by downed power lines. For most of the day much of Mumbai remained in chaos despite the efforts of the city authorities and the armed forces who were brought in to help.

One of the worst-hit areas was Kalina, in the southern half of the city close to the airport. Here, the waters rose very suddenly to a depth of almost 5m, catching many people unawares. Most of those on foot were able to scramble or swim to safety, but several people trapped in their cars were drowned.

Farther north, in the Goregaon district, Kiran Joshi narrowly escaped a similar fate. 'I took my car towards the main gate of Nirlon Compound. Suddenly, I saw some trees adjacent to the compound wall start bowing exceptionally low and I realised the danger. I was about to turn when the wall at my right side broke and a tremendous amount of water poured into the compound.

'Before I could do anything, my car was afloat – I had lost control of it completely. The flowing water drove my car for more than 100 ft. I tried to balance it by moving from one seat to another to stop it turning upside-down. I was totally helpless. Somehow, my car came to the side of the road. I shut off the engine and shouted for help. Some people rushed from a nearby shop and waded through the water to reach me. They forced the door open and dragged me out of the car. I was saved.'

The following morning, the waters were still high. Although the rain had eased, much of Mumbai remained flooded. There were fresh disasters as waterlogged buildings collapsed, crushing their occupants. Large areas of the city were left without power, and the roads were clogged with abandoned vehicles and the bodies of victims and animals. The final toll was more than 400 dead, and 17,000 homes damaged. The city would eventually recover from the catastrophe, although it would take time. In the words of Srini Viswanathan from his home in the suburb of Mulund: 'Nothing stops the Mumbai spirit.'

Living on borrowed time?

The rains that struck Mumbai on July 26, 2005, were the worst the city had ever known, and the flooding that followed was unprecedented. Although the rain fell much faster and in greater quantities than ever before, it should not have caused the problems it did. Why did it not simply drain away?

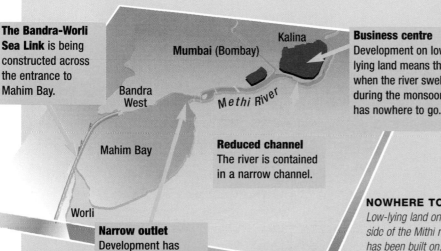

The Bandra-Worli Sea Link is being constructed across the entrance to Mahim Bay.

Kalina

Mumbai (Bombay)

Bandra West

Methi River

Mahim Bay

Worli

Business centre Development on low-lying land means that when the river swells during the monsoon, it has nowhere to go.

Reduced channel The river is contained in a narrow channel.

Narrow outlet Development has created a bottleneck.

NOWHERE TO GO *Low-lying land on either side of the Mithi river has been built on, and the river has been confined to a narrow channel.*

At the time of the deluge, the combination of Mumbai's antiquated and poorly maintained drainage system and closed storm drains prevented rainwater flowing away. The problem was made worse by the fact that, like many Indian cities, Mumbai has grown rapidly, and buildings have replaced the parks and other areas of open ground that used to soak up rainfall.

Development has also affected the city's natural drainage. One of the worst-hit areas, Kalina, lies next to the Mithi river, which divides south Mumbai from most of the suburbs. The Mithi is a seasonal river that swells during the monsoons. Low-lying, marshy land alongside the river used to take up any excess water if the river overspilled its banks, protecting the city. But in recent years, encroaching building developments have reduced the Mithi's width and construction debris has been dumped in the water. One section was recently diverted to make way for the

new Bandra Kurla business district, and this further compromised the river's capacity. On the day of the deluge, as rainwater poured down the narrowed river channel and met the incoming tide, the river burst its banks.

Development around the river was also blamed for the length of time that the floods took to drain away. The Bandra-Worli Sea Link, an eight-lane superhighway currently being built across the entrance to Mahim Bay, further restricts the river at its mouth. Even after the tide had fallen, much of the floodwater remained backed up in the city. It was like emptying a bath through an unusually small plughole.

Once the waters had receded, the problem facing Mumbai was to prevent a repetition of the flooding – a problem most politicians are appearing to ignore. Development continues on the last areas of open land around Mumbai, and the city's drainage system has yet to be overhauled. Roads, which effectively

cover the ground with a waterproof seal, continue to be built even though 88 per cent of the city's population uses public transport.

To further exacerbate the situation Mumbai's last stands of mangrove forest are being cleared to reclaim more land from the sea. This poses a new problem – coastal erosion – and deprives Mumbai of the natural barrier it once had against rising sea levels.

As a result Mumbai's future looks grim. The city is increasingly vulnerable to flooding, and any repeat of the rains of 2005 is likely to have similar consequences.

Some environmentalists believe that Mumbai is on a suicide mission. Bittu Sahgal, one of India's most respected experts on environmental issues, calls it 'a case study for the collapse of urbania in India.'

DOWN THE DRAIN *A city worker stands guard beside a manhole that has been opened to help the floodwaters drain away.*

Hailstorm over Sydney

At about 7.30 on a Thursday evening in 1999, Sydney in Australia came under an extraordinary hour-long bombardment – from hailstones the size of cricket balls. 'It sounded like an aeroplane was going to crash,' recalled one resident, Kim Parrey.

A ferocious storm had swept in off the Pacific and was battering the city, when the colossal lumps of ice came crashing down, smashing windows, denting cars and punching holes through roofs. They carried on falling for 20 minutes.

The timing of the storm on April 14 was fortunate, as most people were home from work and indoors. 'We got no warning,' said John Butt, a resident of the central Rushcutter's Bay district. 'If you were out in the street I am sure you would have been knocked unconscious.' Although no one was killed, much of Sydney was left looking like a war zone. The eastern suburb where Kim Parrey lived was particularly badly hit. Every house on her street was damaged and many roofs were almost entirely destroyed.

An unexpected battering

It was not the kind of weather most Sydneysiders had been expecting that evening. Earlier on, forecasters had predicted mild autumnal conditions. At the time of the broadcast, it looked as if the storm was heading further out to sea. But then it suddenly changed direction and turned inland.

What shocked Sydney residents was its intensity. Violent weather is not unusual in this part of the world, but nobody had seen damage on this scale before. When insurance officer David Jurd was called to Bishopscourt, the official residence of the Anglican Archbishop of Sydney, he found that the building's reinforced skylights had been shattered. 'Those skylights are meant to withstand being walked on, so the force of the hail must have been immense,' he recalled.

The storm proved more expensive than any other natural disaster in Australia. Insurance pay-outs alone totalled 1.7 billion Australian dollars (US$1.25 billion), and the full cost of repairs was much greater, because many homes and cars were not covered against 'acts of God'. More than 32,000 houses and 43,000 vehicles were damaged; lightning sparked at least 25 electrical fires, and around 15,000 homes were left without power. Traffic lights went down, and the emergency services were overrun with calls. Dozens of people were taken to hospital, many with cuts and abrasions from broken glass and splintered roof tiles.

The weight of the hailstones accounted for much of the havoc. Being large, they were unusually heavy. They were formed by powerful updraughts which repeatedly lifted them to high altitudes inside the storm clouds. When they finally became so heavy that the storm clouds could no longer support them, they plummeted to earth like miniature bombs, reaching speeds of over 200 km/h (124 mph).

Death from above

The Sydney storm was a natural disaster of immense proportions, but it was not the worst hailstorm on record in recent times. By a strange coincidence, that happened on April 14, 1986 – 13 years to the day before the Sydney storm – in the Gopalganj district of southern Bangladesh. The hailstones there were the

A PATCHWORK OF TARPAULINS *The hailstones were so large they smashed through roof tiles and slates, causing millions of dollars worth of damage.*

Dense lumps of ice crashed down on Sydney for 20 minutes, causing damage costing more than US$1.25 billion.

217

size of grapefruits; some weighed more than 1kg. And in Bangladesh 92 people died. The storm also destroyed many homes and killed large numbers of livestock.

Another dramatic episode involved an aircraft in South Africa on April 22, 1999 – just over a week after the Sydney storm. Giant hailstones battered a Boeing 727 flying into Johannesburg airport, and although the pilot landed safely and no one was hurt, the plane was so badly damaged it had to be scrapped. Events like this are surprisingly common – so much so that most airlines are insured against damage from hail.

❝ If you were out on the streets I am sure you would have been knocked unconscious. ❞

John Butt, Sydney resident

> **Out of nowhere I saw ... a wave that appeared to be twice the height of the average wave. It was just like a mountain, a wall of water.**
>
> *Göran Persson, First Officer of the Caledonian Star*

T

The biggest search and rescue operation in shipping history began with an SOS signal sent out just after 3 am Greenwich Mean Time (GMT) on December 12, 1978, in the Azores area of the North Atlantic. A severe storm was raging at the time, with winds blowing at near-hurricane strength.

Even so, the signal raised little alarm initially. The seas were terrifying enough to be a threat to smaller vessels, but the ship that sent it was a West German cargo freighter, the *München* – a 43,000 tonne giant, with state-of-the-art equipment and an experienced crew. Even damaged, a ship of her design could float for days. Yet, at the end of a ten-day search, scarcely any trace of the *München* or her 28 crew was found. When the hunt was finally abandoned on December 22, all that had been recovered was four empty life rafts, some lifebelts and a few other pieces of wreckage.

The pride of the fleet

The *München* had set sail from Bremerhaven on Germany's North Sea coast on December 7, bound for Savannah, Georgia, in the USA. The pride of the West German merchant navy, belonging to the Hapag-Lloyd line, she had been launched

only six years earlier and was widely regarded as one of the safest cargo vessels afloat – some had even called her 'unsinkable'.

The first part of the journey was uneventful. Then, near the Azores, the weather took a turn for the worse, and just after midnight on December 11/12 Jörg Ernst, the *München*'s radio operator, mentioned heavy seas and some damage they had caused – he was talking on a 'chat' frequency to his counterpart on a West German cruise liner. But conditions were not bad enough to be of undue concern to a ship of the *München*'s size. So other ships in the area were surprised to pick up her SOS signal after 3 am. The signal was transmitted in Morse code and only parts were intelligible, but it was clear that the ship was in trouble; a search and rescue operation was launched. Further mayday calls were received, the last picked up at a US naval base in Spain as late as 7.14 pm GMT on December 13.

As concern for the *München*'s fate mounted, more than 70 ships lined up 4.8 km (3 miles) apart and combed the ocean. The man in charge was the Dutch Captain Pieter de Nijs. 'We hoped to find the ship, or at least people … or a life raft with people,' he said afterwards. 'We never found a living soul.' The last trace of the *München* ever discovered was an empty lifeboat, salvaged by the Swedish-owned car transporter *Don Carlos* on February 16, 1979, more than two months after the fatal storm.

The disappearance of the *München* seemed inexplicable, and it was not until 1995 that new light was cast on the mystery. On New Year's Day that year, a 26 m high freak wave struck an oil rig in the North Sea. Previously, such giant waves had been known to occur only near the edges of ocean currents, where water flowing one way is

WALL OF WATER *A freak wave in the Bay of Biscay. The waves form in stormy seas and can swamp even the biggest vessels, putting their structures under unbearable strain.*

Freak waves are monsters – some as tall as a ten-storey building. One victim was almost certainly the cargo ship *München*.

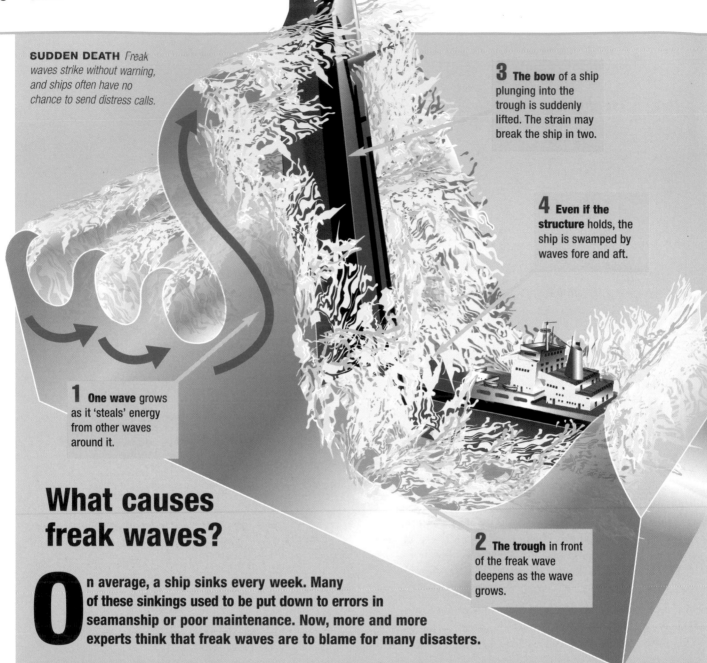

SUDDEN DEATH *Freak waves strike without warning, and ships often have no chance to send distress calls.*

3 The bow of a ship plunging into the trough is suddenly lifted. The strain may break the ship in two.

4 Even if the structure holds, the ship is swamped by waves fore and aft.

1 One wave grows as it 'steals' energy from other waves around it.

2 The trough in front of the freak wave deepens as the wave grows.

What causes freak waves?

On average, a ship sinks every week. Many of these sinkings used to be put down to errors in seamanship or poor maintenance. Now, more and more experts think that freak waves are to blame for many disasters.

Recent research using satellite images has shown that waves of 25 m or over occur somewhere on the planet every few days. Yet freak – or rogue – waves used to be considered a maritime myth, something traditional wave theory could not explain. Waves might vary in height, scientists believed, but they would always do so uniformly around an average. The sudden appearance of waves more than twice the size of those around them was considered almost impossible – scientists reckoned that they might occur, but only once in every 10,000 years or so.

So when the reality of more frequent freak waves became apparent, and in the open ocean away from currents, the hunt was on for new explanations. Texas-born wave mathematician Alfred Osborne has championed one possible answer, involving quantum physics. According to his theory, waves can steal the energy from others next to them. In choppy seas in deep water, where numerous unstable waves are moving at different speeds in different directions, one monster wave may emerge, sucking in energy from the others around it. The process can also

be compared to light being focused by a lens: the energy inherent in the waves is focused in one area, creating the freak wave.

Unlike normal waves, a freak wave forms a giant wall of water, preceded by a deep trough. This can smash into a ship with a force of 100 tonnes per square metre, far more than most vessels are built to withstand.

Osborne has tested his theory by artificially creating freak waves in a huge water tank. He even hopes to offer forecasts, predicting when and where freak waves are likely to occur.

sometimes hit by storm-driven swells moving in the opposite direction. Freak waves in the open ocean had previously been dismissed as impossible. Now one had occurred, and there was damage, along with dozens of eyewitnesses, to testify to it.

In the light of this event, investigators reviewing the evidence about the *München* concluded that something similar might have happened to her. Vital to their conclusion was the lifeboat the *Don Carlos* had picked up in February 1979. When the *München* left port, its lifeboats had hung a full 20 m above the waterline. This boat showed signs of having been ripped from its mount with incredible force. Only a freak giant wave could have battered the ship at that level.

Drama in the South Atlantic

Further evidence for freak waves in the open ocean came in March 2001, when two ships had terrifying encounters with them in the South Atlantic. The first was the *Caledonian Star*, a cruise liner returning from a trip around Antarctica. As a former North Sea fishing vessel converted into a passenger ship specialising in cruises in polar waters, she was designed to cope with the most extreme conditions. 'We had a weather forecast predicting gale force winds,' crew member Karl-Ulrich Lampe recalled. 'That didn't bother us at all.'

As the storm rolled in, the *Caledonian Star* found herself in seas with waves over 12 m high. Then, at 5.30 pm on March 2, First Officer Göran Persson witnessed something extraordinary. 'Out of nowhere I saw ... a wave that appeared to be twice the height of the average wave. It was just like a mountain, a wall of water.' As the wave came towards them, an enormous trough opened up in front of it. 'The ship went down at an angle. People were falling against the bulkheads in the forward part of whichever section they were in.'

The monstrous wave crashed onto the deck. 'The whole bridge was like an explosion,' Persson went on. 'I was washed away to the other side and I had to swim – I actually had to swim – back to the controls to be able to put the ship back on course.' The force of the wave had smashed the navigation equipment. 'It went through my mind,' said Persson, 'that we might not make it.' In fact, the *Caledonian Star* was fortunate. Although the ship had lost much of its instrumentation, the engines were still running. Once the crew had boarded up the smashed windows, Persson was able to guide her back to port.

The German cruise ship *Bremen* underwent a similar pounding the next day and was not so lucky. Like the *Caledonian Star*, the Bremen plunged bow first into a 30 m freak wave, which devastated the bridge. Unlike the *Caledonian Star*, the *Bremen* lost engine power. 'When the engine failed, the ship lay transversely to the sea,' recalled chief engineer Reinhard Fisch. 'The sea rolled crossways to the ship against the big windows of the restaurant.'

These were the ship's most vulnerable point. If they broke, water would pour in, destabilising the vessel and causing her to capsize. It was vital to get the engine running again, but the starter generator lay in bits on the floor. As the ship rolled helplessly in the swell, Fisch battled with the generator in a race against time. Finally, he managed to put it back together. To his relief, the ship's engine roared into life. 'For the first time I had hope we would make it. There are wonderful moments when you know everything works normally again.' The *Bremen* was able to head back to port.

Both experiences shed more light on the probable fate of the *München*. Like the *Caledonian Star* and *Bremen*, her bridge was near the front of the vessel, where it would have felt the full force of a freak wave. Unlike the two other ships, the *München*'s bow had not been reinforced for travel in icy seas. The impact would have mangled the front of the ship, punching in the steel plates of her hull so that torrents of water flooded in and sank her.

5 ships that survived freak waves

The *Caledonian Star* and *Bremen* are not the only ships known to have survived freak waves. Others include the following:

Ramapo, February 7, 1933 A 34 m wave, the highest ever recorded, smashed into the US Navy oil transport ship in the mid-Pacific.

Queen Mary, December 1942 A 23 m wave came close to capsizing the liner during the Second World War, while it was transporting US troops across the Atlantic to Britain.

Queen Elizabeth 2, September 11, 1995 A 29 m wave struck the liner in the North Atlantic during Hurricane Luis. According to Captain Ronald Warwick, 'it looked as if we were going into the white cliffs of Dover.'

Norwegian Dawn, April 16, 2005 Cabins were flooded when a 21 m wave hit the cruise ship off the coast of Georgia, USA.

Pont-Aven, May 22, 2006 The giant car ferry had to put in to the French port of Roscoff, after a 15 m wave struck it in the Bay of Biscay en route from Plymouth to Santander.

Into the Whirlwind

The wind was picking up in the Bass Strait between Tasmania and the Australian mainland, and it was starting to hail. A group of yachts was battling through mounting waves, when a terrifying sight suddenly loomed ahead of them, spiralling between the dark clouds and the heaving sea.

It was Boxing Day, December 26, 2001, and the boats were taking part in one of the world's most challenging yacht races – between Sydney and the Tasmanian capital, Hobart. That year, the Sydney-Hobart race was also part of the Volvo Ocean Race, a round-the-world race held every four years. Leaving Sydney harbour that afternoon, the yachts had entered seas that were already choppy. As the weather worsened and it began to thunder, the leading boats struggled hard to keep stable without losing position. Then they saw it – a waterspout, a twisting, churning funnel of sea water, caused by a tornado and heading directly towards them.

In the path of the twister

As the twister spun closer, even the most experienced sailors began to feel the grip of panic. Lude Ingvall, skipper of the Swedish yacht *Nicorette*, realised that it was on a direct collision course with his boat. 'I really feared for my life,' he recalled. Just before the twister hit, he sent all but three of his 23 crew below. Then it was upon them. 'I felt it was like a wrestler grabbing the back of my jacket and trying to lift me off my feet,' he said. As it roared over the boat, it rained down hailstones the size of golf balls, shredding the mainsail. Luckily, the four sailors managed to cling on to the boat and stay on deck until the waterspout had passed.

On the German yacht *Illbruck*, skipper John Kostecki decided not to take any chances. 'I asked everyone on board to have their harnesses on and to be ready for anything.' As the crew braced themselves, the tornado crept ever closer. 'Now it was only 400 metres away ... We had to change course again, 90 degrees up, so it could pass to leeward.' The

TWO KINDS OF SPOUT

The most dangerous waterspouts form as tornadoes underneath thunderclouds and spiral from the base of the cloud down to the sea. Much more common are 'fair weather' spouts, which form as swirls of cooler air over warm seas. In these, the air spirals upwards from the sea. Fair weather spouts can form almost anywhere over water, including freshwater lakes. The world's waterspout capital is believed to be the Florida Keys, where 400-500 swirl into action each year.

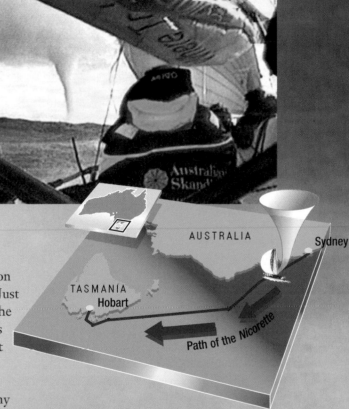

BEARING DOWN *A crew member on the Nicorette captured the approaching twister on video (top). Above: The spout ran into the yachts between Sydney and Hobart.*

SWIRLING DOOM *The base of the waterspout churned up the ocean surface as it spun towards the yachts.*

An unexpected terror screamed down on yachts taking part in the Sydney-Hobart race on Boxing Day 2001 – a towering waterspout.

223

> **It was like a wrestler grabbing the back of my jacket and trying to lift me off my feet.**
>
> *Lude Ingvall, skipper of the yacht* Nicorette

manoeuvre worked, but only just. 'There was a moment where we were all just silent, hoping that it would pass by us. It came very close to us, about 200 metres, and it slowly passed in front of us.' The near miss left them awestruck as well as relieved. 'We had a helpless feeling, where this freak of nature was chasing us down.'

The nearby *Assa Abloy*, another Swedish yacht, was less lucky. 'I was pretty scared,' remembered its British skipper, Neal McDonald. Fortunately, he managed to lower his sails in the nick of time. 'I assumed it would go downwind and it didn't; it came across the wind and we were in the middle of it ... If we had had the sails up, there was every chance that we would have had them all just whipped off.'

According to Gunnar Krantz, skipper of another Swedish contender, *SEB*, the waterspout looked 'like a gigantic vacuum cleaner coming down to suck away all the tiny boats littering the water ... It went for *Wild Thing* and *Nicorette* as they tried to take the sails down. *Wild Thing* ended up right in it and had to retire with torn sails.' 'We expected to see cows and motor homes and everything in it,' was the wry comment of *Wild Thing*'s skipper, Australian Grant Wharington.

Incredibly, although several boats were damaged, nobody was badly hurt. *Assa Abloy* eventually won the race, sailing across the finishing line in Hobart harbour just before 10 am on December 29, closely followed by *Nicorette*. Of the Volvo Ocean Race yachts, only *Wild Thing* was forced to drop out.

El Niño 1997-8

During July 1997, a giant pulse of warmer-than-average water, with a surface area 1.5 times greater than the USA and several hundred metres deep, moved in around the coasts of Peru and Ecuador. The amount of energy it contained was greater than a million Hiroshima bombs.

Meteorologists had first noticed the vast region of warm water in March, when satellites monitoring surface water temperatures in the Pacific Ocean had detected it spreading east from South-east Asia. While this unusually warm pool of water reached the shores of South America, an area of cooler-than-normal water was developing off Australia. All the signs pointed to a major El Niño event that would play havoc with the climate all around the world.

Drought ...

In July 1997, several areas of South-east Asia were suffering unusually dry conditions. In Thailand, rains that should have arrived in May were not now expected until August, and rice farmers had delayed planting. 'The situation is very bad,' said Smith Tumsaroch, the director-general of Thailand's meteorological department. 'Instead of having the rains come to northern Thailand, they have gone eastward into China.'

Similarly, in Indonesia the first hint of the problems ahead occurred when the dry season, which normally lasts from April until September, failed to end. In normal years, monsoon rains coincide with rice planting. The failure of the rains to arrive in October 1997 meant that in most places nothing was planted. Farmers waited anxiously for conditions to change. In December enough rain fell for rice to be planted in Java and

Suddenly we were surrounded from all directions. It took all the little animals, then my house just fell down.

Ipanaqué Silva

EAST AFRICA INUNDATED *Born in the Pacific Ocean, the 1997-8 El Niño caused floods in Kenya's Tana river valley on the other side of the world.*

Kalimantan (Indonesian Borneo), but the delay caused a serious food shortage, and the price of rice rocketed to three times its cost the previous year.

Food shortages were not the only problem caused by the drought. In October, fierce fires raged across the rain forests of Indonesia. Following several months of dry weather and the failure of the monsoon, Indonesia's normally lush forest cover had dried out. Fires started deliberately to clear areas for farming quickly spread out of control. Vast clouds of smoke covered the country and blocked out the sun. The wind blew the smoke across Indonesia's borders to affect Malaysia (see pages 182-3), Singapore and Thailand.

By the time the fires had been put out, they had destroyed an area the size of Portugal. Almost a quarter of all carbon dioxide emissions that winter came from Indonesia's forest fires, and an estimated US$9 billion in revenue was lost across the region as a result of the fires and drought. A thousand people had died and 20 million suffered from respiratory problems.

... and floods

While Indonesia burned, huge storms were brewing on the other side of the world. In normally arid north-western Peru, the rain arrived in December and fell incessantly for weeks. Although used to downpours during El Niño winters, people had never seen weather like this. In some places up to 150 mm was falling every day. In the village of Chato Chico, Isaias Ipanaqué Silva watched the Piura river rise. For Isaias and the other farmers the rain was welcome, but the rising waters of the normally peaceful river were not. Their village, built beside the river, was at risk.

On February 15, 1998, the Piura broke its banks. As a flood surge roared downstream, water poured over the sodden ground and into people's homes. The flood rose from knee-deep to chest height in no time. 'Suddenly we were surrounded from all directions,' Ipanaqué Silva recalls. 'It took all the little animals, then my house just fell

THE TROPICS BAKED DRY *In early 1998, the normally wet Pacaraima region of northern Brazil suffered three months of drought.*

down completely.' Families struggled to save what they could. 'We just grabbed clothes for the children,' says Rosa Jovera Charo, another villager. Everything else that she owned was washed away – livestock, cooking utensils, personal treasures – the water spared nothing. It was a catastrophe for Chato Chico, but most of the villagers survived and were evacuated to a refugee camp in the desert.

Downstream, in Motse, a village of one-room houses on the outskirts of the city of Chiclayo, nobody realised the imminent danger. 'We thought that the water couldn't come here,' explains Flora Ramirez, 'but we lost practically everything.'

The flood struck hard and fast, inundating Motse in a matter of minutes. 'They strung ropes from one house to another to rescue people,' says Manuel Guevara Sanchez. 'Some spent three days on the roof. Those who knew how to swim brought them food.' When the floodwaters receded, ten people in a village of 150 were found drowned.

To the west of the Piura river, the flood run-off drained into the coastal Sechura desert, where it formed a lake covering 5,000 km^2 (1,900 sq miles).

SILVER LINING

New opportunities

Although a disruptive El Niño event causes problems, it also creates opportunities. Poor harvests in one region can increase the value of crops elsewhere. In 1997 and 1998, for example, coffee-growers in Brazil and Indonesia suffered, while Kenyan growers found that demand for their coffee beans soared – as did the prices they could charge.

With systems in place to predict the onset and severity of an El Niño event, people will be able to use their knowledge of its global impact for commercial advantage. Squid stocks off California plummet, as does palm-oil production in Indonesia and the Philippines. Companies or nations that can take advantage of this knowledge will prosper.

The ability to predict El Niños was used to positive effect in Peru in 1997. In the north, cattle were grazed on land normally too dry to support them, and arable farmers planted rice and beans in areas usually barren, resulting in bumper harvests. On the coast, fishermen made plans to catch shrimp in waters that are usually too cold to support them.

> ## 'Some spent three days on the roof. Those who knew how to swim brought them food.'
>
> *Manuel Guevara Sanchez*

Elsewhere, floodwater formed numerous puddles and pools that provided perfect breeding grounds for mosquitoes, leading to an explosion in cases of malaria. Within months, in the Piura river region alone, more than 30,000 people were infected – three times the average for that time of year.

Little of South America escaped El Niño's disruptive effects. Ecuador had severe flooding, with 108 people killed and 28,000 made homeless, as well as outbreaks of cholera, malaria and dengue fever. Neighbouring Colombia experienced its worst drought for years, with crop and livestock losses totalling millions of dollars. A greater number of severe storms raged over Paraguay than at any other time in its history. Floods and high winds caused damage to much of the country's infrastructure. Bridges collapsed, buildings crumbled and roads were washed away. Huge areas of land that had never before been flooded disappeared underwater.

Chile and Argentina also had higher than usual rainfall, yet the normally lush and tropical Amazon basin experienced unusually dry conditions. It had some of its worst forest fires in living memory.

North America

As the intensity of the El Niño increased, its effects spread. During the autumn, the warm surface water that had gathered off the coasts of Ecuador and Peru crept northwards up the Californian coast. In December, the first in a succession of torrential thunderstorms lashed the coast for weeks. Rivers rose and broke their banks, and everywhere the land became waterlogged. By February, conditions became critical. 'California's urban hills and mountains are saturated with water. They can't take any more. Many of them are dangerously unstable and it will take months of dry weather before they are stable again,' reported a Department of Emergency Services spokesperson. Swollen rivers swept away vehicles and their occupants; mudslides blocked roads and railway tracks, and in

CONTINUED ON PAGE 230 »

Causes of El Niño

The unseasonal current of warm water that arrives off the coast of Peru was christened El Niño, or the Boy Child, by Peruvian fishermen because its effects come into full force around Christmas, although the process begins months earlier.

An El Niño is a periodic sustained warming of a very large area of the equatorial Pacific Ocean. It begins between March and June, and reaches maximum impact the following December. El Niño events occur about every two to five years, and vary in intensity and in their impact on patterns of rainfall and drought.

In a normal year, high pressure dominates over Peru and low pressure over South-east Asia. The trade winds blow east to west across the Pacific, pushing warm surface water westwards. This warm water builds up off Indonesia, producing tropical storms over South-east Asia. In some years, the sea level around Indonesia is 50 cm higher than it is off Ecuador and Peru.

The movement of warm water away from South America allows colder, nutrient-rich water to well up along the coast, and causes dry conditions in the north-west of the continent. Around June each year, a small amount of warm water travels back to South America, blocking off the upwelling for a month or two.

Every few years, the difference in atmospheric pressure between the east and west Pacific regions reverses temporarily – a pattern known as the Southern Oscillation. The trade winds begin to slacken, and the warm-water pool in the west spreads back towards South America, where it begins building up. The warmer the water becomes, the more the trade winds slacken, in a cyclical process that sees the warm-water pool in the eastern Pacific swell considerably in a few

months. As warm water piles up in the eastern Pacific, cooler-than-usual water gathers off Australia and South-east Asia.

Because surface temperatures in the ocean directly affect the atmosphere above, weather conditions change on both sides of the Pacific. When the western equatorial Pacific cools, less energy is transmitted into the atmosphere. The air dries out and tropical storms do not materialise.

Meanwhile, warmer-than-usual surface temperatures in the eastern equatorial Pacific cause large amounts of energy to be transferred to the atmosphere, producing heavy storms along the west coast of North and South America. During December 1997 and January 1998, the sea surface temperature off Peru and Ecuador was 28°C, and rainfall was 15 times the seasonal average.

The heat energy associated with a severe El Niño can disrupt weather patterns across whole continents, even on the other side of the world.

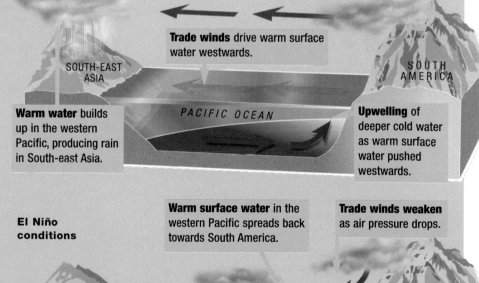

Normal conditions

Trade winds drive warm surface water westwards.

SOUTH-EAST ASIA

SOUTH AMERICA

PACIFIC OCEAN

Warm water builds up in the western Pacific, producing rain in South-east Asia.

Upwelling of deeper cold water as warm surface water pushed westwards.

El Niño conditions

Warm surface water in the western Pacific spreads back towards South America.

Trade winds weaken as air pressure drops.

SOUTH-EAST ASIA

SOUTH AMERICA

PACIFIC OCEAN

Conditions dry out in South-east Asia and cold water gathers around coast.

Cold upwelling is cut off as warm water builds up around coast.

El Niño's global impact

The 1997-8 El Niño disrupted weather patterns all around the world for more than a year, causing drought in normally wet areas and floods in dry areas, and leaving a trail of destruction in its wake.

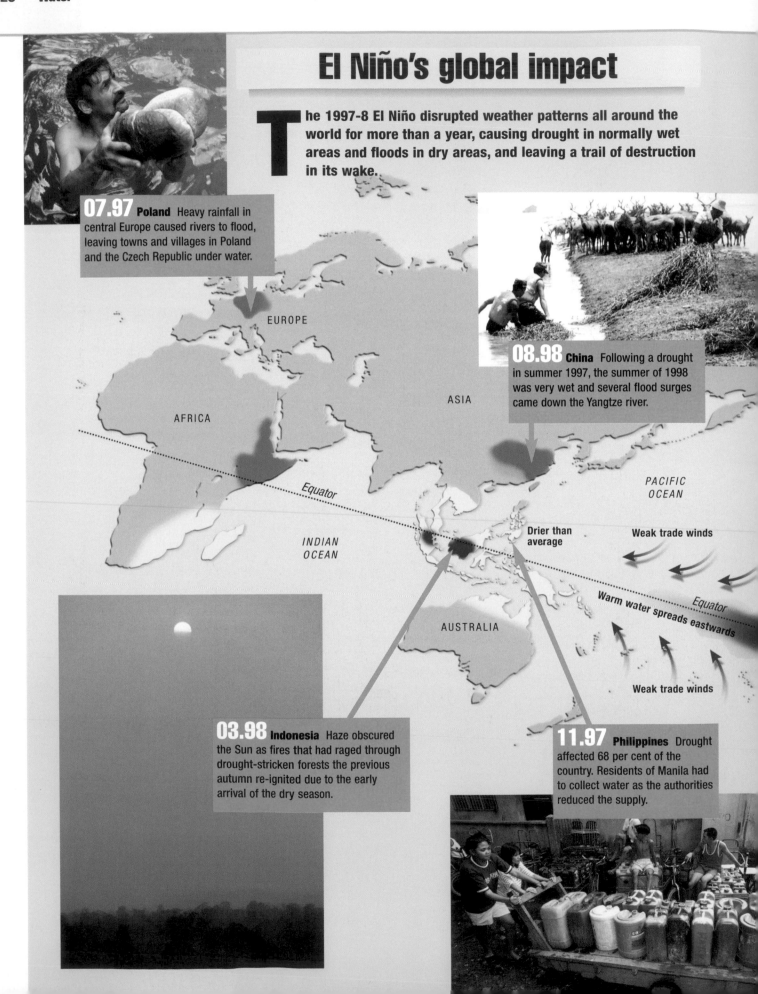

07.97 Poland Heavy rainfall in central Europe caused rivers to flood, leaving towns and villages in Poland and the Czech Republic under water.

08.98 China Following a drought in summer 1997, the summer of 1998 was very wet and several flood surges came down the Yangtze river.

EUROPE

ASIA

AFRICA

PACIFIC OCEAN

Equator

INDIAN OCEAN

Drier than average

Weak trade winds

Equator

Warm water spreads eastwards

AUSTRALIA

Weak trade winds

03.98 Indonesia Haze obscured the Sun as fires that had raged through drought-stricken forests the previous autumn re-ignited due to the early arrival of the dry season.

11.97 Philippines Drought affected 68 per cent of the country. Residents of Manila had to collect water as the authorities reduced the supply.

03.98 California Record rainfall along the coast left hillsides unstable. In Laguna Niguel, a landslide caused several houses to collapse.

01.98 Brazil Tens of thousands of hectares of rain forest burned during a record drought.

Northern branch of jet stream pushes mild air inland

Warmer than average winter

Southern branch of jet stream pushes storms eastwards

NORTH AMERICA

Wetter than average winter

GREENLAND

ARCTIC OCEAN

Weak trade winds

Warm water builds up

ATLANTIC OCEAN

Equator

Weak Peruvian current

SOUTH AMERICA

01.98 Peru Weeks of heavy rain caused overflowing rivers, flash floods and mudslides to cascade through villages and towns in the Andes region.

Wetter than average

Drier than average

Fires

places removed whole hillsides. 'It's frightening, so incredible. Mother Nature puts you in your place', said one resident, driven from her home by an advancing tongue of mud.

In northern California, 6 m waves ate into the coast, washing away the land from beneath beachfront homes. In Los Angeles, dozens of homes were destroyed as their foundations and the land beneath them slipped away. In all, 17 people were killed, 35 of California's 58 counties declared a state of emergency, and damage was estimated at over $500 million.

Disruption around the world

Although the effects of El Niño are at their most intense in regions bordering the Pacific, it can disrupt weather patterns right around the world. In Europe, the problems began with the onset of the El Niño in summer 1997. So much rain fell that river heights reached record levels and the centre of the continent suffered terrible floods. In Poland, 55 people lost their lives after three months of rain fell in less than four hours. In the Czech Republic, 60 people were killed as flash floods swept through the country.

Kenya also suffered flooding when its wet season, which began normally in October 1997, rapidly intensified and overran into January. Floods destroyed crops and disrupted the transport system, with many roads and bridges completely washed away. They also caused a huge increase in disease as water sources became contaminated and sewers overflowed.

Rainfall in Ethiopia, to the north, was similarly disrupted. During the 1997 dry season, from June to September, far less rain fell than usual, and crop planting was delayed. When the rains came in October, they were unusually heavy. Flash floods washed away homes and killed hundreds of people. Thousands more were displaced. In Somalia, the entire Juba river valley was inundated, with homes, and some whole towns,

Predicting El Niño

A severe El Niño in 1982-3 prompted scientists to develop ways of measuring deviations from normal conditions, or anomalies, that occur in the Pacific Ocean. These are used to predict an El Niño about six to twelve months in advance.

Water temperature and wind strength in the Pacific Ocean are measured by a system of 70 buoys moored along the Equator. This system, known as the TAO (Tropical Atmosphere/Ocean) array, was completed in 1994. Each buoy continuously monitors water temperature from the surface down to a depth of 500 m, together with air temperature, wind speed and relative humidity. It transmits this data via satellite to the US Pacific Marine Environmental Laboratory in Seattle. Here, the data is combined with temperature readings taken from research ships to form a detailed picture of the upper ocean and lower atmosphere and to spot any shifts away from average conditions.

The 1997-8 El Niño was tracked by the TOPEX/Poseidon satellite (above),

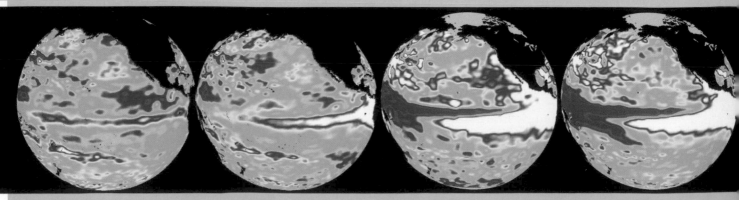

April 25, 1997   May 25, 1997   November 10, 1997   December 10, 1997

submerged up to their roofs. 'It's a terrible disaster. We've got satellite mapping of the rains that have gone right off the rainfall scale,' reported Lyn Geldof, spokesperson for the Somalia Inter-Agency Flood Response. By November, the floods had killed 448 people in Somalia, rendered 150,000 homeless and destroyed much of the country's food reserves.

A sting in the tail

In the summer of 1998, as surface temperatures in the Pacific were returning to normal, the tail end of El Niño generated a huge area of low pressure that swept across eastern China, bringing thunderstorms and torrential rain across much of the region. At the beginning of July, the Chang Jiang (Yangtze) river, which flows from the Tibetan plateau eastwards through the most heavily populated part of the country, burst its banks. Water levels in the river did not drop until the beginning of September, and during those two

months eight successive flood peaks swept down, causing widespread flooding each time. Armies of soldiers and civilians struggled to reinforce the flood-protection dykes in the few days between each peak. The official death toll was 3,656, but many believe the real number was much higher. An incredible 5.7 million homes were destroyed and a further 7 million damaged. Around 14 million people became refugees and were forced to move elsewhere.

The Chang Jiang flood of 1998 was the second-greatest in China for 50 years. At the same time, the Songhua river in the north-east broke its banks, inundating another vast area. The two floods combined covered 3 per cent of all China's agricultural land, destroying crops and drowning livestock. Transport networks were paralysed and factories forced to close as the water spread. The damage done to homes and businesses added up to some US$45 billion, and the effect on China's economy was felt for months.

which has now been discontinued. This mapped the topography of the ocean surface, showing up tiny alterations in sea level. Seawater expands when it warms, so sea level is another indicator of water temperature and allows meteorologists to monitor the currents associated with El Niño and identify build-ups of warm water.

The newest and, some believe, best tool for predicting the onset of El Niño was developed by scientists at the NASA Space Flight Center. It measures subtle differences in the colour of the water in satellite images of the Pacific

Ocean taken over time. The colour is produced by clouds of phytoplankton – microscopic chlorophyl-producing algae that turn the surface water green. They can only survive in cooler nutrient-rich

waters, and disappear when water warms up. Because they change the ocean's colour, they can be used to track the currents linked to El Niño and identify changes in surface temperature.

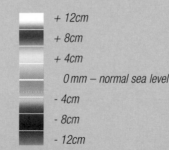

+ 12cm
+ 8cm
+ 4cm
0 mm – normal sea level
- 4cm
- 8cm
- 12cm

TRACKING EL NINO *The TOPEX/ Poseidon satellite recorded the course of the 1997-8 El Niño. The colours indicate sea surface height and temperature relative to normal. The white area, which was 12 cm higher and 2.8°C warmer than normal, shows the build-up and dissipation of the warm-water pool. Purple areas were below average height and temperature.*

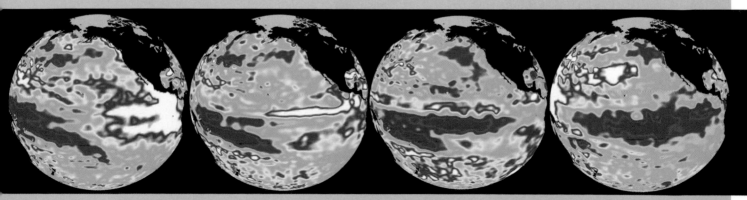

February 5, 1998   March 14, 1998   August 13, 1998   February 27, 1999

Drowned in Sight of Shore

The sea does not have to be wild to be dangerous. On one sunny summer day in 2003, eight people drowned on the Florida coast, dragged to their deaths by sinister, narrow rip currents that flow away from the shore, often with incredible strength.

PULLED TO SAFETY
A lifeguard tows a young couple from the grasp of a rip current on Florida's Daytona Beach.

The previous two days had been stormy in the Florida panhandle in the far north-west of the state. But Sunday, June 8, dawned bright and sunny at Grayton Beach in Walton County. Although red flags were flying, warning swimmers and surfers of hazardous conditions, many people went into the sea. The waves looked fairly small, and in the growing heat, the water was tempting.

'We decided to get the boogie boards out, along with a lot of other people that were out there, and play right in the shoreline,' recalled Sandee LaMotte, who was staying in Walton County. 'The sign next to the red flag said it meant "dangerous currents, like rip tides," but it did not say these could or would occur at the shoreline. I did not know I was in danger in knee-deep water.'

There were no lifeguards to enforce or explain the rules, and Sandee was not worried about leaving her husband, Larry, and their children, Ryan and Krysta, while she went back to their holiday home to prepare some food. Five minutes later, the door burst open and Krysta came running in: 'Mom! Mom! Ryan got stuck in the water, and Daddy went in after him, and now Daddy's gone.'

Lying on his boogie board, Ryan had been dragged out to sea by a rip current hidden in the surf. His 60-year-old father had also been caught up in the current while trying to rescue him and was now fighting for his own life.

Watching the disaster unfold was another holidaymaker, 36-year-old Ken Brindley from Arkansas. As soon as he saw the father and son in trouble, he dived in and swam out towards them. He was unable to reach Ryan, who had in fact escaped the rip

A holiday in the sun turned to tragedy when treacherous rip currents drowned Larry LaMotte and seven others.

233

current and was drifting with his board parallel to the beach, so he struck out towards Larry instead. Another man reached Ryan and pushed him back to the shore.

By this time, the beach was in panic. 'People were yelling "Call 911! We need help!",' remembered Theo Laurent, a local surfer. He was out in the water at the time and paddled his board towards the two men, who were by now floating face down. 'When I got to those guys, they were 100 per cent unconscious,' he said. 'There was nothing, no response at all.'

He managed to flip them over and was struggling to keep their heads above water, while a sheriff's helicopter circled overhead. Then other surfers arrived, and between them they managed to drag the two men back towards the shore.

'I screamed to the heavens'

The terrified Sandee LaMotte, meanwhile, had run back to the beach. 'It just seemed to go on forever. At one point I screamed to the heavens, but mostly I just stood in the water, praying. I saw a man brought in with red trunks and they started working on him. Then I saw another man out there floating face down, and I knew. It was Larry. Larry was dead.'

Larry LaMotte had drowned; his would-be rescuer Ken Brindley died later in hospital. Both had made the fatal mistake of trying to swim straight back to the beach instead of parallel to the shore (see box, right) and had been dragged farther and farther out. Along the Florida panhandle that day, six other people died in the same way: Robert Heymeyer, 57, from St Louis; Marla Amos, 31, from Indiana; Curtis Cohran, 53, a local resident; David Che-Hsien Huang, 40, from Houston; Marietta Yakstis, 62, from Illinois; and Shalyn Cuadrado, 32, from Louisiana.

According to experts, the storms that hit Florida on June 6 and 7 had caused the rip currents. They whipped up large waves which punched holes through sandbars off the beaches. By June 8, the waves had subsided but the gaps remained, with the currents streaming through them at colossal speeds. Ironically, the water in a rip current looks calmer and less dangerous than the breakers around it.

These dangers are something all lifeguards know about. But even today, says Sandee LaMotte, many of Florida's beaches are unprotected – a situation she is working hard to get changed. 'The current lack of protection is just callous disregard for human life,' she argues. Most people agree, but there is a reluctance to pay for new lifeguards. Meanwhile, Florida dreads a repeat of 'Black Sunday', as it has become known.

WHAT MAKES A RIP CURRENT?

When a sandbar forms along a shoreline, it creates a kind of pool between the bar and the beach. As waves break on the shore, they crash over the bar and onto the beach, but the bar impedes the water's return journey out to sea, trapping it in the pool. Often, the water flows along the shoreline parallel to the beach until it finds a gap in the sandbar, through which it rushes out as a rip current. These are usually narrow, up to 9 m wide, but can be very fast – 8 km/h (5 mph) or faster.

They can knock people off their feet, but because they form on the surface, they do not drag swimmers underwater. People drown when they exhaust themselves trying to swim back against the current. Rip currents are relatively narrow, and you can escape one by swimming parallel to the shore. Once out of it, you can strike back towards the beach.

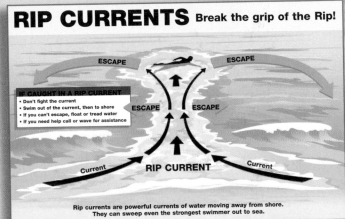

RIP CURRENTS Break the grip of the Rip!

ESCAPE   ESCAPE

IF CAUGHT IN A RIP CURRENT
• Don't fight the current
• Swim out of the current, then to shore
• If you can't escape, float or tread water
• If you need help call or wave for assistance

ESCAPE   ESCAPE

Current   RIP CURRENT   Current

Rip currents are powerful currents of water moving away from shore. They can sweep even the strongest swimmer out to sea.

AWARENESS *The US National Weather Service and Lifesaving Association are seeking to raise awareness of the dangers of rip currents.*

Central Europe Under Water

At around 4 am the sirens started to wail in the Karlin district of the Czech capital, Prague. The worst had happened – the defences had been breached. Early though it was, people were soon pouring onto the streets, dragging their belongings to the safety of higher ground.

Most were prepared and had already packed. A few stragglers rushed to bundle their most valuable large possessions upstairs, before throwing what they could into suitcases. As they hurried along, the floodwaters of the Vltava river followed after them, creeping relentlessly, inch by inch, to the doors of their homes.

By the time day broke on Tuesday, August 13, 2002, whole sections of the city were under water, basements flooded, homes awash and businesses destroyed. Miraculously, no one had been killed – the citizens of Prague had been forewarned of the danger, unlike less fortunate people living farther upstream. Even so, the speed of events took many by surprise. 'I live about 300 metres from the river,' one man said later. 'We had to evacuate very quickly. I was afraid because I didn't know what would happen.'

Scenes evoking the war

By early afternoon, the full extent of the flood damage was becoming clear. More than 50,000 people had been forced from their homes, and there were reports that the worst was yet to come. From her workplace more than a kilometre (0.6 miles) from the city centre, office-worker Monika Vegh sent an email describing events. 'The city is panicking and people are buying food like crazy,' she wrote. 'No one knows what to expect ... The people carrying suitcases as they flee evoke scenes from World War II.'

While most were fearful, some found the floods grimly fascinating. As the day progressed, crowds built up on riverside embankments, defying the authorities who wanted them to move to higher ground. Many tourists visiting Prague gathered near the city's historic Charles Bridge, the tops of whose normally towering arches were now just a few metres above the surging surface of the river. 'I could see fridges, chairs and other furniture being carried ... underneath,' one visitor wrote later.

The waters also threatened the Old Town. This district is what draws most tourists to Prague – its beautiful buildings adorn countless postcards and the covers of most guides. Efforts to keep the flood out were particularly intense here. Nevertheless, by late afternoon with rain pouring down and the river still rising, things were looking bad, and the mayor gave the order to evacuate the Old Town.

> ❝ **The city is panicking and people are buying food like crazy. No one knows what to expect.** ❞
>
> *Monika Vegh, Prague office-worker*

HIGH WATER *Prague's Charles Bridge just cleared the Vltava even when the districts at each end of it were threatened with flooding.*

MAKE-SHIFT RAFT *Floodwaters swept down three major rivers: the Vltava, Elbe and Danube. They rose nearly a storey high here, in Meissen on the Elbe.*

Torrential rain in August 2002 unleashed floods across central Europe, causing an estimated 12 billion euros of damage.

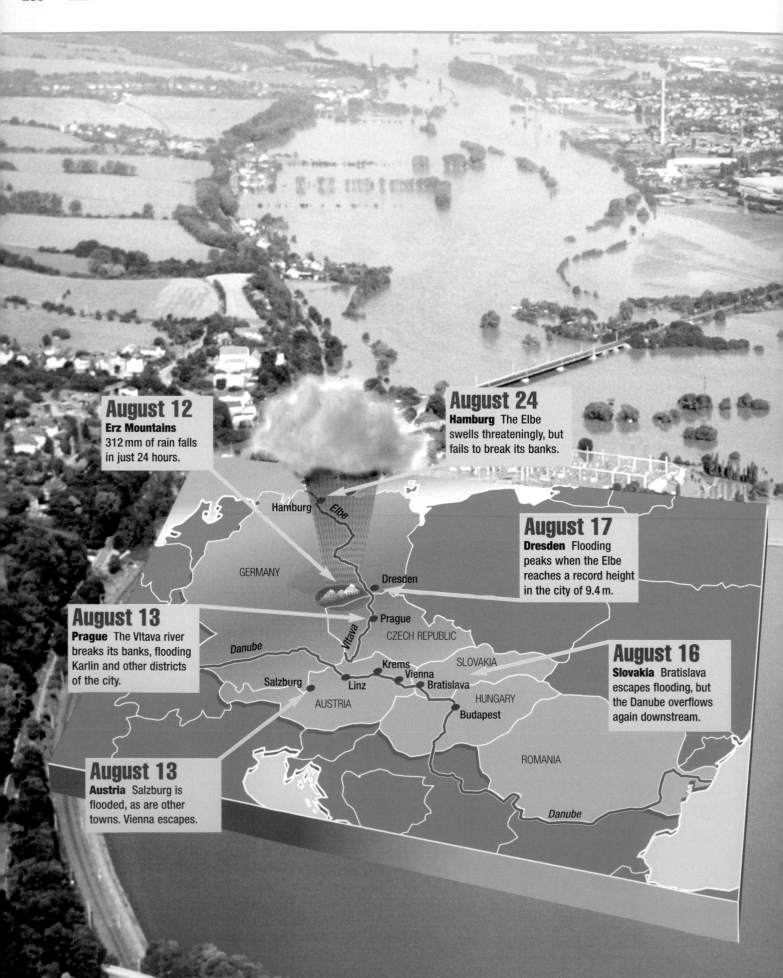

August 12
Erz Mountains
312 mm of rain falls
in just 24 hours.

August 24
Hamburg The Elbe
swells threateningly, but
fails to break its banks.

August 17
Dresden Flooding
peaks when the Elbe
reaches a record height
in the city of 9.4 m.

August 13
Prague The Vltava river
breaks its banks, flooding
Karlin and other districts
of the city.

August 16
Slovakia Bratislava
escapes flooding, but
the Danube overflows
again downstream.

August 13
Austria Salzburg is
flooded, as are other
towns. Vienna escapes.

Hamburg   Elbe

GERMANY

Dresden

Prague

Vltava

Danube   CZECH REPUBLIC

Krems   SLOVAKIA

Vienna

Salzburg   Linz   Bratislava

AUSTRIA   HUNGARY

Budapest

ROMANIA

Danube

As darkness fell, Prague felt like a city under siege. Streets which had been bustling with people the day before were now deep under water, and more looked set to disappear during the night. The river had virtually split the city in half. Only one bridge remained open and much of the subway network was flooded.

Daybreak on Wednesday brought relief for some and heartbreak for others. The Old Town had been spared – its hastily assembled defences had held. But people elsewhere had not been so lucky. In the city's Kampa district, the water now reached the first floors of buildings, flooding many apartments. In Karlin, one of the lowest-lying and worst-affected areas, the floods were lapping at the buildings' upper floors.

During the course of the day, the river gradually dropped and the floods receded. Only then could people return to their homes and begin to survey the damage. Many had lost almost everything. Yet there was a feeling of solidarity as friends, families and neighbours faced the crisis together. As one local man said, with typical Czech good humour: 'It has stopped raining and there has been no big humanitarian disaster – they have even caught the seals that escaped from the zoo!'

KEEPING IT IN OR OUT?
Dresden's water purification plant on the outskirts of the city is besieged by floodwaters, which spilled over from the swollen Elbe.

A crisis that crossed borders

The floods that hit Prague that August devastated much of central Europe. Generated by the second of two vast storm fronts, they followed another flood, which only days before had struck the area around Novorossiysk on Russia's Black Sea coast, sweeping through a beach resort and leaving 58 people drowned in the sea. Although fewer lives were lost in central Europe than in Russia, the floods there caused more widespread destruction, as they surged down the Vltava, Elbe and Danube rivers and threatened no fewer than four capital cities – Prague, Vienna, Bratislava and Budapest.

They began with torrential rain on Monday, August 12. In the Erz Mountains of Germany, 312 mm fell in 24 hours – three times the usual rainfall for the whole of August. This downpour was by far the largest ever recorded in Germany, smashing the previous record: 260 mm in Saxony in 1906. Storms, unlike anything seen for a century, also hit the western Czech Republic, south-eastern Germany and north-eastern Austria. Even after the worst had passed, more rain fell, turning mountain streams into raging torrents that poured into the tributaries of the great rivers below.

The first places to feel the effects of the deluge were towns and villages along those tributaries. In the Erz Mountains, a flash flood roared down the normally diminutive Müglitz river, smashing the dam of a flood-retention reservoir and pouring into the village of Weesenstein. At one point, the water there was rising at a rate of 1 m every hour. By the time the flood passed, a quarter of all the houses in the village were destroyed.

In the state of Upper Austria, several towns and villages were immersed as tributary rivers broke their banks. People were forced to take refuge on rooftops. Some were rescued by helicopter, but many had to wait until the floods receded, sustained by food baskets lowered from the air. There were similar scenes across the western Czech Republic. With roads and railway lines under water and bridges washed away, many places remained cut off for days.

Throughout Monday, August 12, floodwaters surged into the major rivers. Before reaching the Danube, they washed through the Austrian city of Salzburg, where the Salzach river broke its banks and water poured into more than 1,000 homes. As Salzburg was declared a disaster area, cities along the Danube braced themselves for the worst. Linz and Krems both suffered flooding, with hundreds of homes and businesses damaged or destroyed. In Lower Austria, the Kamp, which flows into the Danube downstream of Krems, also burst its banks, flooding parts of the state. Farther east, Vienna's well-maintained flood defences saved it. These are based around an enormous flood-relief channel called the New Danube, which is normally half-empty and closed off from the main river by locks.

Devastation in Dresden

In the early hours of Tuesday, August 13, as floodwaters poured along the Vltava river into Prague, another flood wave was rolling down the Elbe, which has its source in the Krkonoše mountain range in the north-west of the Czech Republic. The two rivers join at Mělník, north of Prague, where the Vltava flows into the Elbe. The next major city, just over the German border, is Dresden.

RHINO RESCUE *Keepers haul a white rhino from its flooded enclosure in Prague's zoo. When water entered their compound, several seals escaped into the river.*

ART SAVED *In Dresden's Zwinger Palace art gallery, priceless paintings had to be moved to safety on higher floors.*

the North Sea. As a result, all building development along the river had been constructed to withstand severe flooding in mind. The banks of the river are raised high above its normal level and the port area contains more than 40 purpose-built drainage channels and basins, connected to the Elbe by sluice gates.

By August 13, Dresden had already experienced its first taste of flooding. It stands where a normally small tributary, the Weisseritz, joins the Elbe. The day before, the Weisseritz had burst its banks and swamped the west of the city. This was a disaster, but worse was to come. As the floodwaters of the Vltava rushed into the already swollen Elbe, they overflowed onto the surrounding countryside, while in the midst of it all, the water in the river's main channel surged on towards Dresden.

Unlike the flood in Prague, the inundation of Dresden was relatively gradual. It was just as relentless, however, and in the end Dresden suffered even deeper flooding than the Czech capital. At its peak on Saturday, August 17, five days after the flood began, the Elbe was running through Dresden at a height of 9.4 m – in August its average height there is just 2 m.

Mayor Ingolf Rossberg compared the disaster to the infamous fire-bombing of the city near the end of World War II. 'This is our most difficult time since February 1945,' he said. The emergency services and volunteers were at full stretch saving not only people but also the city's art treasures, many of them housed in the 18th-century Zwinger Palace, former residence of the Electors of Saxony. Wheelchair-bound 92-year-old Hans Nadler witnessed the scene. 'I have photos of the Zwinger under water in 1896 but I have never experienced anything like [this],' he said.

Downstream from Dresden, the Elbe flooded smaller towns and villages, but the other major city in its path, Hamburg, weathered the worst of the high waters, thanks to its flood defences. Positioned near the mouth of the Elbe, Hamburg is subject to frequent tidal storm surges forcing large quantities of water upstream from

Floodwaters of the Danube

With Dresden under water and the communities lying to its west still waiting for the worst of the floods to hit them, the Danube in the east was beginning to inundate regions downstream from Vienna. The next large city in the flood's path was Bratislava, the capital

Better prepared

There is nothing new about catastrophic floods, and thanks to advances in science, technology and engineering, they are, in many ways, less of a problem now than in the past. The 2002 floods are a good example. Although vast areas were inundated, relatively few people died. Vienna, Bratislava and Budapest all managed to contain the Danube. Even where defences did not work, early-warning systems meant that most people were evacuated from their homes before the floods hit.

Since 2002, other cities along the Danube have improved their defences. In 2003, work began on a new system for the Austrian river port of Krems; Linz has also improved its flood protection. Floods in April 2006 put both cities' defences to the test and both proved effective.

A new flood-forecasting scheme, based on continuously updated rainfall records, also helped to prevent damage elsewhere in Austria and farther down the Danube in Hungary. The advance warning enabled people in areas which were at risk to erect temporary defences and barriers.

SILVER LINING

PICKING UP THE PIECES
In Glashütte, on a tributary of the Elbe south of Dresden, residents search for their belongings as the floodwaters recede.

10 most deadly floods

Some of the most catastrophic floods on record have been along China's great rivers. Generally speaking, the worst disasters have been in less developed parts of the world, with less money to spend on flood-prevention and protection schemes.

	LOCATION	DATE	CAUSE	ESTIMATED DEATHS
1	Huang He (Yellow River), China	1931	Natural	1-3.7 million
2	Huang He, China	1887	Natural	0.9-2 million
3	Huang He, China	1938	Man-made – levees destroyed to halt advance of Japanese forces	500,000-900,000
4	Bangladesh	1970	Natural	300,000-500,000
5	Huang He, China	1642	Man-made – destruction of dykes by anti-government troops	300,000
6	Ru river, China	1975	Dam collapse after torrential rain	230,000
7	Henan, China	1939	Natural	200,000
8	Chang Jiang (Yangtze), China	1931	Natural	145,000
9	Chang Jiang, China	1911	Natural	100,000
10	Bengal, India	1942	Natural	40,000

of Slovakia. It was well prepared for the worst the Danube could throw at it, with a sophisticated system of embankments and discharge channels, combined with a recent widening of the river where it flows through the city. This meant that there was capacity enough to contain the torrent, and even with the river at the highest level ever recorded in Bratislava, the surging waters passed through without incident. Downstream, however, the Danube burst its banks once more, swamping many smaller settlements and drowning huge areas of farmland.

The Hungarian capital Budapest also straddles the Danube. Down the centuries, its city planners, like those of Vienna and Bratislava, have built to ensure that the river can be contained even when it is at its most violent. The defence system there has two layers. The first consists of a massive lower wall, sufficient to contain the river's waters in all but the most exceptional circumstances. If it rises higher than this wall, as happened in August 2002, a second wall keeps it out of the city. During the floods of 2002, the only inconvenience Budapest suffered

More – and worse – floods to come?

The floods that struck central Europe in 2002 were extreme, but not unique. Similar surges have affected the same rivers in the past and will happen again in the future. Floods approaching the size of those in 2002 have tended to occur at the rate of about one every century.

The Danube has been particularly susceptible, which explains why the major cities on its banks were much better prepared in 2002 than Prague and Dresden.

The fear is that future floods may be more frequent and more severe as a result of human activity. In the wake of the 2002 events, for example, it became clear that deforestation may have played a part in making the disaster worse. In Austria, people blamed local mayors who had approved the widespread felling of trees for lucrative housing and business projects. Tree cover soaks up rainfall and prevents the rapid run-off that characterised the early stages of the 2002 floods.

Another factor, which may have added to the scale of the disaster in 2002, is global warming. Scientists have long predicted an increase in extreme weather events as the Earth's average temperature rises. If this is so, freak storms and floods are likely to become more common in Europe than in the past, and the evidence is swinging in favour of this theory.

In March and April 2006, the Elbe again broke its banks and inundated parts of Dresden. At the same time, the Danube flooded large areas of Austria and Hungary, setting a new record height of 8.6 m in Budapest, while other floods caused several deaths in Slovakia and the Czech Republic.

HOLDING BACK THE WATERS *In Dresden, volunteers assist rescue workers as they pile up sandbags to reinforce existing flood defences.*

was the closure of the roads along the top of the lower wall on each bank.

As the waters spread across Hungary, the flood wave began to lose momentum. Croatia, Serbia and Romania were mostly spared – although in Romania tornadoes and localised flash floods linked to the extreme weather system caused some casualties.

Counting the cost

Considering the sheer scale of the floods that swept Europe in August 2002, it is astonishing that more people were not killed. Across the nations affected, and discounting the disaster in Russia, fewer than 40 people lost their lives. The material and financial costs of the floods, however, were considerable. As the waters receded, tens of thousands of people returned to their homes to find them ruined by water and mud. Some had nothing to return to – the buildings they had lived or worked in were reduced to rubble and everything they once owned had been washed away. In Germany alone, the floods forced more than 100,000 people from their homes. Even beyond the reach of the floods, the rising water table inundated countless cellars and basements.

A year after the floods, the financial cost was worked out. In total, damage of more than 12 billion euros (US$14 billion) had been caused, three-quarters of it in Germany. Fewer than 10 per cent of the people affected were adequately covered by insurance. Many had no insurance covering flood damage at all and faced ruin.

When Diana Wrightson bought her guesthouse in Happisburgh on the Norfolk coast in 1980, a road and row of bungalows separated it from the cliffs and beach. Since then the sea has claimed the road and bungalows – and most of her garden.

> **It can be frightening in a really bad storm. You hear the sea, and occasionally you hear the plonk of a bit of cliff falling down.**
>
> *Diana Wrightson,*
> *Happisburgh resident*

Cliff House, which Diana runs with her partner Jill Morris, is literally teetering on the edge. The sandy cliffs on which Happisburgh (pronounced HAYS-borough) is built are eroding away, and the entire village is tumbling bit by bit into the North Sea – it has become known as the 'disappearing village'.

North Norfolk is one of Britain's longest-inhabited regions. Archaeological digs outside Happisburgh have unearthed stone tools made some 700,000 years ago by *Homo erectus*, a direct ancestor of our own species – a revolutionary find, because it used to be thought that the earliest human ancestors arrived in Britain less than 500,000 years ago. At that time the area looked out over an open plain stretching all the way to what is now the continent of Europe. By contrast today, says Diana Wrightson with an ironic smile, 'The sea views are getting better and better.'

Hanging on

'There is less than 20 metres between us and the cliff edge,' she says. 'We are living on borrowed time.' But unlike others who abandoned their properties as the cliffs retreated, she says she will not move out 'unless forced to do so … We have known since about 2002 that this was coming but were determined to stay open as long as possible. We did reluctantly decide this year to close the teashop and no longer advertise the bed and breakfast accommodation – not because it would be dangerous for visitors to come but because we were no longer prepared to invest any more money in the upkeep and maintenance of a business which has no market value at all.'

At first the erosion brought unexpected benefits. The teashop they opened on the ground floor of the guesthouse was thriving, as tourists and day trippers flocked to see the beleaguered village. 'People love coming to see the coast, how it has changed.'

Over the Edge

ON BORROWED TIME
Diana Wrightson, with her guesthouse, Cliff House, in the background.

LAND'S END *Happisburgh's wooden sea defences, called revetments, have been crumbling since the early 1990s.*

Happisburgh in Norfolk is disappearing into the North Sea, as coastal erosion gnaws away at its cliffs.

But time is running out. As long ago as 2003, council officials called and asked her to fill out a homelessness form. 'That brought me up with a bit of a jolt!' she exclaims. In fact, she has lined up a place to rent inland when the end finally comes. 'Until then, we live from day to day.'

Diana's long association with the village dates back to her childhood. 'My grandmother lived here when I was young. This is the same road where she used to live, and I used to come for my holidays.'

Even though the village is gradually falling into the sea, this section of the Norfolk coastline has a unique and compelling beauty. 'It's a lovely, remote area where the air is clean and the skies are wonderful. That hasn't changed,' says Diana. 'The only change has been in the coastline. For 50 or 60 years, nothing happened. Then, suddenly, it just galloped. In 1993, the revetment – the barrier built to keep the sea at bay – began to deteriorate. That seemed to be fatal.'

SILVER LINING

Restoring wetlands

Holding back the sea is an endless task. Dykes, sea walls and other man-made defences have to be regularly repaired or replaced if they are to do their job properly. Nature, however, has its own defence against the encroaching sea – coastal wetlands. Their networks of channels dissipate the energy of storm surges and waves, and so protect inland areas.

Restoring wetlands is a relatively cheap and environmentally friendly way of protecting our coasts. One such project is being tried at Wallasea Island in Essex, England. Here, 110 hectares (272 acres) of new coastal wetlands are being created to improve existing sea defences. As well as protecting the land, the new wetlands provide havens for wildlife and recreational spaces for people. Wallasea Island is already attracting resident wetland birds and will provide an important stopping off point for migrating species. A footpath will ensure that birdwatchers and other visitors can enjoy the wetland.

The concept of wetland restoration is relatively new, but it is being applied in many parts of the world. In Louisiana it has been proposed as a way of mitigating the impact of future hurricanes (see page 107), and in Sri Lanka mangrove forests are being restored, following the Boxing Day tsunami of 2004.

> **We look over the edge almost every day to check what is happening. It's rather like a terminal disease.**
>
> *Diana Wrightson*

No longer protected

Since 1993, Happisburgh has lost 26 homes to the sea. The people who lived in them have all been rehoused or found new places to live, but the loss of their old homes is still a painful memory.

Many ex-residents suffered financially, too. Diana explains: 'When the bungalows got to within about 6 metres of the edge, people were asked to leave. They were given council accommodation, but householders were expected to pay for the destruction of their own houses. That's an awful thing, isn't it?'

Things are not much better for the owners of the remaining properties in Happisburgh. These are now worthless, as it is impossible to insure them and there will be no government compensation when they eventually disappear.

'Behind us we've got about 14.5 metres of garden. They say that when it gets to 10 metres the house needs to be demolished. And we've got no garage at all. Obviously you do feel that you're in a very precarious position. It can be frightening in a really bad storm. You can hear the sea, and occasionally you hear the plonk of a bit of cliff falling down. We look over the edge almost every day to check what is happening. It's rather like a terminal disease. It may sound strange, but you get used to it.'

When ghostly bells toll

People in this part of the world have been living with the threat of erosion for centuries. In medieval times, the thriving port town of Dunwich lay just over the county border in Suffolk; it now lies deep beneath the waves, the best part of 1 km (0.6 miles) out to sea. Several smaller settlements have also disappeared, including a village called Shipden, which vanished into the sea 700 years ago and is now submerged 400 m off the Norfolk coast – according to local legend, you can still hear its church bells tolling out on stormy nights, calling long dead parishioners to worship.

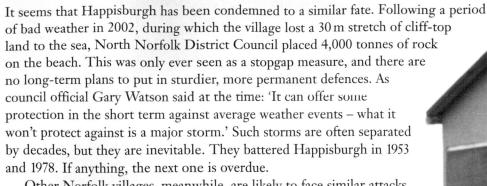

It seems that Happisburgh has been condemned to a similar fate. Following a period of bad weather in 2002, during which the village lost a 30 m stretch of cliff-top land to the sea, North Norfolk District Council placed 4,000 tonnes of rock on the beach. This was only ever seen as a stopgap measure, and there are no long-term plans to put in sturdier, more permanent defences. As council official Gary Watson said at the time: 'It can offer some protection in the short term against average weather events – what it won't protect against is a major storm.' Such storms are often separated by decades, but they are inevitable. They battered Happisburgh in 1953 and 1978. If anything, the next one is overdue.

Other Norfolk villages, meanwhile, are likely to face similar attacks from the sea, although they are not yet under the same imminent threat. On the edge of Winterton, near Great Yarmouth, for instance, 64 m of land was lost between 1997 and 2003. Early in 2004, the coastguard watchtower there had to be demolished because the land beneath it was beginning to fall away. At the time of writing, the beach café, once set well back from the edge, is just metres away from tumbling onto the beach.

Financing the fight

A large part of the problem for Happisburgh and other small coastal communities fighting erosion is economic. It is hard for local authorities and governments to justify the cost of keeping the waves back when that cost is greater than the value of the property being protected. Every year, the British government spends an estimated £500 million on coastal defences, and typically the money is allocated to the places where it can be used most efficiently and effectively.

For this reason, larger communities often fare better than their smaller neighbours. Great Yarmouth, for example, is home to more than 90,000 people and is the centre of North Norfolk's tourist industry. Any money put aside for maintaining sea defences or building new ones is almost always allocated to it or the nearby town of Cromer. Unfortunately for Happisburgh, home to just over 1,000 people, it lies far down on a list filled with larger villages, towns and coastal cities. The resources to spend on coastal defences are inevitably limited. As the sea relentlessly gnaws away at the coast, somebody, somewhere, is bound to lose out.

TEETERING CHALET
Boarded up and left to nature, this holiday home on the Norfolk coast clings to land that could soon fall into the sea.

GLOBAL EROSION

- **Tuvalu: The South Pacific nation is threatened by drowning**
- **The Carolinas: Day by day, the US states lose territory to a foe they cannot defeat**

Tuvalu Saufatu Sopoanga, prime minister of Tuvalu in the South Pacific, spoke bluntly about his country's future at the United Nations General Assembly in 2003: 'We live in constant fear of the adverse impacts of climate change. For a coral atoll nation, sea-level rise and more severe weather events loom as a growing threat to our entire population.'

Tuvalu is tiny – nine islands with a total area of 26 km² (10 sq miles), whose highest point is just 5 m above sea level. In recent years, it has had a taste of what is to come if sea levels continue to rise as a result of global warming. High tides have caused flooding across many of the islands, with water surging over the beaches and rushing inland. In some places, sea water has also risen up though the islands' porous rock.

The results can be bizarre. After an exceptionally high tide on February 28, 2006, Monise Laafai, manager of the Tuvalu Cooperative Society, visited a friend on the island of Fogafale. 'Molu Tavita didn't have to go anywhere to catch dinner,' he commented. 'He netted quite a school of tilapia (fish) in his kitchen.'

Laafai's good-natured reaction is typical of Tuvaluans, but the increasing regularity and severity of the floods is causing concern. Many scientists predict that much of Tuvalu will be uninhabitable by the end of the century, either lost to the sea completely or flooded twice daily with every high tide. Some of its people have already decided to leave, giving rise to a new term – 'climate refugees'.

THE FUTURE *Children gaze at the sea water surrounding their home during high tides in 2005. For them, such floods are likely to become more common.*

North Carolina

Every year, North Carolina loses a little more land to the sea – it is one of the USA's shrinking states. At Cape Hatteras, the shoreline is moving back by around 4 m a year. In 1999, the US Park Service was forced to shift the famous Cape Hatteras lighthouse – they had to dismantle the structure and rebuild it a kilometre (0.6 miles) further back from the surf to prevent it falling victim to the sea.

Erosion is not just about crumbling cliffs – low-lying areas are just as susceptible, and climate change is making matters worse. In North Carolina, small but measurable rises in the sea level have combined with more severe storms and hurricanes to strengthen the age-old assault on the state's sandy shores.

Yet, despite the fact that the coast is receding, people continue to build on it. Often, the actions of new home-owners put their properties at increased risk. 'A lot of people don't like vegetation on their shoreline,' explains coastal geologist Stan Riggs, 'but the minute they clear it and open up their view, they create the opportunity for erosion. Any vegetation you maintain on the shoreline is better than none. The moment you open it up, it becomes like a wound, and it festers.' Dredging for sand offshore is also taking its toll. It removes the sediment that the sea would normally deposit back onto the shore to replace sand lost during storms.

As the sea marches onward, more and more people are finding their properties gobbled up, and the problem is not confined to North Carolina. At Edisto Beach, South Carolina, the shoreline is receding by as much as 13 m every year. Local resident Rie Rone recalls what the town was like when she was a girl. 'I can remember in the late '50s walking down a boardwalk across the dune to reach the beach.' Now the dune has gone; the boardwalk has gone; even her former home has disappeared.

The story is the same in parts of Georgia and farther south in Florida. The US coastline is ever-changing but the pace of change has increased.

RIGHT ON THE BEACH
A house at Cape Hatteras, North Carolina, photographed in 2004. When it was built, it was flat on the ground inland.

FUTURE PROFILE

Age-old processes in the era of global warming

Coastal erosion is a worldwide problem. Along Europe's shores, an area of around 15 km² (5.8 sq miles) is lost to the sea each year. In the four years between 1999 and 2002, some 250-300 homes had to be abandoned in Europe because of disappearing coastlines.

At the same time, for millions of people living in low-lying communities along Asia's coasts and the deltas of its great rivers, erosion confronts them with the ever-growing prospect of seeing their homes and livelihoods washed away. In the USA, Louisiana's coastal wetlands are disappearing at a rate of 75 km² (30 sq miles) a year. In France, coastal landslides have destroyed large sections of the famous white cliffs at Étretat in Normandy, much loved and painted by the Impressionists. Across the Channel, nearly 2.5 km (1.5 mile) of 45 m cliffs near Lyme Regis on England's south coast crashed into the sea in December 2000; a few months later, a 70 m chalk stack, the Devil's Chimney, collapsed at Beachy Head in East Sussex. The coast of Holderness in Yorkshire is retreating at an average rate of 1.5 m a year.

There is, of course, nothing new about coastal erosion – our shorelines have always changed. The processes involved are complex, depending not only on rock type, but also on the shape of a coastline. Even the most crumbly sandstone or chalk cliff will stand firm if protected by a wide beach, while the gradient of the slope beneath the surf is another key factor. A shallow slope helps to dissipate wave energy, whereas a steep one can cause waves to rear up and crash with greater force than they otherwise would.

Nor is erosion the only process at work. Others include longshore drift, by which the same sediments eroded from one stretch of shoreline are moved along the coast to other spots, where they are washed up and expand the coastline. In the UK, the results of this process can be seen at Harlech in North Wales, famous for its medieval castle, built by King Edward I of England in the 1280s. In those days, the castle stood on a cliff directly overlooking a beach; today, it is more than 1 km (0.6 miles)

EVER-CHANGING SHORES
The world's coasts are dynamic and alter through time. In the European Union, as elsewhere, areas are disappearing through erosion, while in other places new land is formed as sediment is dumped through aggradation.

- Erosion
- Aggradation
- Stable

Eastern England With every major North Sea storm, sections of this coast are washed away.

Southern Bay of Biscay The granite of the Pyrenees, which reach the shore, is resistant to erosion.

Algarve Portugal's southern coast is receding, battered by waves whipped up by ocean storms.

Mediterranean Erosion is less than on Atlantic coasts, as waves and tidal ranges are smaller.

inland. Centuries of longshore drift and sediment build-up have pushed the coastline farther out into the Irish Sea.

In recent times, however, other factors have become important, working alongside these age-old processes and almost certainly modifying them. One is sea-level rise caused by global warming. As the planet heats up, its ice caps, glaciers and snow cover melt, adding new water to the oceans. Records show that sea level rose by 19.5 cm between 1870 and 2004, and that the rate of increase accelerated in the last 50 years of that period. Scientists predict that it will continue to increase, raising the high tide marks on beaches around the world and putting more coastlines at risk of erosion. Higher sea levels will also put more places at risk of flooding when storms batter the coast.

Another factor is climate change. As the average global temperature rises, so local climate and weather patterns change. There is evidence that this is already happening. Measurements in the north-west Atlantic show that waves there are becoming bigger and the storms causing them more frequent. Between 1985 and 1995, the average wave height during winter in the area west of Shetland increased by 15 per cent. This has serious implications for coastal communities around the north-west Atlantic. As Dr James Hansom of the University of Glasgow explains: 'Because sea levels are continuing to rise and larger waves are hitting the cliffs, the rate of modification of the coastline is increasing.'

These factors point towards a more difficult future for coastal communities.

STORM SURGE *Waves crash over a sea wall in Winthrop, Massachusetts. This region takes the brunt of North Atlantic storms.*

Fortunately, our ability to measure and predict coastal erosion is improving. Scientists such as Dr Jon Mills from the University of Newcastle upon Tyne in England are pioneering new techniques to generate highly accurate, three-dimensional computer models of coastlines, which allow them to monitor erosion and forecast where it is most likely to happen. The problem looks set to grow, but Dr Mills hopes that with more accurate figures we will have a clearer picture of what is happening around our coastlines. And this will enable governments to plan appropriate strategies for coastal defence.

The *Hans Hedtoft* was the pride of Denmark, described as 'the safest ship afloat', and ever since her launch at the Frederikshavn shipyard in August 1958, her exciting new technology had kept her in the headlines. Now, it was time for her to set sail on the first leg of her maiden voyage.

> **This ship means a revolution in Arctic navigation.**
>
> *Captain P.L. Rasmussen*

Built by the Royal Greenland Trading Company to link Denmark with its dependency Greenland, she had been designed, at the request of the Danish government, to withstand the worst the North Atlantic could throw at her. Until then, it had only been possible to sail between the two places in summer; in winter thick ice in the ocean around Greenland made the journey impossible. The *Hans Hedtoft*, named after a former Danish prime minister, was supposed to change all that.

'This ship means a revolution in Arctic navigation,' said Captain P.L. Rasmussen. He was not exaggerating. Her bow and stern were reinforced with riveted steel plates for smashing through ice, and she had a double steel bottom – a normal outer layer and an inner layer a few feet apart. The inner layer provided a barrier to prevent sea water getting in if the bottom was holed. The hull had seven separate watertight compartments: if one filled completely with water, the ship would still stay afloat. As well as being the toughest vessel in the Danish fleet, she was the best equipped, carrying state-of-the-art instrumentation, including gyro, radar and the sophisticated Decca Navigator System. She also had several radio-equipped lifeboats and rafts. She was no ocean liner, but the *Hans Hedtoft* was still an impressive sight to the crowd of onlookers gathered in Copenhagen harbour on the afternoon of January 7, 1959 –

Denmark's *Titanic*

LAST FAREWELL *Onlookers wave goodbye to passengers on board the* Hans Hedtoft *as she sails out of Copenhagen harbour on Wednesday, January 7, 1959.*

HIDDEN DANGER *Typically, 90 per cent of an iceberg's volume is under water, as shown in this composite image, combining overwater and underwater photographs. Even if the tip is spotted, it is hard to predict the shape of the underwater portion.*

In an eerie echo of the fate of the *Titanic*, the Danish ship *Hans Hedtoft* sank after striking an iceberg during her maiden voyage.

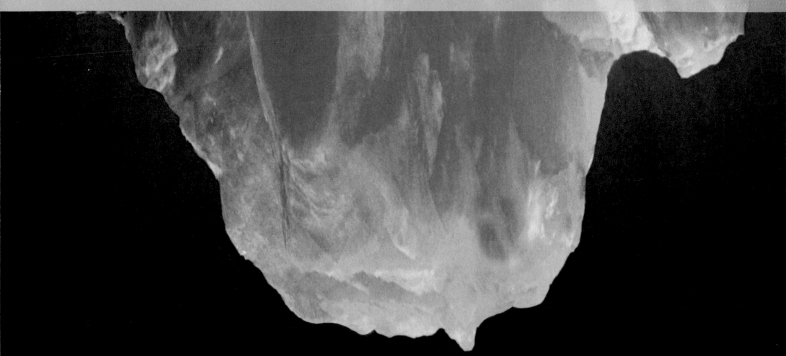

2,900 tonnes of new metal shining in the cold winter sun. The last of the cargo was brought on board and her diesel engine roared into life. The crowd cheered as the huge ropes tying her to the dock were cast off and she headed out into the North Sea.

ALL THAT REMAINED *Icelandic farmer Magus Haflidasson with a lifebuoy from the* Hans Hedtoft, *the only item from the ship ever found. It is now on display in Qaqortoq (formerly Julianehaab).*

Safe journey

Twelve days later, she arrived at Godthaab (now called Nuuk), the capital of Greenland. Not only had she made the journey in the depths of winter, but she had also done so in record time. The crew unloaded the ship's cargo, and the next morning, she cruised up Greenland's icebound west coast, stopping at Sisimiut and Maniitsoq to pick up passengers and new cargo. Just over a week later, she returned to Godthaab and collected more passengers, including Augo Lynge, one of Greenland's two members of the Danish parliament, the Folketing. Lynge's presence marked something of a political climb-down. In the past, he had argued

strongly against the Folketing's plans for winter sailings to Greenland on the grounds of navigational risk.

On January 29, the *Hans Hedtoft* was ready to return to Copenhagen. On board were 40 crew, 55 passengers and a cargo of frozen fish. She stopped briefly at the southerly town of Julianehaab (Qaqortoq). Then, at 9.45 pm, she left the Greenland coast behind and headed out into the North Atlantic.

As she set off into the darkness, the sea was calm. There was a light, changeable wind, but the forecast was good. By the next morning, however, the sea had grown choppy. Snow was falling and visibility had dropped to about 1 km (0.6 miles). As the morning progressed, the

'We are slowly sinking. Need immediate assistance of all vessels in the neighbourhood.'

Last signal received from the Hans Hedtoft

weather worsened, with a strong wind blowing from the north-east. A storm was brewing. But Captain Rasmussen would probably have felt confident that he could sail the *Hans Hedtoft* safely through the storm, relying on his sophisticated navigation equipment.

As it happened, there were other ships in the area, despite the increasingly dangerous conditions. One was the German trawler *Johannes Krüss*, lunging through towering waves about 40 km (25 miles) away. Her crew had hauled in their nets and battened down all hatches. To compound the danger, drift ice crackled around their bows, and icebergs loomed above the swell, like mobile mountains. Sea ice is rare in this area and the *Johannes Krüss* had not been built to deal with it, so its captain, Albert Sierck, radioed his fishing company to alert them to the trawler's predicament. Headquarters radioed back that he should ride out the storm and then head home.

Disaster strikes

At 1.36 pm, a weather station at Prince Christian Sound on the south-eastern tip of Greenland picked up an SOS: '*Hans Hedtoft*. Collision with iceberg. Position 5930N-4300W.' At 3.12 pm came a second SOS: '*Hans Hedtoft*. Position 5930N-4300W. Leaking under waterline. Water has penetrated engine room.' Over the horizon, the *Johannes Krüss* picked up the signal and headed towards the position it gave. Farther off, another German trawler, the *Justus Haslinger*, and a US coastguard cutter, the *Campbell*, also picked up the signal and started to sail towards the stricken ship. At 5.41 pm came a third SOS: '*Hans Hedtoft*. We are slowly sinking. Need immediate assistance of all vessels in the neighbourhood.'

By the time the *Johannes Krüss* reached the position several hours later, no trace of the *Hans Hedtoft* or any of its lifeboats remained. All around were large chunks of ice, while the sea rose and fell in a terrifying swell. The crew could barely see the water in front of them through the driving snow. Despite their heroic efforts, the German fishermen had arrived too late. Like the *Campbell* and the *Justus Haslinger*, both still some way

off, they had been hampered by the terrible conditions. The next morning, with the storm still raging, the captain of the *Campbell* reported that conditions were worse than anything he had ever encountered. The sea was littered with icebergs and smaller blocks of ice. Not far off, they had sighted a single, enormous ice floe, 60 km (37 miles) long and 1 km (0.6 mile) wide.

The search and rescue mission that followed lasted several days, with aircraft from the Canadian and US air forces combing the area for wreckage and survivors. They found nothing. All 95 souls on board the *Hans Hedtoft* had perished. The only surviving record of their fateful journey was a single lifebuoy washed ashore on Iceland nine months later.

Floating danger

Ice is not that hard, relatively speaking – its strength is around 10 per cent that of concrete – but the huge momentum of an iceberg, combined with the potentially large contact area, can generate hundreds of tonnes of force against a ship's hull, causing it to dent and buckle and even rip open. Also, because an iceberg's underwater section is much larger than the area above the surface, a ship can crash into the submerged part before spotting the 'tip'. In the case of the *Hans Hedtoft*, the conditions were so bad and the force of the impact would have been so great that the ship's navigational aids and additional strengthening would have been useless. But the wreck has never been found, so its full story may never be known.

5 ships that hit icebergs

Collisions with icebergs still occur, despite systems for tracking them, set up after the sinking of the *Titanic* in 1912.

Overseas Ohio, Jan 1994 The oil tanker suffered damage worth $1 million after hitting a berg in Prince William Sound, Alaska.

Kastela, Aug 1963 The Yugoslav freighter sank after striking a berg off northern Canada. No known survivors.

Svend Foyn, Mar 1943 Like the *Hans Hedtoft*, the tanker struck a berg off Cape Farewell, Greenland. It sank.

Hugo, May 1927 Believed to have sunk after hitting a berg, also off Cape Farewell. All hands are thought to have been lost.

Titanic, Apr 1912 The liner sank during its maiden voyage, after hitting a berg in the North Atlantic. More than 1,500 lives lost.

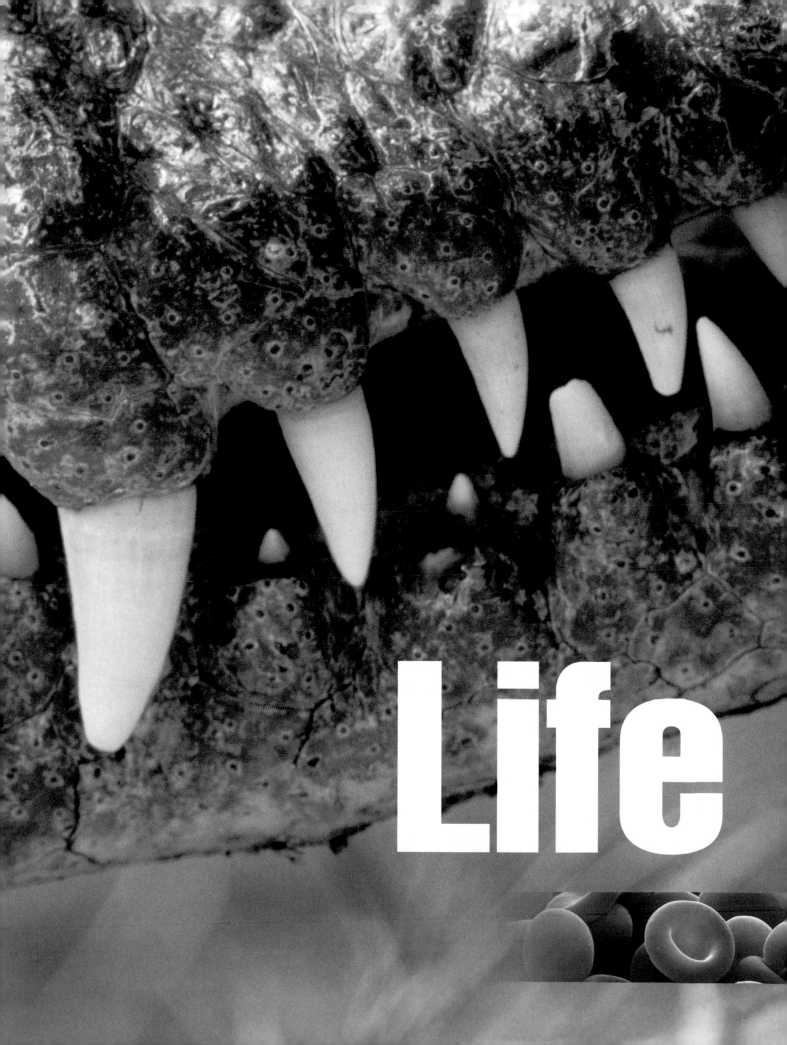

Life

Shark Attack

MENACING *The great white shark's formidable jaws contain up to 3,000 teeth, embedded in rows, although only the front row is functional at any one time. New teeth lie flat and rotate upright as they move forwards to replace worn ones.*

Every year, tens of thousands of people encounter the ocean's number-one predator. For a few, the experience is fatal.

257

Rick LePrevost was swimming with his three children in 7 m of water near a friend's yacht in Florida's Tampa Bay when he felt a bump on his leg. Then something grabbed his left thigh and tried to pull him under.

'As soon as I felt it, I kicked away,' says LePrevost. There was no pain, and he believes that his life jacket kept him buoyant and prevented the shark from dragging him below the surface. Then the beast released its grip. He shouted at the children to get out of the water, and swam after them to the yacht, where he hauled himself up. 'I got in the boat and laid on the deck,' he remembers. 'There was blood everywhere. I was lying there and could just see over the side. I could see the shark under the water, circling the boat. ... They bite and maim you, then circle you and wait until you are weak,' said LePrevost. 'Then they eat you.' He survived because he managed to get out of the water before the creature – later identified as a bull shark or lemon shark, and thought to be about 9 m long – made a second attack. The surgeon who treated him counted five bites, in the thigh, abdomen, ankle and calf, and he needed 120 stitches.

Rick LePrevost was fortunate. The shark had bitten once and then retreated, giving him time to escape. And his wounds, although serious, did not prevent him reaching safety. Others have not been so lucky. In August 2004, Randy Fry was diving for abalone in 4 m of water off the California coast, near Fort Bragg. Cliff Zimmerman, Randy's old friend and diving partner, was in the water with him at the time. The two were at the surface catching their breath after a free dive taken without SCUBA equipment. 'I heard a "whoosh", like a submarine, like a boat going by fast,' Zimmerman says. 'It was a shark. It almost brushed me. I saw its dorsal fin. I don't know what kind it was; all I know is, it was big – big enough to kill.' The shark – later identified as a great white – powered into Fry, and the water instantly filled with blood. Seconds after Zimmerman had first seen the shark, his friend had disappeared; his remains were found the next day.

On the attack

There are dozens of reported shark attacks on people annually worldwide, leading to as many as 15 deaths in a bad year. The majority of attacks are made by great whites, tiger sharks and bull sharks, all of which are large and strong enough to keep hold of a human and drag them underwater. Their teeth are designed to tear through flesh, and cause massive blood loss and loss of limbs. The great white can bite with a pressure of 3 tonnes per cm^2. It clamps its jaws onto a victim and tosses its head from side to side to extract a lump of flesh. Humans are not a good food source for sharks, being too boney, and attack victims are usually released, but in some cases not before the person has lost too much blood to survive, or has drowned.

Unprovoked shark attacks fall into one of three types. The most common is the 'hit and run': the shark comes from nowhere and inflicts a single wound, then disappears. These attacks occur mainly close to shore and may be the result of mistaken identity, as when a feeding shark sees splashing at the surface that could resemble prey in distress. 'Bump and bite' and 'sneak' attacks occur in deeper water. In a 'bump and bite' attack, the shark circles and bumps into its victim before homing in. A 'sneak' attack occurs without any warning. In both cases, repeat attacks are common, and they result in worse injuries and more fatalities than 'hit and run' attacks.

Inadvertent intruders

The popularity of beach holidays and watersports have led humans into the shark's domain in far greater numbers than in the past, and this has increased the chances of an encounter. Surfers, in particular, can find themselves in the danger zone as the largest waves form over shelves and seamounts, places that attract a lot of fish and the sharks that feed on them. The rugged western coast of South Australia is one such place, dotted with quiet bays where swells rolling in towards the shore hit a rock shelf and form breakers. In September 2000, two surfers were killed in the area by great white sharks in as many days.

New Zealander Cameron Bayes was on honeymoon when he was taken while surfing off Cactus Beach. Jeff Hunter, who has surfed the area for over 25 years, saw it all from the beach. 'It was a ferocious attack,' he says. 'I saw the shark quickly circle the man before knocking him into the water. It took him in a circular motion.' Bayes managed to scramble back onto his board before the shark returned and

TOO CLOSE FOR COMFORT
A bull shark cruises off Miramar Beach, Florida. The previous day, a 14-year-old girl was badly injured by a bull shark at a nearby beach.

dragged him under. 'It looked horrendous. There was blood and board everywhere. It was just a blur of shark and thrashing water.' The great white returned to the surface and spat out a piece of surfboard before disappearing. The day after Bayes died, a local surfer was killed by a shark off Black Point, 200 km (125 miles) farther along the coast. On average, one person is killed every year by sharks in Australia, but this stretch of coast is popular with great whites, which are attracted inshore by the presence of salmon and colonies of seals.

Out of the blue

Most attacks on surfers are made by great whites, which normally feed on seals, sea lions and small whales as well as fish, rays and other sharks. Seals and sea lions are particular favourites because their blubber-rich bodies provide great whites with high-energy food, and it is possible that sharks mistake the outline of a surfer on a board for a seal. When taking seals and sea lions at the surface, great whites often power into them from

10 most dangerous sharks

Shark attacks are rarer than many people suppose. Just over 1,000 unprovoked attacks have been recorded since records began in 1580. But attacks are many times more common than in the past, mainly because more people now spend time in the sea, swimming, surfing or diving. The most dangerous shark to humans is the great white, although attacks by 42 species out of a total 368 have been recorded.

	SPECIES	UNPROVOKED ATTACKS ON PEOPLE	DEATHS
1	Great white	323	75
2	Tiger	131	29
3	Bull	99	22
4	Sand tiger	70	2
5	Requiem	48	8
6	Nurse	47	0
7	Blacktip	40	1
8	Hammerhead	32	1
9	Blue	32	4
10	Shortfin mako	25	2

TAKING A RISK *A tiger shark cruises below a snorkeller (above left). Tiger sharks feed on a wide variety of creatures, including sea turtles. As turtles spend time drifting at the surface, attacks on humans may begin as cases of mistaken identity.*

'**They bite and maim you, then circle you and wait until you are weak. Then they eat you.**'

Rick LeProvost

BACK IN THE WATER
Despite losing his arm in a shark attack, Chuck Anderson returned to competitive swimming.

below. Sometimes they smash into a victim with such force that it is thrown out of the water.

Sharks were the last thing John Gilbert was thinking about when he was surfing off Stinson Beach, north of San Francisco, in May 2002. 'We were out there kidding around, talking, waiting for the next wave,' he recalls. 'Then all of a sudden, we heard a scream. I looked over and this guy was about 3 or 4 feet out of the water in a shark's mouth. You could see its teeth, its gums. Its eyes were shut and its gills were wide open,

like shutters. The whole dorsal fin on its back was out of the water.' The shark had grabbed Lee Fontan, an experienced surfer, who was about 4 m further out from the beach than the others. 'You see sharks on TV, where seals are attacked,' Gilbert says. 'It was just like that, straight up like a missile. The shark hit him and launched him straight out of the water.' Rather than give in, 24-year-old Fontan fought back, punching the shark hard on the snout until it let go. As he clung to his board other surfers managed to get him back to the shore. He had a huge gash in his left thigh and three tooth holes below his ribs, but he survived.

Tourist attraction

South Africa has a species of fur seal that draws great whites to its shores in abundance, and the sharks have become a major tourist attraction. People pay high prices to dive with them, protected by thick steel cages, while others go on shark-spotting boat trips. To entice the sharks to come closer, a bloody mixture of dead fish is scattered in the water. Some shark specialists have suggested that this is causing the sharks to associate boats and humans with food, increasing the possibility of attacks, especially as several surfers and swimmers

DANGER – SHARK HAZARD

There are several measures people can take to reduce the risk of encountering a shark when they go in the water.

- Many species, including bull and tiger sharks, hunt for food around dawn, at dusk or during the night. These times are best avoided in places frequented by sharks.
- Sharks feed among sandbars, reefs and drop-offs, where prey fish live.
- They also feed where dead fish or fish remains are regularly dumped in the water, such as in harbours or around fishing fleets, and places popular for baitfishing.

- Polluted or murky waters, where visibility is reduced, are danger spots.
- Splashing at the surface can cause irregular ripples, which can resemble an injured fish or seal.
- Anything that gleams or flashes, or which creates a strong contrast, such as shiny jewellery, multi-coloured swimwear and uneven, stripey tans, may look like a fish moving at the surface.
- Sharks prefer to attack a lone victim, so swimmers and surfers are safer in a group.
- Sharks can detect blood in the water from 500 m away, so people should not enter the water if they are bleeding.

Fighting back

Bernard Connor Jr saw his attacker before it struck. In May 2004, he was surfing at Salmon Creek Beach, off Bodega Bay, California, when he spotted a great white shark coming at him. By driving it off with his surfboard, he gave himself time to get away.

'Hearing a strange splash, Connor glanced over his right shoulder to see a large fin jutting out of the water. 'It was just like in the movie,' he says. 'My first thought was, that's a really big dolphin. But then I noticed it was swimming side to side rather than up and down. I thought I was dust.'

Connor was lying chest down on his board when the shark turned and struck his left thigh, tumbling him into the water. As he fell, the shark began thrashing its head and tail. 'I felt like I was in a boiling cauldron,' Connor says. 'I was spinning like I was in a whirlpool.' Next, the shark started circling, as if preparing to make another attack. Connor also turned, keeping his board between himself and the fish. Then, after the fourth circuit, the shark swam straight towards him. When it was almost on him, Connor rammed the nose of his board into its face and it began thrashing violently around him again. 'I thought the guy was going to die,' says Noel Robinson, who was watching from the beach. 'I couldn't believe how much water the shark was displacing.' Onlookers estimated that it was over 4 m long.

As the thrashing stopped, Connor, still uninjured, climbed back on his board and started paddling. It was then that he sensed a third approach. 'That was probably the scariest time,' he says. 'I remember thinking that I needed to calm down.' Connor stopped and the shark circled behind him. As it did so, he started paddling for the beach. The attack had lasted about 30 seconds, but it took 5 minutes for him to sprint to safety. 'The longest 5 minutes of my life,' Connor says.

Bernard Connor Jr

have been attacked in the past few years. Tyna Webb was killed and, more unusually, eaten by a great white in the area while taking an early-morning swim, which she had done daily for the past 17 years. One of her friends, Brian de Jager, saw the attack. 'I took my usual walk and saw Tyna swimming,' Brian says. 'The next minute I saw this fin coming through the water and then the discoloration in the water. It was so quick, it all took place in only 30 seconds.'

Swimming into danger

The warm waters of the Gulf of Mexico along the southern coast of the USA are popular for watersports. They are also prime hunting grounds for bull sharks, whose prey includes tarpon, dolphins and turtles. Territorial and highly aggressive, bull sharks follow prey close inshore, and sometimes venture into water shallow enough for people to walk in. Despite this, at the beginning of June 2000, no one had been attacked by a bull shark along the Alabama coast in 100 years.

One morning, triathlon athletes Chuck Anderson and Richard Watley went for a pre-training swim. 'About 5 minutes into my swim, something ran into me and flipped me over in the water,' Chuck recalls. He looked down and saw a shark just in front of him. 'I put my hands out and the shark took the four fingers off my right hand. He then came back at me and took a chunk out of my stomach.' Chuck lifted his head to breathe. 'I could see the fin come straight at me. I went to push off [the shark] and my right hand went completely into his mouth. When it did, he rolled straight to the bottom and dragged me across it, gnashing his head back and forth, just swinging me around like a rag doll.' They ended up on a sandbar with the shark on top of Chuck. 'As I pulled and tugged, my arm actually broke off in his mouth. I fell backwards over the sand bar, then got up and ran to the beach.'

At this point, the shark turned on Richard Watley. 'It came up under me, and I looked down and saw him staring me right in the face ... It bit my thigh and would have taken a chunk out of me, but I hit it,' Watley says. 'I thought it might leave me alone but it came at me again and again. I would punch him, he would retreat, and then I would swim as fast as I could for about 5 to 10 seconds. Then I would have to turn around and face him again.' Watley survived by swimming, between charges, back to the beach. 'He chased me all the way to the shore.'

YOUNG TARGETS

- A teenager surfing with friends is killed by a great white shark in Adelaide, Australia
- A 17-year-old survives attack by a tiger shark in Kauai, Hawaii

Nick Peterson In December 2004, 18 year-old Nick Peterson and three friends – Adam Floreani, Andrew Tomlin and Ty Wheeler –were towing a surfboard behind a dinghy off West Beach in Adelaide, Australia. Nick jumped off the boat and was swimming towards the board when a 5 m great white shark attacked. 'It came up from nowhere – he didn't

> **By the time it hit me what it was, he was being dragged under. This thing grabbed him by the arm and took him underneath the boat.**
>
> *Andrew Tomlin*

REMEMBERING A FRIEND *Adam Floreani, Ty Wheeler and Andrew Tomlin (inset above) remember Nick Peterson, who was killed by a shark within sight of shore.*

LOST AT SEA *Police search for Nick Peterson's remains.*

see it for a second before it happened,' said Adam. 'It happened so fast,' Andrew said. 'I didn't know what it was – I thought it was just a dolphin. By the time it hit me what it was, he was being dragged under. This thing grabbed him by the arm and took him underneath the boat.' They did their best to make the shark let go of Nick, striking at it with the dinghy's oars, but they could not save their friend and the shark disappeared with Nick's body.

'The attack was very quick, they lost sight of him very quick and the only remains was a lot of blood in the water,' said police chief Inspector Dave Lusty. A search for Nick's body and for the shark began early next morning as police and boats combed the area, but Nick's remains were never found.

Nick's father thanked his friends for their bravery. 'At great risk to themselves they endeavoured to save Nick,' he said.

> # The skin was all torn up and all my flesh was just torn up. I didn't really notice my foot was gone until I was in the ambulance. '
>
> *Hoku Aki*

Hoku Aki

In March 2002, 17 year-old Hoku Aki had a run-in with a tiger shark while he was bodyboarding off Brennecke Beach in Hawaii. Tiger sharks inhabit coastal and deep waters in tropical and semi-tropical regions, and feed on a wide variety of prey. In Hawaii they come near to the shore in pursuit of green turtles. They do not swim as fast as great whites, and their victims often see them before they close in.

HAPPY TO BE ALIVE
Hoku Aki waves as he leaves hospital. The teenager lost most of his left leg in an attack by a tiger shark.

'I opened my eyes and I could see the shark,' Aki says. 'It was just tossing me all over the place. I remember hearing my leg break – I heard the bones snap.

'I tried to open the [shark's] mouth to get it off me, but that didn't work. In the end, I just grabbed the shark's eye and ripped it out, then it let me go.'

Hoku thought he was going to die, but he managed to struggle to the beach and call for help. Nancy Roberts, a registered nurse, immediately grabbed a towel and used it as a tourniquet on Aki's leg while her son called a lifeguard.

'I had a look at my leg and I just noticed the skin was all torn up and all my flesh was just torn up. I didn't really notice my foot was gone until I was in the ambulance. I would like to thank the nurse that was at the beach. She saved my life.'

Aki's left leg was amputated above the knee, but he remained positive about the future. 'I never thought this would happen to me ... I can't stop my life because of it. I just gotta keep going and just make the best of it.' But he didn't have plans to go back in the water. 'I'll just sit on the beach and watch the waves or something.'

Cholera thrives in places where sanitation is poor and the water supply untreated. The disease is rare in the industrial world, but in other places it is an ever-present threat, waiting to explode into an epidemic when conditions are right, as they were in Angola in 2006.

The outbreak began in the capital, Luanda, in February. In just a few weeks it had spread from there to all but four of Angola's 18 provinces. At its peak, in May, 500-700 new cases and 10 deaths were being reported each day. Around a third of the victims were children under five. Maria André lost three members of her family in just two days: her 15-year-old daughter, her 13-year-old niece, and a nephew who was just four. Five other young relatives fell ill, but recovered. 'I don't know what happened,' she says. 'I heard about the disease on the radio and all of a sudden it was here. They were all healthy and now they are dead. It's not easy to lose three children at once.'

A disease of poverty

The cholera bacterium, *Vibrio cholerae*, causes infection of the intestines, and is passed on through contact with contaminated water and food. It spreads rapidly in places where drinking water and sewage are untreated. Victims experience severe diarrhoea, vomiting and cramps, and lose body fluids rapidly – at the rate of up to 1 litre per hour. Without treatment in the form of rehydration salts, death due to dehydration can follow within hours. Children and the old are particularly vulnerable, yet in healthy people the symptoms may be quite mild.

In Angola's outbreak, Luanda was the worst-hit place. Originally built to house 200,000 people, by the beginning of 2006 it was home to more than 4.5 million, most of them driven from the surrounding countryside by Angola's 27-year civil war. Two-thirds of Luanda's population live in vast shanty towns, such as Boa Vista.

Conditions in the shanty towns make them a breeding ground for cholera. Less than half the inhabitants have even an outside lavatory, and the streets are filled with human excreta and rubbish. 'I have never seen anything like it,' says David

Something in the Water

SOURCE OF THE PROBLEM
Children collect water from a filthy stream in Luanda.

BOA VISTA *Around 10,000 people live in this neighbourhood, where the epidemic started, without clean drinking water or a sanitation system.*

In 2006, Angola experienced the worst recorded cholera epidemic in its history. More than 2,000 people died.

DESPERATE WAIT
*A mother sits with her ill son
in a treatment centre run by
Médecins Sans Frontières.*

Weatherill, a water and sanitation expert working for Médecins Sans Frontières (MSF) in Angola. 'You see conditions like this on a smaller scale, but I have never seen it on such a huge scale. It is quite shocking.'

The cholera bacteria takes between 6 and 72 hours to incubate, and was carried around the country by people yet to realise they were infected. Benguela, on the Atlantic coast, saw more than 500 die, and another 241 lost their lives in the northerly town of Malanje. The situation worsened in April, when heavy rains caused widespread flooding. Luanda, which lies on the coast, was particularly badly affected. 'When it rains here,' explains David Weatherill, 'the rain washes all the rubbish off the slopes down towards the houses by the sea. These people get flooded, the water level rises in their houses and it mixes with all the excreta that is lying around because the people don't have access to latrines. One family told us that they had 1 metre of standing water, contaminated with excrement, [in their home] for two days.'

Most people who contract cholera do so by drinking or washing in contaminated water. For Luanda's slum-dwellers, this is almost impossible to avoid. In the shanty towns there is no piped water. Fresh water is brought in by tankers operated by private companies, who get their supplies from the rubbish-strewn Bengo River to the north of the city. The water is sold on, usually untreated, to Luanda's 10,000 or so water vendors.

> **❛One family told us that they had 1 metre of standing water, contaminated with excrement, [in their home] for two days.❜**
>
> *David Weatherill, Médecins Sans Frontières*

This water, despite being potentially unsafe, is expensive, costing up to 12 US cents for 4.5 litres – a large amount of money in a country where two-thirds of the population lives on less than US$2 a day. As a result, most people ration what they use to around 9 litres a day, far less than the United Nations' recommended minimum of 23 litres, and 4 per cent of the amount used daily by the average Westerner.

Three months into the epidemic, the Angolan government, with the help of the United Nations, set up a limited number of distribution points for free, clean water. Long before dawn each day, thousands rose to plant their buckets in organised lines that stretched out through the slums like spiders' legs. Many people travelled miles to reach these few centres. Crowds remained long after the water had gone. 'People waited for the last drop,' says José Mateus, a neighbourhood co-ordinator.

For many, the distribution points were too little, too late. In March, 27 year-old Vieira Muieba, a construction worker living in Boa Vista, lost his wife, Ombrina Cabanga, to cholera. Ombrina, he says, did everything she could to protect herself, her husband and her daughter from the disease, washing plates,

RELIEF ACTION *A water tank is installed outside a cholera treatment clinic in Malenje as part of the fight to control the epidemic.*

rinsing vegetables and cleaning out the shared latrine, used by three other families. She even disinfected the water she bought from the neighbourhood vendor, using bleach as recommended by the Health Ministry. But it was not enough. Her home, like many in the slums, backs onto a rubbish-strewn gully. One Tuesday evening she came home from her job selling soap in the market and vomited. Two days later, she was dead. 'I am just a working man. I don't know why the government doesn't help us,' says Vieira. 'I don't know where the money goes. We become angry but we don't know what to do.'

The 2006 epidemic, which lasted until July, put more than 50,000 people in hospital. According to official statistics, it claimed just over 2,000 lives. In reality, it is almost certain that many more people died. 'The figures are likely to be under-reported,' says Richard Veerman, MSF's country co-ordinator for Angola. 'Actual numbers are likely to be two or three times more because many people will have just died at home without the opportunity to come to a treatment centre.'

Barriers to change

Angola's cholera epidemic of 2006 was the first major outbreak of the disease in the country for 11 years. Medical experts are surprised that it did not happen sooner. They are also concerned that it will happen again if the authorities do not install a safe water supply.

'Cholera is right in its element in the shanty towns of Luanda,' says David Noguera of Médecins Sans Frontières (MSF). To stop future outbreaks, 'preventative measures, such as a massive intervention to provide free-of-charge water, are needed.' David Weatherill, also of MSF, agrees. 'Water is the most critical factor in a cholera outbreak. Without having clean water, it's impossible to stop the spread of the disease.'

With its oil-based economy booming, Angola has the money to clean up the shanty towns and provide safe drinking water, but government finance for proposed changes has been miniscule.

Many critics blame institutionalised corruption. A 2002 report by the US State Department found that most of Angola's wealth was in the hands of a tiny elite that included a significant number of government officials. It is not just the US administration that holds

this view. Angola is officially recognised as the seventh most corrupt nation in the world by Transparency International, an independent organisation that promotes good governance.

If the barriers to change are not broken down, cholera is likely to become ever more of a problem. Angola had not had a major cholera outbreak since 1995. 'Now we expect it to reappear every year,' says Karen Godley of MSF. 'It will become endemic.'

FUTURE PROFILE

Lethal Injection

Snakes are worshipped as gods in some cultures and despised in others; but they are almost universally feared. Although the majority of species are non-venomous, some snakes can inject powerful toxins that have the potential to kill humans.

Until recently, antivenins for snake bites did not exist, and even today they are not available in many parts of the world. The nightmare of being bitten when miles away from help came true for Joshua Taylor when he was working on a scientific survey deep in the Borneo rain forest in 2001. As Joshua reached up to grab the branch of a tree, he felt a sharp, stabbing pain on the back of his arm. 'I thought it was just biting ants,' he remembers, but when he turned to look, coiled on the branch next to his hand was a small, green, highly venomous pit viper.

Joshua knew it was serious when he saw the dismayed look on the face of his local Penan guide, Johnnie. The snake was small but potentially deadly. Johnnie killed it, then immediately set to work on the bite, smearing it with saliva and pinching it between his fingers to squeeze out the venom. He then rubbed the snake's brains into the wound 'to counteract the venom' – all the time, he was muttering a long prayer in Penan.

Johnnie helped Joshua to his feet. They had to get to the nearest village, which was a 25-minute walk away. 'He told me that he had survived a bite from a similar snake as a child,' Joshua says. 'He said that as long as I was still alive after 20 minutes, I would survive.' When they reached the village, everyone sprang into action. Joshua's arm was wrapped with medicinal plants and he was given three cups of bitter-tasting juice to gulp down. He had survived the first 20 minutes and was showing no signs of serious poisoning. That night, he slept fitfully and was almost surprised when he woke up alive in the morning.

Joshua stayed at the village and made a full recovery. Within two days, he was back on his feet and ready to return to work. Although he felt better, he was a little jumpy. 'Every single twisted vine was a snake – or so I envisioned!'

Poisonous saliva?

Pit vipers, which include the rattlesnakes of North America, are among the most dangerous snakes to humans although they do not have the deadliest venom. As well as being numerous in the areas they inhabit, they have large venom glands and hollow fangs that can inject large quantities of venom quickly. They have hemotoxic venom, which attacks blood-vessel walls and seeps into surrounding tissue, where it causes blood clotting. This produces swelling and intense pain; victims usually die from shock. The other main type of venom is neurotoxic: it attacks the nervous system, causing a prickly sensation, and kills by paralysing the heart and lungs. Cobras, coral snakes and black mambas are among the species with neurotoxic venom. Some species' venom contains both types.

Venom is modified saliva, and snakes use it for immobilising and digesting food. Venom production uses up a lot of energy, and adult snakes can control the amount they inject, using a little on small prey, more on larger victims. If a snake bites because it is startled, it often injects only a small amount of venom and in some

> **'I thought it was just biting ants ... He said that as long as I was alive after 20 minutes, I would survive.'**
>
> *Joshua Taylor*

POISON SPRAY *Most venomous snakes use their fangs to inject venom. Spitting cobras, such as this Mozambique spitting cobra from Africa, fire venom at the eyes of anything that threatens them.*

Of the 450-500 species of venomous snakes, about 250 can kill humans. An estimated 50,000 people die from snakebites each year.

cases none at all, although even a 'dry' bite can cause infection due to bacteria in the snake's mouth.

Many snakes have toxic venom, but have small fangs at the back of the mouth so cannot inject it into humans. Large constrictors, such as pythons and boas, are non-venomous, but can deliver bites that require stitches. These snakes kill prey by biting hold, coiling themselves around the victim and squeezing until it suffocates. Although constrictors attack and sometimes kill humans, these instances are relatively rare.

Occupational hazard

Snake bites kill over 100,000 people in Asia and Africa each year. India has neither the largest number of venomous snakes nor the most deadly species, but it has the greatest annual number of snake-bite deaths. According to official estimates, 2.5 million people in India are bitten each year, and 50,000 die. Most snake-bite incidents happen in rural areas, where snakes are abundant and human activities, especially farming and hunting, bring snakes and people into regular contact. People working in the fields do not wear heavy clothing, which would give them some protection. And lack of transport may prevent them reaching medical help quickly.

Deadly fascination

Not all snake bites occur in the wild. In developed countries, many herpetologists and enthusiasts are bitten while handling snakes. But even here, medical staff may not have the correct antivenin for treating a snake-bite victim.

In August 2000, snake-keeper Micah Stancil was putting a 1 m long sedge viper into a bag in order to clean its cage when it bit him on the thumb. 'I didn't feel any pain from the bite, but I knew it had happened.' After putting the viper back in its cage, he told his wife to rush him to the hospital. 'About half way to the hospital, my hand began to feel as if it were on fire.'

By the time he saw a doctor, his hand had swollen like a balloon and he was in

> **After four hours I awoke to discover, to my dismay, that the swelling was past my shoulder and into my chest.**
>
> *Micah Stancil*

10 most venomous snakes

All ten of the snakes with the most toxic venom live in Australia. The deadliest, the fierce snake or inland taipan, has venom 50 times more potent than an Indian cobra's, but it lives in remote areas and rarely bites people.

	SPECIES	LENGTH (m)	NATURAL HABITAT
1	Fierce snake/inland taipan	2	Dry plains and grasslands
2	Eastern/common brown snake	2	Forest, woodland, pasture, scrub
3	Coastal taipan	2.9	Forest, scrub, coastal heath, dunes
4	Eastern tiger snake	2	Rain forests, swamps and waterways
5	Tasmanian tiger snake	2	Thick forest to open grassland
6	Sea krait	2	Coral reefs and coastal waters
7	Western tiger snake	1.2	Forests and grasslands
8	Black tiger snake	1.2	Coastal dunes and dry, rocky areas
9	Death adder	0.5	Open woodland and scrub
10	Western brown snake	1.5	Forests, grasslands and deserts

INLAND TAIPAN *One bite can produce 110 mg of venom, enough to kill 100 people, but there are no recorded human fatalities. It is a shy and docile snake that feeds on small rodents, which it kills with a single bite of neurotoxic venom.*

EASTERN/COMMON BROWN *This snake can be very aggressive. Its venom is 12 times more toxic than an Indian cobra's. It is responsible for the most deaths from snake bites in Australia, although this is only one or two per year.*

COASTAL TAIPAN *This is the largest venomous snake in Australia. It is an aggressive hunter and inflicts several rapid bites. It has long fangs and a large venom supply, and survival from a bite is not certain even with antivenin.*

EXTRACTING VENOM
A snake-handler collects venom from a fer-de-lance, or velvet killer, in Costa Rica. The venom will be used to create antivenin to treat bites from this deadly snake.

excruciating agony. The doctor administered antivenin, but it was the wrong type. Before long, the arm was swollen past Micah's elbow and he was blacking out from the pain. 'As they were taking me to my hospital room from the ER, I lost consciousness,' he says. 'After 4 hours I awoke to discover, much to my dismay, that the swelling was past my shoulder and into my chest. The pain had subsided due to a morphine drip, but my hand was so swollen that my fingers were spaced out as far as they could go.'

A hand surgeon was called but was not keen to operate. The snake's venom had affected Micah's blood, destroying most of its platelet cells. If he was cut, his blood would no longer clot and he could bleed to death. 'I was technically a haemophiliac,' Micah explains. 'My blood was very thin and the doctors were worried that I could start bleeding internally. I couldn't even get out of bed because they were scared I might fall or bump into a table and bleed to death.' It was more than a week before he could go home. He still bears the scars on his left arm and he cannot bend his left thumb as the ligaments were destroyed.

Narrow escape

While leading a zoology field trip in south Texas, Bret Welch came across a large western diamondback in the road and decided to catch it to show the class. 'Now, I have caught over 200 large rattlesnakes before, but this one was different. He was right out of hibernation, hungry, grouchy, and I found him in the middle of the day. I had no grabbers or hooks with me and all I could

use was a shirt to give him a target.' Brett distracted the snake with his shirt and grabbed it by the tail, pulling it into the road so that everyone could see it. At that moment the rattlesnake attacked, injecting a large quantity of venom into his hand. 'I've been bitten before and knew I had to start sucking out as much venom as possible.' For the size of the snake that bit him – over 2 m long with a 6 cm span between its fangs – Bret should have been given 18 vials of antivenin within two hours and another 18 vials over the next three days.

On the way to hospital, Bret's hand swelled up severely and his skin began to turn yellow. When he arrived half an hour later, he was barely able to get out of the truck. To his dismay, the hospital had no antivenin. Bret's body started to shut down and his lungs stopped working. He remembers being put on a respirator and rushed to a second hospital. He is not sure whether they gave him any antivenin. The following day he was transferred to a third hospital, where he was given five vials of antivenin.

Bret survived, despite being given so little antivenin so late, but he has little use of his hand. He believes he lived because he had been bitten before and had developed some immunity.

COBRAS

Cobras inhabit tropical and desert regions in Asia and Africa, and are among the most dangerous snakes to humans. The Indian or common cobra, along with Russell's viper, is responsible for the most snake-bite deaths in the world each year. In Africa, the Egyptian cobra is a major killer.

Cobras include the largest venomous snakes. Their neurotoxic venom is not the most poisonous, but they can inject a large quantity. The king cobra can inject enough venom in one bite to kill an adult elephant. Some cobras spit venom at potential threats. They aim for the eyes, and can hit a victim accurately from a distance of 2.4 m, causing a severe stinging pain and temporary blindness.

Trouble Breathing

The patient seemed to be suffering from an unusual case of pneumonia. But doctors who saw him in a hospital in China's southerly province of Guangdong in November 2002 were puzzled. His symptoms were strange – high fever, dry cough, aching and shortness of breath.

None of the tests they ran could pinpoint what was making him ill. Before long, four healthcare workers who had been treating him also fell sick, complaining of the same strange symptoms. The man is now believed to have been the first victim of Severe Acute Respiratory Syndrome (SARS), although at the time the disease had no name. The Chinese authorities never released his identity.

By February the next year, the mystery illness had begun to spread. At first, the authorities tried to suppress news of it, but on February 11, 2003, the Ministry of Health finally submitted a report to the Beijing office of the World Health Organization (WHO), which admitted that there had been an outbreak of an unknown 'acute respiratory syndrome' in Guangdong. Just over a month later, on March 15, the WHO announced that this new disease, which it called Severe Acute Respiratory Syndrome, was a virus and a 'worldwide health threat'. It revealed that possible cases had been identified in Indonesia, the Philippines, Singapore, Thailand, Vietnam and as far afield as Canada. There had already been an outbreak among hospital workers in Hong Kong. What had begun as a localised problem was quickly turning into a potential pandemic.

Within two weeks, the WHO had issued a recommendation that departing travellers from affected areas should be screened for SARS, and some financial analysts trimmed their short-term economic forecasts for the South-east Asian nations. Although the number of reported deaths was still small, people were frightened because so little was known about the disease. On March 29, Dr Carlo Urbani, the Italian

ISOLATION WARD *A child SARS victim waves to thank doctors in Beijing's Ditan Hospital for 'get well' gifts they gave him. By the time this picture was taken, in May 2003, SARS was declining in China.*

There was worldwide panic in 2003 as SARS, a new and deadly respiratory disease, threatened to turn into a global pandemic.

273

WHO official who had first identified the SARS virus, died of the disease himself in Vietnam.

At the outset, SARS was thought to be spread only through so-called droplet transmission – via coughing and sneezing. Droplets produced like this are quite heavy and travel just a metre or so before falling to the ground. The theory was that SARS could be transmitted only through relatively close contact, including through shared central ventilation systems. In April 2003, that theory was dismissed as SARS tore through a Hong Kong apartment block that had no central ventilation.

Superspreaders

Dr William Schaffner of Vanderbilt University in Nashville, Tennessee, explains the second mechanism by which SARS may have spread – through 'superspreaders', infected individuals who seemed to be more contagious than most others. 'It is very likely this virus was usually spread by droplet transmission,' he says, 'but from time to time it may have been embedded in a "superspreader" who may have also spread the virus through airborne transmissions.' Airborne transmissions are tiny particles

NO WAY OUT *A policeman stands guard at the entrance to a quarantined apartment block in Hong Kong.*

5 worst affected countries

According to WHO estimates, by the end of July 2003, there had been 8,096 SARS cases worldwide and 774 people had died. Outside Asia, the worst-hit country was Canada, where the first death was that of a 78-year-old woman on March 5, 2003. She was of Chinese ethnic origin and had recently returned from a trip to Hong Kong.

	COUNTRY	CASES	DEATHS
1	China	5,327	349
2	Hong Kong	1,755	299
3	Canada	251	43
4	Taiwan	346	37
5	Singapore	238	33

that emerge with our breath and may travel long distances suspended in the air. A 64-year-old doctor may have been the superspreader who brought SARS from mainland China to Hong Kong – he infected eight people on his floor in the Metropole Hotel before dying of the disease himself.

As the weeks passed, intensive study began to yield results. Canadian researchers managed to sequence the genome of the SARS virus, and vaccines were developed. And where there were outbreaks, they were successfully contained. For example, when SARS appeared to be spreading through Beijing, the Chinese government ordered the closure of all schools and entertainment venues, such as theatres and cinemas.

In the end, the SARS pandemic never materialised. On June 5, 2003, less than eight months after the first death in Guangdong, the WHO announced that the outbreak had peaked around the world. After that, one by one, all the affected countries were declared SARS-free. In the year that followed, there were three small outbreaks of SARS from medical research facilities, but all of these were contained. Finally, in February 2005, SARS was officially described as eradicated outside laboratories. The first new major disease of the 21st century had come and gone.

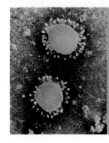

2002

Nov First known case of 'atypical pneumonia' (SARS) occurs in Foshan, Guangdong, China.

2003

Feb China reports 305 cases and five deaths. The virus spreads to Hong Kong, Taiwan and Vietnam.

Mar WHO issues a global SARS alert. Cases are reported in Canada, Germany, Singapore Thailand and the UK.

May There have been more than 6,000 cases worldwide by May 2 and more than 8,000 by May 22.

July Taiwan, the last area with a recent outbreak, is declared SARS-free. SARS has been contained.

The purplish-black berries of deadly nightshade – a plant that lives up to its name – are so toxic to humans that people can be poisoned merely by touching them. Eating a few berries causes death from respiratory failure. Lower doses cause a racing heartbeat, dilation of the pupils and vomiting.

Deadly nightshade is native to Europe and northern Asia, but also grows in many other parts of the world. Its unusual properties have long been recognised, and it has been used over the centuries as an ingredient in everything from herbal anaesthetics to nerve gas. Ladies once used drops made from an extract of deadly nightshade to beautify themselves by dilating the pupils of their eyes – hence its other name, belladonna, from the Italian for 'beautiful lady'.

Because it is so familiar, deadly nightshade rarely causes accidental poisonings – most people who find it growing near them know to leave it alone. Nonetheless, one case was recorded in a British medical magazine in 2002. A 70-year-old woman was admitted to a hospital in Leicester with symptoms that included hallucinations, dizziness, an inability to concentrate, sudden fits of laughter and dilated pupils.

Beautiful but Deadly

Something similar had happened on three previous occasions and she had been diagnosed as suffering from recurrent psychosis. But the doctors who examined her were puzzled. They carried out tests, and these did not reveal anything that could fully explain her symptoms. Then, the day after, her daughter brought in some berries from a plant growing near the woman's home – it was deadly nightshade. On this and the three other occasions, the woman – who was from South Asia, where the plant is not a native – had eaten its berries. Further tests confirmed this diagnosis and the woman recovered fully.

Fatal fungi

Unlike deadly nightshade and other poisonous plants, many fungi are hard to identify accurately and are generally less well understood. The mushrooms and toadstools most people think of as fungi are, in fact, just the fruiting bodies of much larger organisms made up of threads of tissue, which run through dead wood, leaf litter and soil. Unlike the fruits of most plants, fungal fruiting bodies are not intended to be eaten, which is why so many more of them are poisonous. Some advertise the fact with bright colours, warning animals to stay away. Others, however, look innocuous and closely resemble the edible mushrooms of non-poisonous species.

Accidental poisoning by fungi happens more often than with plants. In most cases, it takes several hours before symptoms appear – it may even take days. The first signs of poisoning include vomiting, diarrhoea and dehydration, followed by a period in which the patient feels well again. After that, if the patient is not treated, the kidneys and liver start to suffer damage and can fail completely, leading to death.

FOUR TO FEAR *All four of these species (clockwise, from top left) are poisonous: deadly nightshade, the death cap mushroom, poison ivy and the castor oil plant. Oil extracted from the seeds of the castor oil plant is used in industry as a lubricant and even in some medical products, but the seeds are deadly poisonous if eaten raw, because they contain high concentrations of the toxin ricin.*

Nature's bounty can be deceptive. A number of plants and fungi are dangerous to humans, causing serious injury or even death.

BRUSH WITH DANGER
Stinging spines cover the stems and leaves of Australia's nettle trees, and can injure anybody brushing against them. Inhaling the plant's shed hairs causes nosebleeds.

The deadliest of all mushrooms is the death cap, native to Europe but now also found in many other parts of the world. It contains a cocktail of toxins of which the most lethal is alpha-amanitin, which attacks the liver and kidneys. In October 1988, five people in Oregon, USA, stir-fried some death caps, mistaking them for an edible variety. Three of them suffered irreversible liver damage and had to undergo life-saving transplants. In just over a week around the New Year of 1997, nine people in northern California were hospitalised after eating death caps – two died. The most famous historical victim of death cap poisoning was the Renaissance Pope Clement VII, who died in 1534 after eating one – it is possible that he was fed it deliberately by enemies.

One group of mushrooms, the 'false morels', can poison by vapour. 'Real' morels (*Morchella* species) are much prized by gourmets, especially in France. False morels (*Gyromitra* species) look similar but need to be treated with caution. When cooked, they release a toxic compound, called monomethylhydrazine. At 87.5°C, this rises from the fungi like steam. The cook is enveloped in toxic fumes, but does not immediately succumb to the effects. When symptoms do appear, they may be mild or severe, depending on the dose. Small doses can cause dizziness, fatigue, headaches, vertigo, stomach pain or bloating. More serious cases can lead to convulsions, liver damage, destruction of red blood cells and coma. Once cooked, false morels are, in fact, edible, so for those determined to taste them, they should be prepared

in a well-ventilated kitchen, to avoid breathing in the monomethylhydrazine vapour, and the cooking liquid should be thrown away.

Other mushrooms, such as the common inkcap, are poisonous only if eaten with alcohol. The common inkcap, found in Europe and North America, contains a toxin called coprine, similar to the key ingredient in a drug sometimes used to treat alcoholics. Eaten on its own, it is completely harmless, but with alcohol it causes vomiting, rashes and dizziness.

Formidable foliage

Plant leaves can also contain toxins. Leaves are the factories in which plants produce their food, so protecting them from browsing animals is important if the plant is to thrive. Many plants produce toxins which build up in their leaves, making them virtually inedible; others have leaves that exude toxins when damaged or inject them directly through tiny spines.

The stinging nettle is the most common example in Western Europe. Tiny hairs, tipped with brittle glassy spines, cover the surfaces of its leaves. These break off at the slightest touch, embedding themselves in the skin. As they break, they squirt poison into the wounds from small chambers at the base of each spine. After the initial pain, each sting swells up into a little bump, leaving a rash. The effect is unpleasant, but the European stinging nettle has relatives in other parts of the world that are downright dangerous. Tropical Australia has three ferocious species, one of which grows into a tree up to 15 m high. Even brushing against one of these causes rashes and extreme pain, which can last for days. Another tree nettle, the New Zealand ongaonga, has been known to kill dogs, horses and at least one human.

In North America, poison ivy is well known for its toxic leaves. Not a true ivy, it grows as a small shrub or climbing vine, containing the poison urushiol in its leaves and stems. Contact with an undamaged plant causes no reaction, but poison ivy is extremely brittle, and where it breaks, its toxic sap oozes out. Even the tiniest amount can cause a rash and severe irritation. Humans are particularly susceptible. While cats and dogs are unaffected by urushiol, they often bring the sap into the home on their fur. Owners may contract a poison ivy rash simply by stroking their pets.

Poison ivy has two close cousins in North America: the poison sumac and the poison oak. The latter is common on the West Coast, where it is a hazard for fire-fighters tackling forest fires. As poison oak burns, it releases urushiol into the air, which can affect both the skin and the lungs. Although urushiol is not life-threatening, it causes painful rashes and lung irritation that can persist for several days afterwards.

Prickly defences

Instead of using chemicals to fight their battles, some plants develop sharp thorns, spines or blades. Many coarse grasses, for example, have tiny but fearsome silica blades along the edges of their leaves. These are sharp enough to cut through the skin and draw blood.

Most acacia trees bristle with long, sharp spines, forming a defensive barrier fearsome enough to deter all but the toughest browsers. One African acacia, known appropriately as the wait-a-bit thorn, has such ferocious thorns that it can actually hold people or animals captive. Its long,

whiplike branches are covered with large, backward-pointing thorns that stab through the skin and grip like meat hooks. Any creature that gets snagged becomes more entangled as it tries to escape. In parts of Africa, villagers plant hedges of wait-a-bit thorns and other acacias around their settlements and fields, as a protection against wild animals.

A few plants have gone a step further and evolved ways to capture animals. They tend to be found in areas where there are few, if any, nutrients in the soil. The plants need the animals to provide them with essential minerals. Among them are pitcher plants, which have evolved in such a way that their leaves fuse together to form a tube-shaped trap. Nectar attracts insects and other small animals to the plant; then, once inside the lip of the pitcher, they slide into the pool of water and digestive juices at the bottom. Sundew plants also trap flying insects, using beads of sticky liquid on the ends of flexible hairs. When an insect lands on one of these it becomes stuck and other hairs wrap around it, holding it fast. The plant can then digest its meal at leisure.

Perhaps the most elegant of all the carnivorous plants is the venus flytrap. Its leaves have trigger hairs which, when tripped, cause them to snap together. All it takes is a touch from the legs of a fly or other insect against the hairs to seal the creature's fate.

STICKY END *The beads of sticky liquid on this sundew plant trap insects, which the plant then digests.*

In the Blood

Every year more than a million people die from malaria — that is, one person every 30 seconds. It is one of the world's biggest killers. Many more millions — an incredible 10 per cent of the world's population — carry the disease, living with its recurring and debilitating bouts of fever.

The vast majority of new malaria cases occur in sub-Saharan Africa, where it is the greatest single cause of death, although it is also prevalent in South America and many parts of Asia. George Owino Osiga, a cobbler from the village of Nina, 48 km (30 miles) from Lake Victoria in western Kenya, describes its effects on their lives. 'Two weeks ago our aunt died from malaria,' he says. 'She was ill on Tuesday, complaining about a bad headache and fever, and on Wednesday she was dead. It is not unusual like that. At least with AIDS it can take you a long time to die, but malaria is quick. In the past three years, 25 of my family and friends have died in this way.' In his village, he continues, 'everyone has malaria. ... Recently, we have buried ten people from this disease ... because it is so bad.'

In places such as Nina, where malaria is endemic, people are often infected again and again. Over time, they may build up an immunity, which is one reason that there are so many more living malaria sufferers than malaria deaths. But although sufferers survive, they do so at a cost. 'For myself,' George Owino Osiga says, 'it comes and goes. Last year, I was affected almost all year with malaria, so I could not work well. The headaches were very bad. But this year, it is better.'

Microscopic killers

Malaria is an ancient disease which has evolved alongside humans over thousands of years. Tiny single-celled parasites belonging to four different species within the scientific genus *Plasmodium* cause it, each species infecting people with a slightly different form of the disease. Of these parasites, the most widespread and dangerous is

SAFE AND SOUND
An Ethiopian father carries his daughter home after she has been successfully treated for malaria. The disease killed 300,000 people in Ethiopia in 2005.

INSECT HOST *Mosquitoes transmit the malaria parasite in their saliva. The disease declined in Europe and North America with the draining of swamps and mill ponds in the 19th century. Today, it is confined mainly to the tropics.*

Malaria blights the lives of millions living in the tropics. It is a killer that also helps to trap whole nations in poverty.

PREVENTING INFECTION
A health educator in Djibouti shows trainee workers how to soak mosquito nets in insecticide.

GOOD NIGHT'S SLEEP
A Ghanaian mother and her son with their net. Mosquitoes are most active at night, so sleeping beneath a mosquito net reduces the chances of being bitten.

Plasmodium falciparum, which causes cerebral malaria. Left untreated, this is almost always fatal.

Mosquito bites transfer the parasites to humans. *Plasmodium* parasites live in the guts of about 60 species of anopheline mosquitoes, found throughout the tropics. When a female mosquito of one of these species takes a drink of human blood before laying its eggs, it passes the parasite to the person it is biting via its saliva. Mosquitoes lay their eggs in still, fresh water, which is why the incidence of malaria tends to be higher near stretches of fresh water and during the rainy season. Male anopheline mosquitoes feed only on plant juices and so are harmless to humans.

Once in the human bloodstream, the parasites are carried to the liver, where they invade the cells and multiply. They may spend up to 30 days there, hiding inside red blood cells to avoid the white blood cells of the host's immune system, before re-emerging into the bloodstream. Here, they multiply once more until the red blood cells can no longer contain them. The red cells burst, inducing anaemia and bouts of fever in the infected person. In cerebral malaria, the bloated red blood cells can block the tiny vessels in the brain, leading to coma and death. Other vital organs can also be damaged in this way, even when the brain is not. Again, the outcome is often death if the person is left untreated.

The disease can be treated and even cured. A variety of antimalarial drugs are available, but they are often expensive – too expensive for most of the people who are at risk. Even after treatment, malaria can recur. Often, some *Plasmodium* parasites remain, lying dormant in the cells of the liver, out of reach of the drugs. They may reappear in the bloodstream years later, causing symptoms including fever and joint pain.

Economic impact

By affecting so many people's health, malaria also has an impact on national economies. In Africa, its effect on the workforce is recognised as a major impediment to development. 'Since 1990, the per person GDP in many sub-Saharan African countries has declined,' says Dr Jeffrey Sachs, Director of the Center for International Development at Harvard University, 'and malaria is an important reason for this poor economic performance.'

According to the World Health Organization (WHO), the gross domestic product (GDP) of sub-Saharan Africa would be almost a third higher if malaria had been eradicated 35 years ago. In other words, without malaria, the region would earn an extra US$100 billion a year, almost five times the amount it receives in development aid. 'Malaria is hurting the living standards of Africans today and is also preventing the improvement

> **❝Malaria is hurting the living standards of Africans today and is also preventing the improvement of living standards for future generations.❞**
>
> *Dr Gro Harlem Brundtland*

SICKLE CELL ANOMALY

Sickle cell anaemia can be lethal. During periods of high muscular activity, the blood cells of people who suffer from it warp into a sickle shape. These can then block small blood vessels, causing pain, tissue damage, even death. Sufferers, however, are more likely to survive malaria, which may explain why the condition is common in parts of Africa. In most people, the malaria parasite evades the immune system by hiding inside red blood cells. In sickle cell sufferers, however, it makes them warp out of shape. They are then destroyed, along with the parasite, when they pass through the spleen.

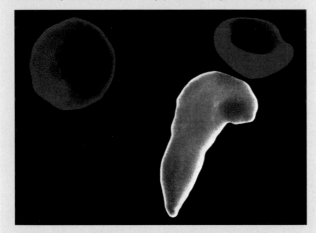

BLOOD DISORDER *Sickle cell anaemia is an inherited condition, which causes red blood cells to change shape.*

of living standards for future generations,' says Dr Gro Harlem Brundtland, former Director General of the WHO. 'This is an unnecessary and preventable handicap on the continent's economic development.'

The saddest fact is that the disease can be prevented by relatively simple measures, but these, again, are beyond the means of the majority of people living in malaria-prone regions. Sleeping under a mosquito net treated with insecticide halves the chance of becoming infected, but a net costs on average US$5, which makes it too expensive for most families in the poorest developing countries.

In sub-Saharan Africa, just 2 per cent of children sleep under mosquito nets, yet children are more at risk than anyone else: three-quarters of all the people who die from malaria are under the age of 16. 'Everyone knows mosquitoes are the danger, but the problem is that people are poor,' says George Owino Osiga. 'Even if you tell them about bed-nets, they are thinking about how they will eat. Nobody uses nets.'

Living with malaria

Four decades ago, the disease was on the decline. A new insecticide had proved so successful at eliminating mosquitoes that it was being used around the world in a bid to wipe out malaria for ever. It was DDT, today more often associated with environmental and potential human health problems than with the eradication of disease. Its over-use by farmers as a pest control was decimating wildlife populations, particularly among

most deadly infectious diseases

Rare new diseases are the ones that usually hit the headlines – bird flu, Ebola, SARS and the like. But while these fill the pages of newspapers and catch the public's imagination, other, much bigger killers quietly do their work, wiping out humanity on a scale that even wars and the worst natural disasters cannot match. According to the World Health Organization, the following seven diseases kill more people than any others:

	DISEASE	TYPE	TRANSMISSION	DISTRIBUTION	DEATHS ANNUALLY (estimated)
1	Pneumonia	Viruses	Airborne	Global	3,500,000
2	HIV/AIDS	Virus	Sexual contact, blood transfusion, mother to baby	Global	2,800,000
3	Diarrhoea diseases	Bacteria	Contact with infected food or person	Global	2,220,000
4	Tuberculosis (TB)	Bacterium	Airborne, infected cow's milk	Global	1,500,000
5	Malaria	Protist	Mosquito bites	Tropical and subtropical Africa, Asia and South America	1,110,000
6	Measles	Virus	Airborne	Global	890,000
7	Whooping cough	Bacterium	Airborne droplets from infected person	Global	350,000

New hope

Developing an effective vaccine against malaria is tricky. Few people know this better than Dr Joe Cohen of the pharmaceuticals giant GlaxoSmithKline (GSK), whose Belgian-based team has spent more than 20 years dedicated to the task. 'I think the main challenge is the complexity of the parasite itself,' he says. 'Parasites have devised ways of escaping the immune system of the host which are exquisite, and I think that is the major reason why we haven't been able up to now to develop any vaccine against any parasitic disease.'

In the case of malaria, however, there are high hopes of a breakthrough. Trials indicate that one potential vaccine, called RTS,S, developed by GSK with the Walter Reed Army Research Institute in the USA, is particularly promising. In 2003, it was tried out on 1,442 children in Mozambique. Results released in 2005 showed that, over an 18-month period, it had reduced malaria cases by 35 per cent and severe cases by 49 per cent. 'The unprecedented response demonstrated in this study,' said Dr Pedro Alonso of the University of Barcelona, 'is further evidence that an effective vaccine to help control the malaria pandemic … is very possible.' Further trials are being carried out in six African countries among both adults and children.

Another boost has come from the world's richest man, Microsoft chairman, Bill Gates. In 2003, he gave US$168 million to research facilities and companies working to develop a malaria vaccine, more than doubling the amount spent globally on investigating the disease. 'Malaria is robbing Africa of its people and potential,' he said. 'Beyond the extraordinary human toll, malaria is one of the greatest barriers to Africa's economic growth, draining national health budgets and deepening poverty.' The Bill & Melinda Gates Foundation, headed by Gates and his wife, donated a further US$258.3 million in 2005.

These huge cash injections have helped to change attitudes. 'Gates is … telling us this is doable,' says Regina Rabinovich, former director of the Malaria Vaccine Initiative (MVI). In the fight against malaria, she adds, the 'world should have a sense of impatience rather than a sense of resignation'. Evidence of this new spirit can also be seen in research into new antimalarial drugs. 'Five years ago, the malaria drug research pipeline was virtually empty,' says Dr Chris Hentschel of the Geneva-based Medicines for Malaria Venture (MMV). 'Now we're developing 20 promising compounds …' Among them are drugs that will cost just US$1 or less and cure malaria with three simple one-a-day doses and a cherry-flavoured antimalarial pill that dissolves in water for children.

SILVER LINING

birds. The empty landscapes this created inspired the US biologist Rachel Carson to write her bestselling book *Silent Spring*, published in 1962, which attacked the widespread use of DDT and helped to launch the modern environmental movement. But DDT was, in fact, a very effective weapon against malaria. Controlled targeting of anopheline mosquitoes using DDT wiped out malaria in the USA, and other nations came close to eliminating it. In India, annual incidence of malaria was reduced from around 75 million cases to to just 50,000 by 1961.

Eventually, however, experts realised that they could never defeat malaria completely by targeting its carriers. That goal was too ambitious, considering the vast areas of wilderness in which anopheline mosquitoes could still hide. In 1969, the WHO, which had launched the Global Malaria Eradication Programme 14 years earlier, officially ended it. Although great strides had been made and millions of lives saved, malaria had clung on, and it soon started to make a spectacular resurgence.

Today, it is a brave, desperate or politically isolated government that attempts to tackle malaria with DDT.

International pressure against the use of the chemical for any reason is so great that few are willing to try it. Most countries have signed an international convention banning its use. When in 2004 Uganda proposed DDT spraying to control its malaria problem, it sparked considerable concern among the country's international development partners.

The best hope is that a vaccine against malaria will be discovered (see box, above). Unlike spraying, an effective vaccine could provide a realistic way of eliminating the disease for good. In the meantime, some prevention campaigns are bringing success. In a remote region of Senegal in western Africa, for example, 20-year-old Oumoul Khary Sow and her family drive round villages, distributing free plastic-wrapped packs of insecticide-treated mosquito nets – part of a government-sponsored drive to try to control the disease. The initiative works and has also boosted morale. 'When we started out, people here were resigned to having malaria – to dying from malaria,' she says. 'They thought it was something they just had to accept. Now they know how to fight it – by sleeping under insecticide-treated nets and seeking medical care at the dispensary when they have a fever.'

An adult locust eats its body weight in plant matter every day. A swarm of them, which may contain 80 million of the insects over an area of 1 km² (0.4 sq miles), can bring devastation to entire communities, wiping out their crops and destroying the foliage their livestock need to feed on.

Th Eighth Plague

In 2004, north-west Africa suffered its worst locust plague in 15 years. Between April and November, trillions of the insects swept through ten countries in swarms of almost unprecedented size – a few were more than 70 km (40 miles) long. Storms even blew some out over the Atlantic to the Canary Islands, where astonished tourists were driven indoors to escape them. On the mainland, people faced something far worse than a spoiled holiday – ruined crops and the prospect of hungry months ahead.

Black with locusts

Unlike many insects, locusts are not fussy eaters, which means that when a swarm arrives very few plants escape its attentions. Swarms can cover several square miles,

and they are constantly on the move, the locusts' appetites forcing them on in a continuous search for food. In their wake they leave bare branches, destroyed livelihoods and the prospect of famine. The Old Testament book of Exodus is scarcely exaggerating when it describes a plague of locusts, the eighth in a succession of ten different 'plagues' that are supposed to have afflicted Egypt: 'They covered the surface of the whole land till it was black with them; they devoured all the vegetation and all the fruit of the trees … ; there was no green left on tree or plant throughout all Egypt.'

Locusts' lives are divided into three distinct stages. As eggs, they lie buried in the sandy soil for 10 to 65 days. They then hatch out as wingless larvae, called

INVASION FORCE *Locust swarms are a recurrent nightmare in north and west Africa. Here, a Senegalese man sweeps the insects from his face during an earlier plague in 1989.*

The plague of locusts that swept across Africa in 2004 was of biblical proportions, leaving stripped fields and hungry villages.

MOVING CARPET *A few last blades of grass stick up through a writhing mass of locusts in Senegal during the 2004 plague. One tonne of locusts – a small portion of most swarms – can eat as much in a day as 2,500 people.*

SPREADING OUT *In June and July, locusts that had hatched in north-west Africa in the spring spread southwards across the Sahara to the Sahel, where their swarms merged with swarms of newly hatched insects.*

hoppers, which form swarms for defence against predators such as birds. These march over the land, eating as they go. Even at this stage, they are extremely destructive, but since they cannot fly they are easier to contain and destroy. It is when they become adults, around 36 days after hatching, that their swarms pose the greatest threat. By now the insects are larger and developing eggs of their own, so they become even more voracious. And they have wings, so they can travel much farther in search of food. Adult locusts can cover as much as 200 km (124 miles) in a day, and they may live for five months.

Clouds over Africa

The 2004 plague began in Morocco and Algeria during April. Ironically, a wet winter and spring triggered it by creating unusually good growing conditions for plants between the Mediterranean coast and the Sahara desert. Locust larvae hatching out found themselves surrounded by a rare bounty of food, and far more survived to adulthood than in most previous years.

As the locusts turned into adults, their swarms began to exhaust the food supplies around them, forcing them to migrate south and east across the Sahara on the summer winds. When they reached the Sahel along the Sahara's southern edge, they mingled with new swarms there and spread out in a band

HOLIDAY FROM HELL *At the end of 2004, many locusts were blown out to sea. Some landed on the tourist beaches of the Canary Islands, where the authorities declared a state of alert.*

roughly 4,000 km (2,485 miles) long, stretching from Mauritania to Chad. They then began moving slowly southwards again, reaching Senegal in late September. Their timing could not have been worse.

'We were three weeks away from the harvests and people had sunk all their savings into the seeds they planted,' explains Mame Dieng, a village chief from Rao district in northern Senegal. The locusts destroyed the peanut crops that provide most rural people with their only source of income, and many villagers had no choice but to uproot and head for the cities in search of work. Those who remained had to cut their costs in order to buy food, and many were forced to sacrifice their children's education, as they could no longer afford to pay for it.

Once locusts arrive, they are hard to eliminate. People do their best to frighten them away, but when the swarms are thick, almost as soon as one swarm is airborne, another is replacing it. Djiby Diop was working on a maize and pepper farm on the Mauritania-Senegal border when the locusts came. 'The swarms came several times here and for hours we chased by waving flags,' he says, 'but they were too many. They ate half of the crops.' Luckily, the farm's owner managed to contact

> **The swarms came several times here and for hours we chased by waving flags, but they were too many. They ate half of the crops.**
>
> *Djiby Diop, Senegalese farm worker*

BARE BRANCHES
A Moroccan apple farmer surveys the damage to his orchard. The locusts devoured his entire crop and with it his income for the year.

Senegal's Directorate of Rural Development and alert them. At the same time, he and other local landowners and farmers pooled their resources to buy pesticide. The government sent in soldiers armed with portable sprayers.

Unlike Djiby's employer, many poorer farmers lost almost everything. In the nearby village of Thill Peulh, Marie Diop tried in vain to clear the locusts from the plot of land she works. Before the swarms came, it was full of ripening produce; within days, the locusts had stripped it almost bare. Unable to afford pesticide, Marie's only option was to try to frighten the locusts away. Day after day, she marched up and down, banging a cooking pot with a wooden spoon. But the insects kept returning. 'It's been going on for three weeks,' she said. 'This must be the tenth time they've come to this field since they arrived. Usually we clap them away with the pots, but they are too many. It's no use.'

SILVER LINING

Sky prawns

Locusts devastate crops, but they themselves can provide a tasty meal. In parts of Africa, they have long been considered a delicacy. The Tswana people of southern Africa, for example, remove their wings and legs, then sauté them to create a dish known as *tinjiya*, while the Swazi roast them as *sikonyane*. Locusts are even used to create a high-energy travellers' food. The South Sotho people roast headless locusts, then grind them into a fine powder, to make them easier to carry. Further afield, in Cambodia, locusts are stuffed with peanuts, then lightly grilled.

Australians, too, have started turning the tables on the locusts that often sweep across New South Wales. *Cooking with Sky Prawns* by Edward Joshua and Chris Carr contains more than 20 recipes for locust-based dishes. Joshua calls locusts 'home delivery bush food', and says they are more nutritious than beef. 'If you've eaten a lobster, crab or crayfish, you've already eaten Arthropoda, of which insects are a part,' he says. 'So popping a big juicy locust in your mouth is only a step away!'

Moving on

Locusts are a fact of life in this part of Africa, but the swarms of 2004 were unusually large. Banging pots when there are fewer locusts is often effective. Other techniques include driving the insects away with smoke, but this requires a steady wind for as long as the swarms remain in the area. In 2004, the locusts stayed for weeks.

The plague as a whole spread out and contracted as the individual swarms comprising it exhausted certain areas and moved on to find more food. In early November, many began moving north again, back to Algeria and into Libya. Some then moved on towards the Middle East, while storms blew others west across the Atlantic, with the tourist-filled beaches of the Canary Islands directly in their path.

For North Europeans who had flown south to the Canaries to enjoy the winter sun, sunbathing suddenly became a pastime only for the stubborn and brave, as millions of battered, dying locusts descended on the islands in search of a few final meals. Some were missing legs and others had damaged wings. Many began eating each other in order to survive – locusts often turn to cannibalism to provide the energy to set off and find more food. Others crashed into the sea, and every wave washed more up onto the islands' beaches.

Elsewhere in November, the locusts also gradually started to die. But it was too late for many families in northern Africa, whose crops the swarms had decimated. In the end, widespread famine was avoided, but most people went hungry. Many were forced to eat the seed corn they had bought to plant the following year.

Early prevention is the key

The plague of 2004 caused terrible devastation. In Mauritania, the nation that suffered most, locusts consumed half of the entire cereal crop. The tragedy was that timely action could have prevented much of the suffering. In theory, at least, most locust plagues can be avoided.

Edouard Tapsoba, head of the UN Food and Agriculture Organization (FAO) in Senegal, voiced his frustration in November 2004. 'It's been more than a year that we've been warning the countries and the donor community [of the growing crisis], without any success, until now,' he said.

As early as the summer of 2003, there had been reports of large locust swarms forming in parts of North Africa. According to the International Red Cross, US$1 million spent in July 2003 would have contained the swarms and prevented the next year's plague. But nothing was done and the consequent damage cost US$100 million to put right. Problems included a failure in international co-operation – the relevant

TOO LITTLE TOO LATE *Senegalese workers spray a swarm with insecticide. Action taken earlier could have prevented the plague.*

agencies in each country had no system for communicating with one another – and an inability to take responsibility and see the size of the problem ahead.

Can such a situation be avoided in the future? The FAO's Locust Group is blunt about the difficulties. These include the sheer size and remoteness of many of the areas where locusts are found. The transport infrastructure is often primitive, and in some places there is the added hazard of land mines, the legacy of regional conflicts.

But there is also much that can be done. The FAO issues regular reports and forecasts of locust activity, based on sources including local information and satellite imagery. It also provides training and technical backup. When, in October 2006, it warned that a potential infestation was developing on the border between Mauritania and Mali, officials responded promptly, and experts were

confident that the crisis was being contained. At the same time, they were able to test a new control method. The insects are most vulnerable at their larval, or hopper, stage. Unable to take to the air, they can easily be killed by spraying or driven into trenches and buried. In Mauritania, experts tested a new environmentally friendly pesticide, using the fungus *Metarhizium anisopliae*. When this infects hoppers, it stops them feeding and they die within three weeks.

Ironically, the conditions in which locusts thrive are the same as those that produce bumper harvests. Given better co-operation among governments and non-governmental organisations, prompt action and the development of new control methods, there is no reason why swarms should not be dealt with early on, allowing regions such as North Africa to prosper, rather than suffer, during their best growing years.

The Swarm

Once 'killer' bees were the stuff of bad movies and science fiction. Now, Africanised bees, popularly known as 'killer' bees, are established in large parts of the Americas. By 2002, they had spread from South America into the south-west USA. They currently have a foothold in six US states.

TOUGH CUSTOMERS
Africanised honeybees produce more honey in tropical regions than their European counterparts, and many South and Central American beekeepers prefer them, despite their aggressiveness.

Hybrid honeybees, dubbed 'killer' bees, hit the headlines in 2005 after swarms made a number of savage attacks on people in the USA.

291

Africanised bees are just that – hybrids created by cross-breeding European honeybees with honeybees from Africa. In nature, European and African honeybees are distinct subspecies, which never meet. But in the 1950s, a Brazilian of Scottish ancestry, Warwick Estevam Kerr, wanted to create productive honeybees for tropical conditions. European honeybees, which had been introduced to the Americas in colonial times, did not thrive in Brazil. Kerr hoped that genes from the African subspecies would toughen them up. He was right.

In 1957, 26 Tanzanian queen bees escaped from Kerr's hives. They began interbreeding with European honeybees in the wild, and swarms of Africanised bees soon started to spread. These have several traits that make them unusually dangerous. They tend to swarm more frequently and are far more aggressive than other bees. If their hive is disturbed, they defend it ferociously, pouring out in huge numbers to sting the person or creature who roused them. They also chase perceived threats much farther from their hives than other bees do.

American Robert Rupe discovered all this in October 2005, when he encountered some Africanised bees while quail hunting in the wilds of Arizona. It was a hot day, and he was planning a dip in a stream to cool off. 'When I got near Kayler Springs, they attacked me. They were on me before I could get to the water,' Rupe says. The bees swarmed around him, then landed on him, stinging repeatedly. 'They were just like dive-bombers, kamikazes,' he says. Trying to escape them, Rupe scrambled uphill, crossing two barbed wire fences

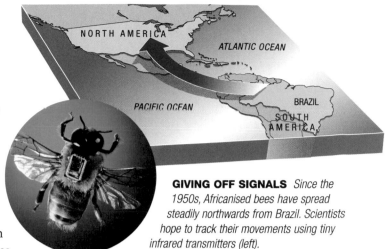

GIVING OFF SIGNALS *Since the 1950s, Africanised bees have spread steadily northwards from Brazil. Scientists hope to track their movements using tiny infrared transmitters (left).*

and falling backwards into some cactus as he went. When the swarm finally left him, he was in agony but still alive. In his weakened state, it took him five hours to get back to his vehicle. At home, his wife counted 50 stings and he was later admitted to hospital.

Ready to attack

And yet, despite their fearsome reputation, it is rare for killer bees to live up to their name. Their venom is no more powerful than that of other bees; it is just that they sting more readily and in greater numbers. The average person in good health can tolerate 20 bee stings per kilogram of body weight. Considering that the average male human weighs more than 70 kg, it would take well over 1,000 individual stings to kill.

Children, pets and the elderly are more vulnerable. In September 2005, 82-year-old Connie Bermes narrowly escaped death, when bees living in a hollow tree near her home in El Paso, Texas, stung her more than 100 times. Fortunately, her neighbour, Johanna Puga-Martinez, had just returned home in the car with her children, when the bees attacked. One stung Johanna's son, 10-year-old Sergio, at the front door. He turned and came sprinting back. 'As soon as I looked up, a swarm of bees was coming after him,' Johanna says. She bundled Sergio back into the car, then saw Mrs Bermes stumbling towards them with bees all over her body. 'All she did was tap my car like to say, "Help me".'

Johanna ran out and grabbed a water hose, which she turned on the bees, and that finally stopped them attacking. She herself was stung more than 20 times in the process. Another witness was horrified to see the bees completely covering Mrs Bermes' face, getting into her mouth, ears and hair. Several bees even made it to the hospital, carried along in the ambulance.

LUCKY SURVIVOR *Robert Rupe shows some of the stings he received while out hunting. If he had been stung many more times, he would probably have died.*

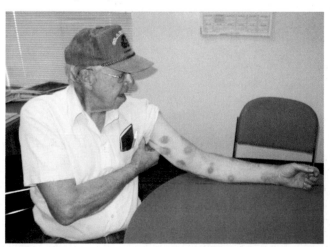

When Nguyen Thanh Hung came home to his native city of Thai Binh, Vietnam, in December 2004, his family decided to celebrate his return with a feast. Tragically, it ended with the death of one of Hung's brothers, and Hung himself fell seriously ill.

One of the delicacies at the feast was a family favourite – *tiet canh*, a kind of thick soup made with raw duck's blood mixed with herbs. 'The duck was plump and looking healthy,' recalls Hung, 'so we didn't have the slightest suspicion that it might be sick.' The next day, however, his brother, Nguyen Hung Viet, became ill and developed a temperature. The duck was, in fact, infected with a deadly disease that was causing

The Next Pandemic?

alarm across East Asia – the H5N1 strain of avian or bird flu. Unfortunately, the family, unsure what was wrong with Nguyen Hung Viet, kept him in bed at home for a week, before finally taking him to hospital.

'It was New Year's Day,' says Hung. 'The hospital was running on minimal staffing and only got back to normal operating schedule three days afterwards. It was unfortunate timing for him. … He couldn't breathe, his left lung was totally damaged. Yet the doctors didn't think he had bird flu.'

They were wrong, and on January 10, 2005, he died. Later that day, Hung himself developed a fever. 'I got really worried, so the next day I went to a clinic where they took a scan of my lungs.' By this time, other people had died of avian flu in southern Vietnam and the doctors took his case seriously. 'I was immediately put into quarantine. My concern grew each day, as my temperature was staying extremely high. At the worst moment, two-thirds of one lung was severely affected.

'Still, when the doctors told me I had bird flu I was totally shocked. I knew nothing about it and it scared me. … I got into such a panic, even though my fever was beginning to subside. For two nights, I didn't sleep. I told myself I should not doze off at any point – something may happen inside me, inside my brain, and I may never wake up. Only when my fever had gone and the doctors told me my lungs had made a miraculous recovery did I feel a little relieved.' He was later released from hospital in perfect health – he was one of a lucky few in Vietnam who caught the disease and survived.

Outbreaks in Hong Kong

The first known human death from avian flu had occurred eight years earlier in Hong Kong. The victim was a three-year-old boy, who died in May 1997 – just two months before the British returned the territory to Chinese rule. By December, another five people in Hong Kong had died from the disease, and 12 more had been infected. Fears grew that this could be the start of an epidemic.

The Chinese government acted decisively. The disease had been linked to chickens, and in one of their first major operations after regaining Hong Kong, the authorities

CLOSE PROXIMITY
Chickens in a cage at a poultry market in Hanoi, Vietnam's second largest city. In 2004, avian flu swept through the country, wiping out flocks, infecting 29 people and killing 20.

After an earlier outbreak in 1997, the deadly H5N1 strain of avian flu re-appeared in 2003, raising fears of a global pandemic.

ordered the mass slaughter of all chickens there. Ducks, geese and other poultry kept in close proximity to chickens were also killed. The government paid breeders and vendors for their stock, and within three days 1.4 million birds had been slaughtered, disinfected and buried. No new cases appeared in the subsequent months, and the disease was declared eradicated.

Five years later, avian flu was back. In February 2003, a father and son in Hong Kong both tested positive for the H5N1 strain of the virus that had caused the earlier deaths and infections. While human cases remained rare, the disease spread rapidly in poultry and, before long, started crossing borders. By early 2004, it had been detected in Thailand, Laos, Vietnam, Cambodia, Indonesia, South Korea and Japan, and the first human cases outside Hong Kong had begun to appear. By June, there had been 12 confirmed cases among people

in Thailand, eight of whom died. In Vietnam there had been 23 confirmed human cases, and 16 people had died.

One of the major concerns about avian flu is the relative speed with which it could spread not just through a particular region, but across the entire world. The virus causing it is shed in the saliva, nasal secretions and excrement of infected birds and passed on to other birds through them. Clearly, the potential for infection among birds is greatest in places where they are crowded together, such as poultry farms. But wild birds also carry the virus, and many of them travel thousands of miles each year, migrating between different parts of the globe. Although it has yet to be proved, it seems extremely likely that they have helped to spread the disease.

The risk of cross-infection from wild birds to humans is, however, low, mainly because people rarely have close physical contact with them. The advice of most governments in areas at risk is simply, 'If you see a dead wild bird, leave it alone'. Cross-infection is much more likely from domestic poultry. These, too, travel long distances across borders as part of the international trade in poultry. So far, the vast majority of human cases of avian flu have been transmitted by poultry.

Another concern is the difficulty of treating the disease. The two most common antiviral influenza

drugs, amantadine and rimantadine, have proved ineffective. Hopes are high, however, that other drugs, notably oseltamavir and zanamavir, will be more successful, and tests are currently underway. No fully protective vaccine has yet been developed.

The fear of mutation

Medical experts' biggest fear is the possibility of human-to-human transmission of the disease. As long as people can only be infected by close contact with birds, the number of cases will remain relatively low. Human-to-human transmission would mean that the virus has mutated and developed a much greater potential to spread among people.

This made the case of Nguyen Thanh Hung particularly important. Although Hung believes he caught

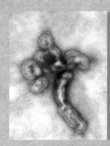

1997 The H5N1 strain of the avian flu virus (left) infects 18 people in Hong Kong – the first known human victims. Six die.

2003 Avian flu breaks out again. By the year's end, there have been four human deaths – in Hong Kong (1) and Vietnam (3).

2004 The disease spreads – 46 human cases are reported during the course of the year, 29 in Vietnam and 17 in Thailand.

2005 Human cases are reported in five Asian countries, including 42 deaths. First cases recorded in birds in Europe.

2006 The first cases appear in birds in Africa. People are also infected, including six Egyptians who die from the disease.

LESSONS LEARNED *Birds can be vaccinated against avian flu, although no vaccine has yet been found for humans. Here, animal health workers in northern Vietnam herd vaccinated chickens back into their enclosure.*

MIGRANT CARRIERS
Wild swans fly over the Anzali marshlands in Iran, where avian flu arrived in February 2006. Migrating wildfowl have the potential to carry the disease around the globe.

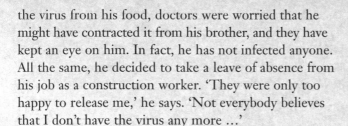

the virus from his food, doctors were worried that he might have contracted it from his brother, and they have kept an eye on him. In fact, he has not infected anyone. All the same, he decided to take a leave of absence from his job as a construction worker. 'They were only too happy to release me,' he says. 'Not everybody believes that I don't have the virus any more …'

The disease, meanwhile, has continued to spread, but in nothing like pandemic proportions. By late 2005, it had been found in birds in Russia and eastern Europe. On March 29, 2006, it was discovered in Britain, in the body of a swan washed up in the harbour of Cellardyke, a coastal village in Fife in Scotland. Human cases have also spread. By October 2006, people had died from avian flu in nine different countries: China, including Hong Kong (a total of 14 deaths to date), Vietnam (42), Thailand (17), Cambodia (6), Indonesia (55), Azerbaijan (5), Iraq (2), Egypt (6) and Turkey (4). A non-fatal case had also occurred in Djibouti in East Africa.

The threat of an avian flu pandemic remains. But although poultry farmers are rightly worried, experts believe the general public can remain calm. So long as the virus does not mutate – a possibility medical scientists are watching closely – most people have little to fear.

BRINGING BIRD FLU HOME

Although human-to-human transmission of avian flu remains unproven, it has passed between mammals. Domestic cats in several countries have contracted the disease and many have passed it on before dying.

The first report came in 2004 from Thailand, where 14 cats from the same Bangkok household died in quick succession. Post-mortem examinations of the cats revealed the presence of the H5N1 strain of the avian flu virus. One cat had fed on the carcass of a chicken killed by avian flu at a nearby farm, then returned home and passed on the virus. Since then, cats in Indonesia, Iraq and Germany, as well as Thailand, have died of avian flu. It has also been detected in cats in Austria. The German and Austrian cats caught the disease from wild birds.

The fear is that cats may be able to transmit the virus to their owners. Experts recommend keeping domestic cats indoors in places where avian flu is endemic and avoiding any contact with cats that appear to be sick.

Superbug

Drugs are chemical weapons that fight the micro-organisms causing disease, and in the war against illness, they have brought countless triumphs. But some micro-organisms fight back, evolving to cope with drugs and creating new medical problems. One is the MRSA 'superbug'.

MRSA is a strain of the potentially lethal *Staphylococcus aureus* bacterium, which has evolved a frightening resistance to most antibiotics, including methicillin – hence its full name methicillin-resistant *Staphylococcus aureus*. Methicillin, a kind of penicillin, used to be regarded as a virtual cure-all for infectious bacteria, able to combat even ones that had built up resistance to other types of penicillin.

Staphylococcus aureus infections, including non-methicillin-resistant ones, can be extremely unpleasant. The bacteria are widespread, and many people carry them on their skins or in their noses without suffering any harm. Infections occur when the bacteria get inside the body, often through an open wound – although people with reduced immunity, such as the elderly or those already suffering from another disease, can be infected even if the skin is not broken.

Symptoms range from tenderness, swellings or boils at the site of the infection to a condition called necrotising fasciitis (sometimes known as flesh-eating disease), in which toxins are released that destroy living tissue. In some cases, they lead to death. MRSA infections are worse than infections by other strains of *Staphylococcus aureus* because their resistance to methicillin makes them much harder to treat.

Drawn-out trauma

Living through an MRSA infection is a drawn-out and traumatic experience, and even when cured, patients may be left with scars, stiffness or more serious physical disabilities. British financial adviser Tony Field was infected with MRSA in a Birmingham hospital in August 2000, while recovering from a broken leg, and he remained infected for three years.

Just before he left the hospital, he was informed that he had the infection but told it was nothing to worry about. 'Six weeks after being discharged, my thigh became swollen … ,' he remembers. 'I pointed it out to the doctor who was on a routine visit that day. An immediate call was arranged to the clinic. A sample of fluid was drawn off and analysed. I still had MRSA.' Two days later the swelling on his thigh burst, pouring out a horrific trail of blood and other discharge. In the end, Tony had to undergo an operation, in which the infected part of his leg was removed, finally eradicating the MRSA. Determined to help others in a similar position, Tony now heads up a support group, MRSA Support.

For another victim, Helena Glenn from South Carolina, USA, the

WIDESPREAD *A third of people worldwide are estimated to carry* Staphylococcus *bacteria on their bodies. Infections usually occur when the skin is broken, allowing the bacteria to enter the body.*

The MRSA 'superbug' kills more than a thousand people each year in Britain alone, and is still evolving new strains worldwide.

297

LITTLE MIRACLES *Carolyn Moretto from Nottingham, England, holds her triplets, Alex, Georgina and Max. Born prematurely, they contracted MRSA, but survived.*

MRSA bacteria, but it does at least help to prevent them from being transferred from patient to patient.

At the same time, the bacteria are still evolving. Methicillin-resistant infections are usually treated with the drug vancomycin, traditionally seen as an antibiotic of 'last resort'. Worryingly, however, a new strain of MRSA has recently emerged, which is resistant to vancomycin and so, for the time being at least, incurable. In the USA, meanwhile, another strain has appeared in the wider community, not just hospitals. Called community-acquired or CA-MRSA, it is common in prisons, gyms and other places where people are crowded together, although it can be picked up just about anywhere.

In October 2005, nine-year-old Jewaun Smith from Chicago became infected with CA-MRSA after scraping his left knee when he fell off his bike. In a few days, the infection spread right through his body, leaving him with dozens of holes in his lungs. He barely survived. Other cases have recently been reported of CA-MRSA infections arising from tattoos made by tattoo artists using unsterilised equipment. Although this new strain of the superbug is currently confined to the USA, its spread around the world seems inevitable.

symptoms of her infection started with bumps on her leg, which were initially diagnosed and treated as insect bites. Later, her left knee started to swell until, she says, it 'looked like a very large blister waiting to burst'. They were no ordinary bumps, she adds. Each one was 'deep red on the outside but on the inside, it was black'. In fact, she was suffering from necrotising fasciitis. The knee did burst, but after a number of operations, she has survived.

Still evolving

In Britain, MRSA first appeared in 1961 and spread slowly until the early 1990s, when rates started to rise rapidly. Today, it is a major problem both in Britain and other parts of the world, particularly in some hospitals. In Britain, many people blame the rise in infections on cost-cutting measures in the National Health Service, particularly the removal of ward sisters, which is widely believed to have led to a decline in standards of cleanliness and hygiene. Good hygiene does not destroy

CLEAN SHEETS *MRSA bacteria, like all others, thrive in dirty conditions. By keeping hands, uniforms and bed linen clean, hospital staff can help to prevent it from spreading.*

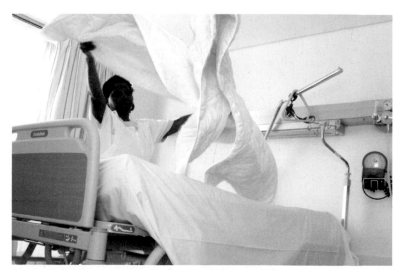

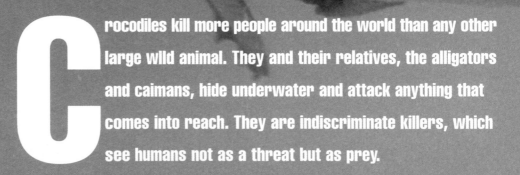

Crocodiles kill more people around the world than any other large wild animal. They and their relatives, the alligators and caimans, hide underwater and attack anything that comes into reach. They are indiscriminate killers, which see humans not as a threat but as prey.

When these monstrous reptiles strike, they do so with surprising speed and incredible force – once in their jaws, few escape. Australian environmentalist Val Plumwood was one of the lucky few. A saltwater crocodile attacked her while she was canoeing alone through Kakadu National Park in the country's Northern Territory in 1985.

Its first target was the canoe itself. 'I was totally unprepared for the great blow when it struck the canoe,' Val recalls. 'Again it struck, again and again, now from behind, shuddering the flimsy craft. … I realised I had to get out of the canoe or risk being capsized.' She looked around for the best place to escape to. The banks of the channel were steep and slippery with mud, but then she spotted a paper bark tree. 'I made the split second decision to leap into its lower branches and climb to safety,' she says.

Cold-blooded Killers

'I steered to the tree, tensed for the jump and leapt. Before my foot even tripped the first branch, I had a blurred vision of great toothed jaws bursting from the water. Then I was seized between the legs in a red-hot pincer grip and whirled into the suffocating wet darkness. In that split second I thought I was going to die. I was rolled under the water for what seemed like an eternity, but when I seemed all but finished, the rolling suddenly stopped. My feet touched bottom, my head broke the surface, and, coughing, I sucked at air, amazed to be alive.'

JAWS AGAPE *A saltwater crocodile cruising in the waters off Papua New Guinea. The 'saltie' is as at home in estuaries and rivers as it is in the sea.*

The nightmare repeats

Fortunately for Val, the water was too shallow for the crocodile to drown her. But her ordeal was not over. 'The crocodile still had me in its pincer grip between the legs. I had just begun to weep for the prospects of my mangled body when the crocodile pitched me suddenly into a second death roll.

'When the whirling stopped again I surfaced, still in the crocodile's grip, next to a stout branch of a large sandpaper fig growing in the water. I grabbed the branch, vowing to let the crocodile tear me apart rather than throw me again into that spinning, suffocating hell. For the first time I realised that the crocodile was growling, as if

Most fearsome of crocodiles is the saltwater crocodile, or 'saltie', the world's largest reptile, which kills around 2,000 people each year.

angry. I braced myself for another roll, but then its jaws simply relaxed; I was free. I gripped the branch and pulled away, dodging around the back of the fig tree to avoid the forbidding mud bank, and tried once more to climb into the paperbark tree.'

But getting away would not be that easy. 'As in the repetition of a nightmare, the horror of my first escape attempt was repeated. As I leapt into the same branch, the crocodile seized me again, this time around the upper left thigh, and pulled me under. Like the others, the third death roll stopped, and we came up next to the sandpaper fig branch again. I was growing weaker, but I could see the crocodile taking a long time to kill me this way. In despair, I grabbed the branch again. And once again, after a time, I felt the crocodile's jaws relax, and I pulled free.

TOGETHERNESS *Plumwood is now an ecological campaigner. 'In the West,' she says, 'there is a strong effort to deny that we humans are also animals positioned in the food chain.'*

'I knew I had to break the pattern; up the slippery mud bank was the only way. I scrabbled for a grip, then slid back toward the waiting jaws. The second time I almost made it before again sliding back, braking my slide by grabbing a tuft of grass. I hung there, exhausted. "I can't make it," I thought. … The grass tuft began to give way. Flailing to keep from sliding farther, I jammed my fingers into the mud. This was the clue I needed to survive. I used this method and the last of my strength to climb up the bank and reach the top. I was alive!'

Val had survived the attack; now she had to get to safety. The ranger station she had left earlier was several kilometres away, but fear drove her on. 'After putting some distance between me and the crocodile, I stopped and realised for the first time how serious my wounds were. … I tore up some clothing to bind the wounds and made a tourniquet for my bleeding thigh, then staggered on.'

Eventually, Val realised she could go no farther. She dragged herself to the edge of the swamp, where she felt she was most likely to be found, then collapsed. Hours later, she was discovered and taken to Darwin Hospital, where she slowly recovered. She developed a severe leg infection, but no amputation was necessary.

> **The crocodile still had me in its pincer grip between the legs. I had just begun to weep for the prospects of my mangled body when the crocodile pitched me suddenly into a second death roll.**
>
> *Val Plumwood*

Death in the Finniss River

The fact that Val Plumwood survived a saltwater crocodile attack is a miracle. These massive creatures – the world's largest reptile, growing up to 7 m long and weighing as much as a tonne – are responsible for around 2,000 deaths every year. Some of the killings take place in Australia, but many more in Indonesia and other parts of South-east Asia. As the name implies, saltwater crocodiles are common along coasts and are capable of travelling long distances at sea. But they also colonise freshwater habitats and are just as much at home in swamps and rivers.

Two days before Christmas in 2003, three young Australians encountered a large 'saltie' in the swollen Finniss River near Darwin, Northern Territory. They were washing mud off in the river after a day quad biking, when one, Brett Mann, slipped and fell in. Seeing their friend being swept away, the others – Shaun Blowers and Ashley McGough, both aged 19 – dived in to save him. All three were drifting downstream when they spotted a large and ominous shape swimming towards them.

'Ashley screamed out, "Croc, croc!"' says Shaun Blowers. 'We just swam to the nearest tree and straight up we went. We were looking around for Brett but we didn't hear a thing, didn't hear a scream, no splashing or anything. Two minutes later the croc brought Brett to the surface and pretty much showed him off to us.' After that, they never saw Brett again.

Ashley and Shaun remained in the tree for 22 hours while the crocodile circled below. 'He just hung around all night and pretty much all the next morning,' Shaun

recalls. Eventually, they were rescued by helicopter. A friend, concerned that they had not come home, had raised the alarm and a search team had been sent out.

Nile crocodiles

Africa's Nile crocodile is a close rival of the saltwater crocodile in size and deadliness. It lives in rivers and water holes across most of Africa and has no fear of humans. Nile crocodiles kill people every day. Like many of their relatives, they hunt creatures that come down to the water's edge, bursting out and grabbing their prey before it has time to react. They also hunt anything that ventures into the water. They drag their victims under and roll them over and over to drown them.

Elspeth Harley, an 18-year-old British gap year student, witnessed this in March 2002, while swimming with friends in Kenya's supposedly safe Lake Challa

OUT IN THE OPEN
On land, the Nile crocodile poses little threat, but in the water it can move and strike with terrifying speed and power.

when a Nile crocodile grabbed another girl, Amy Nicholls. 'Amy swam a stroke and turned round to face the bank, then she suddenly started screaming,' she recalls. 'I held out my hand to her but in a few seconds she disappeared.' Before she died, Amy resurfaced, screaming: 'It's got my feet. It's a crocodile!' Her body, missing an arm, was recovered three days later.

Alligators in America

The crocodile's North American equivalent is the alligator, which inhabits the continent's subtropical south, from Florida to Texas. This too is a formidable beast – adult males can grow to more than 5 m long – capable of tackling almost any prey. In the past, alligators' paths rarely crossed those of humans, as the wetlands they prefer were wild and sparsely populated by people. Lately, however, the situation has changed, especially in Florida. As more people move to the state, so more new homes are needed. Florida's great wetland habitat, the Everglades, has been partially drained, forcing its natural inhabitants into direct conflict with humans.

Alligators are less aggressive than crocodiles and do not pose so much of a threat to people. But attacks, including fatal ones, are increasing. Many blame construction workers and others who feed wild alligators, leading them to associate humans with food.

In May 2004, a 1.5 m alligator attacked 12-year-old Malcolm Locke while he was swimming in Lake Diana, north of Orlando. He escaped by fighting off the reptile. 'It took a bite out of my head and a big chunk out of my ear,' Malcolm says. But after he punched the alligator, 'it just squirmed away'. Malcolm swam to shore and a neighbour then drove him to hospital. 'Malcolm did the right thing,' says Joy Hill of the Florida Fish and Wildlife Conservation Commission.

CATCHING A KILLER
Trapper Curtis Lucas (left) and US Forestry Service officer Jim Ellis bring ashore an alligator shot after it killed Annmarie Campbell in May 2006.

Struggling, Hill explains, is the best way to react. If an alligator feels it might get injured, it will release its grip and search for easier prey.

Two months later, a 3.7 m alligator attacked Janie Melsek from Sanibel, Florida, dragging the 54-year-old into a pond. A quick-thinking neighbour, Jim Anholt, saved her. 'The lady was in the pond and the alligator had a hold of her,' Jim remembers. 'Just her face was showing.' He held onto her neck to keep her head above water until the police arrived. It took three officers along with Jim to wrestle her free. 'It was a kind of tug-of-war,' Jim says. Janie Melsek had serious injuries to her thigh, buttocks and right arm, which later had to be partially amputated. The alligator was shot.

Others have been less fortunate. In May 2006, alligators killed three people in Florida in less than a week. The first, Yovy Suarez Jimenez, disappeared while out jogging in Broward County, just north of Miami. Her dismembered body was discovered in a canal the next morning, and an alligator was later shot and found to have her two arms in its stomach. Unusually, it seems that the alligator attacked and killed her on land, then dragged her body into the canal.

A few days later, two other women died. An alligator attacked Annemarie Campbell while she was snorkelling near Lake George, in northern Florida. Judy Cooper was discovered, covered in alligator bites, in a canal north of the city of St Petersburg, on Florida's west coast. She had been dead for three days.

True survivors

Crocodiles and their relatives were here long before humans evolved, and they will almost certainly still be here long after we are gone. These hardy reptiles have barely altered in millions of years – their design is so perfect that they have had little need to evolve any further.

The members of the scientific order Crocodilia look primeval, because they are. They include the crocodiles and alligators along with their relatives, the Indian gharial and the caimans of South and Central America. Species much like these lived alongside the dinosaurs more than 65 million years ago: some even hunted them. In fact, the two groups – crocodiles and dinosaurs – were quite closely related, having both evolved from the same distant ancestor. Unlike dinosaurs, crocodiles survived. The cataclysm that wiped out their land-living cousins (see pages 190-1) and more than half of all the other life forms then existing on Earth left them virtually unscathed.

Their incredible toughness may partly explain their survival. They are unfussy eaters, which will feed on rotting meat as well as live prey, and they can go for months between meals. Despite their association with water, they can also live for up to four months without drinking. If the pools or rivers they are inhabiting dry up, they go into aestivation (like hibernation, but triggered by hot, dry conditions), waiting in burrows or beneath overhanging banks for the rains to return.

Crocodiles and the other members of their order, then, are unlikely to disappear, and as our numbers increase, so will our encounters with them,

JURASSIC ANCESTOR
The crocodile Steneosaurus bollensis *lived 180 million years ago in what is now Germany.*

including fatal ones. People in Australia, South-east Asia and Africa have always shared their homes with crocodiles, but there are now more fatal attacks, simply because the human population in these regions is greater than it was in the past. In 2002, this trend led the Uganda Wildlife Authority to start a cull of crocodiles in Lake Victoria, after they had attacked and killed more than 40 people in seven months. In other places, such as Florida, alligator attacks are increasing because people are moving into the animals' natural habitat, building homes alongside the waterways they live in. Tourism, too, has had an impact. There are now few places that adventure-seeking holiday-makers cannot go, and some actively seek the danger of the wildest places. Many fatal attacks in recent years have been on people who were canoeing along and even swimming in waters that are home to crocodiles.

FEEDING THE PROBLEM *A golfer throws a biscuit to a young alligator in Florida. Acts like this have been blamed for the rise in alligator attacks on people.*

Africa's Darkest Secret

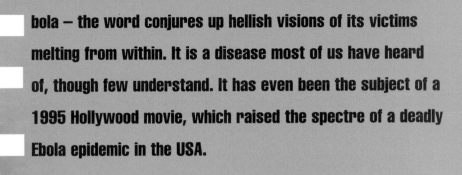

E

bola – the word conjures up hellish visions of its victims melting from within. It is a disease most of us have heard of, though few understand. It has even been the subject of a 1995 Hollywood movie, which raised the spectre of a deadly Ebola epidemic in the USA.

There is no doubt that Ebola is a terrible disease. Most people infected die within two weeks, and the way they die is gruesome. The disease breaks down their living body tissue, destroying blood vessels and organ linings. Before they die, some bleed from every orifice. In the words of BBC reporter Pascale Harter, who covered an outbreak in Congo in 2003, 'Ebola is a messy, undignified death of uncontrollable vomiting, diarrhoea and bleeding.' There are few more horrific ways to go. But an epidemic, as depicted in the film *Outbreak*, seems unlikely. Usually, the disease kills its victims faster than it can spread and so burns itself out before travelling too far.

Spreading by contact

Its full name is Ebola haemorrhagic fever, and medical experts first recognised it as a distinct disease in 1976, when outbreaks occurred in Sudan and the Democratic Republic of the Congo (then Zaïre). They named it after a tributary of the Congo river. Later that year, they found that two closely related but slightly different viruses – called Zaïre ebolavirus and Sudan ebolavirus – had caused the outbreaks.

The 1976 outbreaks were confined to relatively small areas and lasted just a few months. But within those areas a large number of people were infected, of whom a high proportion died. In Sudan, 284 people were infected, of whom 151 died – that is, 53 per cent. Most people were infected by personal contact within hospitals, and many of those who died were doctors or nurses. In Zaïre, even more people died. There, the first patients were treated in a hospital in the village of Yambuku in the north of the country, but the re-use of contaminated needles meant that the infection spread to several surrounding villages. Of 318 people who contracted the disease, 280 died – a mortality rate of 88 per cent.

Since 1976, there have been several major outbreaks in Africa. Hundreds more people have died, and yet the disease is still poorly understood. We do not know, for example, exactly where it comes from. Scientists believe that there must be a 'reservoir' animal species or group of species in the wild which carry the disease without symptoms, but what that reservoir is remains a mystery.

> **Ebola is a messy, undignified death of uncontrollable vomiting, diarrhoea and bleeding.**
>
> *Pascale Harter*

FRIGHTENING RESPONSIBILITY
Red Cross workers carry away young victims of an Ebola outbreak in Zaïre (now the Democratic Republic of the Congo) in 1995.

Since the Ebola virus was first identified in 1976, more than 1,200 people infected by it have suffered horrific deaths.

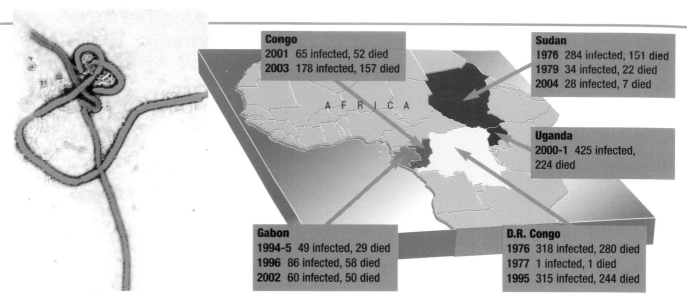

Congo
2001 65 infected, 52 died
2003 178 infected, 157 died

Sudan
1976 284 infected, 151 died
1979 34 infected, 22 died
2004 28 infected, 7 died

A F R I C A

Uganda
2000-1 425 infected,
224 died

Gabon
1994-5 49 infected, 29 died
1996 86 infected, 58 died
2002 60 infected, 50 died

D.R. Congo
1976 318 infected, 280 died
1977 1 infected, 1 died
1995 315 infected, 244 died

VIRUS *There are four known strains of Ebola – the two that affect humans and two others, which have apparently killed only non-human primates.*

EBOLA OUTBREAKS *In human terms, Ebola haemorrhagic fever is a relatively new disease. The first recorded outbreaks were in 1976.*

Similarly, we have yet to develop any kind of vaccine or cure. The only hope of surviving Ebola lies in the victim's own immune system. People do survive it, but once infected they are more likely to die.

Although Ebola remains incurable, the medical profession has learned much about containing it. They know that it is highly contagious and can be passed on by the least physical contact – such as a handshake. Now, every time there is an outbreak, the World Health Organization (WHO) immediately gets involved. In

August 2000, for example, Ebola appeared in Uganda for the first time, and within hours a WHO rapid response team had been despatched. Clad from head to toe in biologically secure protective suits, they did everything possible to prevent the infection from spreading. The remote area where the outbreak had occurred was put under quarantine – nobody was allowed in or out. These measures prevented the outbreak from spreading, but they failed to stop new cases within the affected area. There is a local tradition of close contact with the dead at funerals, and more people were infected after touching the corpses of earlier victims. By the time the outbreak finally subsided in January 2001, 425 people had been infected and 224 had died.

A living virus

In 2003, the BBC's Pascale Harter had a frightening encounter with Ebola after reporting on an outbreak in the village of Kéllé in northern Congo. When she returned to the capital, Brazzaville, she found she had some of the symptoms – tiredness, fever and vomiting – and was examined in a military hospital in the city. 'When a disembodied voice from behind a mask asks you how often you're vomiting, and examines your body for signs of blood beneath the skin from internal haemorrhaging, you know you've got something very bad,' she wrote later. 'The gloves and goggles worn by the doctor let you know you are no longer a healthy body to be protected from illness but a living virus to be protected against.'

ULTIMATE SACRIFICE *Italian nun Sister Dina Rosa Belleri died from Ebola in 1995 after treating infected patients in the Orders Aid Hospital in Kikwit, Zaïre.*

In the end she turned out to have malaria, but it gave her an insight into what it is like to be an Ebola victim. While the hospital staff still suspected the disease, they were terrified of any contact with her. The doctors 'eventually decided that I should be given a malaria test. The most junior medic to be found was forced to perform the task. He stood outside my isolation room trembling visibly. As he pricked my finger hurriedly, I saw the sweat gathering behind his goggles.

'Major illnesses usually elicit sympathy and caring, but Ebola just creates fear and panic. … Although I am fine now – and over the malaria – the government cannot let me go until they have a negative result. In the meantime, I have friends to bring me water and food. But most of the Ebola patients dying in the isolation ward in Kéllé are not so lucky. Even their families are too scared to bring them water. Ebola is not only a gruesome death but a lonely one.'

An outbreak in Sudan, in 2004, showed that more positive lessons have also been learned. In May, four people died of Ebola in the southern town of Yambio, and the WHO sent in a team of experts. By August, the outbreak was over, and only three more people had died. One thing experts had learned was the need to educate people about the disease. 'Once the people of Yambio were convinced of the very real risks Ebola posed and they understood what they could do to protect themselves and their families, the outbreak response was greatly accelerated,' says WHO official Asiya Odugleh. Other new measures taken in Yambio included setting up an isolation ward surrounded by a low fence. This enabled friends and relatives to see patients and talk to them from a safe distance, without putting themselves at risk.

'The lessons we learned in Yambio … will strengthen our responses to future outbreaks,' says another WHO official, Dr Hassan El Bushra. 'WHO cannot predict where or when the next Ebola outbreak will happen, but we can continue building on what we have learned in Yambio.'

EBOLA'S DEADLY COUSIN

Compared to Ebola, which is familiar to most people by name at least, the Marburg virus is virtually unknown. Yet it poses as much of a threat as Ebola does, if not a greater one. Like Ebola, the Marburg virus is a so-called filovirus, a virus that causes haemorrhagic fever – a fever accompanied by bleeding. The symptoms of infection are very similar, with high fever, diarrhoea, vomiting and severe internal bleeding. There is often also bleeding from the eyes, nose, ears and other external bodily orifices. Like Ebola, the Marburg virus has no known vaccine or cure. Mortality rates from infection are equally high, ranging from around 50 per cent to over 90 per cent.

In 2005, there was an outbreak of Marburg virus in the northern Angolan province of Uige. By the time it was over, more than 300 people had died, the vast majority of them children. At one point, it was feared that the disease might spread to the capital Luanda, as several infected people had come there from Uige and died in the city. Antonio, a Luanda garage worker, articulated the mood at the time: 'Everybody is afraid of this virus,' he said. 'We don't know what it will do to us.'

In the end, the Angolan outbreak was contained. Experts from the World Health Organization (WHO) arrived and measures were implemented, similar to those used with Ebola. Community leaders were enlisted to help inform local people of the risks of cross-infection and what they could do to prevent the spread of the disease. Local musicians even recorded a song to help raise awareness.

The experience in Angola showed that the Marburg virus can be contained even if it cannot be cured. However, it still remains largely mysterious. As with Ebola, its natural host remains unknown, as does the method by which it jumps to humans.

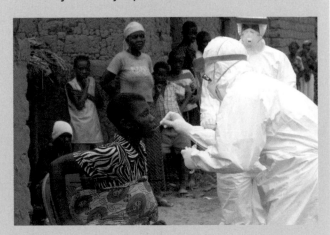

TAKING NO CHANCES *Dressed in full protective clothing, a doctor takes a sample from a woman suspected of being infected with the Marburg virus.*

A Grizzly End

Timothy Treadwell spent 13 summers with the grizzly bears of Alaska. He saw himself as an eco-warrior, who devoted much of his life to the animals and considered them his friends. In October 2003, one of the bears he loved so much killed and ate him and his girlfriend.

Grizzly bears are a North American subspecies of the brown bear, which is native to Europe, Asia and North America. They are huge animals – male grizzlies can weigh up to 680 kg, more than ten times the average weight of North American human males. They are now confined to North America's north-western corner, from Alaska through western Canada and into the US states of Idaho, Montana and Wyoming.

Treadwell's dedication to the animals was unquestionable. In 1997, he and film producer Jewel Palovak had co-written a book called *Among Grizzlies: Living With Wild Bears in Alaska*. A year later, he founded Grizzly People, dedicated to protecting bears and their natural habitat. But although his death was tragic, some people had seen it it coming. Unlike most field biologists – and contrary to the advice given by his own Grizzly People organisation – Treadwell often approached grizzly bears in the wild and seemed to have no fear of them. After his first few summers visiting Alaska,

ON THE PROWL *Grizzly bears are omnivores. Generally, they feed on a combination of plant roots and berries, fungi, insects, fish and small mammals.*

Timothy Treadwell and Amie Huguenard were camping by a lake in Alaska, when a grizzly bear attacked and ate them.

309

he stopped carrying pepper spray with him, commonly used to repel bears if they attack. 'He just felt that was an invasive, aggressive mechanism that translated into a kind of attitude,' says Joel Bennett, an old friend. 'He didn't want to have that attitude. He kind of wanted to resign himself to whatever happened.'

Treadwell's relationship with the bears he shared his life with was certainly unusual. As the years passed, he felt he got to know them and he gave several of them names. He captured many of his encounters with them on home video. Rebecca Dmytryk recalls footage she saw of him standing in a stream near an older bear he had named Quincy. 'Quincy,' he was saying, 'do you remember when you stood over me? You were so hungry, and you should have eaten me, but you didn't. Thanks for not eating me, Quincy.'

Caught on tape

Treadwell and his girlfriend Amie Huguenard died on October 4, 2003, on the shores of Kaflia Lake in south-western Alaska. Air taxi pilot Willy Fulton found their remains two days later, having flown in, as agreed, to pick them up from their camp.

After landing on the lake and making his way to shore, Willy shouted for Tim and Amie to let them know he had arrived, but got no response. He decided to hike up the path from the shore towards the camp, but soon stopped and turned around. 'Something just didn't feel right,' he says. 'Something seemed strange, hollering with no answer.' He made his way back towards the plane 'at a pretty good clip' and when he got there turned to see 'a pretty nasty-looking bear' sneaking down the path with its head down. 'It was just the meanest-looking thing,' he says.

As the bear headed to the camp, Willy took off and flew over the animal, trying to chase it away. Looking down, he could see the bear feeding from what appeared to be a human rib cage. Every time he flew past, it began to feed even faster. Realising he was going to need help, Willy called in the park rangers.

They found Amie's body in front of the tent, half eaten and buried beneath a large pile of mud and sticks – a food cache built by the bear. Very little of Tim remained at all. All that was found was his head, with what investigators describe as a 'frozen grimace' on his face, and, nearby, his right arm and hand. They also found a video camera with its lens cap still on.

When the tape inside was played back, investigators were shocked. The last six minutes had captured the

AT HOME IN THE WILD
Tim Treadwell and Amie Huguenard on one of the floats of Willy Fulton's air taxi. They were never seen alive again.

sounds of the bear attacking Tim and his frantic screams as he tried to fight it off. 'It's pretty disturbing,' says Chris Hill, one of the investigators. 'I keep hearing it in my mind.'

It seems that the couple heard a bear outside their tent at night and Tim went out to investigate. 'His way of operating was to get out of the tent immediately when he heard a bear around,' says Joel Bennett. 'He subscribed to the theory that the worst thing you could do was stay in the tent.'

The first sound on the tape is Amie's voice, apparently after Tim had asked her to turn the camera on. 'She sounds surprised and asks if it's still out there,' says Chris Hill. The next voice is Tim's, picked up by a remote microphone he was wearing. He is screaming the words: 'Get out here! I'm getting killed out here!' The next sound is of the tent zip going up and the

> ❝ **Get out of here! I'm getting killed out here!** ❞
>
> *Timothy Treadwell*

front flap of the tent opening. It is obviously stormy and there is the noise of rain battering the tent. 'They are both screaming,' Hill says. 'She's telling him to play dead, then it changes to fighting back. He asks her to hit the bear. There's so much noise going on. I don't know what's him and what might be an animal.'

The tape runs out while Tim is still alive. Amid his moans are the sounds of his microphone scraping along the floor as the bear drags him away.

No one knows how long it took for him to die, nor how much later Amie died. Biologist John Schoen believes her screams may have drawn the bear back. According to him, they 'sound eerily like a predator call' – a device that mimics the sound of an injured animal, used by hunters to lure coyotes, wolves and bears into shooting range. The look on her face, at least, suggests that her death was quick. Those who uncovered her said she looked as though she was sleeping peacefully.

Page numbers in **bold** indicate
main entries.

A
acacia trees 277
Aceh (Sumatra) 201
   see also Banda Aceh
Acheson, Sir Donald 130, 131
acid 128, 130
Acraman Crater (Australia) 190
ActionAid International 29
Adapazari (Turkey) 14
Adelaide 180, 262
Aeta (Philippines) 160, 162, 163
Africa 35, 149, 168, 199, 224, 268, 270,
   271, 277, **284–289**, 294, 301, 303,
   304–307
   East Africa **28–35**, 197, 224, 295
   North Africa 60, 112, 285, 286, 288,
      289
   southern Africa 228, 288
   sub-Saharan **278–283**
   West Africa 124–127, 283, 285, 286
   see also individual countries, places
African plate 24, 149
agriculture 35, 123, 164
   agricultural losses 117
   see also crops; farming
Ahsan, Syed Mohammad 121
aid *see* relief aid
AIDS 279, 282
Air Pollution Index (API) 182
air pressure *see* atmospheric pressure
aircraft 36
   damage to 111, 170–171, 217
   in firefighting 177
   lightning strikes on 170–171
   loss of 170–171, 183
   for relief missions 121
airport closures 44, 98, 100, 115, 130,
   148
Aki, Hoku 263
Alabama 44, 45, 76, 78, 79, 96, 98,
   102, 261
Alaska 50, 93, 158, 253, **308–309**
Algarve (Portugal) 248
Algeria 286, 288
alligators 298, 302, 303
   attacks by 302, 303
   see also caymans; crocodiles; gharials
Alonso, Dr Pedro 283
Alpide belt 24
Alpine villages 53, 55, 56
Alps 54, 57, 61
Alsace (France) 61
Amazon river 209
Amcrica *see* USA
American Midwest **40–43**, 84
American Red Cross 81
Amite (Louisiana) 84
*Among Grizzlies: Living With Wild
   Bears in Alaska* 308
Anatolian plate 17
Ancash (Peru) 50, 51
Anchorage (Alaska) 50
Andaman Islands 194, 199, 202
Andermatt (Switzerland) 61
Anderson, Chuck 260, 261
Andes 51, 152, 229
Andrea Gail 113
Angeles City (Philippines) 158, 162
Angola **264–267**, 307
animal life, loss of 30, 140, 174, 177,
   178
   see also livestock, loss of

Antarctic plate 24
Antarctica 70
antelopes 31
anticyclones 70, 131, 133
antivenin 271
Apophis asteroid 191
Arabian plate 24
Arabian Sea 212
Arbajahan (Kenya) 32
Arctic 250
   Arctic air 68, 70, 71, 73, 108, 112
Argentina 226
Arizona 166, 190, 291
Asclepius asteroid 191
ash, volcanic 136, 138, 140, 141, 142,
   143, 144, 146, 150, 151, 154, 155,
   156, 158, 160, 161, 162, 163, 164,
   165
Asia 25, 88, 248, 270, 271, 274, 279,
   282, 294, 308
   South-east Asia **182–183**, **194–205**,
      224, 227, 301, 303
   see also individual countries, places
asteroids 186, 190–191
   2002MN asteroid 191
   2004FH asteroid 191
   2004MN4 asteroid 191
   99942 Apophis asteroid 191
Astrodome, Houston 105
astronomers 191
Athens 73
Atlanta 45
Atlantic Ocean 25, 39, 45, 60, 93, 99,
   100, 112, 113, 117, 205, 221, 285,
   288
   Atlantic tsunami 205
   North Atlantic 160, 218, 249, 250,
      252, 253
atmosphere 93, 160, 184, 186, 188, 190
atmospheric pressure 102, 227
   high 39, 60, 62, 70, 96, 113, 131
      see also anticyclones
   low 44, 73, 116, 117, 212
      see also depressions
Augulis, Richard 82
Australia 122, **180–181**, 190, 203,
   216–217, **222–223**, 224, 227, 228,
   258, 259, 262, 270, 276, 288, 298,
   301, 303
Australian plate 24
Austria **52–55**, 57, 236, 237, 238, 239,
   241, 295
avalanches **52–57**, 140
   in Austria 57
      Galtür avalanche (1999) **52–55**, 57
      avalanche protection 54, 55
   deadly avalanches since 1900 57
   Hochfugen avalanche 57
   in Italy 57
   in Peru 57
   prevention of 56
   in Switzerland 57
avian flu 282, **292–295**
Aviation Safety Network 170
Azerbaijan 295
Azores 60, 218, 219
Azores High 60, 62
Azufrado river (Colombia) 154, 155

B
bacteria 282, 296
Bahamas 96, 98, 99
Baird-Murray, Fiona 111
Balad airbase (Iraq) 171

Bam (Iran) 24, 25, **27**
Banda Aceh (Sumatra) 194, 198, 201,
   204
Bandra Kurla (Mumbai) 215
Bandra-Worli Sea Link 215
Bangkok 201, 295
Bangladesh 84, **87**, **118–123**, 197,
   202, 217, 240
Barabhita (Bangladesh) 87
Barbados 99
Barcelona, University of 283
Barringer Crater (Arizona) 190
Bashial (Bangladesh) 87
Bass Strait 222
Bathurst Bay (Australia) 122
Baum, Frank 82
Bay of Bengal 118, 120, 121, 202
Bay of Biscay 112, 113, 219, 221, 248
Bay St Louis (Mississippi) 98, 102,
   122
Bayes, Cameron 258, 259
Beachy Head 248
bears 140
   brown bears 308
   grizzly bears 308, 309
      attacks by **308–309**
bees
   Africanised 290, 291
   honeybees 290, 291
   killer bees **290–291**
   Tanzanian 291
Beijing 88, 90, 91, 92, 93, 272, 273
   Beijing fogs 88
   Beijing sandstorms 88
   Beijing Weather Modification Office
      93
Belarus 73
Belize 99
belladonna 274
Belleri, Sister Dina Rosa 306
Bengal 240
Bengo river (Angola) 266
Benguela (Angola) 266
Bill & Melinda Gates Foundation
   283
Biloxi (Mississippi) 94, 98, 102
bird flu 282, **292–295**
Birmingham (Alabama) 45
Bishop (California) 93
bison 177, 178
Black Dragon tidal bore (China)
   206–209
Black Mountain (Washington State)
   142
Black Point (Australia) 259
Black Saturday (in Yellowstone NP)
   174, 176
Black Sea 17, 73, 237
Black Sunday (American Midwest) 42,
   43
Blackburn, Reid Turner 143
Blair, Tony 62
Blanco, Governor Kathleen 105
Bleak House 131
blizzards
   in eastern USA (1993) **44–45**
Blons (Austria) 57
blood 278, 281, 282, 292, 305, 307
Blowers, Shaun 301
Boa Vista (Luanda) 264, 267
Bodega Bay (California) 261
Boise City (Oklahoma) 41
bolides 189, 190
Bolu-Gerede (Turkey) 17
Bordeaux 62

boreholes 32, 43
bores *see* tidal bores
Borneo 182, 183, 225, 268
Boston (Massachusetts) 205
Bourque, Pierre 39
Boxing Day (2004) tsunami 25,
   194–205, 244
   anatomy of 198–199
Brahmaputra river 121
Branxholme (Australia) 180
Bratislava 236, 237, 239, 240
Brazil 209, 225, 226, 229, 291
Brazzaville (Congo) 306
Bremen 221
Brennecke Beach (Hawaii) 263
Brighton 108, 112
Brindley, Ken 232, 233
Brinkley, Douglas 94
Britain 63, 67, 73, 113, 121, 295, 296,
   297
   see also England; Scotland; UK;
      Wales
British Columbia 136
British Geological Society 164
bronchitis 131
Bruntland, Dr Gro Harlem 281, 282
Bryan, Scott 163
Budapest 236, 237, 239, 240, 241
Bukavu (DRC) 149
Buras (Louisiana) 98, 102
Burke, John 80
Burma (Myanmar) 202, 301
Burundi 28, 29
Buryatia (Siberia) 73
Bush, President George W. 97, 98, 99

C
CA-MRSA 297
Cactus Beach (Australia) 258
Calcutta 123
calderas 138, 164, 165
Caledonian Star 218, 221
California 24, 25, 43, 93, 107, 136,
   142, 165, 226, 229, 230, 257, 261,
   276
Cambodia 288, 294, 295
camels 33
Cameroon **124–127**
   Cameroon's Institute for Geological
      and Mining Research 127
Campbell, Annemarie 302
Campbell (US coastguard cutter) 253
Campi Flegrei (Italy) 164, 165
Canada **36–39**, 42, 50, 56, 66, 73, 79,
   82, 136, 141, 145, 190, 203, 209,
   253, 272, 273, 308
Canal do Norte Pororoca tidal bore
   (Brazil) 209
Canary Islands 205, 285, 286, 288
cannibalism (of locusts) 288
Cape Cod 168
Cape Farewell (Greenland) 253
Cape Hatteras (North Carolina) 247
   Cape Hatteras lighthouse 247
Cape Verde 286
carbon dioxide 93, 124, 125, 126, 127,
   132, 182, 225
cardiac arrest (after lightning strike)
   168, 169
Caribbean 99, 113, 150
Caribbean plate 150
Carson, Rachel 283
Cascade mountain range (USA) 57,
   136, 142
castor oil plant 274

cats 295
cattle 28, 29, 30, 32, 33, 42, 61, 120, 122, 123, 124
  see also livestock, loss of
Cayman Islands 99
caymans 298, 303
  see also alligators; crocodiles; gharials
Central America 290, 303
Chad 286, 287
Chadwick, Alex 178
Chalmette (New Orleans) 103
Chang Jiang (Yangtze) river 231, 240
  Chang Jiang flood (1998) 231
Ch'angwon (South Korea) 117
Channel Islands 111
Charles Bridge (Prague) 234
chars 121
Chato Chico (Peru) 225, 226
cheetahs 31
Cherrapunji (India) 210
Chesapeake Bay Crater 190
Chicago 113
  University of Chicago 81
chickens 61, 292, 294, 295
Chicxulub Crater (Mexico) 190, 191
Chile 24, 200, 226
China 17, 25, 27, 50, 67, **88–93**, 114, 116, 117, 203, **206–209**, 224, 228, 231, 240, 272, 273, 292, 295
Chinchiná (Colombia) 154, 155, 156
Chinchiná river (Colombia) 152, 154, 156
Chirac, President Jacques 62
chlorine 124, 126
cholera 226, **264–267**
Ch'ungch'ong-Bukto (South Korea) 117
Clark Air Base (Philippines) 160, 161
Clayton (New Mexico) 83
Clean Air Acts (UK) 132
Clement VII, Pope 276
climate change 63, 92, 93, 160, 164, 247, **248–249**
  see also global warming
clouds 216
  dust clouds 40, 41, 42
  thunderclouds 169
Clover Mist fire (Yellowstone NP) 174, 176
coal smoke 88, 128, 129, 131, 132
coastal erosion 215, 230, **242–249**
  Happisburgh (Norfolk) **242–245**
  North Carolina **247**
  Tuvalu **246**
cockle-pickers, Chinese 64–67
Cohen, Dr Joe 283
Coja (Portugal) 181
cold air *see under* weather
Coldwater (Washington State) 143
Colfax (Washington State) 144
Colombia 50, **152–157**, 226
  Geology and Mines Bureau (INGEOMINAS) 154, 155
Colorado 41
comets 185, 186
composite volcanoes 138
Congo 306
Congo river 305
Connecticut 45
Connor Jr, Bernard 261
contaminated water 264
continental plates
  African 24, 149
  Antarctic 24
  Australian 24

Eurasian 17, 24
  North American 24, 150
  South American 24, 152
  see also tectonic plates
Cooper, Judy 302
Copenhagen 250, 252
Cordillera Central (Andes) 152
Cornwall (Ontario) 39
Costa Rica 271
costs *see* economic losses
Cowlitz river (Washington State) 144
cows 28
cramps 264
Crater Lake (Oregon) 142
craters
  impact craters 190, 191
    10 largest 190
  volcanic 140, 141, 146, 148, 152, 155, 160
Croatia 241
crocodiles 33
  attacks by **298–303**
  Nile crocodiles 301–302
  saltwater crocodiles 298, 299, 301
  see also alligators; caymans; gharials
Cromer (Norfolk) 245
crops 43, 63, 183, 212, 226
  crop failure 28, 29, 61, 62, 164, 226
  destruction of 43, 115, 120, 146, 162, 212, 230, 231, 284, 285, 287, 288, 289
Cuba 97, 99
Cudgee (Australia) 180
Cumbre Vieja (Canary Islands) 205
currents
  Peruvian current 229
  rip currents **232–233**
cyclones
  Cyclone Bhola (2003) **118–123**
  Cyclone Mahina 122
  cyclone shelters 122, 123
  deadliest western Pacific 117
  see also typhoons
Cyparis, Auguste 151
Czech Republic 73, 228, 230, 234, 236, 237, 238, 241

D
Dacca (East Pakistan) 121
  see also Dhaka (Bangladesh)
Dallas 107
damage, cost of *see* economic losses
Dandenong Ranges (Australia) 180, 181
Danish Institute of Agricultural Sciences 63
Danube river 61, 234, 236, 237, 238, 239–241
Darwin 301
  Darwin Hospital 300
Daytona Beach (Florida) 232
DDT 282, 283
de-gassing 127
deadly nightshade 274
deaths 166, 225
  in air crashes 170, 171, 183
  from alligator attacks 302
  in avalanches 53, 55, 57
  from bear attacks 308–309
  in bush fires 180
  from crocodile attacks 298, 299, 301, 302, 303
  from diseases 282
    from avian flu 292, 293, 294, 295
    from cholera 264, 265, 266, 267

from Ebola 305, 306, 307
    from malaria 279, 281, 282
    from Marburg virus 307
    from MRSA 297
    from SARS 272, 273
  in earthquakes 14, 15, 18, 19, 21, 22, 24, 25, 26, 27
  from electrocution 117, 214
  in floods 94, 96, 103, 117, 118, 119, 120, 121, 123, 210, 212, 214, 226, 230, 231, 237, 240, 241
  in forest fires 180, 181
  in heatwaves 59, 60, 61, 63
  in landslides 50, 66, 117, 214
  from lightning strikes 166, 167, 168, 169, 170, 171
  in mudslides 47, 50, 51, 152, 154, 156, 157
  from poisoning 274, 275, 276
  in rip currents 232, 233
  at sea 183, 218, 219, 220, 250, 251, 252, 253
  from shark attacks 256, 257, 258, 259, 261, 262–263
  in smogs 129, 131, 132, 133, 183
  from snakebites 150, 269, 270, 271
  in storms 108, 111, 113
    in cyclones 117, 118, 119, 120, 121, 123
    in hailstorms 217
    in hurricanes 94, 96, 99, 102
    in ice storms 37
    in tornadoes 76, 78, 79, 80, 82, 84, 87
    in typhoons 115, 116, 117
  from tidal bores 205, 207, 208
  on tidal sands 65, 66, 67
  in tsunamis 194, 195, 197, 200, 201
  in volcanic eruptions 136, 137, 143, 144, 146, 147, 148, 149, 150, 151, 152, 154, 156, 157, 158
  from carbon dioxide 124, 125, 126
  in winter weather 37, 45, 53, 55, 57, 68, 69, 72, 73
  see also animal life, loss of; livestock, loss of
Decca Navigation System 250
deer 140, 174, 178
deforestation 35, 88, 126, 241
Degirmendere (Turkey) 21
dehydration 58, 264, 274
Del City (Oklahoma City) 84
Delaware 45
Democratic Republic of the Congo (DRC) 126, **146–149**, 305, 306
dengue fever 226
Denmark 63, 250
depressions 39, 96, 115
  tropical 96
deserts 270
  desertification 92
  expanding 88, 89, 90, 91
  formation of 91
Devil's Chimney (Beachy Head) 248
Devon 110
Dhaka (Bangladesh) 87, 123
  see also Dacca (East Pakistan)
diarrhoea 264, 274, 282, 305, 307
Dickens, Charles 131
dinosaurs, extinction of 190, 191, 303
Disasters Emergency Committee 203
diseases 29, 30, 226, 230
  avian flu **292–295**
  cholera **264–267**
  Ebola **304–307**

malaria **278–283**
  Marburg virus 307
  most deadly infectious 282
  MRSA **296–297**
  SARS **272–273**
  water-borne 213
displaced people 22, 42, 94, 98, 107, 123
  see also evacuation; homelessness; refugees
Ditan Hospital (Beijing) 272
Djibouti 281, 295
DNA 164
Dodge City (Kansas) 42
dolphins 261
Dominican Republic 99, 113
Don Carlos 219, 221
donkeys 28
Doppler radar 81, 82
Dover harbour 110
DRC *see* Democratic Republic of the Congo (DRC)
Dresden 236, 237, 238–239, 241
drought **28–35**, 41, 43, 61, 62, 87, 88, 92, 93, 172, 174, 176, 180, 183, 224–225, 226, 227, 228, 229
drugs 281, 296, 297
ducks 292, 294
Dunwich (sunken town) 244
dust 41, 51, 89
  dust bowls 91
    America's dust bowl (1930s) **40–43**
  dust clouds 40, 41, 42
  dust storms 40, 41, 42, 43, 89, 90
  see also sandstorms
Düzce (Turkey) 17, 19, 20
dykes 244

E
earth tremors 17, 149, 154
earthquakes **14–27**, 50, 51, 57, 138, 140, 146, 149, 154, 160, 191, 194, 198, 199, 205
  in Bam (2003) 24, 25, **27**
  deadliest of 20th century 25, 27
  earthquake resistance 23
  forecasting of 25
  Great Chilean 24
  in Kashmir (2005) 24, 25, **26**, 27
  in Kobe 23, 24, 25
  Loma Prieta 23, 24
  regions at risk from 24–25
  in San Francisco 23, 24
  in Tangshan (China) 24, 25, 27
  in Turkey (1999) **14–22**
East Africa **28–35**, 197, 224, 295
East China Sea 207
East Pakistan 118, 121, 122
Ebbert, Terry 107
Ebola haemorrhagic fever 282, **304–307**
Ecevit, Bülent 18
economic losses
  due to coastal erosion 245
  due to disease 281
  due to drought 61, 225
  due to earthquakes 24
  due to El Niño 225, 226, 230, 231
  due to flooding 94, 116, 231, 235, 241
  due to forest fires 225
  due to heatwaves 61
economic losses (*cont'd*)
  due to locusts 289
  due to mudslides 116

due to sandstorms 88
due to storm damage 45, 79, 80, 84,
    94, 96, 102, 108, 109, 115, 116,
    117, 123, 216, 217
due to volcanic eruptions 136, 137
Ecuador 224, 226, 227
Edisto Beach (South Carolina) 247
Edmonton (Canada) 73
Egypt 34, 187, 285, 294, 295
El Bushra, Dr Hassan 307
El Chichón (Mexico) 156
El Líbano (Colombia) 154, 156
El Molo people 32, 33
El Niño
    causes of 227
    El Niño (1997-8) 183, **224–231**
    global impact of 228–229
    predicting 230–231
El Paso (Texas) 291
El Salvador 99
Elbe river 234, 236, 237, 238, 239,
    240, 241
electrical storms 169–170
    see also lightning
electricity
    electricity consumption 72
    electricity generation 34, 62, 126
    electricity pylons 169
        collapse of 38, 39
electrons 169
elk 140, 178
Ellis, Jim 302
Emergency Doctors Association 60
emphysema 131
Empire State Building 168
England 60, 62, **64–67**, **108–113**,
    128–132, 168, 209, **242–245**, 248
    see also individual counties, places
English Channel 110, 113
Enhanced Fujita Scale 81
    see also Fujita Scale
epidemics 264–267
Equator 230
erosion
    coastal 215, 230, 242–249
        Happisburgh (Norfolk) **242–245**
        North Carolina 247
        Tuvalu **246**
    soil 41, 43, 92, 112
Ershad, President Hussain
    Mohammad 87
Erta Ale volcano (Ethiopia) 145
eruptions, volcanic
    deadliest 156
    explosive eruptions 138, 140
    phreatic eruptions 138, 155
    super-eruptions **164–165**
        biggest 165
    see also gas, volcanic; steam
        explosions; volcanoes
Erz Mountains (Germany) 236, 237,
    238
Erzincan (Turkey) 17
Essex 169, 244
Eta Aquarids meteor shower 186
Ethiopia 28, 30, 145, 228, 230, 279
Étretat cliffs (France) 248
Eurasian plate 17, 24
Europe 27, **58–63**, 160, 185, 187, 230,
    242, 248, 274, 276, 279, 294, 308
    central Europe 68, 73, 228,
        234–241
    eastern Europe 295
    northern Europe 63
    western Europe 17, 276

see also individual countries, places
European Union presidency 62
evacuation 97, 98, 99, 100, 102, 105,
    106, 107, 156, 160, 162, 163, 178,
    234, 241, 244
    see also displaced people;
        homelessness; refugees
Evenki people 188, 189
Everglades (Florida) 302
Exodus, book of 285
explosive eruptions 138, 140

F
factories 128, 131, 132
Falls fires (Yellowstone NP) 176
famine 164
    see also drought
Fan fire (Yellowstone NP) 172, 176
farming 28, 29, 32, 34, 43, 121, 124
    contamination of farmland 123
    devastation of farms 61
    loss of farmland 42, 51, 90, 92, 155,
        212
    over-farming 41, 92
    poultry farms 61
    see also agriculture; crops; livestock,
        loss of
Farnborough (Hampshire) 108
fault lines 16, 21
    Great Rift Valley 149
    in Indian Ocean 196, 197, 198
    North Anatolian Fault 16, 17, 18
    San Andreas Fault 23, 24, 25
    see also tectonic plates
Federal Emergency Management
    Agency (FEMA) 97, 105, 106,
    107
The Ferris Flotel (South Korea) 114
Fessenheim (Alsace) 61, 63
Field, Tony 296
Figueiró Dos Vinhos (Portugal) 181
Finisterre (Spain) 111
Finniss river (Northern Territory) 301
fire 27
    from fireball explosions 188, 189
    forest fires 61, 180, 189, 225, 226,
        228, 229
        in Australia (1983) **180–181**
        in Portugal (2005) **181**
        in South-east Asia (1997)
            182–183
        in Yellowstone Nat'l Park (1988)
            172–179
    in New Orleans (2005) 98
    smog from fires **182–183**
    volcanic fires 151
fireballs **184–187**, **188–191**
firefighters 72, 172, 174, 175, 176, 177,
    178, 179, 181
firestorms 150, 151, 172, 173, 174, 175
Fish, Michael 108
Fish Canyon (USA) 165
fishing 32, 33
    fishing fleets 260
    fishing industry losses 117, 200, 226
'flesh-eating disease' 296, 297
Flint (Michigan) 84
flood defences 104, 117, 234, 238, 239,
    240
    see also levees
floods 17, 18, 21, 22, 35, 46, 115, 116,
    117, 151, 166, 224, 225–226, 228,
    229, 230, 231, 266
    in Bangladesh (1970) **118–123**
    in central Europe (2002) **234–241**

flash floods 34, 117, 230, 238, 241
    most deadly 240
    in Mumbai (2005) **210–215**
    in New Orleans (2005) **94–107**
Floreani, Adam 262, 263
Florida 44, 45, 93, 94, 96, 98, 99, 112,
    168, 205, **232–233**, 247, 257, 258,
    302, 303
    Florida Fish and Wildlife
        Conservation Commission 302
    Florida Keys 222
    Florida Panhandle 102
fluoride 33
fluorine compounds 132
fogs 88, 128
    see also smogs
Folkestone harbour 110
Fontan, Lee 260
forests 35, 88, 92, 126, 180, 189, 241,
    270
    forest fires see under fire
    mangrove forests 244
    see also trees
Fort Bragg (California) 257
France 57, **58–63**, 121, 209, 248
freak waves **218–221**
freeze, Russia's big (2006) **68–73**
frost 70, 73
Fry, Randy 257, 258
Fujita, Dr Ted 81
Fujita Scale 78, 81, 82
Fulton, Willy 309
fumaroles 138, 160
fungi 289
    poisonous 274–276

G
Gabon 306
Gainesville (Georgia) 84
Galtür (Austria) **52–55**, 57
Galveston (Texas) 99, 107
Ganges river 121
    Ganges delta 118
Ganpu (China) 208, 209
Gansu (China) 27
Garcia, Albert 159
gas, natural 73
gas, volcanic **124–127**, 136, 138, 140,
    148, 150, 158, 160, 164
    piping of 127
Gates, Bill 283
geese 294
Geminids meteor shower 186
Geological Survey of Canada 145
Geological Survey of India 186
geologists 138, 140, 144, 146, 148, 150,
    160, 161, 164, 190
Georgia (USA) 45, 76, 78, 79, 84, 102,
    247
Germany 63, 73, 121, 236, 237, 241,
    273, 295, 303
Ghana 281
gharials
    Indian 303
    Malayan 303
    see also alligators; caymans;
        crocodiles
Gibbon River valley (Yellowstone NP)
    176
Gien (France) 60
Gilbert, Dick 80
Gilbert, John 260
Gironde Mascaret tidal bore (France)
    209
Gisenyi (Rwanda) 148, 149

Glacier Park (Washington State) 142
glaciers 43
    Gurschen glacier 61
    melting of 61
Glasgow, University of 249
Glashütte (Germany) 240
GlaxoSmithKlein (GSK) 283
Glencoe (Alabama) 44
Glenn, Helena 296
global cooling 160
global warming 35, 63, 93, 100, 123,
    241, 246, 248–249
    see also climate change
goats 30, 33
Gobi desert 90, 92
Godley, Karen 267
Godthaab (Greenland) 252
Gölcük (Turkey) 17, 18, 21, 22
Goliad (Texas) 84
Goma (DRC) 146, 148, 149
Gomez, Efraín 157
Gopalganj (Bangldesh) 217
Gore, Vice-President 82
Goregaon (Mumbai) 214
Gottbreht, Jeff 106
Grant Village (Yellowstone NP) 176
The Grapes of Wrath 43
grasslands 43, 92, 270
    see also savannah
Grayton Beach (Florida) 232
'Great Green Wall' (China) 92, 93
Great Lakes 77, 113
Great Plains 40, 43
Great Rift Valley 149
Great Yarmouth 245
Green Party 62
Green river (Washington State) 139
greenhouse gases 93
Greenland 250, 252, 253
grizzly bear attacks **308–309**
Grizzly People 308
Grootfontein (Namibia) 187
Guadeloupe 99
Gualí river (Colombia) 152, 154
Guam 115
Guangdong (China) 272, 273
Guatemala 99
Guinsaugon (Philippines) **46–50**
Gulf Coast 94, 98, 99, 100, 107
Gulf of Izmit (Turkey) 17, 20, 21, 22
Gulf of Mexico 36, 44, 76, 77, 84, 96,
    97, 98, 100, 102, 261
Gulf Stream 97
Gulfport (Mississippi) 98, 102
Gurschen glacier (Switzerland) 61
Gutenberg, Beno 25
Gyromitra species 276

H
H5N1 strain of avian flu 292, 293,
    294, 295
haemorrhaging 305, 306, 307
Hagermen, Jess 144
hailstorms 222
    hailstones 62, 216, 217
    Sydney hailstorm (1999) **216–217**
    worst on record 217
Haiti 99
Hamburg 236, 239
Hampshire 108
Hampstead Heath 129
Hangzhou Bay tidal bore (China)
    206–209
Hanoi 292
Hans Hedtoft, sinking of the 250–253

Hansom, Dr James 249
Happisburgh (Norfolk) **242–245**
Harlech (North Wales) 248
Harter, Pascale 305, 306
Harvard University 281
Harwich 111
Hawaii 145, 262, 263
Heathrow airport 108
heatwaves
 in Europe (2003) **58–63**
Heicheng (China) 25
helicopters 80
 rescue helicopters 49, 54, 66, 106,
  121, 142, 144, 152, 238
Hellroaring fire (Yellowstone NP)
  174, 176, 177
Henan (China) 240
Hengist 110, 112
Henry, Jeff 175
Hentschel, Dr Chris 283
herdsmen 28, 29, 32
Hermes asteroid 191
Hickson, Dr Catherine 145
Highdown Hill (South Downs) 113
highs *see* anticyclones; atmospheric
  pressure
Hill, Chris 309
Himalayas 25, 26, 87
hippopotamuses 30
HIV/AIDS 279, 282
Hoba meteorite 187
Hobart (Tasmania) 222
Hoffman, Dustin 305
Hohhot (Inner Mongolia) 89
Holderness (Yorkshire) 248
Holmes, Sherlock 131
homelessness 18, 26, 87, 115, 202
 see also displaced people; evacuation;
  refugees
Homo erectus 242
Honda (Colombia) 154, 156
Honduras 99
Hong Jiang, Professor 93
Hong Kong 272, 273, 292, 294, 295
Honshu (Japan) 117
hospitals 34, 35, 58, 73, 88, 102, 130,
  131, 181, 182, 183, 201, 216, 267,
  272, 274, 296, 297, 300, 305, 306,
  307
 lack of 26
Houghton, Sir John 123
Houston 107
 Astrodome 105
hovercrafts, rescue 66
Huang He (Yellow River) 240
huayco 51
Huck fire (Yellowstone NP) 177
Hugli bore (India) 209
Hugo 253
Huguenard, Amie 309
humanitarian aid 202, 203
 see also relief aid
Hungary 236, 239, 240, 241
hunger 29, 121, 285
hunting 33
Hurricane Alley (USA) 100
hurricanes 44, 108, 109, 110, 161, 166,
  244
 deadliest Atlantic 99
 Hurricane Betsy 104
 Hurricane Camille 122
 Hurricane Emily (2005) 100
 Hurricane Fifi 99
 Hurricane Flora 99
 Hurricane Floyd 112

Hurricane Grace 113
Hurricane Katrina (2005) **94–107**,
  122
Hurricane Luis 221
Hurricane Mitch 99
Hurricane Pam (training exercise) 97
Hurricane Rita (2005) 100
Hurricane Wilma (2005) 100
Hydro-Québec 39
hydrocarbons 21, 133
hydrochloric acid 132
hyenas 31
hypothermia 53, 72, 73
Hyundai Heavy Industries 117

I

Ibagué (Colombia) 154, 155, 156
ice 51, 72, 73, 112, 154
 Canada's ice storm (1998) **36–39**
 ice caps 35, 138, 152, 154, 156
 ice particles in clouds 169
 icebergs **250–253**
  ships colliding with 251, 253
 sea ice 73, 250, 253
Ice Age 43, 66
Idaho 142, 172, 308
Illinois 76, 77, 79, 84, 166
impact craters 190, 191
 10 largest 190
India 57, 122, **184–187**, 199, 202, 209,
  210–215, 240, 270, 283
Indian Ocean 28, 34, 118, 196, 198,
  200, 205, 212
Indian plate 24
Indiana 76, 78, 79, 82, 84
Indonesia 25, 156, 164, **182–183**,
  194–205, 224, 225, 226, 227, 228,
  272, 294, 295, 301
Industrial Revolution 131
Ingvall, Lude 222, 223
insecticides 289
 see also pesticides
Intracoastal Waterway (New Orleans)
  94, 99
Iran 25, 26, **27**, 295
Iraq 171, 295
Ireland 63
iridium 190
Irish Sea 249
Islamabad 122
isolation wards 272
Istanbul 14, 16, 25
Italy 27, 50, 57, 63, 164, 165, 203
Izmit (Turkey) 14, 16, 17, 19, 21

J

Jack and Jill (windmills) 112
jackals 31
Jackson Hole (Wyoming) 56
Jade Sea (Lake Turkana) 30, 32
Jaffe, Professor Dan 92
Jamaica 99, 113
Jambi (Indonesia) 183
Japan 17, 23, 24, 25, 27, 92, 114, 115,
  116, 117, 145, 165, 200, 203, 294
Java 224
Jersey 111
jet streams 112, 229
Jimenez, Yovy Suarez 302
Johannes Krüss 253
Johannesburg 217
Johnston, David 143
Julianehaab (Greenland) 252
Junger, Sebastian 113
Justus Haslinger 253

K

Kaflia Lake (Alaska) 309
Kakadu National Park (Australia) 298
Kalimantan (Indonesia) 182, 225
Kalina (Mumbai) 214, 215
Kalutara (Sri Lanka) 199
Kamchatka Peninsula 117
Kamp river (Austria) 238
Kampa district (Prague) 237
Kansas 41, 42, 43, 82, 84
Kapellner, Helmut 53, 54
Kaptipada (India) 184
Kara Crater (Russia) 190
Karlin district (Prague) 234, 236, 237
Karliova (Turkey) 17
Kashmir 24, 25, **26**, 27
Kastela 253
Katchall Island (Andaman Islands) 194
Katowice (Poland) 72, 73
Katrina *see under* hurricanes
Kauai (Hawaii) 262
'Keeper of the Fire' 136
Kéllé (Congo) 306, 307
Kelut (Indonesia) 156
Kendrapara district (India) 184
Kent 168
Kentucky 45, 76, 78, 79, 80, 82
Kenya 28, 29, 30, 33, 34, 35, 202, 224,
  226, 228, 230, 279, 301
Kerr, Warwick Estevam 291
Khait (Tadzhikistan) 50
Kikai (Japan) 165
Kikwit (Zaïre) 306
Kingston University (London) 163
Kobe (Japan) 23, 24, 25
Koh Phi Phi (Thailand) 200
Korea 92, 117
 Korean peninsula 114, 116
 see also North Korea; South Korea
Korea Meteorological Administration
  116
Krabi (Thailand) 197, 200, 201
Kraft, Katia & Maurice 145
Krakatau 164, 165, 200
Kreifels, Susan 158, 162
Krems (Austria) 236, 238, 239
Krkonose mountains (Czech Republic)
  238
Kuala Lumpur 183
Kuching (Sarawak) 183

L

La Niña 82
 see also El Niño
La Palma (Canary Islands) 205
Labrador 36, 113
Laguna Miguel (California) 229
Lagunillas river (Colombia) 152, 154
lahars 136, 138, 139, 140, 141, 150, 151,
  152, 154, 162, 163
 secondary lahars 163
Lahaul Valley (India) 57
Lake Borgne (Louisiana) 98
Lake Challa (Kenya) 301
Lake Diana (Florida) 302
Lake Edward (DRC) 149
Lake George (Florida) 302
Lake Kivu (DRC/Rwanda) 126, 148,
  149
Lake Monoun (Cameroon) 126, 127
Lake Nyos (Cameroon) **124–127**
Lake Pontchartrain (Louisiana) 97,
  98, 103
Lake Taupo (New Zealand) 164, 165

Lake Turkana (Africa) 30, 32, 33
 shrinkage of 32–33
Lake Victoria 34, 303
lakes, volcanic 124, 126
LaMotte, Sandee 232, 233
landslides 27, 46, 66, 117, 140, 141,
  205, 214, 229, 248
 biggest since 1900 50
 largest recorded 136
 see also mudslides
Langtou Gou (China) 90
Laos 294
Las Nereidas river (Colombia) 154
Lassen Volcanic National Park
  (California) 142
lava 30, 126, 138, 145, 146, 147, 148,
  149
 lava domes 138, 141
Le Morne Rouge (Martinique) 151
Le Prêcheur (Martinique) 150
Leeward Islands 99
Leicester 274
Leonids meteor shower 186
LeProvost, Rick 257, 259
Lerias, Governor Rosette 50
Lesser Antilles volcanic arc 150
levees 94, 96, 97, 98, 99, 102, 103,
  104, 107
Leyte Island (Philippines) 46, 48, 50
Libya 286, 288
lightning 34, 44, 45, 62, 92, 142,
  166–171, 176, 216
 ball lightning 169, 170
 effects of 166
 lightning safety 170
 lightning strikes 172
 strikes on aircraft 170–171
Lin Langren (Chinese gangmaster)
  67
Linz (Austria) 236, 238, 239
lions 31
livestock, loss of 28, 29, 30, 32, 34, 42,
  87, 120, 123, 124–125, 130, 226
 see also animal life, loss of
Locke, Malcolm 302
locusts
 as food 288
 plagues of **284–289**
Loire river 60
London 107, **128–132**, 133
Long Valley (California) 165
Longbaoshan (China) 91
longshore drift 248, 249
The Loop (warm water) 97
looting (in New Orleans) 98, 105
Lorenz, Manfred 54, 55
Los Angeles 133, 230
Louisiana 84, 94, 97, 98, 99, 100, 102,
  107, 244, 248
 Louisiana Department of Wildlife
  and Fisheries 105
 Louisiana State University 94, 97,
  104
Louisville (Kentucky) 79, 80, 82
Lower Austria 238
lows *see* atmospheric pressure;
  depressions
Luanda (Angola) 264, 266, 307
Lucas, Curtis 302
Lumpur, Seth 183
Lupar Benak tidal bore (Malaysia)
  209
Luzon (Philippines) 160, 162
Lyme Regis 248
Lyrids meteor shower 186

M

McGough, Ashley 301
Macmillan, Harold 132
Madison, University of (Wisconsin) 93
Magadan (Siberia) 70, 73
magma 138, 140, 144, 146, 150, 158, 160, 161, 164, 165
Maharashtra (India) 210, 212
Mahim Bay (India) 215
Maine 45, 113
maize 28
Malanje (Angola) 266, 267
malaria 226, **278–283**, 307
  immunity from 279
  Malaria Vaccine Initiative (MVI) 283
Malaysia 182, 183, 202, 209, 225
Maldives 197, 199, 202
Malé (Maldives) 197
Mali 286, 289
Malik, Ghulan 120
mangroves 244, 301
Manicouagan Crater (Canada) 190
Manikganj (Bangladesh) 87
Manila 25, 50, 183, 228
Manitsoq (Greenland) 252
Manizales (Colombia) 154, 155
Mann, Brett 301
Manotick (Ontario) 36
Marburg virus 307
Marcellinus, Ammianus 21
Mariquita (Colombia) 154, 156
Marshall Islands 122
Martin, Gerald 143
Martinique 99, **150–151**
Masai Mara Reserve 30
Masai people 28, 29, 30
Masan (South Korea) 116, 117
Massachusetts 45, 249
Mauritania 287, 289
Mayfield, Max 96
Mayurbhanj district (India) 184
measles 282
Médecins Sans Frontières 266, 267
Medicine Lake (California) 142
Medicines for Malaria Venture (MMV) 283
Mediterranean 17, 25, 248
Meissen 234
Melbourne 180
Melsek, Janie 302
meltwater 61, 152, 154, 156
Meraux (New Orleans) 103
Merrow (Surrey) 111
Messina (Italy) 27
Met Office, UK 63, 108, 110, 111, 113, 123, 168, 170
Metarhizium anisopliae 289
Meteor Crater (Arizona) 190
meteorites 190
  over Orissa (2003) **184–187**
meteorologists 63, 73, 76, 77, 81, 92, 97, 115, 212, 224, 231
  see also weather forecasting
meteors 186
  meteor showers 186
  meteor storms 185
methane 126
methicillin 296, 297
Mexico 190, 191
Mexico City 25, 133
Miami 96, 107, 302
Michigan 78, 79, 82, 84

Middle East 27, 185, 288
Middlesex Hospital (London) 131
Midwest City (Oklahoma City) 84
migrating wildfowl 295
Milan 133
Mills, Dr John 249
Mink Creek fire (Yellowstone NP) 176
Miramar Beach (Florida) 258
Mirpur (Kashmir) 26
Mirror Plateau (Yellowstone NP) 172
Mississippi 78, 79, 84, 94, 97, 98, 100, 102, 122
Mississippi river 77, 94, 97, 98, 102, 104, 107
  Mississippi delta 102
  Mississippi River-Gulf Outlet (MR-GO) 99, 104
Mississippi Sound 102
Missouri 84
Mithi river (India) 215
Miyako, island of (Japan) 115, 116
Mohanty, Basant Kumar 186
Molinos river (Colombia) 154
molten rock 138
Mongolia 88
  Inner Mongolia 89, 90, 93
monsoon rains 120, 121, 163, 166, 224, 225
  monsoon vortices 212
  Mumbai monsoon (2005) **210–215**
Mont Pelée (Martinique) **150–151**, 156
Montana 142, 172, 308
Monticello (Indiana) 79, 82
Montreal 36, 38, 39
Moore (Oklahoma City) 84, 86
Morchella species 276
Moretto, Carolyn 297
Morocco 286, 288
Morokweng Crater (South Africa) 190
Morris (Illinois) 76, 79
Moscow 68, 71
mosquitoes 279, 281, 283, 301
Motse (Peru) 226
Mount Adams (Washington State) 142
Mount Baker (Washington State) 140, 142
'Mount Fuji of the West' 136
Mount Hood (Oregon) 142
Mount Huascarán (Peru) 50, 51, 57
Mount Jefferson (Oregon) 142
Mount Kazbek (North Ossetia) 57
Mount Kenya 35
Mount Kilimanjaro (Tanzania) 35
Mount Lofty Ranges (Australia) 180
Mount Nyamuragira (DRC) 149
Mount Nyiragongo (DRC) 126, **146–149**
Mount Pinatubo (Philippines) 144, **158–163**, 164, 165
Mount Rainier (Washington State) 142
Mount Royal (Montreal) 39
Mount St Helens (Washington State) 50, **136–144**, 165
Mount Shasta (California) 142
Mount Unzen (Japan) 145
Mozambique 149, 283
MR-GO (Mississippi River-Gulf Outlet) 99, 104
MRSA **296–297**
  community-acquired (CA-MRSA)

297
Mtera reservoir (Tanzania) 34
mudslides 117, 136, 139, 140, 150, 151, 162, 163, 226, 229
  Guinsaugon (Philippines) **46–50**
  Nevado del Ruiz (Colombia) **152–157**
  Yungay (Peru) 50, **51**, 57
  see also lahars; landslides
Mudurnu (Turkey) 17
Müglitz river (Germany) 238
Mumbai **210–215**
München, sinking of the 218–219, 221
Munigi (DRC) 148
Murillo (Colombia) 154, 156
mushrooms 274
  death cap 274, 276
  inkcap, common 276
  morels, false 276
  morels, real 276
mutation 294–295
Myanmar (Burma) 202, 301
Mymensingh (Bangladesh) 87

N

Nagin, Mayor Ray 97, 98, 107
Nakdong river (South Korea) 117
Nakhla meteorite 187
Namibia 187
NASA 93, 160, 168, 231
  satellite observation department 93
Nashville 273
Natchez (Mississippi) 84
National Center for Atmospheric Research, US 100
National Gallery (London) 131
National Geographic Magazine 83, 139, 143
National Guard, US 99, 105, 107
National Health Service 297
National Hurricane Center (NHC), US 96, 97
National Space Centre, UK's 191
National Weather Service (NWS), US 80, 81, 82, 97, 233
  see also Weather Service, US
Native Americans 136
Nazca oceanic plate 152
Near Earth Objects (NEOs) 191
Nebraska 42, 83
necrotising fasciitis 296, 297
nettle trees 276, 277
Nevado del Ruiz (Colombia) 50, **152–157**
New Danube river 238
New Deal 43
New Hampshire 45
New Jersey 45
New Mexico 83
New Orleans
  Canal Street 95
  canals 99, 102, 103, 106
  Convention Center 99, 105, 106
  French Quarter 103
  Hurricane Katrina (2005) **94–107**
  Intracoastal Waterway 94, 99
  maps of 98–99
  Superdome 98, 99, 102, 105, 106
New Richmond (Wisconsin) 84
New South Wales 288
New York 43, 93, 168, 187, 205
New York State 39, 78, 79
New Zealand 164, 165, 277
Newberry Crater (Oregon) 142
Newcastle upon Tyne, University of

249
Nguyen Hung Viet 292, 294
Nguyen Thanh Hung 292
Nicaragua 99
Nicholls, Amy 302
Nicobar Islands 202
Nicomedia (Izmit) 21
Nicorette (yacht) 222, 223
Niger 286
Nijs, Captain Pieter de 219
Nile river *see* White Nile river
Nina (Kenya) 279
Ningxia (China) 50
nitrogen oxide 133
nitrous oxide 182
Noguera, David 267
nomads 28, 29, 30, 34
Norfolk **242–245**
Normandy 248
Norris Junction (Yellowstone NP) 176
North Africa 60, 112, 285, 286, 288, 289
North America 43, 90, 92, 93, 136, 142, 150, 165, 205, 226, 227, 230, 269, 276, 277, 279, 302, 308
  see also individual countries, states, places
North American plate 24, 150
North Anatolian Fault 16, 17, 18
North Carolina 44, 45, 78, 79, 81, 113, 246, **247**
North Fork fire (Yellowstone NP) 174, 175, 176, 177, 179
North Korea 92
North Ossetia 57
North Sea 219, 239, 242, 243, 248, 252
Northern Territory (Australia) 298, 301
Norway 66
Norwegian Dawn 221
Nova Scotia 113
Novarupta (Katmai) 158
Novorossiisk (Russia) 237
Novosibirsk (Russia) 71
Nuuk (Greenland) 252

O

Observation Point (Yellowstone NP) 175
oceans 93
  see also Atlantic Ocean; Indian Ocean; Pacific Ocean
Odugleh, Asiya 307
Ogallala Aquifer (USA) 43
Ohio 45, 76, 77–80, 81
  Ohio National Guard 81
Okinawa 115, 116
Oklahoma 41, 43, 84, **84–87**, 171
Oklahoma City 84–87
Old Faithful geyser (Yellowstone NP) 172, 179
Old Faithful Inn (Yellowstone NP) 175, 177, 179
Old Town (Prague) 234, 237
Omsk (Siberia) 71
ongaonga 277
Ontario 36
Orders Aid Hospital (Kikwit) 306
Oregon 142, 276
Orionids meteor shower 186
Orissa (India) **184–187**
Orlando 302
Osborne, Alfred 220
Ottawa 36, 39
Outbreak (film) 305

overgrazing 88
Overseas Ohio 253
Oxfam 149
ozone, ground level 133
ozone layer 160

P

Pacaraima region (Brazil) 225
Pacific Marine Environmental
    Laboratory, US 230
Pacific Ocean 82, 92, 93, 100, 114,
    115, 116, 117, 122, 142, 164, 205,
    216, 221, 224, 227, 230, 231, 246
    'Ring of Fire' 24, 50, 140, 142, 164
Pacific plate 24
Pakistan 26, 27, 212
Palawan (Philippines) 183
PAN AM flight 214 170
pandemics 273, 283, 292, 293, 295
Papua New Guinea 299
Paraguay 226
parasites 279, 281, 282, 283
Paris 58, 59, 60, 63, 133
Pathani Samant Planetarium (India)
    184
Paun, Owen 71
peasoupers 131
Pelloux, Dr Patrick 60
penicillin 296
Pennsylvania 45
Pereira, William 23
The Perfect Storm 113
Perkins, Phil 178
Perseids meteor shower 186
Persson, Göran 221
Peru 50, **51**, 57, 224, 225, 226, 227,
    229
Peruvian current 229
pesticides 88, 282, 288, 289
    see also insecticides
Peterson, Nick 262–263
Petitcodiac bore (Canada) 209
Philippine Institute of Volcanology
    and Seismology (PHIVOLCS)
    158, 160, 161
Philippines 25, **46–50**, 114, 117,
    158–163, 183, 226, 228, 272
phreatic eruptions 138, 155
Phuket (Thailand) 196, 197, 200, 201
phytoplankton 93
Piccadilly Circus 129
Pinatubo *see* Mount Pinatubo
pitcher plants 277
Piura river (Peru) 225, 226
plagues of locusts **284–289**
plants, poisonous **274–277**
Plasmodium parasites 279, 281
plates *see* tectonic plates
Plumwood, Val 298–300, 301
Plymouth (England) 110
pneumonia 131, 272, 273, 282
poison ivy 274, 277
poison oak 277
poison sumac 277
poisonous plants **274–277**
Poland 72, 73, 228, 230
pollution 88
    air pollution 58, 129, 132, 182, 183
    Air Pollution Index (API) 182
    from coal smoke 88, 128, 129, 131,
        132
    industrial 128, 131
    London's great smog (1952)
        128–132
    from oil spillages 21, 103

in South-east Asia (1997) **182–183**
from vehicle emissions 58, 70, 88,
    133, 182
of water supplies 164
Pont-Aven 221
Popigai Crater (Russia) 190
population growth 123
Portugal 61, 180, **181**, 248
poultry 294, 295
power failures 21, 36, 37, 39, 44, 45,
    68, 98, 105, 108, 115, 117
power stations 62, 126, 128
    nuclear 61, 62, 63, 117
Prague 234, 236, 237, 238, 239, 241
pressure, atmospheric *see* atmospheric
    pressure
Prince Christian Sound (Greenland)
    253
Prince William Sound (Alaska) 50,
    253
Puchezh-Katunki Crater (Russia) 190
Puerto Rico 99
pumice 136, 138, 140, 156, 158, 161,
    163
Purvis (Mississippi) 84
Pusan (South Korea) 114, 116, 117
pyroclastic flows 136, 138, 140, 141,
    151, 152, 154, 156, 158, 164

Q

Qaqortoq (Greenland) 252
Qiantang river (China) 207, 208, 209
Qiantang bore **206–209**
Quadrantids meteor shower 186
Québec 39
Queen Elizabeth II 221
Queen Mary 221
Quetta (Pakistan) 27
quick clay 66
quicksand 65, 66, 67

R

rain 28, 34, 35, 36, 39, 46, 98, 102,
    113, 117, 120, 155, 156, 162, 209,
    224, 226, 228, 230, 231
    rainmaking 93
    record rainfall **210–215**, 229, 236,
        237, 238
    supercooled 38
    see also monsoon rains; storms
Ramapo 221
Ramree (Myanmar) 301
Ranrahirca (Peru) 50, 57
Rao district (Senegal) 287
Rasmussen, Captain P.L. 250, 253
Ray, Governor Dixie Lee 138
rays 259
Red Crescent, Turkish 22
Red Cross 48, 105, 121, 156, 289, 305
    see also American Red Cross
Red fire (Yellowstone NP) 176
Red Square (Moscow) 68
refugees 149, 231, 246
    see also displaced people; evacuation;
        homelessness
relief aid 22, 29, 34, 99, 107, 121, 124,
    149
    humanitarian aid 202, 203
    see also rescue workers
reptiles, world's largest 298, 301
rescue workers 16, 20, 22, 46–47, 49,
    50, 52–53, 65, 66, 72, 100, 106, 152,
    157
    search-and-rescue operations 97,
        98, 219, 253

see also relief aid
respiratory problems 88, 131, 133,
    146, 183, 225, 272–273, 274
rhino rescue 238
Rhode Island 45
    University of 126
Rhône valley 62
Richter, Charles 25
Richter scale 14, 15, 17, 19, 26, 27, 50,
    51, 138, 140, 194, 198
    magnitudes on 25
ricin 274
'Ring of Fire' (Pacific Ocean's) 24, 50,
    140, 142, 164
rip currents **232–233**
Roanoke (Alabama) 44, 45
Robinson, Edwin E. 168
Romania 73, 236, 241
Roosevelt, Franklin D. 43
Rossberg, Mayor Ingolf 239
Rotterdam 107
Royal London Hospital 130, 131
Royal Melbourne Hospital 181
Ru river (China) 240
Rupe, Robert 291
Rushcutter's Bay (Sydney) 216
Russia 57, **68–73**, 116, 117, 188, 189,
    190, 237, 241, 295
Rwanda 126, 146, 148, 149
Ryukyu Islands (Japan) 117, 165

S

Sachs, Dr Jeffrey 281
Sacramento river (California) 107
Sadler's Wells theatre 130
Saffir, Herbert 96
Saffir-Simpson scale 96, 100, 116
Sahara Desert 286
Sahel 286
Sahgal, Bittu 215
St Bartholomew's Hospital (London)
    131
St Christopher 110
St Elmo's fire 170
St Louis (Missouri) 84
St Petersburg (Florida) 302
St Petersburg (Russia) 68, 71
Saint-Pierre (Martinique) **150–151**
Sake (DRC) 149
Saki Naka (Mumbai) 212
Sallanches (France) 57
Salmon Creek Beach (California) 261
Salzach river (Austria) 238
Salzburg 236, 238
Samar (Philippines) 161
San Andreas fault 23, 24, 25
San Antonio 107
San Francisco 23, 24, 260
San Joaquin river (California) 107
sand 66, 67
sandstorms **88–93**
sanitation, poor 264
Santa Maria (Guatemala) 156
Santarém (Portugal) 181
Sarawak 182–183
SARS **272–273**, 282
satellites 93
    mapping by 231
    monitoring by 160, 224
    satellite pictures 45, 92, 112, 113,
        115, 121, 160, 199, 220, 230–231,
        289
    tracking by 93, 230, 231
    weather satellites 45, 82, 121
Saudi Arabia 121

savannah 29, 32, 34
    see also grasslands
Save the Children 27
Scandinavia 66
scavenging animals 31
Schaefer, Joseph 82
Schaffner, Dr William 273
Scholes, Maureen 130, 131
scorpions 301
Scotland 295
sea defences 107, 242, 244, 245
sea levels, rising 107, 123, 246, 247,
    249
sea lions 259
Sea of Marmara 17, 18, 20
Sea of Okhotsk 73
seals 259, 260
search-and-rescue operations *see under*
    rescue workers
Seattle 92, 140
Sechura Desert (Peru) 226
Seine Mascaret tidal bore (France)
    209
seismic activity 140, 146, 205
    see also volcanoes
seismographs 25, 160, 189
seismometers 138, 160, 161
Senegal 283, 285, 286, 287, 288,
    289
Serbia 241
Sevastopol (Ukraine) 73
Severe Acute Respiratory Syndrome
    (SARS) **272–273**
Severn bore (England) 209
sewage, untreated 264
Seychelles 202
Shaheru Crater (Mount Nyiragongo)
    148
Shanghai 107
shanty towns 264, 266, 267
sharks
    attacks by **256–263**
    blacktip sharks 259
    blue sharks 259
    bull sharks 258, 259, 260, 261
    great white sharks 256, 258, 259, 262
    hammerhead sharks 259
    nurse sharks 259
    requiem sharks 259
    sand tiger sharks 259
    shortfin mako sharks 259
    tiger sharks 258, 259, 260, 262, 263
Shaturia (Bangladesh) 87
Shea, Dennis 100
sheep 28
Shetland Islands 249
shield volcanoes 138
Shipden (sunken village) 244
ships
    adrift in severe winds 110
    capsized 114, 116
    collisions between 183
    cross-Channel ferries 110, 112
    hitting icebergs 251, 253
ships *(cont'd)*
    sinking of 110, 113, 115, 116,
        218–221, 250–253
    surviving freak waves 221
    swept inland 21
    volcanic destruction of 151
shooting stars 186
shores, changing 248
    see also coastal erosion
Shoshone fire (Yellowstone NP) 176
Shoshone Lake (Yellowstone NP) 176

Shubenacadie bore (Canada) 209
Siberia 68, 70, 71, 73, 188
sickle cell anaemia 282
Sigurdsson, Haraldur 126
sikonyane 288
Silent Spring 283
silt 67
Simpson, Bob 96
Singapore 182, 183, 225, 272, 273
Sinigame (Sri Lanka) 203
Sint Eustatius (Caribbean) 99
Sisimiut (Greenland) 252
ski resorts 53, 54, 55, 56, 61
sky prawns (locusts) 288
Slovakia 236, 240, 241
slums *see* shanty towns
Smith, Jewaun 297
smogs 58, 133
  London's great smog (1952)
    128–132
  in South-east Asia (1997) **182–183**
  see also fogs
smoke
  coal smoke 88, 128, 129, 131, 132
  from forest fires 172, 174, 178, 179,
    182
Snake Complex (Yellowstone NP) 176
snakes **268–271**
  10 most venomous 270
  adders 270
  black mambas 269
  boas 270
  brown snakes 270
  cobras 269, 270, 271
    black spitting cobras 268
  constrictors 270
  coral snakes 269
  diamondbacks 271
  fer-de-lance snakes 150, 271
  fierce snakes 270
  pit vipers 269
  pythons 270
  rattlesnakes 269, 271
  sea kraits 270
  taipans
    coastal taipans 270
    inland taipans 270
  tiger snakes 270
  vipers 270, 271
snow 52, 53, 54, 55, 56, 57, 72, 73,
  112, 152, 154, 177, 178
  in eastern USA (1993) **44–45**
  thundersnow 45
Sochi (Russia) 73
Soi (Tadzhikistan) 50
Soil Conservation Act (in US) 43
soil erosion 41, 43, 92, 112
Solar System 186–187
Somalia 28, 29, 32, 33, 34, 35, 197,
  199, 202, 228, 230, 231
soot 128
Sopoanga, Saufatu 246
SOS signals 218, 219
South Africa 190, 217, 260
South America 224, 227, 279, 282,
  290, 303
  see also individual countries, places
South American plate 24, 152
South Australia 180, 258
South Carolina 44, 45, 247
South China Sea 200
South Downs 112, 113
South-east Asia **182–183**, **194–205**,
  224, 227, 301, 303
South Korea **114–117**, 294

South Sotho people 288
southern Africa 228, 288
Southern Oscillation 227
space, outer 184–187
  impact from **188–191**
Spain 60, 63, 181
Spirit Lake (Washington State) 143
Sri Lanka 197, 199, 200, 201, 203,
  204, 244
Stalingrad *see* Volgograd
Stancil, Micah 270, 271
Staphylococcus aureus bacterium 296
steam explosions 137, 138, 140, 150,
  151, 155, 160, 161
Steinbeck, John 43
Steneosaurus bollensis 303
stepped leader (in lightning) 169
Stevens Pass (Cascades) 57
stinging nettles 276
Stinson Beach (California) 260
Stoney Tunguska river (Siberia) 188,
  190
Storm Creek fire (Yellowstone NP)
  174, 176
storms 62, 209, 218, 225, 237, 242,
  244, 245, 248, 253
  Beijing sandstorms 88
  Black Sunday storm 42, 43
  Canada's ice storm (1998) **36–39**
  Cyclone Bhola (2003) **118–123**
  dust storms 40, 41, 42, 43, 89, 90
  England's great storm (1987)
    108–113
  firestorms 151, 172, 173, 174, 175
  Hurricane Katrina (2005) **94–107**
  meteor storms 185
  The Perfect Storm 113
  sandstorms **88–93**
  storm chasers 83
  Storm Prediction Center
    (Oklahoma) 82, 84
  storm surges 94, 95, 98, 102, 104,
    107, 116, 117, 118–123, 239, 241,
    249
    top 5 storm surges 122
  superstorms 45
  Sydney hailstorm (1999) **216–217**
  tornado super outbreaks **76–87**
  tropical storms 96, 98, 118
  Typhoon Maemi (2003) **114–117**
  waterspouts **222–223**
  see also blizzards; cyclones;
    hailstorms; hurricanes; lightning;
    thunderstorms; tornadoes
Straits of Malacca 183
Stratford (Texas) 41
stratosphere 160
stratovolcanoes 138, 152
Su-Bum (Cameroon) 124
sub-Saharan Africa **278–283**
subduction 150, 152
Subic Bay Naval Station (Philippines)
  161
subtropical air 108
subtropical seas 96
Sudan 28, 305, 306, 307
Sudan ebolavirus 305
Sudbury Crater (Canada) 190
Suffolk (England) 244
sulphur 88, 124, 126, 131, 150, 187
sulphur dioxide 131, 132, 160, 165, 182
sulphuric acid 131, 160
Sumatra 27, 164, 165, 182, 183, 194,
  196, 197, 198, 199, 201, 205
Sumnia 110

sundew plants 277
Suniti (India) 184
super outbreak tornadoes *see*
  tornadoes
'superbug' (MRSA) **296–297**
Superdome, New Orleans 98, 99, 102,
  105, 106
superspreaders (of SARS) 273
surfing (on tidal bores) 208–209
Surrey 111, 129
Surusuria (India) 184, 186
Sutherland, Donald 305
Svend Foyn 253
swans 295
swarms
  of bees **290–291**
  of locusts **284–289**
Swazi people 288
Sweden 63
Switzerland 57, 61
Sydney **216–217**, 222
Sydney-Hobart race (2001) **222–223**
Syria 149

T

Tadzhikistan 50
Taegu city (South Korea) 117
Taipei 101 Tower (Taiwan) 23
Taiwan 273
Taklimakan desert (China) 92, 93
Tambora (Indonesia) 164, 165
Tamil Nadu (India) 200
Tampa Bay 257
Tana river (Kenya) 224
Tangail (Bangladesh) 87
Tangshan (China) 24, 25, 27
Tanzania 28, 34, 35, 197, 202
Tapsoba, Edouard 289
tar 128
Targhee National Forest (Wyoming)
  176
tarpons 261
Tasmania 222
Taylor, Joshua 268, 269
tectonic plates 16, 146, 150, 198
  African plate 24, 149
  Anatolian plate 17
  Antarctic plate 24
  Arabian plate 24
  Australian plate 24
  Caribbean plate 150
  Eurasian plate 17, 24
  Indian plate 24
  Nazca oceanic plate 152
  North American plate 24, 150
  Pacific plate 24
  South American plate 24, 152
  see also continental plates; fault lines
Tehran 25
Telwatta (Sri Lanka) 201
Tempel-Tuttle comet 185, 186
temperatures
  falling 128
  freezing 36–39, **68–73**
  heatwaves **58–63**
  rising 108
  temperature inversion 129–130, 131
  temperature swings 108
Tennessee 44, 45, 76, 78, 79, 84, 273
Texas 41, 43, 77, 83, 84, 99, 105, 107,
  271, 291, 302
Thai Binh (Vietnam) 292
Thailand 182, 183, 194, 196, 197, 199,
  200, 201, 202, 204, 224, 225, 272,
  273, 294, 295

thirst 29, 31, 33, 121
Three Sisters (Oregon) 142
thunderstorms 44, 76, 77, 82, 84, 87,
  115, 142, 156, 166, 168, 169, 170,
  172, 176, 226
tidal bores
  Black Dragon tidal bore (China)
    206–209
  Canal do Norte Pororoca (Brazil)
    209
  Gironde Mascaret (France) 209
  Hangzhou Bay tidal bore (China)
    206–209
  Hugli bore (India) 209
  largest bores 209
  Lupar Benak (Malaysia) 209
  Petitcodiac bore (Canada) 209
  Qiantang bore (China) **206–209**
  Seine Mascaret (France) 209
  Severn bore (England) 209
  Shubenacadie bore (Canada) 209
  surfing on 208, 209
  Turnagain Arm bore (USA) 209
  Wager Bay bore (Canada) 209
tides
  high tides 118, 120, 246
  spring tides 209
  storm tides 123
  tidal sands in Morecambe Bay
    64–67
tiet canh 292
tinjiya 288
Titanic 250, 253
toadstools 274
Toba (Sumatra) 164, 165
Tokyo 25, 27, 93
Tomlin, Andrew 262, 263
TOPEX/Poseidon satellite 230–231
tornadoes 44, 45, 102, 166, 222, 241
  in Bangladesh (1989, 1996) **87**
  forecasting of 82, 84, 87
  super outbreak tornadoes **76–87**
  tracking of 80
  in USA **76–87**
    deadliest in US history 84
    Tri-State Tornado 84
  see also twisters
Toronto 36, 39, 170
Tosya (Turkey) 17
tourism, effects of 303
Toutle river (Washington State) 139,
  141, 144
toxins 88, 268, 276, 277, 296
trade winds 227, 228, 229
traffic pollution *see* pollution
Transamerica Pyramid (San Francisco)
  23
Transparency International 267
transport, paralysis of 130
  see also airport closures
Treadwell, Timothy 308, 309
trees
  destruction of 36, 39, 46, 87, 108,
    111, 112, 120, 136, 139, 144,
    172–179, 180, 181, 188, 189, 190
  'Great Green Wall' (China) 92, 93
  planting of 55, 92, 93
  regeneration of 112, 178
Treidl, Dr Friedrich 54, 55
tremors, volcanic 138, 172
  harmonic tremors 138, 140, 160
Trenberth, Kevin 100
Trevino, Lee 166
tropics 34, 279, 281
  tropical air 113

tropical cyclones *see* cyclones
tropical storms 96, 98, 118
  see also cyclones
troposphere 160
Truman, Harry R. 143
Tsinghai (China) 27
tsunamis 17, 18, 21, 27, 151, 191
  10 worst tsunamis 200
  Atlantic tsunami 205
  Boxing Day tsunami (2004) 25, **194–205**, 244
    anatomy of 198–199
Tswana people 288
tuberculosis 282
Tumsaroch, Smith 224
Tunguska (Siberia) 190
Tunisia 286
Tupelo (Mississippi) 84
Turkana people 30, 32
Turkey **14–22**, 295
  Turkish Red Crescent 22
Turkmenistan 27
Turks and Caicos 99
Turnagain Arm bore (USA) 209
Turtle Mountain (Canada) 50
turtles 259, 261, 263
Tuvalu **246**
Twain, Mark 39
twisters 82, **84–87**, 222
typhoons 122
  Super Typhoon Tip 117
  Typhoon Ike 117
  Typhoon Lucille 117
  Typhoon Maemi (2003) **114–117**
  Typhoon Mike 117
  typhoon rains 163
  Typhoon Rananim 117
  Typhoon Rusa 117
  Typhoon Thelma 117
  Typhoon Yunya 161, 162
  see also cyclones

U

Uganda 34, 149, 283, 306
Uganda Wildlife Authority 303
Uige (Angola) 307
UK 60, 203, 273
  see also Britain; England; Scotland; Wales
Ukraine 73
Ulsan (South Korea) 116, 117
UN 34, 205
UN aid 99, 267
UN Disaster Relief Organization 154
UN Environment Programme 35
UN Food and Agriculture Organization (FAO) 289
UN General Assembly 246
UN resolutions 123
UNICEF 118, 122, 203
universities 81, 93, 94, 97, 104, 126, 163, 249, 273, 281, 283
Upper Austria 238
Ural Mountains 70
Urbani, Dr Carlo 272
Urir Island (Bay of Bengal) 120
urushiol (poison) 277
US Army 121
  US Army Corps of Engineers 102, 107
US Coast Guard 98, 105, 106
US Forestry Service 302
US Geological Survey (USGS) 143, 158, 160
US Lifesaving Association 233

US Navy 49
US Park Service 247
US State Department 267
USA 36, 39, **40–43**, **44–45**, 57, **76–87**, 90, 92, **94–107**, 113, 121, 136, **136–144**, 137, 141, 164, 165, 168, **172–179**, 187, 190, 203, 205, 209, **232–233**, 247, 248, 253, 261, 276, 283, **290–291**, 296, 297
  see also individual states, places

V

vaccines 273, 283, 294, 295, 307
Vaiont (Italy) 50
Val d'Isère 57
van Heerden, Ivor 94, 97, 104
Vanavara (Siberia) 188
vancomycin 297
Vancouver (Washington State) 143
Vanderbilt University (Nashville) 273
Veerman, Richard 267
venom **268–271**, 291
  extraction of 271
vents *see* fumaroles
venus flytraps 277
Verdalen (Norway) 66
Vermont 39, 45
Vesilind, Pritt J. 83
Vibrio cholerae 264
Victoria (Australia) 180
Vienna 236, 237, 238, 239, 240
Vietnam 182, 272, 273, 292, 294, 295
vineyards 62
Virginia 45, 78, 79
Virunga mountain chain (Africa) 149
viruses 272, 273, 282, 294, 305, 306, 307
Vltava river 234, 236, 237, 238, 239
volcanoes 145, 172, 205
  composite 138
  Cumbre Vieja (Canary Islands) 205
  extinct 30, 124
  monitoring of 144
  Mont Pelée (Martinique) **150–151**, 156
  Mount Nyiragongo (DRC) 126, **146–149**
  Mount Pinatubo (Philippines) 144, **158–163**, 164, 165
  Mount St Helens (Washington State) 50, **136–144**, 165
  Nevado del Ruiz (Colombia) 50, **152–157**
  stratovolcanoes 138, 152
  super-eruptions **164–165**
  types of 138
volcanic craters 140, 141, 146, 148, 152, 155, 160
volcanic explosivity index (VEI) 156, 165
volcanic lakes 124, 126
  see also ash, volcanic; eruptions, volcanic; gas, volcanic; lava; magma; tremors, volcanic
volcanologists 126, 143, 145, 205
volcanology 138, 163
Volgograd 72
Volvo Ocean Race 222, 223
vomiting 264, 274, 276, 305, 307
Vredefort Crater (South Africa) 190
vultures 31

W

Waco (Texas) 84

Wager Bay bore (Canada) 209
Wajir (Kenya) 33
Wales 248
Wallasea Island (Essex) 244
Waller, Dr Robert 131
Walter Reed Army Research Institute 283
warm air *see under* weather
Washington DC 43
Washington State 50, 57, **136–144**
  University of Washington 93
water
  contamination of 30, 264
  shortages of 28, 29, 30, 31, 32
water holes 29, 31, 33, 34
  see also boreholes; wells
waterspouts **222–223**
Watley, Richard 261
waves 21–22, 65, 94, 102, 110, 113, 116, 117, 230, 233, 248, 249
  freak waves **218–221**
  shock waves 51
  see also tidal bores; tsunamis
weather
  cold air 36, 39, 54, 62, 68, 70, 71, 73, 76, 87, 108, 112, 113, 128, 129
  collision of weather systems 111
  disrupted weather patterns 160, 164, 228–229
  warm air 36, 39, 62, 84, 87, 108, 113, 122, 129
  see also anticyclones; atmospheric pressure; depressions
weather forecasting 36, 44, 45, 54, 70, 77, 82, 84, 87, 96, 111
  see also meteorologists
Weather Service, US 44
  see also National Weather Service (NWS), US
Weatherill, David 266, 267
Webb, Tyna 261
Webster, Ranald 180, 181
Weesenstein (Germany) 238
Weisseritz river (Germany) 239
Wellington (Washington State) 57
wells 33
  well wars 33–34
  see also boreholes; water holes
West Africa 124–127, 283, 285, 286
West Pakistan 122
West Sussex 111
West Virginia 45, 78, 79
Western Ghats (India) 212
wetlands 35, 302
  disappearance of 107, 248
  restoration of 107, 244
whales 259
Wheeler, Ty 262
whirlwinds **222–223**
the White House 43, 97
White Nile river 34
whooping cough 282
wildlife boom 112
windmills 112
winds 22, 41, 43, 65, 88, 123, 174, 176, 180, 212, 218, 226, 253
  altered wind patterns 160
  hurricane-force 108, 109, 110
  prevailing winds 183
  trade winds 227, 228, 229
  whirlwinds **222–223**
  wind speeds (Fujita Scale) 81
  see also cyclones; hurricanes; storms; tornadoes; trade winds; twisters; typhoons

wine 62
Winterton (Norfolk) 245
Winthrop (Massachusetts) 249
Wisconsin 84, 93
Wizard of Oz 82
Wolfe Creek Crater (Australia) 190
woodlands 112, 270
Woodward (Oklahoma) 84
World Bank 92
World Food Programme 149
World Health Organization (WHO) 272, 273, 281, 282, 283, 306, 307
World Meteorological Organization 63
Worthing (England) 111
Wrightson, Diana 242, 244
Wyoming 56, **172–179**, 308

X

Xenia (Ohio) 76, 77–80, 81, 82

Y

yacht races 222, 223
Yambio (Sudan) 307
Yambuku (Zaïre) 305
Yangtze river 228, 231, 240
Yanguan (China) 207, 208, 209
Yekaterinburg (Russia) 70
Yellow River 240
Yellowstone Lake 176, 179
Yellowstone National Park 164, 165, **172–179**
Yorkshire 248
Yucatán peninsula 97, 191
Yungay (Peru) 50, **51**, 57

Z

Zaïre 305, 306
  see also Democratic Republic of the Congo (DRC)
Zaïre ebolavirus 305
Zambales mountain range (Phillipines) 160
Zhu Rongji, Premier 91
Zimmerman, Cliff 257, 258
Zumbado, Tony 94
Zwinger Palace art gallery (Dresden) 239

Acknowledgments

Abbreviations:
T = top; M = middle; B= bottom;
L = left; R = right

Front cover: Fred K. Smith
Back cover: digitalvision
1 Empics/AP/Curtis Compton. 2-3 Olivier Grunewald. 4 digitalvision/ARC/ Deserts, 1; digitalvision, 3; Bradbury and Williams, 2, 3; Science Photo Library/ Andrew Syred, 4. 5 Empics/AP. 6 Empics/ AP/J. Pat Carter. 7 Yellowstone National Park/Jim Peaco. 8 Newspix (News Limited)/Hellmut Issels. 9 Corbis/John Conrad. 12-13 digitalvision/ARC/ Deserts. 14-15 Empics/AP, BL; National Geographic Image Collection/Reza. 16 Empics/AP. 17 Empics/AP/Seth Rossman, B. 18-19 Impact Photos/Yann Arthus-Bertrand. 20 National Geographic Image Collection/Reza. 22 Empics/AP/ Oktay Cilesiz/Anatolia,T; Empics/AP/ Enric Marti, B. 23 Corbis/Sygma/Patrick Robert. 25 Corbis/Tom Bean. 26 Empics/ AP/Richard Vogel. 27 Getty Images/AFP. 28-29 Panos/Dieter Telemans, background, TL. 30 Empics/AP/Karel ardea.com/Clem Haagner. 32-33 Corbis/Jeffrey L. Rotman. 33 Empics/AP/Karel Prinsloo, TR. 36 Auscape/Ferrero-Labat. 37 Empics/AP/ Tom Hanson. 38-39 Getty Images/AFP/ Robert Laberge. 40-41 Empics/AP/ NOAA George E. Marsh Album. 42 Corbis/Bettmann. 44-45 Empics/AP/ Curtis Compton. 45 NOAA/National Climatic Data Center/NESDIS, TL. 46-47 Empics/AP/Bullit Marquez. 48-49 Getty Images/US Navy/Michael D. Kennedy. 49 Empics/AP/Bullit Marquez, TR. 51 Getty Images/Time & Life Pictures/NASA, MM; Corbis/Lloyd Cluff, B. 52-53 Corbis/epa; 54 Reuters. 56-57 Karsten Wenke. 58-59 Camera Press/Gamma/Alexis Duclos. 59 Empics/ AP/International Photos, BR. 60 Getty Images/AFP/Thomas Coex. 60-61 Camera Press/Gamma/Eric Dessons. 62 Reuters/Jeane Philippe Arles. 63 Getty Images/AFP/Olivier Morin. 64-65 Collections Picture Library/Robert Estall. 65 Empics/AP/Paul Ellis, BR. 66 Empics/AP/John Giles. 68 Empics/AP/ Dmitry Lovetsky, BL. 68-69 Empics/AP/ Alexsander Zemlianichenko. 70 Empics/ AP/Alexei Vladykin. 71 Owen Paun. 72 Empics/AP/Bela Szandelsky, TL; Empics/ AP/Alik Keplicz, B. 73 Sun Media Corp/ Brendon Dlouhy. 74-75 National Geographic Image Collection/Carsten Peter. 76-77 Empics/AP/Fred Stewart. 78 John Hultgren. 80 Dick Gilbert Foundation. 83 National Geographic Image Collection/Carsten Peter. 85 Reuters/Sue Ogrocki. 86 Empics/AP/J. Pat Carter. 87 Reuters/Sue Ogrocki. 89 Empics/AP/Xinhua/Li Xin. 90-91 Panos/ Mark Henley. 91 Getty Images/AFP/ Peter Parks, MR. 92 Empics/AP/Xinhua, Wang Chengxuan. 94-95 Reuters/Mark Wallheiser. 95 Getty Images/Mario Tama, TR. 96 Rex Features/NASA. 97 Reuters/Rick Wilking. 98-99 Rex Features/NASA. 100 Reuters/David J. Phillip. 101 Reuters/CN/Richard Carson. 102-03 Reuters/Rick Wilking. 104 Reuters/Marc Serota. 105 Reuters/Jason Reed, TL; Reuters/Richard Carson, R. 106 Empics/AP/Kevork Djansezian. 108, 109 *The Argus*, Brighton/Simon Dack. 110, 111 Jersey Evening Post. 112 Paul

Amos. 114-115 Getty Images. 116 Empics/AP/Yonhap/Cho Jung-Ho. 118-119 Corbis/Bettmann. 120, 121 Empics/ AP. 124 George F. Kling. 125 Corbis/ Peter Turnley. 127 Empics/AP/Christine Nesbitt. 128-9 Getty Images/Hulton Archive. 130 Getty Images/Hulton Archive/Monty Fresco. 131 Royal London Hospital Archives/Maureen Scholes. 133 Reuters/Gareth Watkins. 134-5 Olivier Grunewald. 136 USGS/ Robert Krimmel. 136-7 USGS/Donald A. Swanson. 138 naturepl.com/ARCO/ Lucasseck. 139 USGS/Lyn Topinka. 140 USGS/US Forest Service/Jim Nieland. 141 USGS/Lyn Topinka. 143 USGS/ Harry Glicken, T; USGS/Dan Dzurisin, B. 144 National Geographic Image Collection/Carsten Peter, T; Robert Cocking (Natural Resources Canada/ Geological Survey of Canada), ML. 146-7 Empics/AP/Karel Prinsloo. 148 Empics /AP/Sayyid Azim. 149 Reuters/Jacky Naegelen. 150-1 Corbis. 152 mount-pelee.com/Lacroix, A. – La Montagne Pelée et ses Eruptions, BM; Corbis/ Rykoff Collection, BR. 152 Corbis/AFP/ Jonathan Utz. 153 Rex Features/Sipa Press. 154-5 Rex Features/Mauro Carraro. 157 Rex Features/Mauro Carraro. 158-9 Corbis/©Alberto Garcia. 161 Corbis/Roger Ressmeyer. 162-3 Corbis/NASA. 166 Empics/AP. 167 Getty Images/Ralph Wetmore. 168 Empics/Marty Lederhandler. 169 Corbis/Robert Llewellyn. 170-1 oaklahomalighting.com/Charles Allison. 171 Empics/AP/James Croxon. 172, 173 Yellowstone National Park/Jim Peaco. 174 National Geographic Image Collection/Michael S. Quinton. 175 Yellowstone National Park. 176, 177 Yellowstone National Park/Jeff Henry. 178, 179 Yellowstone National Park/Jim Peaco. 180 Newspix, T. 180-1 Empics/ Sergio Azenha. 182-3 Camera Press/ Gamma/Buu Alain. 185 Getty Images/ AFP/Jamal Nasrallah. 187 Sara Eichmiller, T; R.A. Langheinrich meteorites/ www.nyrockman.com/Photo taken by Iris Langheinrich. 189 Empics/AP. 190 Auscape/Jean-Paul Ferrero. 192-3 Getty Images/Sean Gallup. 195 Getty Images/ AFP/John Russell. 196-7 Newspix/ Hellmut Issels (sequence); Getty Images/ AFP (background). 197 Newspix/ Hellmut Issels, R sequence. 199 Getty Images/DigitalGlobe. 200-201 AKG/ Ullstein/Ex-Press. 201 Getty Images/ AFP/Pornchai Kittiwongsakul. 202 Reuters/Arko Datta. 202-203 Getty Images/AFP/Jimin Lai. 206-207 Reuters/ China Daily Information Corp. 208 Reuters/China Daily Information Corp. 209 Reuters/Sergio Moraes. 210, 211 Reuters/Punit Paranjpe. 212-213 Empics/AP/Aijaz Rahi. 213 Reuters/ Punit Paranjpe, MR. 215 Empics /AP/ Aijaz Rahi. 216-217 Newspix/Nathan Edwards. 217 Newspix/Michael Perini, BL. 219 NOAA Photo Library. 222 Newspix, M. 222-3 Corbis/Reuters/ Handout Team Nicorette. 224-5 Getty Images/AFP, T; Still Pictures/Christian Aid/G. Griffiths, B. 228 Reuters/Poland Press Photo/Andrzej Iwanczuk, TL; Rex Features/Sipa Press, TR; Reuters/Erik de Castro, BL; Getty Images/Liaison/Paula Bronstein, BR. 229 Rex Features/ Keystone USA, TL; Getty Images/AFP/ Marie Hippenmeyer, TR; Reuters/Silvia

Izquierdo, B. 230-1 NASA JPL/TOPEX/ Poseidon. 232-3 *Daytona Beach News-Journal*/Nigel Cook. 234 Camera Press/ Gamma/Rossi Xavier. 235 Reuters/ Fabrizio Bensch. 236-7 Empics/AP/Jan Bauer. 238 Rex Features/Sipa Press. 239 Reuters/Alexandra Winkler. 240 Camera Press/Gamma/Piel Patrick. 241 Reuters/ Alexandra Winkler. 242-3 Albanpix.com/ Alban Donohoe. 245 Alamy/Photofusion Picture Library/Jim Hodson. 246-7 worldviewofglobalwarming.org/Gary Braasch. 249 Empics/AP/Michael Dwyer. 250 Scanpix Denmark. 251 Corbis/Ralph A. Clevenger. 252 Scanpix Denmark. 254-5 SeaPics.com/V & W/Fritz Poelking. 256-7 SeaPics.com/James D. Watt. 258 Empics/AP/Jason C. Miller. 259 SeaPics.com/Doug Perrine. 260 Empics/AP/John Reed, T; ardea.com/ Valerie Taylor, B. 262 NewsPics/Jo-Anna Robinson, T; Empics/AP/Lindsay Moller, B. 263 basetwoproductions.com/Dean Sensui. 264 Empics/AP/MSF/Paco Arevalo. 264-5, 266 Magnum Photos/ Paolo Pellegrin. 267 Médecins Sans Frontières/Barry Gutwein. 268-9 Corbis/ Rod Patterson. 270 NHPA/ANT Photo Library, TL; Auscape/John Wombey, M; Auscape/Pavel German, B. 271 Empics /AP/Mariano Matamoros. 272 Empics /AP/Xinhua/Wang Chengxuan. 273 Reuters/Kin Cheung, T; Science Photo Library/Dr Steve Patterson, B. 275 Science Photo Library/Bob Gibbons, TL; Science Photo Library/G. Tomsich, TR; naturepl.com/Jose B. Ruiz, BL; Science Photo Library/G.A. Matthews, BR. 276 naturepl.com/Juergen Freund. 277 Science Photo Library/Claude Nuridsany & Marie Perennou. 278-9 SeaPics.com/Petterik Wiggers. 279 Science Photo Library/ Mona Lisa Production, BR. 280, 281 Panos/Giacomo Pirozzi. 282 Science Photo Library/Dr Gopal Murti. 284-5 Camera Press/Gamma/Christian Dumas. 286 Camera Press/Gamma/Etienne de Malglaive. 286-7 Corbis/Reuters/Juan Medina. 288 FAO/G. Diana. 289 Camera Press/Gamma/Etienne de Malglaive. 290 naturepl.com/Premaphotos. 291 Science Photo Library/Department of Energy, T; *Payson Roundup Newspaper*/Carol La Valley, BL. 293 Empics/AP/Nick Ut. 294 Science Photo Library/Dr Gopal Murti, B. 294-5 Empics/AP. 295 Empics/AP/ Tran Van Minh. 296 Science Photo Library/CDC. 297 Rex Features/ Gary Roberts, T; Science Photo Library/HOP Americain/AJ Photo, B. 298-9 SeaPics.com/Franco Banfi. 300 Newspix, L. 300-301 FLPA/Frants Hartmann. 302 Empics/AP/Tom Benitez. 303 Natural History Museum, London, T; Reuters/Joe Skipper, B. 304-305 Camera Press/Laif/Ulutuncok. 306 Still Pictures/Ron Occalea, T; Camera Press/Cassati/Grazi neri, B. 307 WHO/Christopher Black. 308 Corbis/John Conrad. 309 Willy Fulton.

Artworks:
Bradbury & Williams for pages 142, 164. Glyn Walton for pages 17, 24, 36, 57, 67, 79, 90, 98-99, 108, 116, 123, 127, 141, 154, 165, 176, 177, 182, 188, 198, 199, 205, 208, 212, 215, 220, 222, 227, 228-9, 236, 248, 286, 291, 306.
NASA/Sage II for page 160.
NOAA-USLA Rip Current Task Force for page 233.

The publishers are grateful to the following individuals, publishers and websites for their kind permission to quote material:

14, 16 Zeynep Uygun, Nihat Ozen, Kadir Bahcecik, BBC News website. 21-22 Cengic Tayfur, NOAA. 22 Bulent Ertekin, www.info.turk.be; Beat Kunzi/Andrew Buncombe © *The Independent*, 19 August 1999. 26 Nabeel Ahmad, Faiz Din, BBC News website. 27 Rob Macgillivray/James Astill; Hamideh Khordoosta/James Astill; Parisa Damandan, The Power of Culture, www.powerofculture.nl. 28 Kiteleik Kasale, ActionAid International. 29 Naila Namposo, Kimere Nampaso, Pelgiya Kabanyiginya, ActionAid International. 31 Michael Koikai, Agence France Press. 32 Denge Galgalla, permission to reproduce 'Bleak future for ancient traditions' was granted by Richard Wainwright and CAFOD, the full article can be read online at www.cafod.org.uk/new_and_events/ emergencies/east_africa_emergency/ bleak_future_for_ancient_traditions; Mursal Mohammed, www.oxfam.co.uk/ what_we_do/where_we_work/kenya/ camel_crisis.htm/Mursal; Sheik Ibrahim Khail, Fatuma Ali Mahmood, *The Washington Post*; Christian Lambrechts, excerpt from the UN Environment Programme's Press Release 'Life Saving Anti-Drought Measures Must Include Investment in Nature – Rainfall Patterns in East Africa at Risk from Loss of Forests, Grasslands and other Ecosystems', 12 January 2006, www.unep.org/dewa/mountain. 36 Ken W. Watson, www.rideau-info.com; Pat Drummond, boatingincanada.com/ icestorm.html. 39 Hydro-Québec. 41 Margie Daniels, PBS, www.pbs.org. 42 J.R. Davison, PBS, www.pbs.org. 43 Lawrence Svobida, PBS, www.pbs.org; Clifford Hope, www.kancoll.org; Melt White, PBS, www.pbs.org. 44 Don Strength, NOAA; Paul Kocin, www.weather.com; Michael Leach, NOAA. 45 Don Strength, NOAA; Alicia Miravalles, AP. 48 Florencio Libaton, AP. 48-49 Rosette Lerias, AP. 49 Edmund Abella, BBC News website; Florencio Libaton, AP. 50 Dag Navarette, BBC News website; Wangyu Abieva, BBC News website. 51 Local child, www.rumbosonline.com. 53-54 Georg Walter, Luggi Salner, Christa Kapellner, Jason Tait, BBC *Horizon*, 'Anatomy of an Avalanche', 25 November 1999. 54 Manfred Lorenz, www5.ur.se. 54-55 Friedrich Treidl, BBC *Horizon*, 'Anatomy of an Avalanche', 25 November 1999. 55 Manfred Lorenz, Jörg Heumader, www5.ur.se. 58 Michel Cannesant/David Burnie. 60 Patrick Pelloux/Stefan Steinberg, International Committee of the Fourth International, World Socialist Web Site, www.wsws.org, 14 August 2003. 62 Les Verts Alsace. 63 Jørgen Olesen, *New Scientist*, www.NewScientist.com; François Roumiguières/David Burnie. 65 Emergency services, BBC News website. 66 Alex Bottomley, BBC News website; Harry Roberts, David Ward Copyright Guardian News & Media Ltd 2004; Alex Bottomley, BBC News website. 68, 70 Owen Paun, www.lexlibertas.com. 70 Nikolai Firyukov, www.rin.ru.

71 Owen Paun, www.lexlibertas.com. 72-73 Vladimir Grebenkin, BBC News website. 76-77 Irene Hale, www.xeniatornado.com. 78 Eyewitness, www.democraticunderground.com; Homer Ramby, www.xeniatornado.com. 78-79 Shirley Stamps, www.xeniatornado.com. 79-80 Irene Hale, www.xeniatornado.com. 80 Dick Gilbert/WHAS. 81 Don Halsey, www.xeniatornado.com. 82 John Forsing, Joseph Schaefer, Richard Augulis, NOAA. 83 Priit J. Vesilind, *National Geographic*, April 2004. 84 Scott and Susan Carlin/Paul Simons. 87 Barabhita and Bashial quotes, Tom Grazulis, The Tornado Project. 88 Francisco Little, www.bjreview.cn; Dai Qing, BBC News website. 91 Zhang Rui, The Official Xinhua News Agency; Li Ming Jiang, BBC News website. 92 Juergen Voegle, BBC News website. 92-93 Dan Jaffe, Science@NASA. 93 Duane Hilton, Science@NASA; Jay Herman, Science@NASA; Zhang Qiang, *The Daily Telegraph*, 1 July 2005; Professor Hong Jiang, BBC News website. 94 William Morrow & Co from *The Great Deluge: Hurricane Katrina, New Orleans, and the Mississippi Gulf Coast* by Douglas G. Brinkley, 2006; Elizabeth English, courtesy of CNN. 96 Chris Abbott, from *The Great Deluge*; Max Mayfield, courtesy of CNN. 97 Max Mayfield, ABC News, Ivor van Heerden, Viking Books from *The Storm: What Went Wrong and Why During Hurricane Katrina – The Inside Story from One Louisiana Scientist* by Ivor van Heerden and Mike Bryan, 2006. 102 *The Great Deluge*. 103 Gene Alonzo, Michael Brown, *The Great Deluge*. 104 *The Storm*. 105 Jaqui Goddard, Times Online. 106 *The Great Deluge*; Wil Haygood and Ann Scott Tyson, *The Washington Post*. 107 *The Great Deluge*. 108 Michael Fish, BBC News website. 110 Sid Bridgewater. 111 Fiona Baird-Murray, Froglets Publications from *In the Wake of the Hurricane* by Bob Ogley, 1988. 112 Harry Fordham; Simon Potts. 113 David Vallee, courtesy of CNN. 115 Yoshitaka Sunagawa, *Okinawa Times*. 116 Yoon Seok-hwan, Korean Meteorological Administration. 117 Choi Joong-kwon, YTN TV; Devon Rowcliffe, John Quirk, BBC News website; Grace Morris, www.lifeway.com. 118-120 Francis Smethwick/Paul Simons. 120 Ikram Sehgal, *The News* Internet Edition, 8 September 2005, www.jang.com.pk. 121 Lifeboat crews, RNLI. 122 Muhammad Bulu Mia, Shahinur Begam, ActionAid International. 123 Survivor, *New Scientist*; Mesbahur Rahman, *New Scientist*, www.NewScientist.com. 124 David Chia Wambong, Papa Nyako, Ahadji Abdou, BBC *Horizon*, 'Killer Lakes', 4 April 2002. 126 Haraldur Sigurdsson/Paul Simons. 127 Greg Tanyileke/Kevin Krajick, 'Defusing Africa's Killer Lakes', *Smithsonian* magazine, September 2003. 128-9 Barbara Fewster, BBC News website. 130 Betty Crowhurst, Peter Prentice, BBC News website; Donald Acheson, 'The Big Smoke: Fifty Years After the 1952 London Smog', seminar held 10 December 2002 (Centre for History in Public Health, 2005, www.icbh.ac.uk/witness/hygiene/smoke); Maureen Scoles, Jenel Farrell, NPR Rights and Reuse

Associates, p202.513.3622, f202-513-4017, www.npr.org. 131 Donald Acheson, 'The Big Smoke'; Robert Waller, BBC News website. 138-9 Bill Closner/Pat Moser, *The Columbian*, 28 May 1980; Nancy Ashutz, *The Columbian*, 'Remember Mount St Helens'; Rowe Findley, *National Geographic*, January 1981. 142 Mike Moore/Ley Garnett, © Copyright 2006, Oregon Public Broadcasting; Dave Millar, BBC News website. 142, 144 J. Marc Johnson, *The Columbian*, 'Remember Mount St Helens'. 143 Harry R. Truman/Rowe Findley, *National Geographic*, Jan 1981; David Crockett, KOMO-TV. 144 Jon Blundy; Rowe Findley, *National Geographic*, January 1981; Jess Hagerman, *The Daily News of Longview*, Washington. 145 Catherine Hickson/Celia Coyne. 148 Awete Emilie, Copyright © 2002 by The New York Times Co., reprinted with permission. 149 Richard Mwambo, BBC News website; James Astill; Rob Wilkinson, courtesy of CNN. 151 Father Mary, Stein & Day from *The Day the World Ended*, by Gordon Thomas and Max Witts, 1969; Auguste Cyparis, Yale University Press from *Vulcan's Fury* by Alwyn Scarth, 1999. 152, 154, 156, 157 José Luis Restrepo, reprinted from *The Journal of Volcanology & Geothermal Research*, vol 44, issue 3-4, B. Voight, 'The 1985 Nevado del Ruiz Volcano Catastrophe', pp349-386, Copyright 1990, with permission from Elsevier. 157 Ediliberto Nieto, Marina Franco de Huez, Felix Rojas, *Los Angeles Times*. 158, 162 Susan Krcifcls, *Honolulu Star-Bulletin*. 162-3 Beby Tolentino, Copyright © 1991 by The New York Times Co., reprinted with permission; Scott Bryan/Celia Coyne; Tubag Hagatan, 'Return of the Natives' by Saranyoo Samakrathgit, under the Journalism Fellowship Programme of the South-east Asian Press Alliance. 164 Reproduced by permission of The Geological Society of London, all rights reserved. 166 Jennifer, NOAA. 168 Mike, NOAA; Edwin E. Robinson. 169-70 Vivienne Coyne/Celia Coyne. 170 Lauren, BBC News website. 172 Joan Anzelmo, Danny Bungartz, *Los Angeles Times*; Phil Perkins/Celia Coyne; from 'Yellowstone on Fire!' *The Billings Gazette*, 1995. 175 Jeff Henry, Roche Jaune Press from *Crown Jewel of National Park Lodges* by Karen Wildung Reinhardt and Jeff Henry, 2004. 178 Norm Beul, 'Troops Train to Fight Wildfires', *The Washington Post*, 26 July 1988; Phil Perkins/Celia Coyne; Don Despain, Radio Expeditions @ nationalgeographic.com, 1998, www.nationalgeographic.com/radix/yellowstone/yellow_post_transcript_2.html. 178-9 Joan Anzelmo, AP. 179 Frank Marley, 'A Trip to Yellowstone National Park 1988', *A Yellowstone Notebook*, www.yellowstone-notebook.com. 181 Ranald Webster, *The Daily Telegraph*, 22 October 2002, © Jen Kelly; Ranald Webster, *The Age*, 19 February 1983 © Mark Metherell; Paul Henry, BBC News website; Elder Silvano, Reuters; Paulo Tavares, firefighter, 25 August 2005. 182-3 Hatta Morsidi, Hadiah vıntı Nasır, Khavita Kaur and Vincent Wee, from 'Shifting Winds Lowers Malaysian Pollution', by Thomas Fuller © 2006

IHT/iht.com; Seth Mydans, Copyright © 2006 by The New York Times Co., reprinted with permission. 184 Bandita Das, BBC News website; Orissa resident, BBC News website; Dr Jayadev Kar, www.tajanews.com; Bishwa Bhushan Harichandan, BBC News website. 186 Basant Kumar Mohanty, BBC News website. 188-190 Semen Semenov, Chuchan, Leonid Kulik, reprinted from *Giant Metorites*, E.L. Krinov, Copyright 1966, pp147-148, with permission from Elsevier; Wilhelm Fast/Richard Stone, *Discover* Magazine. 191 Kevin Yates/Celia Coyne. 196 Don Howie, Beverley Howie, Alan Morrison, *The Age*. 197-200 Warren Lavender, courtesy of CNN. 200 Deepa, Les Boardman, courtesy of CNN; Boree Carlsson; Alan, www.tsunamistories.net. 200-201 Fiona, www.tsunamistories.net. 201 Tilly Smith, BBC News website. 204 Jerome Kerr-Jarrett. 208-209 Stuart Matthews. 213 Sanjay Shah, Sunita Masapi, Rediff.com India Ltd ('Worst Rains Mumbai Has Seen', 27 July 2005, www.rediff.com/news/2005/jul/27rain5.htm). 213-214 Ganesh Nadar, Rediff.com India Ltd ('Worst Rains Mumbai Has Seen', 27 July 2005, www.rediff.com/news/2005/jul/27rain5.htm). 214 Bharat Mahajan, BBC News website; Akshay Khatri, BBC News website; Aslam Khan, BBC News website; Kiran Joshi, Rediff.com India Ltd ('Worst Rains Mumbai Has Seen', 27 July 2005, www.rediff.com/news/2005/jul/27rain5.htm). 215 Bittu Sahgal, BBC News website. 216 Kim Parrey, Anglican Communion News Service; John Butt; David Jurd, Anglican Communion News Service. 219 Pieter de Nijs, 'Freak Waves', BBC *Horizon*, 14 November 2002. 221 Karl-Ulrich Lampe, Göran Persson, Reinhard Fisch, 'Freak Waves', BBC *Horizon*, 14 November 2002; Ronald Warwick, copyright 2000-2006 © European Space Agency, all rights reserved. 222-3 Lude Ingvall, John Kostecki, courtesy of CNN; Neal McDonald; Gunnar Krantz; Grant Wharington, courtesy of CNN. 224 Smith Tumsaroch, from 'El Niño Threatens Rice Crops Across Asia' by Thomas Fuller © 2006 IHT/iht.com. 225-6 Ipanaqué Silva/Curt Suplee, *National Geographic*, www.nationalgeographic.com/elnino/mainpage.html. 226 Rosa Jovera Charo, Flora Ramirez, Manuel Guevara Sanchez/Curt Suplee, *National Geographic*, www.nationalgeographic.com/elnino/mainpage.html; California Department of Emergency Services spokesperson, courtesy of CNN. 230 California resident, courtesy of CNN. 231 Lyn Geldof, courtesy of CNN. 232-3 Sandee LaMotte; Theo Laurent, *The St. Augustine Record*. 234 Monika Vegh, www.radio.cz; Luke Allnutt, courtesy of CNN. 237 Courtesy of CNN. 239 Ingolf Rossberg, BBC News website; Hans Nadler, Museum Security Network. 242, 244 Diana Wrightson. 245 Gary Watson, BBC News website. 246 Saufatu Sopoanga, Monise Laafai, TuvaluIslands.com. 247 Stan Riggs/Jack Betts, Charlotte Observer; Rie Rone, *Coastal Heritage*, The Magazine of the South Carolina Grant Consortium (www.scseagrant.org). 249 James Hansom, BBC News website. 257 Rick

LePrevost © *St. Petersburg Times* 2000. 257-8 Cliff Zimmerman, *The San Francisco Chronicle*. 258-9 Jeff Hunter, 'Shark Takes Surfer off SA Beach' by Stephen Cauchi, *The Age*. 260 John Gilbert, *The San Francisco Chronicle*. 261 Bernard Connor Jr, *The San Francisco Chronicle*; Brian de Jager/Andrew Meldrum; Chuck Anderson and Richard Watley, AP. 262-3 Adam Floriani, Dave Lusty, Nick's father, *The Age*, 18 December 2004. 263 Hoku Aki, *Honolulu Star-Bulletin*. 264 Maria André, Copyright © 2005 by The New York Times Co., reprinted with permission. 266 David Weatherill, Copyright © 2005 by The New York Times Co., reprinted with permission. 267 José Mateus, Vieira Muieba, Copyright © 2005 by The New York Times Co., reprinted with permission; Richard Veerman, BBC News website; David Noguera, Médecins Sans Frontières; David Weatherill, Copyright © 2005 by The New York Times Co., reprinted with permission; Karen Godley, www.irinnews.org. 268-9 The Borneo Project. 270-1 Micah Stancil, www.VenomousReptiles.org. 272 Bret Welch, www.VenomousReptiles.org. 273 Dr William Schaffner/Stefan Lovgren, *National Geographic*, April 2003. 278 George Owino Osiga/James Astill. 281-2 Jeffrey Sachs, Gro Harlem Brundtland, Press Release WHO/28, 25 April 2000, World Health Organization. 282 George Owino Osiga/James Astill. 283 Joe Cohen, BBC News website; Pedro Alonso, www.medicalnewstoday.com; Bill Gates, Regina Rabinovich, Chris Hentschel, Bill & Melinda Gates Foundation; Oumoul Khary Sow, 'Fighting Malaria: Stories from Two Villages', 3 May 2005, World Health Organization. 287-9 Mame Dieng, Djiby Diop, Marie Diop, Edouard Tapsoba, UN Office for the Coordination of Humanitarian Affairs, Integrated Regional Information Networks (IRIN), www.irinnews.org. 288 Edward Joshua, *The Sunday Herald*. 291 Robert Rupe/Carol LaValley, Payson Roundup, 2005; Johanna Puga-Martinez/Daniel Borunda, El Paso Times, 15 September 2005. 292 Nguyen Thanh Hung, BBC News website. 296 Tony Field, MRSA Support, www.mrsasupport.co.uk; Helena Glenn, National Necrotizing Fasciitis Foundation (NNFF). 298-300 Val Plumwood, www.AislingMagazine.com. 301 Shaun Blowers, BBC News website. 302 Elspeth Harley, BBC News website; Malcolm Locke, Joy Hill, Jim Anholt, AP. 305, 306-7 Pascale Harter, BBC News website. 307 Asiya Odugleh, Hassan El Bushra, press release, 7 August 2004, World Health Organization; Antonio, BBC News website. 309 Joel Bennett, *Anchorage Daily News*; Rebecca Dmytryk, CBS News; Willy Fulton, copyright Kevin Sanders, Yellowstone Outdoor Adventure 2006; Chris Hill, CBS News.

When Nature Turns Nasty was published by
The Reader's Digest Association Limited, London

First edition copyright © 2007
The Reader's Digest Association Limited,
11 Westferry Circus, Canary Wharf,
London E14 4HE
www.readersdigest.co.uk

We are committed to both the quality of our products
and the service we provide to our customers. We value
your comments, so please feel free to contact us on
08705 113366 or via our website at:
www.readersdigest.co.uk

If you have any comments or suggestions about the
content of our books, email us at:
gbeditorial@readersdigest.co.uk

When Nature Turns Nasty was edited and produced by
Toucan Books Ltd, London for the Reader's Digest
Association Limited, London

For Toucan Books Ltd

Contributing authors
David Burnie
Celia Coyne
Daniel Gilpin
Paul Simons

Editors
Helen Douglas-Cooper
Ellen Dupont
Andrew Kerr-Jarrett
Conrad Mason

Picture researchers
Mia Stewart-Wilson
Christine Vincent
Caroline Wood

Proofreader
Marion Dent

Indexer
Michael Dent

Design
Bradbury and Williams

For Reader's Digest

Project editor
Rachel Warren Chadd

Art editor
Julie Bennett

Editorial director
Julian Browne

Art director
Anne-Marie Bulat

Head of book development
Sarah Bloxham

Managing editor
Alastair Holmes

Picture resource manager
Sarah Stewart-Richardson

Pre-press account manager
Penelope Grose

Product production manager
Claudette Bramble

Senior production controller
Deborah Trott

Origination
Colour Systems Limited,
London

Printing and binding
Partenaire Fabrication, France

Concept Code: UK2014/G
Book Code: 400-263-UP0000-1
ISBN: 978 0 276 44196 7
Oracle Code: 250002648H.00.24